814 BES

1-10

Praise for

BEST AFRICAN AMERICAN ESSAYS
2009

"A cracking good read, something that all too few essay
anthologies manage to be."
—*Kirkus Reviews*

"This fascinating collection offers a look at the
variety of perspectives on the African diaspora and
larger human experience."
—*Booklist*

"Both intensely personal and political."
—*Boston Globe*

"These short stories, excerpts from novels, and thoughtful
essays cover a broad range of subjects, experiences and
perspectives from many of the best writers working today."
—*Sacramento Bee*

Best

African
American
Essays

2010

ONE WORLD

BALLANTINE BOOKS • NEW YORK

Best
African
American
Essays
2010

———————————— ✳ ————————————

GERALD EARLY, SERIES EDITOR

RANDALL KENNEDY, GUEST EDITOR

Published in the United States by One World Books, an imprint of The Random House
Publishing Group, a division of Random House, Inc., New York,
in simultaneous hardcover and trade paperback editions.

ONE WORLD is a registered trademark and the One World colophon is a trademark of
Random House, Inc.

Permissions credits are located beginning on page 359.

978-0-553-80692-2 (hardcover)
978-0-553-38537-3 (trade paperback)

Library of Congress Cataloging-in-Publication Data
Best African American essays, 2010 / Gerald Early, series editor ;
Randall Kennedy, guest editor.
p.   cm.
Includes bibliographical references.
ISBN 978-0-553-80692-2 (hardcover : alk. paper)—
ISBN 978-0-553-38537-3 (pbk. : alk. paper)
1. African Americans—Literary collections.   2. African Americans—
Politics and government.   3. African Americans—Social conditions.
4. African Americans—Intellectual life.   5. American essays—21st century.
I. Early, Gerald Lyn.   II. Kennedy, Randall.
PS683.A35B47 2010
814'.0080896073—dc22   2009043525

Printed in the United States of America

www.oneworldbooks.net

2 4 6 8 9 7 5 3 1

Book design by Diane Hobbing

I dedicate my efforts in this volume to Tina and Alvin Poussaint:
Exemplary physicians, parents, and friends
—Randall Kennedy

To Stanley Oliver, Long May You Run
—Gerald Early

Preface

After Debra Dickerson and I finished *Best African American Essays of 2009*, it was hard to imagine that I and my new guest editor, Randall Kennedy, could find enough good essays to fill another volume in a matter of months. Of course, we were both aware that the successful presidential campaign of Barack Obama would generate a great deal of writing by both African Americans and non-African Americans on race and politics and on Obama himself. The fear was that there would be little else available because Obama would have, figuratively, sucked all the topical oxygen out of the room.

Understandably, this volume reflects the dominance of Obama as a topic in 2008, the year in which nearly all these essays were published. Indeed, as in our 2009 book, we have included a speech by Obama, this one the famous response to the Reverend Jeremiah Wright flare-up, a turning point in the primary campaign. But we also found many essays written on other subjects, including a number on the arts, among them noted biographer Wil Haygood's trilogy of *Washington Post* appreciations on three significant black musicians who died in 2008: South African singer Miriam Makeba, soul singer and *South Park* voice/actor Isaac Hayes, and actress/singer Eartha Kitt. If anything, this new volume is as rich as its predecessor, if not richer in range of subject matter and style, including pieces on sports.

It is a particular pleasure to have Randall Kennedy as the guest editor. One of our leading public intellectuals and certainly one of our nation's most accomplished legal scholars, Kennedy's published works include *Sellout: The Politics of Racial Betrayal* (2008), *Nigger: The Strange Career of a Troublesome Word* (2002), *Interracial Intimacies: Sex, Marriage, Identity, and Adoption* (2003), and *Race, Crime, and the Law* (1997), all dealing with controversial topics and all of them, in various ways, provocative but remarkably thoughtful and important books. I reviewed both *Nigger* and *Sellout*, having some quarrels with the first but liking the second very much. As I read his books, I always felt that I was experiencing a wonderfully incisive mind and, in these texts, was in the presence of a singularly courageous man. The topics he chose to take on, and the angles he chose to engage them, are not especially easy to discuss among African Americans—that is, without occasionally degenerating into blustering emotion, ideological posturing, rank hypocrisy, or pretentious over-intellectualizing, common afflictions among any intelligentsia and especially intriguing ones among the intelligentsia of a persecuted minority. In the writing trade, it doesn't take long for a skilled practitioner (or even a mediocre one) to gauge what any particular audience wants to hear. Every audience, insecure about defending what it believes or thinks but secure in the rightness of what it thinks and believes, seeks confirmation as the cheapest form of collective identity formation and psychotherapy. It is a more strenuous act to tell an audience what it doesn't quite want to hear or read. Kennedy is no curmudgeonly Mencken or acerbic Stanley Crouch, but he does challenge his readers, especially African Americans, to look at their assumptions anew. I greatly appreciate Randall Kennedy for his quest for honesty and clarity in an uncertain, muddled, and highly compromised world of contesting opinions.

There are some new features here, including a scholarly essay, footnotes and all, by a law professor, which is the result of the intellectual predisposition of the guest editor. Debra Dickerson's volume reflected her own quirks and interests. I suspect that all the volumes in the future will be just as individualized. The other changes, reflections of the series editor's attempt to refresh the book from year to year, include listing the sources for all the pieces in the table of contents instead of only in an acknowledgments page in the back of the book and including an excerpt from a nonfiction book: an autobiography by Lise Funderburg called *Pig Candy*. It is not my intention to use many excerpts from nonfiction books in the *Best African American Essays* series, but I do want to leave open the option to use a couple from especially engaging nonfiction books that offer good writing and sharp thinking and ought to be brought to the attention of our readers. Of course, as everyone who knows anything at all about me and my own creative inclinations should know, the essay is the thing, the grand prose form of experimentation created by Montaigne, built on the imaginative tension of its contradictions. The use of nonfiction excerpts is meant to serve only as a friendly cousin to the preponderance of essays in this and any future volume in this series. Nothing in nonfiction prose beats an essay, except a better or, sometimes, just a different one.

Finally, as both Debra Dickerson and I mentioned in the first volume, while most of the writers are African American or citizens of the African diaspora, there are a few who aren't. Maybe you can pick out who they are. "It may shock and amaze ya," Muhammad Ali once said, but we really don't pick writers on the basis of the race. "That's so old school, Daddy," my daughter used to tell me. We make our selections on the basis of talent, which is an even older school. Besides, we know where all the smart black people live. Once a year we hope a good many of them live here, in these pages.

Gerald Early
St. Louis, Missouri
April 2009

Contents

Contents

Race Talk

Sports

Rita Dove

African American Literature

Racial Identity, Enslavement, and the Law

In Memoriam: John Hope Franklin

About the Contributors

Short bios of all the contributors to *Best African American Essays 2010*
and *Best African American Fiction 2010* can be found at
www.randomhouse.com and at http:cenhum.artsci.wustl.edu.

Introduction
From Slavery to Freedom

by Randall Kennedy

John Hope Franklin asserted that the story of African Americans is a chronicle tracing a path upward from slavery to freedom. This view embodies the optimistic tradition in commentary about the prospects for blacks in America. That is the tradition that maintains that Negroes shall overcome the daunting impediments they have faced and help to create a society in which pigmentocracy is superseded by multiracial democracy. That point of view is by no means unchallenged. Pessimists have long contended that racial harmony on the basis of racial equality is an impossibility. Thomas Jefferson maintained, for instance, that it is certain that blacks and whites "can never live in a state of equal freedom under the same Government, so insurmountable are the barriers which nature, habit, and opinion have established between them." Alexis de Tocqueville was similarly convinced that prospects for racial equality in America were doomed. "I do not believe," he remarked, "that the white and black races will ever live in any country upon an equal footing. But I believe the difficulty to be still greater in the United States than elsewhere." White–black racial antagonism would be an indelible part of American culture, he predicted, because of the poisonous influence of racial enslavement. In the United States, he observed, "the abstract and transient fact of slavery is fatally united with the physical and permanent fact of color. The tradition of slavery dishonors the [black] race and the peculiarity of the race perpetuates the tradition of slavery. . . . You may set the Negro free, but you cannot make him otherwise than an alien to the European."

Abraham Lincoln, "The Great Emancipator," is one of the few white Americans whose portrait adorns the walls of many African American homes. Yet, Lincoln, too, was deeply pessimistic about the prospects for a multiracial democracy. That is why, even after he freed the slaves in the states rebelling against the United States, he explored the possibility of inducing blacks to leave America and to settle in some other land in which they could live without the stultifying presence of whites.

Blacks, too, have contributed to the pessimistic tradition. Some have urged blacks to flee the United States in search of someplace where they could hope to live free of racial denigration. Others have urged blacks to secede emotionally and psychologically from "white America" and to create as an alternative their own Afrocentric institutions. In 1964, near the high point of the Civil Rights Revolution, Malcolm X defiantly refused to express gratitude, satisfaction, or hopefulness because of the desegregation of the armed forces, the 1954 *Brown v. Board of Education* Supreme Court decision, the Civil Rights Act of 1964, or any of the other milestones of the Second Reconstruction. "I am one who doesn't believe in deluding myself," he declared in his 1964 speech "The Ballot or the Bullet."

> *I'm not going to sit at your table and watch you eat, with nothing on my plate, and call myself a diner. Sitting at the table doesn't make you a diner, unless you eat some of what's on that plate. Being here in America doesn't make you an American. . . . No, I'm not an American. I'm one of the 22 million black people who are the victims of Americanism. One of the 22 million black people who are the victims of . . . nothing but disguised hypocrisy. So, I'm not standing here speaking to you as an American . . . I'm speaking as a victim of this American system. . . . I don't see any American dream; I see an American nightmare.*

Some black activists have championed struggles to obtain the rights promised by America while simultaneously arguing that those struggles will likely fail. Hence Professor Derrick Bell declared in 1992 that "Black people will never gain full equality in this country. Even those Herculean efforts we hail as successful will produce no more than temporary peaks of progress, short-lived victories that slide into irrelevance as racial patterns adapt in ways that maintain white dominance." White racism, Professor Bell insisted, "is an integral, permanent and indestructible component of American society."

Despite the strains of pessimism, most blacks, like John Hope Franklin, have been more upbeat about their future here than they had any right to be, expressing a stronger belief in the democratic possibilities of the country than most whites. Consider, for example, Frederick Douglass, the fugitive slave who became a leading abolitionist, storied orator, pioneering journalist, and probably the most famous black in nineteenth-century America. Speaking in May 1863, before the abolition of slavery, Douglass posed the question whether "the white and colored people of this country can be blended into a common nationality, and enjoy together . . . under the same flag, the inestimable blessings of life, liberty and the pursuit of happiness, as neighborly citizens of a common country?" He answered (anticipating Obama): "I believe they can."

Or consider James Weldon Johnson, a general secretary of the NAACP who was also a poet, anthologist, novelist (*The Autobiography of an Ex-Coloured Man*), and memoirist (*Along This Way*). In 1900, Johnson wrote the lyrics to what has become known as the Negro national anthem, "Lift Ev'ry Voice and Sing." In a year during which a black man was lynched about every three days, Johnson penned one of the most inspirational hymns in the canon of American patriotic song:

> *Lift every voice and sing,*
> *'Til earth and heaven ring,*
> *Ring with the harmonies of liberty;*
> *Let our rejoicing rise*
> *High as the listening skies,*
> *Let it resound loud as the rolling sea.*
> *Sing a song full of the faith that the dark past has taught us,*
> *   Sing a song full of the hope that the present has brought us:*
> *Facing a rising sun of our new day begun,*
> *   Let us march on 'til victory is won.*

In the twentieth century the most eloquent spokesman for the optimistic tradition was Martin Luther King, Jr. In his epic speech of August

28, 1963, at the Lincoln Memorial in Washington, D.C., King charged that the United States had defaulted on its obligations to black Americans. Unlike pessimists, however, who maintained that it was delusional to think that the United States would follow a better path in the future, King declined "to believe that the bank of [American] justice is bankrupt. We refuse to believe that there are insufficient funds in the great vaults of opportunity of this nation." He went on to declare that he had a dream "deeply rooted in the America dream" that one day the sons and daughters of former slaves and former slave owners would sit down together at the table of brotherhood and sisterhood and that his children would "live in a nation where they will not be judged by the color of their skin but by the content of their character." Five years later, on the evening before he was assassinated, King engaged in prophecy again, this time asserting that God had allowed him to go to the mountaintop and to see what lay ahead. "I've seen the promised land" of racial justice, King declared. "I may not get there with you. But I want you to know . . . that we, as a people, will get to the promised land."

Thus far in the twenty-first century, Barack Obama has emerged as the most prominent voice of race-relations optimism in the United States. Rebuking those who portray the United States as irredeemable, Obama insists that America has evolved for the better, can progress still more, and that, indeed, its ability to change in positive directions constitutes its "true genius." At the opening of his victory speech during the evening of November 4, 2008, upon learning of his election to the presidency, Obama declared: "If there is anyone out there who still doubts that America is a place where all things are possible, who still wonders if the dream of our founders is alive in our time, who still questions the power of our democracy, tonight is your answer."

Obama's election buoyed the spirits of the optimists and, perhaps more dramatically, persuaded many who had been stoically or cynically pessimistic to reconsider their judgment of America and invest their hopes in it again, or even for the first time. Following the election, one heard repeatedly from people of all racial backgrounds, but especially blacks, that for the first time in a long time, or perhaps ever, they felt part of America, proud of it, and hopeful that it might be able to overcome its longstanding racial predicament.

Obama's election has not ended debate over the prospects for racial justice. Proponents of the pessimistic tradition continue to maintain that, despite Obama's ascendancy, the United States remains a fundamentally racist society in which blacks continue to be consigned to a separate, dishonored, and deprived condition. They see Obama as an Establishment politician who articulates a vague rhetoric of "change" while refraining from pursuing policies that will fundamentally challenge the hegemony of the white affluent power elite. Moreover, they see his electoral success as a chimera that might well reinforce the tendencies toward complacency and denial that prompt Americans, particularly whites, to believe that their fundamentally unjust society is essentially fair. The proponents of this position, however, are a small presence with little influence. They are consigned to the margins, from which they witness a struggle in the mainstream between two camps of optimists—the conservative optimists and the progressive optimists.

Some conservative optimists declined to vote for Obama but nonetheless welcome (at least rhetorically) his victory. They see it as the confirmation of the triumph of the Civil Rights Revolution, the realization of Martin Luther King's famous dream, the ultimate evidence that America has indeed overcome its history of racial oppression. For conservative optimists, Obama's election represents "mission accomplished." They point to it as further justification for their claim that it is up to individual blacks to take advantage of opportunities that are now widely available. The editorial page of *The Wall Street Journal* voiced this conservative optimism when it declared the day after Obama's election that "perhaps we can put to rest the myth of racism as a barrier to achievement in this splendid country." A respondent to a newspaper articulated the same point more crudely but revealingly when he averred: "I don't want to hear any more crap about whites keeping blacks down. A black man in the oval office renders that argument moot."

Progressive optimists see the pessimists as minimizing unduly the achievements won at tremendous cost over the past fifty years—the repeal or invalidation of the laws that once formally ostracized blacks in every aspect of social life; the nullification of the extralegal violence that once terrorized blacks; the enactment of legislation that prohibits discrimination against blacks in employment, places of public accommodation, and voting; the creation of a consciousness that regards with distaste any major institution in which blacks are absent; the making of an America that could elect a black president. But progressive optimists also eschew what they see as the complacency of conservative optimism. They note, for instance, that while Obama's victory was impressive, it also reflected a notable racial polarization. Obama captured ninety-five percent of the black vote (and sixty-six percent of the Latino vote) but only forty-three percent of the white vote. Had the vote been limited only to whites, Senator John McCain would have become the forty-fourth President of the United States. True, in the recent past, there have been white Democratic presidential candidates who have also failed to win a majority of the white vote. But that, too, is consistent with the story of racial polarization. Just as in the nineteenth century it was white Republicans who were burdened with the image of being excessively sympathetic to black Americans (recall that Abraham Lincoln was widely damned as a "black Republican"!), over the past half century it was white Democrats who were burdened with that image. Some argue that the striking divergence between whites and blacks in partisan preferences, especially in presidential contests, is only *apparently* racial and that it is explainable in terms of all manner of ideological and pragmatic disagreements. As Thomas B. Edsall, Ira Katznelson, Dan T. Carter, and others have convincingly argued, however, racial resentments and anxieties are often present as powerful, if obscured, factors in fights over such nominally nonracial subjects as taxes, welfare, federalism, and crime policy. Racial prejudice and attitudes toward it surely play some role in the current situation whereby the Democratic Party is a refuge for blacks while the Republican Party is conspicuous in the degree to which blacks are absent from its ranks. And surely there is some racial connection to the fact that the states in which racial divergences in voting in 2008 were most stark—Alabama, Mississippi, Louisiana, Georgia, South Carolina—are also the states with the most infamous histories of racial oppression.

Progressive optimists concede that Obama's election shows that, racially, much has changed for the better. They rightly maintain, however, that race was by no means an irrelevant or neutral force in the election. Obama's blackness—or, more precisely, reaction to his blackness—was an impediment around which he had to maneuver. Just as John F. Kennedy had to sidestep prejudice against Catholics to prevail in 1960, Obama had to sidestep prejudice against blacks to prevail in 2008. Obama had to go out of his way to comport himself in a fashion that would avoid offending the sensibilities of whites socialized to view blacks through the prism of derogatory stereotypes. He tried hard to avoid controversies that would highlight racial conflict. And when he felt compelled to confront racial issues, he was forced to do so in ways that whites would find acceptable.

Progressive optimists argue that it is premature to declare "mission accomplished" in terms of the struggle for racial justice in America. For one thing, there still exists a major problem with discrimination against blacks. Careful tests have been constructed to determine whether individuals who are similar in every significant respect except race are treated differently by retailers, employers, and those seeking to lease or sell residential property. With sobering consistency, these tests reveal that whites are treated better than blacks.

Another sort of racial impediment stems not so much from current discrimination as from racial discrimination in the past that created conditions that have the lingering effect of penalizing blackness and privileging whiteness. An important example is the housing market and its relationship to wealth. After the Second World War, the United States assisted millions of Americans to purchase homes on favorable credit terms. But the government insisted upon keeping black and white residential areas separate and offered financing to blacks on terms that were considerably less generous than those offered to whites. This invidious policy not only hurt blacks, who were deprived of the opportunity to enter the housing market on an equal basis as their white fellow citizens, it also hurt the children of those blacks and indeed the children of those children. This unfair policy of a generation ago helps to account for the stark racial separateness that characterizes residential patterns in urban and suburban America. It also helps to account for the egregious inequality in wealth between black and white Americans.

At the outset, then, of the Age of Obama, many Americans feel an urgent need to address long-deferred racial difficulties. They are aware that other concerns—economic recession, reforming the health industry, ecological degradation, wars, and terrorism—will consume much of America's available attention and energy. Yet they are also aware that there now sits at the apex of governmental authority in the United States an African American who is well versed in the sociology of American race relations, committed to effecting lasting change on this front, and aware of the tragic extent to which the just demands of blacks and other racial minorities have been denied or neglected over the course of more than two centuries.

The presidential election is, by far, the most salient single event in the pages that follow. In "A More Perfect Union," candidate Obama explains his relationship with and attitude toward Reverend Jeremiah Wright. In "What Michelle Can Teach Us," Allison Samuels describes the intense feelings of devotion and protectiveness that many African Americans feel toward America's unprecedented black First Lady. In "Finally, A Thin President," Colson Whitehead parodies the initially moving but quickly overused declaration that became so familiar in the hours and days after Obama's election: "I never thought I'd live to see a black president." In "America's Greatest Hits," Lolis Eric Elie uses as his point of departure Cindy McCain's assertion that she has "always" been proud of her country, in contrast to Michelle Obama's more provisional declaration. Elie reminds Americans of certain aspects of their history that many try hard to deny or forget, including the ethnic cleansing of native peoples, the enslavement of blacks, and anti-Asian violence, conduct that might prompt questioning as to whether it is morally healthy to insist that one has *always* been proud of the United States.

In "The End of White America?" Hua Hsu acknowledges that "whiteness is no longer a precondition for entry into the highest levels of public office." Yet he trenchantly sounds a warning about the "growing sense of cultural solidarity among lower-middle-class whites—a solidarity defined by a yearning for American 'authenticity,' a folksy realness that rejects the global, the urban, and the effete in favor of nostalgia for 'the way things used to be.'" Challenging the triumphalism of some who see Obama's victory as part of an ineluctable wave, Hsu contends worriedly that it is "possible to imagine white ideality politics growing more potent and more forthright in its racial identification . . . as 'the real America' becomes an ever-smaller portion of, well, the real America, and as the soon-to-be white minority's sense of being besieged and disdained by a multicultural majority grows apace."

The writings featured here display the wide variety of beliefs found in black communities throughout the country. While the Obamas enjoyed the support of an overwhelming majority of blacks, they were nonetheless the locus of sharp disagreements. Melissa Harris-Lacewell skewers Tavis Smiley because of the grounds on which the multimedia impresario criticized candidate Obama. In Harris-Lacewell's view, Smiley's critique displayed an errant egotism. The title of her essay reveals her main thrust: "Who Died and Made Tavis King?" In "Obama No," Adolph Reed repudiates Obama from the left, denouncing him unsparingly as "a vacuous opportunist." Juan Williams, on the other hand, sounds notes of skepticism heard principally among those on the rightward end of the political spectrum. Suggesting that Obama had received racially selective preferential treatment, Williams complains that "[d]uring the Democrats' primaries and caucuses, candidate Obama often got affectionate if not fawning treatment from the American media. Editors, news anchors, columnists and commentators, both white and black, but especially those on the political left, too often acted as if they were in a hurry to claim their role in history as supporters of the first black president." In "Judge Obama on Performance Alone," Williams insists that if the new president "is to represent the full power of the idea that black Americans are just like everyone else, fully human and fully capable of intellect, courage, and patriotism, then Barack Obama has to be subject to the same rough and tumble of political criticism experienced by his predecessors."

Although the election was extraordinarily dramatic and far-reaching, it does not monopolize the pages that follow. Readers are treated to a celebration of Chester Himes by Michael A. Gonzales and an assessment of Amy Winehouse by Daphne Brooks. They will find acknowledgment of the value and importance of sports and sports writing in pieces by William C. Rhoden, Scoop Jackson, Phil Taylor, and L. Jon Wertheim. Homage is paid to the art of biography in profiles of Eartha Kitt, Miriam Makeba, and Isaac Hayes by Wil Haygood. An autobiographical essay by Rita Dove, the former poet laureate of the United States, brings us face-to-face with the trauma of losing one's home to fire, while a memoir by Erika Meitner offers a glimpse of what it is like to be a student in one of Dove's seminars.

Several of the selections below are by familiar figures who have built notable careers over several decades. In "Family Matters," the ubiquitous Henry Louis Gates, Jr., narrates the unraveling of mysteries lurking in his family's geneology. In "Talking About Not Talking About Race," Patricia Williams explores in her quirky fashion the social psychology of race relations. In "Creature Features" and "This Machine Kills Fascists," Gerald Early, the distinguished writer (*The Culture of Bruising*) and my editorial boss in this enterprise, vividly recounts disturbing encounters he and members of his family have had with police officers. In "The End of the Black American Narrative," the prize-winning novelist Charles Johnson (*Middle Passage*) repudiates the pessimistic—"from plantation to ghetto" story—of African American history. Readers, however, will also find in this volume pieces by writers who are just beginning to receive acclaim and will likely be major voices in the years to come. The essays by Ta-Nehisi Coates, Gary Younge, Gary Kamiya, Jelani Cobb, and Adam Serwer bristle with insight.

This volume also offers space to a genre of writing that is all too inaccessible: professorial discourse that is usually confined to journals and books read by students and scholarly peers but not the general public. The gulf separating academic specialists and civilian generalists is regrettable. There is much that all sorts of people would find of value that is located in the *Journal of African American History*, *Philosophy & Public Affairs*, and *The Quarterly Journal of Economics*. At the same time, academics would sharpen valuable skills—for instance, the ability to snag readers with a strong, seductive leading sentence—if they were forced to try harder to attract and retain the attention of an audience that is under no compulsion to read what they write. Students who are assigned to study an article constitute a captive audience. General readers are not; if a writer does not grab their attention quickly, he or she will likely lose them.

Professor John Hope Franklin was a rare example of an intellectual who was able both to command respect among specialists in his field—he was elected president of the American Studies Association, the Southern Historical Association, the Organization of American Historians, and the American Historical Association—and to win a wide general readership. His classic, *From Slavery to Freedom: A History of African Americans*, originally published in 1947, has been continually in print through various editions for more than half a century and has been widely read inside and outside seminar rooms. In honor of Professor Franklin and in appreciation for the felicity with which he shared his learning and insight, I have included here an essay he first published in 1963, "The Dilemma of the Negro Scholar." The circumstances in which he wrote that essay are far different than those that exist today. Then there were major universities and publishers that were still indifferent or even hostile to black intellectuals. Now institutions of culture are considerably more attentive to black talent. The progressive changes wrought, however, do not render wholly obsolete Franklin's marching orders to himself and his fellow black scholars. "The American Negro scholar," he declared, should "use his knowledge and ingenuity, his resources and talents, to combat the forces that isolate him and his people and, like the true patriot that he is, to contribute to the solution of the problems that all Americans face in common."

The scholarly domain I know best is legal academia. I therefore turned to work by law professors for additional examples of writings that ought to be more widely accessible. In "Multiracialism and the Social Construction of Race: The Story of *Hudgins v. Wrights*," University of Iowa Law Professor Angela Onwuachi-Willig excavates a remarkable lawsuit resolved in Virginia in 1806. The plaintiffs in the case, women held as slaves, sued for their freedom, arguing that they were descended from a free Indian woman. The defendant, the putative owner of the women, argued that they descended from an enslaved black woman. The legal system's determination of their status turned on its assessment of their race and on the rules that should govern in the absence of certainty regarding genealogical facts. Professor Onwuachi-Willig not only illuminates the case in its own historical setting; she also shows how anxieties over racial identification continue to haunt American courtrooms and other arenas of cultural contestation.

In conclusion, a word needs to be said about the relationship between the title of this volume and its contents. Although most of the selections below are essays, some are excerpts from books. Lise Funderburg's moving profile of her great-grandfather is drawn from her memoir *Pig Candy*, while Richard Thompson Ford's acerbic musings about opportunistic claims of racial discrimination are drawn from his volume *The Race Card*.

The title promises the "best." But what does "best" mean? It means that, in consultation with Gerald Early, I have selected outstanding work in a variety of genres, writings that are notable either because of the virtuosity of an author, the subject explored, the significance of a statement, or the usefulness of the piece as a prism for revealing noteworthy sensibilities.

The title also promises "African American" essays. What does "African American" mean? It means that I have sought to gather writings by authors who identity themselves as African American or whom I perceived to be African American. But there is more to it than that. The editorial management of this anthology does not engage in a doctrinaire of racial exclusivity. As in its predecessor volume, this number of *The Best African American Essays* includes contributions from writers who would probably describe themselves as "white." Also included is work by "black" writers who eschew the term "African American," writers who reject any sort of racial classification, and authors who are creating new racial labels. The identity of a writer was never determinative for purposes of deciding whether or not to invite his or her participation. Decisive was the character of what an author produced.

Randall Kennedy
Guest Editor

The
Presidential
Election
of 2008

———————————— ✳ ————————————

A More Perfect Union

Barack Obama

"We the people, in order to form a more perfect union."

Two hundred and twenty-one years ago, in a hall that still stands across the street, a group of men gathered and, with these simple words, launched America's improbable experiment in democracy. Farmers and scholars; statesmen and patriots who had traveled across an ocean to escape tyranny and persecution finally made real their declaration of independence at a Philadelphia convention that lasted through the spring of 1787.

The document they produced was eventually signed but ultimately unfinished. It was stained by this nation's original sin of slavery, a question that divided the colonies and brought the convention to a stalemate until the founders chose to allow the slave trade to continue for at least twenty more years, and to leave any final resolution to future generations.

Of course, the answer to the slavery question was already embedded within our Constitution—a Constitution that had at its very core the ideal of equal citizenship under the law; a Constitution that promised its people liberty and justice, and a union that could be and should be perfected over time.

And yet words on a parchment would not be enough to deliver slaves from bondage, or provide men and women of every color and creed their full rights and obligations as citizens of the United States. What would be needed were Americans in successive generations who were willing to do their part—through protests and struggle, on the streets and in the courts, through a civil war and civil disobedience and always at great risk—to narrow that gap between the promise of our ideals and the reality of their time.

This was one of the tasks we set forth at the beginning of this campaign—to continue the long march of those who came before us, a march for a more just, more equal, more free, more caring and more prosperous America. I chose to run for the presidency at this moment in history because I believe deeply that we cannot solve the challenges of our time unless we solve them together—unless we perfect our union by understanding that we may have different stories, but we hold common hopes; that we may not look the same and we may not have come from the same place, but we all want to move in the same direction—towards a better future for our children and our grandchildren.

This belief comes from my unyielding faith in the decency and generosity of the American people. But it also comes from my own American story.

I am the son of a black man from Kenya and a white woman from Kansas. I was raised with the help of a white grandfather who survived a Depression to serve in Patton's Army during World War II and a white grandmother who worked on a bomber assembly line at Fort Leavenworth while he was overseas. I've gone to some of the best schools in America and lived in one of the world's poorest nations. I am married to a black American who carries within her the blood of slaves and slaveowners—an inheritance we pass on to our two precious daughters. I have brothers, sisters, nieces, nephews, uncles and cousins, of every race and every hue, scattered across three continents, and for as long as I live, I will never forget that in no other country on Earth is my story even possible.

It's a story that hasn't made me the most conventional candidate. But it is a story that has seared into my genetic makeup the idea that this nation is more than the sum of its parts—that out of many, we are truly one.

Throughout the first year of this campaign, against all predictions to the contrary, we saw how hungry the American people were for this message of unity. Despite the temptation to view my candidacy through a purely racial lens, we won commanding victories in states with some of the whitest populations in the country. In South Carolina, where the Confederate flag still flies, we built a powerful coalition of African Americans and white Americans.

This is not to say that race has not been an issue in the campaign. At various stages in the campaign, some commentators have deemed me either "too black" or "not black enough." We saw racial tensions bubble to the surface during the week before the South Carolina primary. The press has scoured every exit poll for the latest evidence of racial polarization, not just in terms of white and black, but black and brown as well.

And yet, it has only been in the last couple of weeks that the discussion of race in this campaign has taken a particularly divisive turn.

On one end of the spectrum, we've heard the implication that my candidacy is somehow an exercise in affirmative action; that it's based solely on the desire of wide-eyed liberals to purchase racial reconciliation on the cheap. On the other end, we've heard my former pastor, Reverend Jeremiah Wright, use incendiary language to express views that have the potential not only to widen the racial divide, but views that denigrate both the greatness and the goodness of our nation; that rightly offend white and black alike.

I have already condemned, in unequivocal terms, the statements of Reverend Wright that have caused such controversy. For some, nagging questions remain. Did I know him to be an occasionally fierce critic of American domestic and foreign policy? Of course. Did I ever hear him make remarks that could be considered controversial while I sat in church? Yes. Did I strongly disagree with many of his political views? Absolutely—just as I'm sure many of you have heard remarks from your pastors, priests, or rabbis with which you strongly disagreed.

But the remarks that have caused this recent firestorm weren't simply controversial. They weren't simply a religious leader's effort to speak out against perceived injustice. Instead, they expressed a profoundly distorted view of this country—a view that sees white racism as endemic, and that elevates what is wrong with America above all that we know is right with America; a view that sees the conflicts in the Middle East as rooted primarily in the actions of stalwart allies like Israel, instead of emanating from the perverse and hateful ideologies of radical Islam.

As such, Reverend Wright's comments were not only wrong but divisive, divisive at a time when we need unity; racially charged at a time when we need to come together to solve a set of monumental problems— two wars, a terrorist threat, a falling economy, a chronic health care crisis and potentially devastating climate change; problems that are neither black or white or Latino or Asian, but rather problems that confront us all.

Given my background, my politics, and my professed values and ideals, there will no doubt be those for whom my statements of condemnation are not enough. Why associate myself with Reverend Wright in the first place, they may ask? Why not join another church? And I confess that if all that I knew of Reverend Wright were the snippets of those sermons that have run in an endless loop on the television and YouTube, or if Trinity United Church of Christ conformed to the caricatures being peddled by some commentators, there is no doubt that I would react in much the same way.

But the truth is, that isn't all that I know of the man. The man I met more than twenty years ago is a man who helped introduce me to my Christian faith, a man who spoke to me about our obligations to love one another, to care for the sick and lift up the poor. He is a man who served his country as a U.S. Marine, who has studied and lectured at some of the finest universities and seminaries in the country, and who for over thirty years led a church that serves the community by doing God's work here on Earth—by housing the homeless, ministering to the needy, providing day care services and scholarships and prison ministries, and reaching out to those suffering from HIV/AIDS.

In my first book, *Dreams from My Father,* I described the experience of my first service at Trinity:

"People began to shout, to rise from their seats and clap and cry out, a forceful wind carrying the reverend's voice up into the rafters. . . . And in that single note—hope!—I heard something else; at the foot of that cross, inside the thousands of churches across the city, I imagined the stories of ordinary black people merging with the stories of David and Goliath, Moses and Pharaoh, the Christians in the lion's den, Ezekiel's field of dry bones. Those stories—of survival, and freedom, and hope—became our story, my story; the blood that had spilled was our blood, the tears our tears; until this black church, on this bright day, seemed once more a vessel carrying the story of a people into future generations and into a larger world. Our trials and triumphs became at once unique and universal, black and more than black; in chronicling our journey, the stories and songs gave us a means to reclaim memories that we didn't need to feel shame about . . . memories that all people might study and cherish—and with which we could start to rebuild."

That has been my experience at Trinity. Like other predominantly black churches across the country, Trinity embodies the black community in its entirety—the doctor and the welfare mom, the model student and the former gang-banger. Like other black churches, Trinity's services are full of raucous laughter and sometimes bawdy humor. They are full of dancing, clapping, screaming and shouting that may seem jarring to the untrained ear. The church contains in full the kindness and cruelty, the fierce intelligence and the shocking ignorance, the struggles and successes, the love and yes, the bitterness and bias that make up the black experience in America.

And this helps explain, perhaps, my relationship with Reverend Wright. As imperfect as he may be, he has been like family to me. He strengthened my faith, officiated my wedding, and baptized my children. Not once in my conversations with him have I heard him talk about any ethnic group in derogatory terms, or treat whites with whom he interacted with anything but courtesy and respect. He contains within him the contradictions—the good and the bad—of the community that he has served diligently for so many years.

I can no more disown him than I can disown the black community. I can no more disown him than I can my white grandmother—a woman who helped raise me, a woman who sacrificed again and again for me, a woman who loves me as much as she loves anything in this world, but a woman who once confessed her fear of black men who passed by her on the street, and who on more than one occasion has uttered racial or ethnic stereotypes that made me cringe.

These people are a part of me. And they are a part of America, this country that I love.

Some will see this as an attempt to justify or excuse comments that are simply inexcusable. I can assure you it is not. I suppose the politically safe thing would be to move on from this episode and just hope that it fades into the woodwork. We can dismiss Reverend Wright as a crank or a demagogue, just as some have dismissed Geraldine Ferraro, in the aftermath of her recent statements, as harboring some deep-seated racial bias.

But race is an issue that I believe this nation cannot afford to ignore right now. We would be making the same mistake that Reverend Wright made in his offending sermons about America—to simplify and stereotype and amplify the negative to the point that it distorts reality.

The fact is that the comments that have been made and the issues that have surfaced over the last few weeks reflect the complexities of race in this country that we've never really worked through—a part of our union that we have yet to perfect. And if we walk away now, if we simply retreat into our respective corners, we will never be able to come together and solve challenges like health care, or education, or the need to find good jobs for every American.

Understanding this reality requires a reminder of how we arrived at this point. As William Faulkner once wrote, "The past isn't dead and buried. In fact, it isn't even past." We do not need to recite here the history of racial injustice in this country. But we do need to remind ourselves that so many of the disparities that exist in the African American community today can be directly traced to inequalities passed on from an earlier generation that suffered under the brutal legacy of slavery and Jim Crow.

Segregated schools were, and are, inferior schools; we still haven't fixed them, fifty years after *Brown v. Board of Education,* and the inferior education they provided, then and now, helps explain the pervasive achievement gap between today's black and white students.

Legalized discrimination—where blacks were prevented, often through violence, from owning property, or loans were not granted to African American business owners, or black homeowners could not access FHA mortgages, or blacks were excluded from unions, or the police force, or fire departments—meant that black families could not amass any meaningful wealth to bequeath to future generations. That history helps explain the wealth and income gap between black and white, and the concentrated pockets of poverty that persist in so many of today's urban and rural communities.

A lack of economic opportunity among black men, and the shame and frustration that came from not being able to provide for one's family, contributed to the erosion of black families—a problem that welfare policies for many years may have worsened. And the lack of basic services in so many urban black neighborhoods—parks for kids to play in, police walking the beat, regular garbage pick-up and building code enforcement—all helped create a cycle of violence, blight and neglect that continue to haunt us.

This is the reality in which Reverend Wright and other African Americans of his generation grew up. They came of age in the late fifties and early sixties, a time when segregation was still the law of the land and opportunity was systematically constricted. What's remarkable is not how many failed in the face of discrimination, but rather how many men and women overcame the odds; how many were able to make a way out of no way for those like me who would come after them.

But for all those who scratched and clawed their way to get a piece of the American Dream, there were many who didn't make it—those who were ultimately defeated, in one way or another, by discrimination. That legacy of defeat was passed on to future generations—those young men and increasingly young women who we see standing on street corners or languishing in our prisons, without hope or prospects for the future. Even for those blacks who did make it, questions of race, and racism, continue to define their worldview in fundamental ways. For the men and women of Reverend Wright's generation, the memories of humiliation and doubt and fear have not gone away; nor has the anger and the bitterness of those years. That anger may not get expressed in public, in front of white co-workers or white friends. But it does find voice in the barbershop or around the kitchen table. At times, that anger is exploited by politicians, to gin up votes along racial lines, or to make up for a politician's own failings.

And occasionally it finds voice in the church on Sunday morning, in the pulpit and in the pews. The fact that so many people are surprised to hear that anger in some of Reverend Wright's sermons simply reminds us of the old truism that the most segregated hour in American life occurs on Sunday morning. That anger is not always productive; indeed, all too often it distracts attention from solving real problems; it keeps us from squarely facing our own complicity in our condition, and prevents the African American community from forging the alliances it needs to bring about real change. But the anger is real; it is powerful; and to simply wish it away, to condemn it without understanding its roots, only serves to widen the chasm of misunderstanding that exists between the races.

In fact, a similar anger exists within segments of the white community. Most working- and middle-class white Americans don't feel that they have been particularly privileged by their race. Their experience is the immigrant experience—as far as they're concerned, no one's handed them anything, they've built it from scratch. They've worked hard all their lives, many times only to see their jobs shipped overseas or their pension dumped after a lifetime of labor. They are anxious about their futures, and feel their dreams slipping away; in an era of stagnant wages and global competition, opportunity comes to be seen as a zero sum game, in which your dreams come at my expense. So when they are told to bus their children to a school across town; when they hear that an African American is getting an advantage in landing a good job or a spot in a good college because of an injustice that they themselves never committed;

when they're told that their fears about crime in urban neighborhoods are somehow prejudiced, resentment builds over time.

Like the anger within the black community, these resentments aren't always expressed in polite company. But they have helped shape the political landscape for at least a generation. Anger over welfare and affirmative action helped forge the Reagan Coalition. Politicians routinely exploited fears of crime for their own electoral ends. Talk show hosts and conservative commentators built entire careers unmasking bogus claims of racism while dismissing legitimate discussions of racial injustice and inequality as mere political correctness or reverse racism.

Just as black anger often proved counterproductive, so have these white resentments distracted attention from the real culprits of the middle class squeeze—a corporate culture rife with inside dealing, questionable accounting practices, and short-term greed; a Washington dominated by lobbyists and special interests; economic policies that favor the few over the many. And yet, to wish away the resentments of white Americans, to label them as misguided or even racist, without recognizing they are grounded in legitimate concerns—this too widens the racial divide, and blocks the path to understanding.

This is where we are right now. It's a racial stalemate we've been stuck in for years. Contrary to the claims of some of my critics, black and white, I have never been so naïve as to believe that we can get beyond our racial divisions in a single election cycle, or with a single candidacy—particularly a candidacy as imperfect as my own.

But I have asserted a firm conviction—a conviction rooted in my faith in God and my faith in the American people—that working together we can move beyond some of our old racial wounds, and that in fact we have no choice if we are to continue on the path of a more perfect union.

For the African American community, that path means embracing the burdens of our past without becoming victims of our past. It means continuing to insist on a full measure of justice in every aspect of American life. But it also means binding our particular grievances—for better health care, and better schools, and better jobs—to the larger aspirations of all Americans—the white woman struggling to break the glass ceiling, the white man who's been laid off, the immigrant trying to feed his family. And it means taking full responsibility for our own lives—by demanding more from our fathers, and spending more time with our children, and reading to them, and teaching them that while they may face challenges and discrimination in their own lives, they must never succumb to despair or cynicism; they must always believe that they can write their own destiny.

Ironically, this quintessentially American—and yes, conservative—notion of self-help found frequent expression in Reverend Wright's sermons. But what my former pastor too often failed to understand is that embarking on a program of self-help also requires a belief that society can change.

The profound mistake of Reverend Wright's sermons is not that he spoke about racism in our society. It's that he spoke as if our society was static; as if no progress has been made; as if this country—a country that has made it possible for one of his own members to run for the highest office in the land and build a coalition of white and black, Latino and Asian, rich and poor, young and old—is still irrevocably bound to a tragic past. But what we know—what we have seen—is that America can change. That is true genius of this nation. What we have already achieved gives us hope—the audacity to hope—for what we can and must achieve tomorrow.

In the white community, the path to a more perfect union means acknowledging that what ails the African American community does not just exist in the minds of black people; that the legacy of discrimination—and current incidents of discrimination, while less overt than in the past—are real and must be addressed. Not just with words, but with deeds—by investing in our schools and our communities; by enforcing our civil rights laws and ensuring fairness in our criminal justice system; by providing this generation with ladders of opportunity that were unavailable for previous generations. It requires all Americans to realize that your dreams do not have to come at the expense of my dreams; that investing in the health, welfare, and education of black and brown and white children will ultimately help all of America prosper.

In the end, then, what is called for is nothing more, and nothing less, than what all the world's great religions demand—that we do unto others as we would have them do unto us. Let us be our brother's keeper, Scripture tells us. Let us be our sister's keeper. Let us find that common stake we all have in one another, and let our politics reflect that spirit as well.

For we have a choice in this country. We can accept a politics that breeds division, and conflict, and cynicism. We can tackle race only as spectacle—as we did in the O.J. trial—or in the wake of tragedy, as we did in the aftermath of Katrina—or as fodder for the nightly news. We can play Reverend Wright's sermons on every channel, every day, and talk about them from now until the election, and make the only question in this campaign whether or not the American people think that I somehow believe or sympathize with his most offensive words. We can pounce on some gaffe by a Hillary supporter as evidence that she's playing the race card, or we can speculate on whether white men will all flock to John McCain in the general election regardless of his policies.

We can do that.

But if we do, I can tell you that in the next election, we'll be talking about some other distraction. And then another one. And then another one. And nothing will change.

That is one option. Or, at this moment, in this election, we can come together and say, "Not this time." This time we want to talk about the crumbling schools that are stealing the future of black children and white children and Asian children and Hispanic children and Native American children. This time we want to reject the cynicism that tells us that these kids can't learn; that those kids who don't look like us are somebody else's problem. The children of America are not those kids, they are our kids, and we will not let them fall behind in a twenty-first century economy. Not this time.

This time we want to talk about how the lines in the emergency room are filled with whites and blacks and Hispanics who do not have health care; who don't have the power on their own to overcome the special interests in Washington, but who can take them on if we do it together.

This time we want to talk about the shuttered mills that once provided a decent life for men and women of every race, and the homes for sale that once belonged to Americans from every religion, every region, every walk of life. This time we want to talk about the fact that the real problem is not that someone who doesn't look like you might take your job; it's that the corporation you work for will ship it overseas for nothing more than a profit.

This time we want to talk about the men and women of every color and creed who serve together, and fight together, and bleed together under the same proud flag. We want to talk about how to bring them home from a war that never should've been authorized and never should've been waged, and we want to talk about how we'll show our patriotism by caring for them, and their families, and giving them the benefits they have earned.

I would not be running for President if I didn't believe with all my heart that this is what the vast majority of Americans want for this country. This union may never be perfect, but generation after generation has shown that it can always be perfected. And today, whenever I find myself feeling doubtful or cynical about this possibility, what gives me the most hope is the next generation—the young people whose attitudes and beliefs and openness to change have already made history in this election.

There is one story in particularly that I'd like to leave you with today—a story I told when I had the great honor of speaking on Dr. King's birthday at his home church, Ebenezer Baptist, in Atlanta.

There is a young, twenty-three-year-old white woman named Ashley Baia who organized for our campaign in Florence, South Carolina. She had been working to organize a mostly African American community since the beginning of this campaign, and one day she was at a roundtable discussion where everyone went around telling their story and why they were there.

And Ashley said that when she was nine years old, her mother got cancer. And because she had to miss days of work, she was let go and lost her health care. They had to file for bankruptcy, and that's when Ashley decided that she had to do something to help her mom.

She knew that food was one of their most expensive costs, and so Ashley convinced her mother that what she really liked and really wanted to eat more than anything else was mustard and relish sandwiches. Because that was the cheapest way to eat.

She did this for a year until her mom got better, and she told everyone at the roundtable that the reason she joined our campaign was so that she could help the millions of other children in the country who want and need to help their parents too.

Now Ashley might have made a different choice. Perhaps somebody told her along the way that the source of her mother's problems were blacks who were on welfare and too lazy to work, or Hispanics who were coming into the country illegally. But she didn't. She sought out allies in her fight against injustice.

Anyway, Ashley finishes her story and then goes around the room and asks everyone else why they're supporting the campaign. They all have different stories and reasons. Many bring up a specific issue. And finally they come to this elderly black man who's been sitting there quietly the entire time. And Ashley asks him why he's there. And he does not bring up a specific issue. He does not say health care or the economy. He does not say education or the war. He does not say that he was there because of Barack Obama. He simply says to everyone in the room, "I am here because of Ashley."

"I'm here because of Ashley." By itself, that single moment of recognition between that young white girl and that old black man is not enough. It is not enough to give health care to the sick, or jobs to the jobless, or education to our children.

But it is where we start. It is where our union grows stronger. And as so many generations have come to realize over the course of the two hundred and twenty-one years since a band of patriots signed that document in Philadelphia, that is where the perfection begins.

A Deeper Black

Ta-Nehisi Coates

To say that Barack Obama is our first serious black presidential candidate drastically understates the matter. When Obama greets his political allies, he does not give a simple, firm, businesslike handshake. Instead he offers the sort of dap—a little English in the wrist and a one-armed hug—that black males spend much of their adolescence perfecting. If elected, surely Obama will be the first President to greet foreign dignitaries with a pound. Obama warms up on election morning not by running a three-miler or swimming laps but by shooting hoops. The Illinois senator sports a flawless and ever-fresh Caesar demonstrative of the razorwork native to only one side of the tracks. Think Jay-Z—"I'm not looking at you dudes/I'm looking past you"—not Jay Rockefeller.

Likewise, Obama's wife, Michelle, is not merely a black woman but a black woman bearing the diction of that particular tribe of overachieving South Side Chicago blacks who, as children, were corrected with old adages like "*ain't* is not a word." Reporters have been stunned by her raw wit, by her unwillingness to fawn and gush over her husband. But that's standard procedure in black America, where conflicts stretching back to slave ships have taught women to spurn the Stepford act and view every alleged Lancelot askance.

At campaign events Obama is known to crack himself up—once at a barbershop he began snapping, unprompted, on a customer's alligator shoes. During a speech in South Carolina, to the amusement of himself and a predominantly black crowd, Obama noted that his opponents were trying to "bamboozle" and "hoodwink" the voters. He pulled up after noting that he was "having too much fun." The schooled observer could have seen through the first layer of laughter and beheld the real fun— here is a black man running for President by paraphrasing Malcolm X.

Obama's favorite TV series is *The Wire*. His favorite character is Omar, the coal-black antihero who prowls the streets of West Baltimore toting a shotgun and robbing drug dealers. Of course, there's the matter of Obama's retired pastor, Jeremiah Wright, and his United Church of Christ, which right-wingers have taken to equating with Louis Farrakhan and the Nation of Islam, respectively. A few months before the professional babblers began frothing at the mouth over Wright, the Obama campaign got wind that it might have an image problem. Its response? Filming a YouTube spot of what must be one of only five white members praising the church's openness. It's the old "some of my best friends are black" misdirection play, but executed from the left side.

At night the cable talk shows are filled with trifling gibberish that either extols Obama's "postracialism" or cautions him against being branded the "black presidential candidate." Usually it's both. These pronouncements are almost always made by men who would most likely be hard-pressed to recall the last time they sat down to dinner with a black family. Their viewpoints are shaped by focus groups, polls and warmed-over bromides like "defense moms" and "NASCAR dads." I can't think of a group more ill equipped to bear witness to humanity, much less a phenomenon as intricate and complicated as race in America.

Meanwhile, African American voters have broken for Obama in margins that make Hillary Clinton look about as popular in the neighborhood as Rudy Giuliani. In this, the hamfisted and befuddled intellects of the world see the "advantages" of being black: chief among them a mindless mass of zombies willing to stumble into poll booths and press a button for the black guy. But what the African American Obama voter sees is so much more than just the first black President. Indeed, she sees the blackest man to take the public stage ever. Forget about reparations, welfare and white guilt. Forget about four hundred years, forty acres and a mule. Forget about the Confederate flag, marching through Jena and Duke lacrosse. Barack Obama is black in the Zen-like way in which white people are white—without explanation. Without self-consciousness. Without permission.

While we're at it, forget the man himself: the clearest evidence of Obama's blackness is his utter invisibility as a black man to the thinking class. The idea that took root as soon as Obama hit the national stage was that the junior senator from Illinois was not really black because he was raised in Hawaii by a white mother and does not scream about race every five minutes. When Obama made his now famous address to the 2004 Democratic convention, most of the earliest reactions denied the man's very existence. In the wake of his speech, most commentators sounded variations on the same false note. Christopher Buckley, in *The New York Times*, called him "the new Tiger Woods of American politics," while William Saletan, in *Slate*, said, "Obama isn't exactly black."

In all justice, the blindness extended across the races. After the campaign for the Democratic presidential nomination was under way, Stanley Crouch asserted that Obama does not "share a heritage with the majority of black Americans," while Debra Dickerson simply stated that Obama wasn't black. Meanwhile, the Civil Rights Industrial Complex (CRIC), firmly allied with Hillary, did its best to dislodge Obama from the community he claimed as his own. Last fall, Andrew Young announced his support for Clinton on a local Atlanta news show; he'd probed his (presumably black) political connections in Chicago about Obama and reported that "they don't know anybody around him." Then Young pushed things further, claiming that Bill Clinton is "every bit as black as Barack."

Since its conception in the guilt-racked minds of slave traders, blackness has repeatedly sucked the light from otherwise intelligent folks, rendering them empty, dim vessels in its presence. But pundits did not simply stop at noting Obama's lack of soul; they went on to charge that their measure was somehow universal, that their pronouncements could be trusted as the Doppler radar of electoral breezes and gusts in the black community.

The result was a flurry of stories, which employed the most preliminary of polls, asserting that Hillary Clinton's roots in the black community would ultimately trump Obama's. The swipe was twofold: it posited a black community racked by xenophobic suspicion of Obama while putting distance between the obvious complexity of Obama and the assumed simple-mindedness of black people.

In fact, the notion that Barack Obama would be banished because of his ancestry is the sort of unlettered theorizing that presumes black people are just a mirror image of whites. But unlike white Americans, blacks have centuries of experience dealing (sometimes not so kindly) with biracial people in their midst. For African Americans, the blessing of the one-drop rule is blackness as a big tent. Indeed, the first Barack Obama was Frederick Douglass, a biracial slave and autodidact who throttled his slave breaker, fled to the North, traveled the world as an abolitionist, became an ally of Lincoln and published his poignant memoir, *Narrative of the Life of Frederick Douglass, an American Slave.* For his troubles, Douglass was vilified in his time. Critics of his day asserted that no slave, current or ex, could write so movingly.

Whites, on the other hand, often tend to be interested only in someone's biracial parentage, as if there's some credit to be taken. As Obama has acknowledged, were he a notorious drug lord—no matter his background—there would be no rush to analyze the impact of his biraciality. He would be black. There'd be no other choice.

More recently, actual black people who do not talk for a living have rarely reached for the tool of public banishment. At our roots, there is something cloying about us. Having masqueraded as the great American pariah for all our collective lives, we are quick to flock to the banner of even those who want nothing to do with us. O. J. Simpson, who seemed to spurn his origins at every turn, was suddenly transformed into Malcolm X after he was accused of murder. The idea that a black community racked by misfortune would reject a handsome, Ivy League–educated civil rights lawyer turned senator turned presidential candidate, who'd married a black woman and made his home on the South Side of Chicago—who actually had a chance to win—is, and was, laughable. The fraud was exposed as soon as South Carolina's exit polls started rolling in.

Here is the lesson of it all: never write a book that can be summed up in a four-minute segment of *Hardball.* Item: Shelby Steele's *A Bound Man: Why We Are Excited About Obama and Why He Can't Win.* Christened "America's foremost black intellectual" by George Will—an unsurpassed authority in these matters—Steele is an artifact of the identity culture wars that plagued the 1980s and '90s. And when charged with analyzing Obama-mania, Steele declines to refit his spectacles for the post-9/11 era and instead reaches for the same rusting frames he's been using for almost two decades. "The post-sixties black identity is essentially a totalitarian identity," he writes. "It wants to be an activist identity; it wants black protest to be built into each black person's sense of self."

What follows is a flat and contemptuous rendering of black America. Steele argues that Obama can't win because blacks will not vote for a man who doesn't yell "white supremacy" whenever he's presented with an open mike. Steele, like his compatriots in the pundit class, isn't one to allow actual people to get in the way of a good argument. Writing on hip-hop, he argues that rappers can never assume the iconic status needed to transcend America's racial divide. This would come as news to Will Smith, the first rapper to win a Grammy and currently the most bankable star in Hollywood. At his roots, Steele lacks the nuance to approach black America not as an idea but as a collection of actual thinking, breathing, contradicting (and self-contradictory) human beings.

This is why so much of what's been said about Barack Obama and African Americans has been so shockingly wrong. Intellectuals examining Obama are trapped in an ancient dynamic—one that even in its heyday was overstated—in which white and black America are constantly at each other's throats, and agree on nothing. The either/or fallacy is their default setting. ("Assimilation, not blackness, is the road to success," writes Steele.) They were made for a world where affirmative action and welfare reform were campaign issues, not one where universal health care and the Iraq War have dominated the debate.

A Bound Man has the whiff of an author who spends very little time around the people he deigns to judge. The book misses the essential power of Barack Obama: that he is revealing for white America the quiet mass of black people who do not spend their days calculating the wages of slavery. Steele can't grasp that blackness, like any cultural force, works quietly and has no desire to be folded into square minds.

Fortunately, it's people, not caricatures, who vote. Thus, if you need any more evidence of Obama's blackness, do nothing more than look at the exit polls where he's dominated most demographics, but especially his own. I would like to say that this is beyond identity politics, but really it isn't. In South Carolina, where Obama's hoarding of the black vote began, Al Sharpton, four years earlier, finished third among black voters. But Sharpton, like his comrades among the CRIC, is weighted to a media-driven definition of blackness defined by opposition. Obama's blackness is at once futuristic and conservative. It recalls the blackness displayed in the novels of Zora Neale Hurston, in which racial paranoia is rendered an afterthought; it also reflects the experience of generations of black people who've encountered white America not as an idea but as a collection of individuals.

Barack Obama hails from Hawaii, but he also has roots in a rather large tribe of African Americans of recent vintage who are intimately acquainted with both Americas. Some of them were raised in the affluent suburbs by parents who'd known only the rot of inner cities. Many others, like Obama, are the product of interracial unions, privileged to experience both white and black people on intimate levels. They are the ones who spurned the Ivy League for Spelman and Morehouse, or who rebuffed offers from corporate law firms for a return to the streets.

I speak not as one of them. I grew up like most of black America, de facto segregated. When I went off to college at historically black Howard University, blackness was only what I'd seen—row houses with shallow porches, a nasty crossover dribble, hard-driving parents and reverence for Nat Turner. But in my first year at Howard, I met all kinds—math majors fluent in Russian, Marilyn Manson fans, kids straight out of Jack and Jill with fond debutante memories. The first girl I ever fell for had an Indian father and a black mother. She would flash pictures from a photo album of her visits to the subcontinent. The next girl had turned down NYU for Howard and now ran the campus's embattled gay and lesbian club.

What they all shared was a flight from bastions of whiteness, where their names were often shackled to the prefixes "first" and "only." What they shared was a constant flurry of backhanded compliments from their white peers, who, having witnessed them succeed at anything nonathletic (AP English, debate team, smile), would assure them that they "were not really black" or at least "were not like other blacks."

From their unspoken variety, from the Alphas and Omegas, from the buoyant Afros and long dreads, from the night-blacks to those who were almost passing, I drew the great lesson that black was a country, a broad, beautiful America refracted through a smoky lens. For sure, they were different from me. I was young and bursting with militancy and nationalism—among my treasured effects were obscure tomes of proto-Afrocentricity, a burgeoning collection of music, a stack of notebooks crowded with bad poetry of the "Kill Whitey" persuasion. But when we talked, I could feel the shared essence between us.

They were some of the most confident black people I'd ever known. All our lives we'd been raised to see white people as wraiths, as demigods worthy of either complete subservience or unrelenting opposition. This was the logic of our parents, who'd never been free to see whites as fully human and thus to see themselves in the same way. It's also the logic that

Shelby Steele thinks still dominates black America. What I learned from the black émigrés who've walked through America, and what I gathered as I aged and walked the land myself, was that the much-ballyhooed powers of white people were neither good nor wicked, just overrated.

This is the blackness of Barack Obama. It is an identity that asserts itself without conscious thought. It has no need of marches and placards. It rejects an opportunistic ignorance of racism but understands that esoteric ramblings about white-skin privilege do not move the discussion further. It does not need to bluster, to scream, to hyperbolize. Obama's blackness is like any other secure marker of identity, subtle and irreducible to a list of demands.

It also lines up perfectly with even those younger blacks who've never ventured beyond the veil but who, minus the shadow of segregation, have concluded that their skin is as worthy as the next man's. This is why all the fuss over how much or how little Obama addresses racism misses the point. Obama mentions white racism about as often as black people actually think about white racism—which is to say rarely.

This is not an endorsement. I came up waving *The Final Call* and convinced that the answer to everything lay in the last words of Frantz Fanon. To which most of my friends would reply, "So, who won the game last night?" Survey the average voter in Harlem, Detroit or West Baltimore, ask her to rank her presidential concerns and see where "reparations" or "abolishing the Confederate flag" compares with, say, "health care" or "ending the war." In the wake of Obama's speech on race in Philadelphia, the pundits swooned, marveling specifically at Obama's willingness to say that those who fled inner-city America, who opposed affirmative action, were not racist.

It is the final insult of segregation that such unthinking logic is allowed to stand. In fact, anyone who knows black folks understands that Obama had nothing to lose—black people have been fleeing those same inner-city neighborhoods since the 1970s. To see Obama's point as a mark of courage or even a concession, you'd have to imagine a black America that woke up, every morning, thinking only about welfare and affirmative action. The olive branch Obama extended to white people came directly from the grove of black America, not from some newly discovered transracial hinterland. This is why Obama was able to secure South Carolina without becoming entrenched in the patronage schemes of various black preachers. Obama is a black man, and thus he needed no surrogates to translate for him, no verification from the crumbling CRIC.

Whatever comes of it from here on out for the larger country, Obama has redefined blackness for white America, has served notice that wherever we are, we are. What he is positing is blackness as a valid ethnic identity with its own particular folkways and yet still existing within the broader American continuum. Already a wave of black politicos—Deval Patrick, Corey Booker, Jesse Jackson, Jr.—have raised a similar banner, and there is nothing "postracial," "postblack" or "transcendental" about it. (By the way, does anyone call Joe Lieberman "post-Jewish American" or Mel Martinez "post-Cuban American"?) Indeed, it is a deeper black, the mark of a less defensive, more self-assured African American leadership. Our forebears, God bless them, held blackness like an albatross, which they sought to affix around the neck of white America. But this generation, Obama's generation, holds blackness like a garland, sure in the knowledge that the only neck it belongs around is our own.

Obama No

Adolph Reed, Jr.

He's a vacuous opportunist. I've never been an Obama supporter. I've known him since the very beginning of his political career, which was his campaign for the seat in my state senate district in Chicago. He struck me then as a vacuous opportunist, a good performer with an ear for how to make white liberals like him. I argued at the time that his fundamental political center of gravity, beneath an empty rhetoric of hope and change and new directions, is neoliberal.

His political repertoire has always included the repugnant stratagem of using connection with black audiences in exactly the same way Bill Clinton did—i.e., getting props both for emoting with the black crowd and talking through them to affirm a victim-blaming "tough love" message that focuses on alleged behavioral pathologies in poor black communities. Because he's able to claim racial insider standing, he actually goes beyond Clinton and rehearses the scurrilous and ridiculous sort of narrative Bill Cosby has made infamous.

It may be instructive to look at the outfit where he did his "community organizing," the invocation of which makes so many lefties go weak in the knees. My understanding of the group, Developing Communities Project, at the time was that it was simply a church-based social service agency. What he pushed as his main political credential then, to an audience generally familiar with that organization, was his role in a youth-oriented voter registration drive.

The Obama campaign has even put out a misleading bio of Michelle Obama, representing her as having grown up in poverty on the South Side, when, in fact, her parents were city workers, and her father was a Daley machine precinct captain. This fabrication, along with those embroideries of the candidate's own biography, may be standard fare, the typical log cabin narrative. However, in Obama's case, the license taken not only underscores Obama's more complex relationship to insider politics in Daley's Chicago; it also underscores how much this campaign depends on selling an image rather than substance.

There is also something disturbingly ritualistic and superficial in the Obama camp's young minions' enthusiasm. Paul Krugman noted months ago that the Obamistas display a cultish quality in the sense that they treat others' criticism or failure to support their icon as a character flaw or sin. The campaign even has a stock conversion narrative, which has been recycled in print by such normally clear-headed columnists as Barbara Ehrenreich and Katha Pollitt: the middle-aged white woman's report of not having paid much attention to Obama early on, but having been won over by the enthusiasm and energy of their adolescent or twenty-something daughters. (A colleague recently reported having heard this narrative from a friend, citing the latter's conversion at the hands of her eighteen-year-old. I observed that three short years ago the daughter was likely acting the same way about Britney Spears.)

Princeton Professor Sean Wilentz, a Clinton supporter, noted that the Obama campaign advisers have tried to have it both ways on the race question. On the one hand, they present their candidate as a figure who transcends racial divisions and "brings us together"; on the other hand, they exhort us that we should support his candidacy because of the opportunity to "make history" (presumably by nominating and maybe electing a black candidate). Increasingly, Obama supporters have been disposed to cry foul and charge racism at nearly any criticism of him, in steadily more extravagant rhetoric.

The campaign's accusation that the Clinton team made Obama look darker in a photo or video clip than he actually is—and what exactly are we to make of that as an accusation?—and the hysterically indignant reaction to Geraldine Ferraro's statement that much of Obama's success stems from the fact that "the country is caught up in the concept" of a black candidacy are no different from the campaign's touting its "historic" character. Obama supporters fulsomely attacked even Clinton's attempts to portray him as inexperienced, which is standard fare in political campaigns. They also charged that she was playing to racism. See most recently Harvard sociologist Lawrence Bobo's characterization that she was "disrespecting" black people, a leftover canard from Jesse Jackson's campaigns (which, lest amnesia overtake us, were also extolled as historic firsts).

The Jackson comparison points to one of Obama's key contradictions: Like Jackson, he wants to appeal to blacks with the "it's our time now" line, and to white liberals with that, as well as with the "I'm black in a different way from Jesse" qualifier and the religious conversion rhetoric. A friend said that Obama's campaign, in stressing his appeal to rapturous children and liberal, glamorous yuppies, offers vicarious identification with these groups, as well as the chance to become sort of black in that ultra-safe and familiar theme park way.

I often tell my students that, even though Paul Wellstone was my good friend from college to his death and an individual for whom I always had great respect, no politician in this system is likely to be a person you'd want for your sister-in-law or brother-in-law. And, as many *Progressive* readers may know, I'm hardly a Clinton fan. I'm on record in last November's issue as saying that I'd rather sit out the election entirely than vote for either her or Obama. At this point, though, I've decided that she's the lesser evil in the Democratic race, for the following reasons: 1) Obama's empty claims to being a candidate of progressive change and to embodying a "movement" that exists only as a brand will dissolve into disillusionment in either a failed campaign against McCain or an Obama presidency that continues the politics he's practiced his entire career; 2) his horribly opportunistic approach to the issues bearing on inequality— in which he tosses behaviorist rhetoric to the right and little more than calls to celebrate his success to blacks—stands to pollute debate about racial injustice whether he wins or loses the presidency; 3) he can't beat McCain in November.

Frankly, I suspect that Clinton can't beat him either, but there's no way that Obama will carry most of the states in November that he's won in the primaries and caucuses. And, while it makes some liberals feel good to think that a majority of the American electorate could vote for a black presidential candidate, we should keep in mind that the Republicans haven't let one dog out of the kennel against him yet. The Jeremiah Wright contretemps is only the first bark.

Obama's style of being all things to all people threatens to melt under the inescapable spotlight of a national campaign against a Republican. It's like what brings on the downfall of really successful con artists: They get themselves onto a stage that's so big that they can't hide their contradictions anymore, and everyone finds out about the different stories they've told different people. And Obama's belonging to Wright's church in the first place was quite likely part of establishing a South Side bourgeois nationalist street cred because his political base was with Hyde Park/University of Chicago liberals and the foundation world.

For now, the Jeremiah Wright connection probably won't hurt him too much, partly because the Republicans at this point mainly may want to keep him and Clinton bleeding each other as long as possible. And his Philadelphia compromise speech—a string of well-crafted and coordinated platitudes and hollow images worthy of an SUV commercial, grounded with the reassuring "acknowledgment" of blacks' behavioral inadequacies—has gained him breathing room by holding out a vague promise of racial "reconciliation" that has appealed to centrist liberals ever since Booker T. Washington's comparably eloquent 1895 accommodation to Southern white supremacy. Obama gets credit for "opening a conversation" on race, for "taking the matter on squarely." But he doesn't really speak to what we ought to be doing to address the injustices, past and present, that he mentions. Despite all the babble about Obama's transcendence, Obama persists in portraying black Americans as a stereotypical monolith: blacks feel x; whites feel y. And the trope of black "anger" is a tired chestnut that neither explains nor characterizes political grievances or aspirations. (By the way, Obama's casting Wright's alleged "anger" as generational is entirely consistent with his earlier praise of Ronald Reagan for sensing Americans' desire to undo the "excesses" of the 1960s and 1970s.)

Because he's tried carefully to say enough of whatever the audiences he's been speaking to at the time want to hear while leaving himself enough space later on to deny his intentions to leave that impression, his record represents precisely the "character" weakness the Republicans have exploited in every Democratic candidate since Dukakis: Another Dem trying to put things over on the American people.

Obama's campaign has been very clever in carving out a strategy to amass Democratic delegate votes, but its momentum is in some ways a Potemkin construction—built largely on victories in states that no Democrat will win in November—that will fall apart under Republican pressure.

And then where will we be?

✳

Correction: Adolph Reed, Jr., apologizes to Katha Pollitt for stating that her daughter influenced her to support Obama. Her daughter did no such thing.

Who Died and Made Tavis King?

Melissa Harris-Lacewell

Who put Tavis Smiley in charge?

Over the past two months African Americans have emerged as equal partners in a multiracial, intergenerational, bipartisan, national coalition led by the most exciting political candidate of the past four decades, who also happens to be the first viable African American presidential possibility in our history. So why is Tavis Smiley throwing a temper tantrum?

He is mad because Obama has not promised to attend Smiley's "State of the Black Union" next week in New Orleans. At last year's SOTBU Al Sharpton, Cornel West and others joined Tavis in roundly criticizing Obama for not attending. Where was Barack that weekend? Oh yeah, he was announcing his bid for the U.S. presidency. This year, Obama is busy trying to win Texas, which has emerged as the firewall state for the Hillary Clinton campaign. Obama wins Texas; Hillary goes home. But Tavis & Co. think Obama should spend precious hours chatting with them about their agenda?

(Jimi Izrael wondered the same thing about him and the other Popes of Blackness.) Let me be clear: I respect the importance of the SOTBU. Tavis performs an essential public service by creating and reproducing a critical black counter-public through this event. The event is decidedly democratic because it is open to a true variety of black voices. Every year it showcases black intellect, commitment and ideological diversity. All this is great, but it doesn't make Tavis the gatekeeper. It certainly doesn't give him the right to act as King-Maker, or in this case Queen-Maker.

Tavis and his guests have every right to criticize Obama if they have substantive disagreements with his policy, his approach to politics or his viability as a general election candidate. They do not have a right to create a false, racial litmus test. All these black leaders who spent the year telling us that Obama is not old enough, not black enough and not angry enough to earn African American votes must have noticed that Obama can deliver the black vote to himself, by himself, with little help from these self-proclaimed racial power brokers.

I can't quite figure out what motivates Tavis. At least I understand the old guard Civil Rights leaders. They are genuinely unwilling to cede power, believing that they have an authenticity claim based on their proximity to Martin Luther King, Jr. I also understand the frightened Democratic insiders who rely on the remnants of the Clinton machine for their bread and butter. But Tavis is not in either category. He is a part of a new generation of journalists who have carved out their own constituency. I am actually surprised to see Smiley join a pile-on led by his former boss Bob Johnson, who tried to silence him with such an ungracious termination a decade ago.

Maybe Tavis legitimately worries that the policy issues of black America will be lost in the excitement of the multiracial coalition. That is fair. But I wonder why Tavis does not trust us to vote in our own interests. Obama won the votes of the people of Louisiana last week. He stood at Katrina's Ground Zero while Hillary blew off the state, assuming she couldn't win it. Now Tavis wants to act as a racial super-delegate by claiming he knows what the people need better than the voters.

Maybe Tavis is just jealous. Maybe it isn't deep at all, just a replay of the old adage about crabs in a barrel.

I do not think that Obama should attend the State of the Black Union. I agree with CNN's Roland Martin (which is rare) that Michelle should go. She should listen to concerns, answer questions from the audience and take seriously the substantive concerns raised there. Barack should be in Texas. I don't think anybody in the room will claim that Michelle is not a good enough surrogate for Barack. If Hillary can claim Bill's presidency as her experience, I am pretty sure Michelle can talk to Tavis on the campaign's behalf.

I usually watch this event every year. It is fun, enlightening and inspiring. This year I will have to TiVo it. Why? Because I will be phoning Texas voters to remind them to head out to the polls on March 4.

What Obama Means to the World

Gary Younge

When author and screenwriter Ronan Bennett was wrongfully imprisoned by the British in the infamous Long Kesh in Northern Ireland in the early seventies, a number of books made the rounds among the Irish Republican prisoners. There was Arthur Koestler's *Darkness at Noon,* which tells the story of a Bolshevik revolutionary imprisoned by the Soviet state he helped create, and *One Day in the Life of Ivan Denisovich,* Solzhenitsyn's account of an ordinary prisoner in a Soviet labor camp. But the one that spoke to Bennett most urgently was *Soledad Brother,* the prison letters of black American militant George Jackson.

"The other books didn't have the visceral impact, but *Soledad Brother* was just something I could relate to completely. I felt I knew the man," Bennett recalls. "There were all kinds of recognizable elements in our struggle. The most powerful part was the way he conducted himself in the jail. . . . It was about dignity. Never, ever folding or letting threats from the jailers make you collapse. . . . It was about being principled, dignified and resistant. I tried as best as I could to replicate that attitude of no compromise, resistance and the emphasis they put on solidarity. Strong standing up for the weak."

Bennett had never met a black person. Indeed, the only ones he'd ever seen had been those serving in the British army. Nonetheless, as an Irish Catholic in occupied Ulster, black America loomed large in his life. "From a very early age my family had supported Martin Luther King and civil rights," he says. "We had this instinctive sympathy with black Americans. A lot of the iconography and even the anthems, like 'We Shall Overcome,' were taken from black America. By about '71 or '72, I was more interested in Bobby Seale and Eldridge Cleaver than Martin Luther King."

For most of the last century, progressives and the oppressed around the world have looked to black America as a beacon—the redemptive force that stood in permanent dissidence against racism at home and imperialism abroad. "No African came in freedom to the shores of the New World," wrote nineteenth-century French intellectual Alexis de Tocqueville. "The Negro transmits to his descendants at birth the external mark of his ignominy. The law can abolish servitude, but only God can obliterate its traces." That "external mark" has acted like a passport to an outside world that ostensibly distinguishes black America from the rest of the country and its policies.

When Kwame Nkrumah came to power in a newly independent Ghana, he sent for black American intellectual W. E. B. Du Bois to edit the *Encyclopedia Africana* and Paul Robeson to take up the chair of music and drama at Accra University. Even as colonial France massacred Algerians by the score, it opened its arms wide to the likes of Josephine Baker, James Baldwin and Richard Wright. For some time during the 1980s and '90s, Jesse Jackson acted as a rogue ambassador, parachuting into trouble spots and freeing hostages.

This affinity found potent expression in sports and popular culture too. For most of the last century, there was an organic connection between black artists and the aspirations of African Americans and other oppressed minorities. Their songs, like Sam Cooke's "Change Is Gonna Come" and McFadden and Whitehead's "Ain't No Stoppin' Us Now," provided a soundtrack for a generation of liberation politics (not to mention Barack Obama's campaign). In sports, Tommie Smith and John Carlos greeted "The Star-Spangled Banner" from the Olympic podium in Mexico City in 1968 with their clenched fists. Their protest has resonated across nations and ages. Margaret Lambert, a Jewish high jumper prevented from competing in the 1936 Berlin Olympics, told NPR last year how delighted that protest had made her feel.

Then there was the inimitable Muhammad Ali. "We knew Muhammad Ali as a boxer, but more importantly for his political stance," says Zairean musician Malik Bowens in the film *When We Were Kings*. "When we saw that America was at war with a Third World country in Vietnam, and one of the children of the U.S. said, '*Me?* You want me to fight against Vietcong?' It was extraordinary that in America someone could have taken such a position at that time. He may have lost his title. He may have lost millions of dollars. But that's where he gained the esteem of millions of Africans."

By the beginning of the new millennium, however, black America's most globally prominent faces were singing and rapping about getting rich. They were playing golf and tennis and staying clear of political controversies that might threaten their record-breaking endorsement deals. And in the figures of Colin Powell and Condoleezza Rice, they were representing the most reactionary U.S. foreign policy in at least a generation. When Secretary of State Powell addressed the Earth Summit in Johannesburg in September 2002, he was jeered. A year earlier, when he refused to show up at a United Nations antiracism summit after the United States resisted all talk of reparations for slavery and stifled criticism of Israel, the cartoonist for the South African newspaper *Citizen* ridiculed him: "Coming, Uncle Tom?" asked two characters representing participants at the conference. "De Massa in de big house says I ain't," responds a Powell dressed up as a house servant.

To the world, black Americans were looking and sounding increasingly like the rest of America—for better or worse.

But on November 4, 2008, black America was once again the toast of the world. Throughout the Caribbean, radios blared Mighty Sparrow's calypso hit "Barack the Magnificent"; firecrackers went off in El Salvador; Liberians danced in the street. The *London Times*'s front page showed a picture of Obama below the words *The New World*. *The Sun*, Britain's top-selling daily tabloid, showed Obama under the headline *One Giant Leap for Mankind*.

In the tiny Romanian village of Rusciori, Obama Sorin Ilie Scoica was born on election day. "When I saw Obama on TV, my heart swelled with joy. I thought he was one of us Roma because of his skin color," said Maria Savu, the baby's grandmother, who hoped his name would bring him luck. In Ghana, John Atta Mills, an opposition candidate running on an agenda of change, produced posters of himself standing next to a life-size cutout of Obama. In Brazil, at least eight black candidates took advantage of a quirk in electoral laws so they could stand as "Barack Obama" in elections in October.

America had a black leader, and suddenly everybody else wanted one. Or at least they wondered how they could get hold of one. Political conversation in France, Britain and Germany, in particular, went almost effortlessly from how to keep immigrants out to how descendants of (mostly) immigrants could ascend to the highest office in the land—or why they could not. "America is a New World again," said Rama Yade, junior minister for human rights and France's only black government member. "On this morning, we all want to be American so we can take a bite of this dream unfolding before our eyes." Cem Özdemir, the first politician of Turkish descent to lead a German political party, was not holding his breath. "In Europe there is still a long way to go," he told *Der Spiegel*. "The message is that it's time to move on in Europe. We have to give up seeing every political figure from an ethnic minority as an ambassador of the country of his forefathers."

In almost every instance the simple, honest answer to the question "Could it happen here?" was no. The Obama story was indeed about race. But at its root it was essentially about white people. Would they vote for him? Would they kill him?

"Millions of whites cannot reconcile in their minds with the idea that a black man with his wife and children would move into the White House," argued Fidel Castro. He was right. It just turned out not to make any substantial difference, since those millions of Americans could not bring themselves to vote for any Democrat. It's not clear whether white Europeans would be any more comfortable with electing a black leader in their own countries than some Republicans were here. Having basked in a smug state of superiority over America's social, economic and racial disparities, Europeans were forced by Obama's victory and the passions it stoked to face hard realities about their own institutional discrimination, which was not better or worse—just different.

With the exception of the Roma in Eastern Europe, levels of incarceration and deprivation of nonwhite people in Europe have not reached the level of African Americans here (although the descendants of Bangladeshis in Britain and Algerians in France come close). Black Europeans enjoy little in the way of black American success. Individuals may break through, but there is nothing on the scale of numbers or wealth comparable with the black American middle class.

It only takes one, though. The question isn't whether nonwhite Europeans are ready to run for national office but whether white Europeans would embrace them. Fascism is once again a mainstream ideology on the continent. When a black woman was chosen as Miss Italy in the mid-nineties, some officials complained that she was "unrepresentative of Italian beauty," and the press crowned her "Miss Discord." Poland's foreign minister, Radek Sikorski, joked that Obama's grandfather was a cannibal. Even though the overwhelming majority of nonwhite Europeans were born in Europe, the fact that they are descendants of immigrants excludes them from the European national stories, which are understood to have only white protagonists.

"Where are you from?" an administrator asked me at university in Edinburgh in what has long been a typical conversation.

"Stevenage," I told him, referring to my hometown thirty miles north of London.

"Where were you born?"

"Hitchin," I said, referring to the town nearby.

"Well, before then?"

"Well, there was no before then."

"Well, where are your parents from?"

"Barbados."

"Ah, you're from Barbados," he said.

To this day "immigrant" and "nonwhite" are often used synonymously in France. Indeed, given the conflation of immigration and race in Europe, the fact that Obama's father was an immigrant was in some ways as significant as the fact that he was black. In that sense every country potentially has its Obama, depending on its social fault lines. For the broader symbolism of his win has less to do with race than with exclusion. Just take the group that in the popular imagination resides furthest from power, pluck one from its number, make him or her the national leader and you have an Obama story. In Bolivia it was Evo Morales, the first poor Amerindian to be elected; South Africa's Nelson Mandela went from jail to president in just four years; in Sweden it could be a Finn; in Bulgaria it could be a Turk. Banel Nicolita, a Roma and member of Romania's soccer team, has become known as "the Obama of Romanian football." For a man who is one of eight children raised in a mud house, the accolade could easily be translated as "a man of unlikely accomplishments." "Obama's victory is a motivation for us," said Gruia Bumbu, chair of the National Agency for the Roma.

There was, of course, more to the euphoria over Obama's victory than the question of exclusion—however and wherever it is framed. The defeat of the Republican agenda, with all the war and global havoc it has brought over the past eight years, was enough to make the world jump for joy. After Bush won in 2004, Britain's *Daily Mirror* ran a headline saying, *Doh: 4 More Years of Dubya . . . How can 59,054,087 people be so DUMB?* The *Guardian*'s features supplement ran a page all in black with tiny words saying, *Oh My God!* Many understand Obama as America's belated but nonetheless more considered, less cavalier response to 9/11.

As one of the few members of America's political class not tainted by the Iraq invasion, he appeared a thinker as well as a decider. Worldly where Bush was parochial, consensual where Bush was confrontational, nuanced where Bush was brash, he struck the outside world as though he regarded dialogue and negotiation as strengths rather than weaknesses. With his Kenyan roots, multiracial upbringing and childhood experiences in Indonesia, he also struck a more global figure. Of twenty-two countries polled by Pew Research last July, in only one nation, Jordan, did a majority say they had more confidence in McCain than in Obama. In the remaining twenty-one, nine (ranging from Tanzania to Japan) backed Obama by more than thirty points. In only six was the margin in single digits.

This enthusiasm was not spread evenly geographically. Western Europe (particularly France) was elated, while the Middle East was wary. "In these nations, suspicions of American power are pervasive and extend beyond President Bush's personal unpopularity," argued Richard Wike of the Pew Global Attitudes Project. "Unlike in many other regions, in the Middle East there is little optimism about the post-Bush era." Nonetheless, with America's international standing at an all-time low, a change of direction was generally welcome.

But while antipathy toward Bush and what he had done to the world explains the breadth of Obama's appeal, it could never explain the depth. Relatives of mine in Barbados and Ireland followed the primaries closely. Children of friends at home in England asked if they could stay up to see the election results. They would never have done that for John Kerry. In the Pew poll, taken during the primary, respondents in Europe favored Obama over Hillary Clinton by significant margins.

"The American Negro has no conception of the hundreds of millions of other non-whites' concern for him," Malcolm X observed in his autobiography. "He has no conception of their feeling of brotherhood for and with him." And yet as Ronan Bennett's account of his time in prison shows, the identification went beyond race. Which brings us back to Obama, whose central appeal was not so much that he looked like other Americans as that he sounded so different—and not just in comparison to Bush. For if Obama represents a serious improvement over his predecessor, he also stands tall among other world leaders. At a time of poor leadership, he has given people a reason to feel passionate about politics. Brits, Italians, South Africans, French and Russians look at Obama and then at Gordon Brown, Silvio Berlusconi, Thabo Mbeki, Nicolas Sarkozy and Vladimir Putin and realize they could and should be doing a whole lot better.

Much of this is, of course, delusional. People's obsession with Obama always said more about them than him. Most wanted a paradigm shift in global politics, and, unable to elect governments that could fight for it, they simply assigned that role to Obama. His silence during the shelling of Gaza, however, was sobering for many. As a mainstream Democrat he stands at the head of a party that in any other Western nation would be on the right on foreign policy, the center on economic policy and the center-left on social policy.

Come inauguration day, that final symbolic set piece, the transition will be complete. The rest of the world must become comfortable with a black American, not as a symbol of protest but of power. And not of any power but a superpower, albeit a broken and declining one. A black man with more power than they. How that will translate into the different political cultures around the globe, whom it will inspire, how it will inspire them and what difference that inspiration will make will vary. From inauguration day people's perceptions of Obama will no longer hinge on what he is but on what he does. While it's unlikely that prisoners in Guantánamo have been passing around *samizdat* copies of *The Audacity of Hope*, Obama has already given Maria Savu a different understanding of what is possible for her grandson and maybe something for little Obama Scoica and the people of Rusciori to look up to.

Finally, a Thin President

Colson Whitehead

Over the coming days and weeks, there will be many "I never thought I'd see the day" pieces, but none of them will be more overflowing with "I never thought I'd see the day"-ness than this one. I'm black, you see, and I haven't gained a pound since college. I skip breakfast most days, have maybe half a sandwich for lunch, and sometimes I forget to eat dinner. Just slips my mind. Yesterday morning, I woke up to a new world. America had elected a Skinny Black Guy president.

I never thought I'd see the day. What were the chances that someone who looked like me would come to lead the most powerful nation on earth? Slim.

Skinny Black Guys of my parents' generation pinned their hopes on Sammy Davis, Jr. His was a big-tent candidacy, rallying Skinny Black Guys, the Rat Pack and the Jewish vote in one crooning, light-footed package. He won South Carolina, but he never gathered momentum. In the end, the Candy Man couldn't.

No one stepped up for a long time. Michael Jackson was black and skinny, but also pretty weird, and after a while he wasn't even black any more, although he did retain his beanpole silhouette. We thought we had a winner in Chris Rock, but then he started in with his infamous "There are Russians, and then there are . . . Georgians" routine and we decided he was too raw for the national stage. So we waited. Some lost faith. Others gorged themselves on protein shakes, believing that America might accept a black mesomorph. And some of us kept hoping. We were hungry for change, if not brunch.

Like many Americans, I first saw Barack Obama at the 2004 Democratic convention. I remember telling my wife excitedly, "This guy is probably stuffed after a cup of minestrone!"

We knew it'd be an uphill battle. America has a long, troubled history. Last summer, *The Wall Street Journal* came out and said what all Americans felt, but were too afraid to say aloud: "In a nation in which sixty-six percent of the voting-age population is overweight and thirty-two percent is obese, could Senator Obama's skinniness be a liability? Despite his visits to waffle houses, ice-cream parlors and greasy-spoon diners around the country, his slim physique just might have some Americans wondering whether he is truly like them." Had he bitten off more than he could chew?

I voted for Mr. Obama, but don't give me that "you're racist" line. Skinny Black Guys vote Democratic ninety percent of the time, through thin and thin. Now our day has come.

On the right, there's been much anxiety over what a Skinny Black Guy administration will look like. Will he paint the White House a warm, Cablinasian caramel, lop off the East Wing for a more svelte profile? Pack his cabinet with Garrett Morris, Dave Chappelle and Jimmie Walker? Such talk is ridiculous, although Mr. Obama doesn't hide the fact that he keeps Urkel on speed-dial "because you never know." I'm confident he'll reach across the aisle to Skinny White Guys, Haven't Been Able to Get to the Gym White Guys, and If They Were Women They'd Be Called Zaftig White Guys.

He is going to raise taxes on the middle class, though. They were right about that. Skinny Black Guys hate the middle class. No reason. Just do.

What else can we expect from a Skinny Black Guy White House? (I never thought I'd live to write those words!) We'll turn the corner, or close the menu, as we like to say, on the war on terrorism. The time may come to sit down at the (under-catered) table with the Taliban. The president-elect has a lot in common with these guys. No, not that. It's hard to get good takeout in the caves of Tora Bora, so you know they're pretty lean by now. Nothing breaks the ice like, "Is that my stomach growling, or yours?"

There's a lot of work to be done to get America back on track. There won't be time for full meals, just light snacking. No problem. With the economy tanking, we'll have to tighten our belts. Again, no prob. When Skinny Black Guys say, "I'll just have the Cobb salad," it's not a calorie thing. We're cheap. It'll come in handy when cutting the fat out of the budget in time for beach season.

A lot of bigots woke up yesterday to the reality of our modern world. To them I say, just because you have a high metabolism, it doesn't mean that you don't have a fierce moral vision and the right ideas to fix this country. It just means that you don't gain weight easily.

Somewhere, the Candy Man is smiling.

Judge Obama on
Performance Alone

Juan Williams

With the noon sun high over the U.S. Capitol, Barack Obama yesterday took the oath of office to become president of the United States. On one level, it was a simple matter of political process—the symbolic transfer of power. Yet words alone cannot convey its meaning.

The callused hands of slaves, the voices of abolitionists, the hearts of generations who trusted in the naïve promise that any child can become president, will find some reward in a moment that was hard to imagine last year, much less fifty years ago. Our history, so marred by the sin of slavery, has come to the day when a man that an old segregationist would have described as "tea-colored"—the child of a white woman and an African immigrant, who identifies as a member of the long oppressed and despised black minority—was chosen by a mostly white nation as the personification of America's best sense of self as a nation of power and virtue.

At the end of the 1965 march calling for passage of the Voting Rights Act, Dr. Martin Luther King, Jr., said politics held the potential to reflect the brilliance of the American creed of justice for all, and a "society at peace with itself, a society that can live with its conscience." Years of hard work lay ahead to shift racist attitudes born of political power being limited to white Americans, he said, then added that "the arc of the moral universe is long, but it bends towards justice. How long? Not long. Because mine eyes have seen the glory of the coming of the Lord!"

It is neither overweening emotion nor partisanship to see King's moral universe bending toward justice in the act of the first non-white man taking the oath of the presidency. But now that this moment has arrived, there is a question: How shall we judge our new leader?

If his presidency is to represent the full power of the idea that black Americans are just like everyone else—fully human and fully capable of intellect, courage and patriotism—then Barack Obama has to be subject to the same rough-and-tumble of political criticism experienced by his predecessors. To treat the first black president as if he is a fragile flower is certain to hobble him. It is also to waste a tremendous opportunity for improving race relations by doing away with stereotypes and seeing the potential in all Americans.

Yet there is fear, especially among black people, that criticism of him or any of his failures might be twisted into evidence that people of color cannot effectively lead. That amounts to wasting time and energy reacting to hateful stereotypes. It also leads to treating all criticism of Mr. Obama, whether legitimate, wrong-headed or even mean-spirited, as racist.

This is patronizing. Worse, it carries an implicit presumption of inferiority. Every American president must be held to the highest standard. No president of any color should be given a free pass for screw-ups, lies or failure to keep a promise.

During the Democrats' primaries and caucuses, candidate Obama often got affectionate if not fawning treatment from the American media. Editors, news anchors, columnists and commentators, both white and black but especially those on the political left, too often acted as if they were in a hurry to claim their role in history as supporters of the first black president.

For example, Mr. Obama was forced to give a speech on race as a result of revelations that he'd long attended a church led by a demagogue. It was an ordinary speech. At best it was successful at minimizing a political problem. Yet some in the media equated it to the Gettysburg Address.

The importance of a proud, adversarial press speaking truth about a powerful politician and offering impartial accounts of his actions was frequently and embarrassingly lost. When Mr. Obama's opponents, such as the Clintons, challenged his lack of experience, or pointed out that he was not in the U.S. Senate when he expressed early opposition to the war in Iraq, they were depicted as petty.

Bill Clinton got hit hard when he called Mr. Obama's claims to be a long-standing opponent of the Iraq War "the biggest fairy tale I've ever seen." The former president accurately said that there was no difference in actual Senate votes on the war between his wife and Mr. Obama. But his comments were not treated by the press as legitimate, hardball political fighting. They were cast as possibly racist.

This led to *Saturday Night Live*'s mocking skit—where the debate moderator was busy hammering the other Democratic nominees with tough questions while inquiring if Mr. Obama was comfortable and needed more water.

When fellow Democrats contending for the nomination rightly pointed to Mr. Obama's thin proposals for dealing with terrorism and extricating the U.S. from Iraq, they were drowned out by loud if often vacuous shouts for change. Yet in the general election campaign and during the transition period, Mr. Obama steadily moved to his former opponents' positions. In fact, he approached Bush–Cheney stands on immunity for telecommunications companies that cooperate in warrantless surveillance.

There is a dangerous trap being set here. The same media people invested in boosting a black man to the White House as a matter of history have set very high expectations for him. When he disappoints, as presidents and other human beings inevitably do, the backlash may be extreme.

Several seasons ago, when Philadelphia Eagles' black quarterback Donovan McNabb was struggling, radio commentator Rush Limbaugh said the media wanted a black quarterback to do well and gave Mr. McNabb "a lot of credit for the performance of this team that he didn't deserve." Mr. Limbaugh's sin was saying out loud what others had said privately.

There is a lot more at stake now, and to allow criticism of Mr. Obama only behind closed doors does no honor to the dreams and prayers of generations past: that race be put aside, and all people be judged honestly, openly, and on the basis of their performance.

President Obama deserves no less.

Obama, the Instability of Color Lines, and the Promise of a Postethnic Future*

David A. Hollinger

The focus of media depictions of Barack Obama as a "post-racial," "post-black" or "postethnic" candidate is usually limited to two aspects of his presidential campaign. First is his self-presentation with minimal references to his color. Unlike Jesse Jackson or Al Sharpton, whose presidential candidacies were more directed at the significance of the color line, Obama has never offered himself as the candidate of a particular ethnoracial group. Second, the press calls attention to the willingness of millions of white voters to respond to Obama. Some of his greatest margins in primary elections and caucuses were in heavily white states like Idaho and Montana. He even won huge numbers of white voters in some

* The bulk of this essay appeared, in slightly different form, as "Obama, Blackness, and Postethnic America," *Chronicle of Higher Education*, February 29, 2008. For conversations that helped me develop the ideas I emphasize in this essay, I wish to thank Mark Brilliant, Jennifer Hochschild, Kenneth Prewitt, and Kim Williams.

states of the old Confederacy, and in the November election carried Florida, Virginia and North Carolina.

But there is much more to it.

The Obama candidacy was a far-reaching challenge to identity politics, and that challenge will only deepen now that Obama will be president. At the center of that challenge is a gradually spreading uncertainty about the significance of color lines, especially the significance of blackness itself. Blackness is the pivotal concept in the intellectual and administrative apparatus used in the United States for dealing with ethnoracial distinctions. Doubts about its basic meaning, boundaries, and social role affected ideas about whiteness, and all other color-coded identities. These uncertainties make it easier to contemplate a possible future in which the ethnoracial categories central to identity politics would be more matters of choice than ascription; in which mobilization by ethnoracial groups would be more a strategic option than a presumed destiny attendant upon mere membership in a group; and in which economic inequalities would be confronted head-on, instead of through the medium of ethnorace.

To denote that possible future, I prefer the term "postethnic" to "postracial." The former recognizes that at issue is all identity by natal communities, including as experienced by, or ascribed to, population groups to whom the problematic term "race" is rarely applied. The reconceptualization affects the status of Latinos and other immigrant-based populations not generally counted as "races." A postethnic social order would encourage individuals to devote as much—or as little—of their energies as they wished to their community of descent, and would discourage public and private agencies from implicitly telling citizens that the most important thing about them was their descent community. Hence to be postethnic is not to be anti-ethnic, or even colorblind, but to reject the idea that descent is destiny.

Obama's mixed ancestry generates some of the new uncertainty about blackness. The white part of his genetic inheritance is not socially hidden, as it often is for "light-skinned blacks" who descend from black women sexually exploited by white slaveholders and other white males. Rather, Obama's white ancestry is right there in the open, visible in the form of the white woman who, as a single mother, raised Obama after his black father left the family to return to his native Kenya. Press accounts of Obama's life, as well as Obama's own autobiographical writings, render Obama's whiteness hard to miss. No public figure, not even Tiger Woods, has done as much as Obama to make Americans of every education level and social surrounding aware of color-mixing in general and that most of the "black" population of the United States, in particular, are partially white. The "one-drop rule" which denies that color is a two-way street is far from dead, but not since the era of its legal and social consolidation in the early 1920s has the ordinance of this rule been so subject to challenge.

But even more important to the new instability in the meaning of blackness in American life is the fact that Obama's black ancestry is *immigrant* rather than U.S.-born. The knowledge that Obama's black father came to the United States from Kenya may have done more than anything else to make Americans in general aware of the distinction within the black population of the United States between those who, like Obama's wife, Michelle, are the descendants of men and women who were enslaved in the United States and lived through the Jim Crow era, and those like Obama himself who are the descendants of immigrants from Africa or from the Caribbean.

To understand why the immigrant-originating blackness of Obama is so significant, we need to view it in relation to other happenings. That well over one-third of African Americans doubt that the black population of the United States is any longer a single people was revealed in a November 2007 report by the Pew Research Center. Although the gap in values between middle-class and poorer African Americans was the focus of the study, black immigrants and their children are especially likely to be identified as middle-class. A study by the Princeton University sociologist Douglas S. Massey and his collaborators shows that black immigrants and their children are overrepresented by several hundred percent among the black freshmen at Ivy League colleges. Such statistics are common at many other institutions, including Queens College of the City University of New York, a public university whose campus is located near a large population of African Americans. Many studies tell us that black immigrants and their children do better educationally and economically than do the descendants of American slavery and Jim Crow.

These studies demonstrate that educational and employment opportunities can be available to black people, even in the context of continued white racism. *This reality calls into question the credibility of blackness as our default standard for identifying the worst cases of inequality, and for serving as the focal point of remedies.* Slavery ended in the British Caribbean three decades before it ended in the United States, and black Caribbeans experienced a better postemancipation educational system than did most black people in the United States. Perhaps the force keeping so many black Americans down is operative not so much in the eye of the empowered white beholder as in that legacy of slavery and Jim Crow, in the form of diminished socioeconomic capacity to take advantage of educational and employment opportunities?

To proceed down the theoretical and policy roads offered by this idea is not to doubt the power of white racism, but to locate more precisely its harmful effects. Our colleges and universities and our remedies for employment discrimination have generally assumed that white prejudice—a legacy, indeed, of slavery and Jim Crow—is the problem. That black people face prejudice today is beyond doubt, and numerous studies show that darker-skinned black people are more likely to be mistreated than those with lighter skin. But skin color does not tell the whole story. If it did, the immigrant/non-immigrant distinction within the black population would not have shown itself to have such striking consequences.

The African American descendants of slavery and Jim Crow are the only population group in the United States with a multicentury legacy of group-specific enslavement and institutionalized debasement, including hypo-descent racialization ("one drop of blood" makes a person black) and antimiscegenation laws (black–white marriages were against the law in most states with large black populations until 1967), carried out under constitutional authority. Neither Obama nor any other African American of immigrant background is a member of this population group. The success of Obama in becoming the presidential nominee of one of the nation's two major political parties is, like the success of other black immigrants in other domains, an indication that something other than color-prejudice in the eye of empowered white people is at the root of structural inequality in the United States.

To be sure, many immigrants from the Caribbean have slave ancestors, too, and slavery also has a history in Africa itself. Other groups have been mistreated in other ways, in this country and in the countries of origin of many immigrants. But the segment of the African diaspora enslaved under American constitutional authority has a unique history, the awareness of which was vital in creating the political will in the 1960s and early 1970s to deploy federal power against racism in general, and to produce the concept of affirmative action in particular.

The differences in history and circumstances among various descent groups were largely ignored during the era when our conceptual and administrative apparatus for dealing with inequality was put in place. As John D. Skrentny, a sociologist at the University of California at San

Diego, has shown—in his important 2002 book, *The Minority Rights Revolution*—conflating Asian Americans, Latinos, and American Indians with African Americans was a largely unconscious step driven by the un-examined assumption that those groups were "like blacks"; that is, they were functionally indistinguishable from the Americans who experienced slavery and Jim Crow. Such conflation was officially perpetuated as late as 1998, when President Clinton's Initiative on Race, *One America in the 21st Century: Forging a New Future,* systematically and willfully obscured those differences. That was done by burying statistics that disproved the all-minorities-are-alike myth, and by fashioning more than fifty recom-mendations to combat racism, not a single one of which spoke to the unique claims of black people.

If we are now going to recognize that even some *black* people—people like Obama—are not "like blacks," how can Mexican Americans and Cambodian Americans be "like blacks"? Can the latter be eligible for en-titlements that were assigned largely on the basis of a "black model" that suddenly seems not to apply even to all black people? If black people with immigrant backgrounds are less appropriate targets of affirmative-action and "diversity" programs than other black people, a huge issue can no longer be avoided: What claims for special treatment can be made for nonblack populations with an immigrant base? Can the genie of the im-migrant/nonimmigrant distinction be put back in the bottle, or are we to generate new, group-specific theoretical justifications for each group? That prospect is an intimidating one, trapping us by our habit of defining disadvantaged groups ethnoracially.

Employers and educators are asked to treat the Latino population as an ethnoracial group, yet the strongest claim that many of its members have for special protections and benefits is specific to economic conditions. The history of mistreatment of Latinos by Anglos is well documented, but the instances most comparable to antiblack racism predate the migration of the bulk of today's Latino population. One need not deny the reality of prejudicial treatment of Latinos to recognize another reality as more salient: immigration policies and practices that actively encourage the formation of a low-skilled, poorly educated population of immigrant labor from Mexico and other Latin American nations. As the recent de-bates over immigration confirm, the United States positively demands an underclass of workers and finds it convenient to obtain most of them from nearby Mexico.

But the service institutions obliged to deal with the needs of that population are held accountable on the basis of ethnoracial rather than economic classifications. Colleges and universities are routinely asked to recruit more Latino students and faculty members, and are accused of prejudice if they do not. People who are encouraged to immigrate to this country, legally or illegally, because they are poorly educated, willing to work for low wages and likely to avoid trade unions, do have a powerful claim on our resources, but it is an economic, not an ethnoracial claim. In the Latino case, more than any other, ethnorace is widely used as a proxy for dealing with economic inequality. The widely debated issue of whether Latinos ought to be regarded as a separate "race" would lose much of its point if the economic circumstances of this immigration-based population were confronted honestly rather than through an ethnoracial proxy.

The Asian American section of our color-conscious system is even more anachronistic. There are historical reasons for the relatively weak class position of immigrants from Cambodia and the Philippines, but our category of Asian American conceals the differences between those groups and those who trace their ancestry to Korea, whose adult immigrants to the United States are overwhelmingly college graduates. Institutions eager to assist the poorest immigrants sometimes do so through the hyper-ethnic step of breaking down the Asian category, enabling them to establish programs for Cambodians but not for Japanese. For example, the undergraduate-admissions forms for the University of California system will soon ask Asian and Pacific-Islander applicants to classify themselves in twenty-three ethnic categories.

These considerations suggest that a historical approach to understanding the dynamics of inequality in American life has much to recommend it. Obama himself pointed in this direction in his epochal speech on race, delivered in March of 2008 in the wake of publicity given to the inflammatory sermons of his pastor, the Reverend Jeremiah Wright. "Many of the disparities that exist in the African American community today can be directly traced to inequalities passed on from an earlier generation that suffered under the brutal legacy of slavery and Jim Crow," Obama declared in a crucial turn in that speech.

Before taking that turn, Obama surprised many people by alluding sympathetically to white workers who, damaged by economic turndowns, tended to blame affirmative action for their problems. Even while describing his own childhood pain upon hearing his white grandmother articulate negative stereotypes about black people, Obama turned the spotlight for a few minutes on whites. Obama offered sympathy and legitimacy to a variety of group-specific complaints without fostering an oppression Olympics, and without indulging the sentimental falsehood that all pains are equal. Hence Obama at once urged Americans to look upon inequality in historical terms, and reached out across the black–white color line, confirming his image as a black politician who did not offer a black-centered message.

Yet we can expect that circumstances will push Obama back and forth between images of "more black than we thought" and "not as black as we thought." When, prior to Wright's having persisted in outrageous public behavior, Obama defended Wright's ministry, there was some buzz that he was farther to the black side of the color spectrum than his previous image had been. Once he renounced Wright, exited from Wright's congregation, and increased the frequency with which photographs of his white grandparents were displayed, there was some buzz that he was farther on the white side of that spectrum than some had supposed. These oscillations do not mean that Obama is lacking in authenticity; they mean that once his blackness is destabilized, it can intensify or diminish in a variety of contexts, including trivial ones.

Does the analysis sketched here mean that blackness is no longer relevant to the dynamics of mistreatment in the United States, and is no longer an appropriate basis for solidarity? Of course not. Black people have plenty of reasons to look to each other for mutual support, and to form enclaves strategically, while refusing to have their lives confined by color. The central postethnic principle, after all, is affiliation by revocable consent. But attention to skin color alone will not carry the United States very far toward diminishing the inequalities for which the extraordinary overrepresentation of black men in American prisons is a commanding emblem. A new, more realistic way to distribute resources and energies, calculated to diminish even those inequalities that owe much to a history of prejudice and violence, is needed. Whether it can be created remains to be seen. The Obama phenomenon makes a real conversation more possible than ever before.

The United States is still a long way from the cosmopolitan society that I sketched as an ideal thirteen years ago in my book *Postethnic America: Beyond Multiculturalism*. I have written this essay in response to many suggestions that I address the Obama phenomenon in the context of my ideas about postethnicity. Today we are closer than before to engaging inequalities that are too often understood in ethnoracial rather than eco-

nomic terms. The energies and ideas flourishing around the Obama presidency may promote a long-overdue breakthrough. Obama's illustration
in his own person of the contrast between immigrant and nonimmigrant
black people, and of the reality of ethnoracial mixing, presents a compelling invitation to explore the limits of blackness especially, but also of
whiteness, and of all color-coded devices for dealing with inequality in
the United States. In the long run, the fact that Obama is the son of an immigrant may prove to be almost as important as the fact that he is the son
of a black man and a white mother. Obama's destabilization of color lines
will be hard to forget. Identity politics in the United States will never be
the same again.

Our
Michelle

———————————— ✳ ————————————

What Michelle Can Teach Us

Allison Samuels

Throughout this long, tense election, everyone has focused on the presidential candidates and how they'll change America. Rightly so. But selfishly, I'm more fascinated by Michelle Obama and what she might be able to do, not just for this country, but for me as an African American woman. As the potential First Lady, she would have the world's attention. And that means that for the first time people will have a chance to get up close and personal with the type of African American woman they so rarely see.

Usually, the lives of black women go largely unexamined. The prevailing theory seems to be that we're all hot-tempered single mothers who can't keep a man and, according to CNN's *Black in America* documentary, those of us who aren't street-walking crack addicts are on the verge of dying from AIDS. As writer Rebecca Walker put it on her Facebook page: "CNN should call me next time they really want to show diversity and meet real black women that nobody seems to talk about."

Like Walker, I too know more than my share of black women who have little in common with the black female images I see in the media. My "sistafriends" are mostly college educated, in healthy, productive relationships and have a major aversion to sassy one-liners. They are teachers, doctors and business owners. Of course, there are those of us who never get the chance to pull it together. And we accept and embrace them—but their stories can't and shouldn't be the only ones told.

Yet pop culture continues to hold a very unevolved view of African American women. Take HBO's new vampire saga *True Blood*. Even in the world of make-believe, black women still can't escape the stereotype of being neck-swirling, eye-rolling, oversexed females raised by our never-married, alcoholic mothers. Where is Claire Huxtable when you need her?

These images have helped define the way all black women are viewed, including Michelle Obama. Before she ever gets the chance to commit to a cause, charity or foundation as First Lady, her most urgent and perhaps most complicated duty may be simply to be herself.

It won't be easy. Since her emergence on the national scene, Obama has been deemed radical, divisive and the adjective that no modern-day black woman can live without: angry. Thankfully, so far, she's endured these demeaning accusations with a smile and shrug—at least in public. But if she does end up in the White House, continuing to dial back her straightforward, vibrant personality isn't the answer. In the same way that Eleanor Roosevelt, Jackie Kennedy and Hillary Clinton each redefined what it meant to be First Lady, Michelle will forge her own path. Not only will she draw the usual criticisms, but she'll be open to some new ones too. I eagerly await the public reaction if Sasha and Malia ever sport cornrows or afro puffs on the South Lawn. And if Michelle decides to champion a program that benefits black youth, will her critics slam her for being too parochial?

To be fair, Hillary Clinton's early involvement in her husband's administration (think health-care reform) brought a major backlash. But there's no real evidence of Michelle Obama's desire to be a huge presence in her husband's potential administration. Besides helping military families, we don't even have many clues about what projects she might tackle.

Whatever she does, I hope she doesn't fall victim to critics with little point of reference. Take this month's issue of *Town & Country* magazine. An article—written by a white female reporter—offers advice to both potential First Ladies. The writer suggests Cindy McCain let her "personality and experience shine" and motivate others to give back.

For Michelle, the writer suggests that she avoid "popping off when your guard is down" and to be careful "about how, when and if she injects her ethnicity . . . into her platform as First Lady."

The underlying message is that the last thing anyone needs to be reminded of is that Michelle Obama is *all* black, unlike her husband, who is mixed—as the writer points out for seemingly no reason.

And that speaks to the larger issue that Michelle Obama could pose for the media. Because few mainstream publications have done in-depth features on regular African American women (and no, Halle Berry, Oprah and Beyoncé don't count), little is known about who we are, what we think and what we face on a regular basis. For better or worse, Michelle will become a stand-in for us all.

Just as she will have her critics, she will also have millions of adoring fans who usually have little interest in the First Lady. African American blogs such as *Sisterlicious, Black Girls Rock* and *That Black Girl Group* have all written about what they'd like to see Michelle bring to the White House—mainly showing the world that a black woman can support her man and raise a strong black family. As contributor Felicia Jones wrote on one blog, "Michelle Obama will be the hero my little girls have been looking for. The hero doesn't have to shake her booty or point her finger to get noticed and respected. My little girls finally have a role model." Michelle will have to work to please everyone—an impossible task. But for many African American women like me, just a little of her poise, confidence and intellect will go a long way in changing an image that's been around for far too long.

Movin' On Up

Margo Jefferson

Last summer, rumor spread that Michelle had been caught—on tape and in the company of Louis Farrakhan—hurling the sneer "Whitey" at the people her husband was busily courting. Already she'd been accused of a lack of patriotism, a near-sullen reserve, a militant fist bump, and a tendency to belittle (or was that to verbally emasculate?) her husband. She'd defended and explained. This time, she just deadpanned.

" 'Whitey?' That's something George Jefferson would say."

It was perfect. She got that some people truly believed she had a secret life as a black supremacist. But many more saw her (and him) as black parvenus, cocky upstarts who were gloating, sitcom style, "We've got degrees from your dee-luxe schools/we're movin' on up to your dee-luxe House/We've finally got a piece of the pie, Whitey!" Along the way she'd been masculinized too, turned into George, not Louise Jefferson. Barack was outgoing and comforting; she was bossy and touchy.

Now she's the Mistress of the ultimate Big House. She presides over art and antiques, guest lists and worthy causes. Her thoughts on china patterns are solicited. It's all so decorous and genteel. She's gone from upstart to feminine role model. After all, "First Lady" isn't a job, it's a cornerstone of the feminine mystique. And since pre-Emancipation, black "females" have had to fight for the whites-only privilege of being deemed "ladies": cultured, educated, sexually desirable in a socially respected way. Michelle Obama has managed to get all this without yielding her right to be smart and strong-willed. And though she's our self-appointed Mom-in-Chief, she's not that old standby, the Black Matriarch whose warmth is linked to her corpulence. (Even Oprah hasn't gotten past that one.)

As the response to Michelle has shifted, people are happily retooling their fantasies. Last week, a friend told me about watching a father show pictures of the inauguration to his very young daughter. "What do you think is going on?" he asked. "He kissed the princess and became president," she answered.

The Other Obama: Michelle Obama and the Politics of Candor

Lauren Collins

One January afternoon at the University of South Carolina's Children's Center, in Columbia, Michelle Obama scrunched her five-eleven frame into a small white wooden rocking chair. The state's Democratic primary, which her husband, Barack, needed badly to win, was in forty-eight hours. Obama picked up a picture book, flared her nostrils, and began sniffing noisily, in the manner of a bear foraging in the woods for dinner.

"Boom! Boom! Boom!" she read to a group of preschoolers. "The bear will tromp through the forest on his big hungry feet and"—sniff, sniff, sniff—"find that strawberry, no matter where it's hidden."

The kids burst into giggles. Obama picked up another book, from the *Olivia* series.

"I have Olivia in my four-year-old class!" one boy yelled.

"Is she a friend of yours?" Obama asked.

"Yes."

"Is she a pig?"

Soon, the story was over. "Let's see," Obama said. "Maybe we have a special guest who will read to us."

She got up from the rocking chair and walked over to a set of French doors. "It's Cocky!" the kids shouted as Obama threw open the doors to welcome an enormous red rooster, dressed in a U.S.C. basketball jersey. She flung her arms around Cocky to give him a hug, a gesture somewhat thwarted by his plush potbelly. "Cocky! Let's read one book together with Cocky."

Obama selected another book and held it up to Cocky's beak. "Here you go, Cocky. Can you read?"

"Cocky, I love you!" a kid screamed.

Sharing the stage with a large, fuzzy piece of poultry might have daunted a more delicate sort of aspiring First Lady, but Obama took her eclipse by Cocky with the seen-it-all aplomb of one of the human characters on *Sesame Street*. That day, she was wearing a pair of high-waisted pin-striped sailor pants, a gray cashmere sweater, and a strand of pearls, but, though she is stylishly appointed, she is not dainty. She is often called "regal"—whether in *The New Republic* or in *Glamour*—but her bearing is less royal than military: brisk, often stone-faced (even when making jokes), mordant.

Obama works out like "a gladiator," a friend has said. When people—they're almost always shorter—ask her to pose for pictures, instead of bending her knees she leans at the waist, like the Tin Man. Her winningly chipmunk-cheeked smile is doled out sparingly, a privilege to be earned, rather than an icebreaker or an entreaty. Obama, who graduated from Princeton, earned a law degree from Harvard, and became, first, a corporate lawyer and, more recently, the vice-president for community and external affairs at the University of Chicago Hospitals, spent all but the first year of her childhood in a four-room bungalow on Chicago's South Side. Having traversed vast landscapes of race and class, often as a solo traveller, she evinces the discipline and, occasionally, the detachment of an Army brat. She can seem aloof from politics. Her mother and her older brother both say that she has never once phoned them in tears.

Obama is cool in temperament. When Stevie Wonder, whom she was escorting to the stage at a rally in February, tripped on a riser, sending her tumbling down next to him in front of thousands of people, she exhibited no embarrassment or alarm, turning what could have been a blooper-reel nightmare into a non-event. She is unquestionably accomplished, but she is not a repressed intellectual, in the mode of Teresa Heinz Kerry. More than anything, she seems to enjoy talking about her husband and her daughters (Malia, nine, and Sasha, six). She can give the impression, in the midst of the campaign's endless roundtables and kaffeeklatsches, that she'd rather be talking to them. Obama seems like an iconoclast precisely because she's normal (the norm for a candidate's wife having been defined, in the past, as nonworking, white, and pious about the democratic process).

Obama is also cool in the other sense of the word; her tastes, references, and vocabulary—"freaky," "24/7," "got my back," *American Idol*, Judge Mathis—if not exactly edgy, are recognizable, which, for a political spouse, makes them seem radical. Of the Iowa State Fair's corn dogs and candied apples, obligingly gushed over by hopeful First Ladies every four years: "Stuff on a stick." Here's Obama, talking to me in her motorcade halfway between Sheboygan, Wisconsin, and Green Bay about Obama Girl, the young woman who professed her crush on Obama's husband all over the Internet: "That was a little weird, because, you know . . . I just assumed, you know, there's no way anybody's gonna hear about that. And one day Sasha comes home and she's, like, 'Daddy has a girlfriend. It's you, Mommy.' And it's, like, 'Oh, shhhhhhhhh—yeah.' " Curse word averted, barely.

Her lack of pretense has made her popular with the portion of the electorate, and the media, for whom prim Laura Bush seems out of touch. Cindy Moelis, who has known Obama since they worked together in Chicago's city hall, in the nineties, told me, "I've actually had girlfriends call me and go, 'You're so lucky. If I'd only met her fifteen years ago, I bet we would be best friends.' " *Can Michelle Obama Be First Lady No Matter What?* pleaded the headline for a post on *Wonkette*, the political blog, about a gathering of candidates' wives. "Please don't get all Botoxed and start acting like some sort of Stepford wife. Please?" the post went on, remarking approvingly on what it termed the " 'bitch, please' look" that Obama had seemed unable to suppress in the wake of a comment by Ann Romney.

It's not that Obama doesn't know the anodyne, wifely things to say (essentially, nothing). She is, after all, a "community and external affairs" professional. But her pride visibly chafes at being asked to subsume her personality, to make herself seem duller and less independent than she is, even in the service of getting her husband elected President of the United States. In Wisconsin, I asked her if she was offended by Bill Clinton's use of the phrase "fairy tale" to describe her husband's characterization of his position on the Iraq War. At first, Obama responded with a curt "No." But, after a few seconds, she affected a funny voice. "I want to rip his eyes out!" she said, clawing at the air with her fingernails. One of her advisers gave her a nervous look. "Kidding!" Obama said. "See, this is what gets me into trouble."

Pundits have portrayed Obama as an oversharer and a taskmaster, demeaning her husband by acknowledging his morning breath and his body odor. But the domestic carping that commentators have taken as some sort of uncontrollable T.M.I. tic serves Obama's husband well, and this may account for her frequent recitation of the mundane details of their housekeeping arrangements. By noting, for example, that Barack is "the *Harry Potter* parent," and that she encourages him to find time to read to Malia and Sasha, Michelle makes Barack seem like a great dad and a guardian of young womanhood. The contrast between their family life and that of the Clintons is implicit. When Michelle remarks—as she did, now famously, at a fund-raiser hosted in Beverly Hills—that Barack forgets to "secure the bread so that it doesn't get stale," she's playing the martinet as hammily as she played the big hungry bear in South Carolina.

"Occasionally, it gives campaign people heartburn," David Axelrod, the Obama campaign's chief strategist, admits. "She's fundamentally honest—goes out there, speaks her mind, jokes. She doesn't parse her words or select them with an antenna for political correctness."

People forget that Barack himself has been working the hapless-hubby routine for a long time: he writes about trying to enjoy the bachelor life as a freshman senator in Washington but finding himself too "fully domesticated, soft, and helpless" to remember to buy a shower curtain. The ordinary card, in fact, may be one of the Obamas' best assets. It assuages fears of difference—"We're just like you" is the cumulative message of all the back-and-forth about the breath and the bread—and inoculates against jealousy, a smart bit of self-deprecation on the part of a young, gifted, attractive couple whose fortunes have risen quickly, like movie stars insisting that they were unpopular in high school.

Besides, Obama's tendency toward deflation isn't limited to Barack. Cindy Moelis recalls commissioning a cookie bouquet with icing in the pattern of the Obama campaign's logo and presenting it to Michelle, who replied, "Oh, great. More sugar for the kids." Obama's dismissiveness is not that of the spoiled princess, as her detractors have suggested, but that of the wary striver: why get used to things being good if they could fall apart at any moment?

"Michelle's always been very vocal about anything," her mother, Marian Robinson, told me. "If it's not right, she's going to say so. When she was at Princeton, her brother"—Craig, now the head basketball coach at Brown, was two years ahead of Michelle—"called me and said, 'Mom, Michelle's here telling people they're not teaching French right.' She thought the style was not conversational enough. I told him, 'Just pretend you don't know her.' "

There is more to the Obamas' relationship, however, than the caricature of Michelle as a ballbreaker to Barack's Obambi (Maureen Dowd's term). Consider the moments leading up to Barack's career-making speech at the Democratic National Convention in 2004. The story that the Obamas like to tell, and that their chroniclers like to repeat, is that Michelle pulled Barack aside just before he took the stage, warning him, "Just don't screw it up, buddy!"

Someone who was involved in the preparation of the speech recalls a more nuanced dynamic, as Michelle calmed an irritable Barack. "We were spending intense sessions tinkering with wording and commas," the person says. "It was pretty tense, because everybody was picking at Barack and making suggestions. He was getting a little irate. Michelle was in the room, and she was kind of handling both him as well as some of the speech." The observer went on, "She was listening intently and, without being overly directive, was somebody that he could glance over to, almost a telepathic kind of relationship. He was clearly looking to her for reaction."

Earlier on the day that Obama visited the nursery school, she addressed a congregation at the Pee Dee Union Baptist Church, in Cheraw, a hamlet of about six thousand known as "The Prettiest Town in Dixie." The church's makeshift gravel parking lot, next to the Pee Dee Ice and Fuel Company and bounded by train tracks, was full. After an invocation by the Reverend Jerry Corbett and an introduction by the mayor of Cheraw, Obama came to the pulpit. "You all got up bright and early just for me?" she asked the mostly elderly, almost all-black crowd. "Yes!" they roared. Obama continued, "On behalf of my church home and my pastor, Reverend Wright, I bring greetings."

Obama opened with some reminiscing. "My people are from South Carolina," she said. "I don't know if y'all knew that. . . . In fact, my brother and I came down last week for a mini family reunion at my grandparents' church, because they retired back down here, and before their death they were living here, attending an A.M.E. Baptist church in Georgetown."

Obama was playing to her audience—later she riffed on "those relatives who have plastic on the furniture" and reminded the churchgoers to get "ten other triflin' people in your life" out of bed and down to the polls on Saturday. Her appearances at the church, and many like it, were a key point of strategy in a state that would be the first real test of whether or not Barack could attract significant numbers of black voters. "In South Carolina in particular, because she had family from there, it made a lot of sense for her to speak in the African American community," David Axelrod said.

✳

After warming up the crowd, Obama launched into her stump speech, a forty-five-minute monologue that she composed herself and delivers without notes. Obama has been open about the value of her ability to speak to black audiences in cadences that reflect their experience, but she makes clear her distaste for the notion that she is a niche tool, wielded by her husband's campaign to woo black voters solely on the basis of their shared racial identity. "I mean, I've been to every early state," she told me, when I asked her about reports that she was "deployed" in the South to reach black audiences. "I was 'deployed' to Iowa," she said, making air quotes with her fingers. "I was 'deployed' to New Hampshire." The four times I heard her give the speech—in a ballroom at the University of South Carolina, from the pulpit of Pee Dee Union, at an art gallery in Charleston, and in the auditorium of St. Norbert College, in De Pere, Wisconsin—its content was admirably consistent, with few of the politician's customary tweaks and nods to the demographic predilections, or prejudices, of a particular audience.

Obama begins with a broad assessment of life in America in 2008, and life is not good: we're a divided country, we're a country that is "just downright mean," we are "guided by fear," we're a nation of cynics, sloths, and complacents. "We have become a nation of struggling folks who are barely making it every day," she said, as heads bobbed in the pews. "Folks are just jammed up, and it's gotten worse over my lifetime. And, doggone it, I'm young. Forty-four!"

From these bleak generalities, Obama moves into specific complaints. Used to be, she will say, that you could count on a decent education in the neighborhood. But now there are all these charter schools and magnet schools that you have to "finagle" to get into. (Obama herself attended a magnet school, but never mind.) Health care is out of reach ("Let me tell you, don't get sick in America"), pensions are disappearing, college is too expensive, and even if you can figure out a way to go to college you won't be able to recoup the cost of the degree in many of the professions for which you needed it in the first place. "You're looking at a young couple that's just a few years out of debt," Obama said. "See, because, we went to those good schools, and we didn't have trust funds. I'm still waiting for Barack's trust fund. Especially after I heard that Dick Cheney was s'posed to be a relative or something. Give us something here!"

First Ladies have traditionally gravitated toward happy topics like roadside flower beds, so it comes as a surprise that Obama's speech is such an unrelenting downer. Obama acknowledged to me that some advisers have lobbied her to take a sunnier tone, with little success. "For me," she said, "you can talk about policies and plans and experience and all that. We usually get bogged down in that in a Presidential campaign, over the stuff that I think doesn't matter. . . . I mean, I guess I could go into Barack's policies and rattle them off. But that's what he's for." In Cheraw, Obama belittled the idea that the Clinton years were ones of opportunity and prosperity: "The life that I'm talking about that most people are living has gotten progressively worse since I was a little girl. . . . So if you want to pretend like there was some point over the last couple of decades when your lives were easy, I want to meet you!"

After the speech, Obama was whisked into the church basement. A clutch of people gathered nearby, hoping to catch a glimpse of her. But when she emerged into the chilly morning air, she didn't linger long with her well-wishers. She can seem squeamish about politicking, put off by the awkward stagecraft of glad-handing and the small-group discussions— Michelle, five or six women, and, as she put it one day in Wisconsin, "five thousand cameras"—that her staff bills as "intimate conversations." But she thrives in large venues. Cindy Moelis said, "The first time she got feedback on being such a wonderful speaker, I think when people said, 'Wow, you're really good at that,' she goes, 'Why's everybody surprised?' "

If Michelle Obama's husband succeeds in garnering the Democratic nomination and then in winning the general election in November, she will be not only the first black First Lady of the United States but also one of the youngest since Jackie Kennedy. Yet, for a potential revolutionary, Michelle Obama is deeply conventional. She exudes a nostalgia, invoking the innocence and order of the past, as much as her husband beckons to a liberating future. Listening to her speeches, with their longing for a lost, spit-shine world, one could sometimes mistake her, were it not for the emphasis on social justice, for a law-and-order Republican. "It's not just about politics; it's TV," she says, of our collective decay. And, wistfully: "The life I had growing up seems so much more simple." She is a successful working mother, but an ambivalent one: "My mother stayed at home. She didn't have to work." Her music of choice is Stevie Wonder, and has been since her childhood. (At the Obamas' wedding, a friend sang "You and I.") One of her favorite foods is macaroni and cheese. In *The Audacity of Hope*, acknowledging the appeal of the Reagan administration, Barack writes, "It was related to the pleasure that I still get from watching a well-played baseball game, or my wife gets from watching reruns of *The Dick Van Dyke Show.*"

Obama draws a straight line from the way her parents, Fraser and Marian Robinson, raised her to the world as it ought to be. For all her modern womanhood, she has not been tempted by rebellion or self-differentiation. "My lens of life, how I see the world, is through my background, my upbringing," she said, in South Carolina.

Fraser Robinson and Marian Shields, who both grew up on the South Side of Chicago, married in 1960. Craig was born two years later, and on January 17, 1964, Marian gave birth to Michelle LaVaughn, whom Fraser nicknamed Miche. She and Craig looked so much alike (and still do) that people often mistook them for twins. Fraser, who was partially handicapped by multiple sclerosis, worked swing shifts as a city pump operator, while Marian tended to the children. The family lived in a modest house that they rented from a relative in the South Shore neighborhood. "If I had to describe it to a real estate agent, it would be 1BR, 1BA," Craig told Peter Slevin, of *The Washington Post*. "If you said it was eleven hundred square feet, I'd call you a liar."

Money was scarce but sufficient. Fraser took pride in providing for his family. "If the TV broke and we didn't have any money to have it fixed, we could go out and buy another one on a charge card, as long as we paid the bills on time," Marian told me. Saturday nights were spent at home playing Chinese checkers, Monopoly, or a game called Hands Down (like spoons, with bluffing). It was a simple time. "I probably had two sleepovers my entire life," Craig said. "We were home folks." Many years, the family drove to Dukes Happy Holiday Resort, in Michigan, for a week's vacation.

The Robinsons went to church occasionally, but if they subscribed to any credo it was that of freethinking. From a young age, Craig and Michelle were encouraged to make choices, and to contend with the consequences. "More important, even, than learning to read and write was to teach them to think," Marian Robinson said. "We told them, 'Make sure you respect your teachers, but don't hesitate to question them. Don't even allow us to just say anything to you. Ask us why.' " Craig recalls, of Michelle, "I wouldn't say she ran roughshod over her friends, but she was sort of the natural leader."

Craig became a basketball star at a parochial school, while Michelle rode the bus, and then the El, to attend classes at Whitney M. Young Magnet High School. Michelle's Class of '81 yearbook—she was treasurer of her class—includes a picture of her as a serious-looking young lady in a bright-yellow silk shirt. She did not play varsity sports, even though people were always telling her she should. Craig told me, "That's the best way to get her not to do something. She didn't want to play just because she was tall and black and athletic." Bernadette McHale, one of her teachers, recalled, "Our first full graduating class was in '78, so it was pretty experimental to come here. She made a decision to choose an integrated environment that had more diversity in both curriculum and population."

Craig was recruited to play basketball at Princeton, and Michelle—who figured she could cut it if he could—followed him there. Princeton in 1981 was not particularly hospitable to minorities of any sort. "It was a very sexist, segregated place," Angela Acree, who was Obama's roommate there for three years, recalled. She continued, "We couldn't afford any furniture, so we just had pillows on the floor, and a stereo." Their social lives revolved around gatherings at the Third World Center, rather than the university's eating clubs. Acree recalled, "The white people didn't dance—I know that sounds like a cliché—and they also played a completely different kind of music, whereas we were playing R. & B., Luther Vandross, Run-D.M.C., at the T.W.C."

Obama majored in sociology, investigating, in her senior thesis, "Princeton-Educated Blacks and the Black Community," the ways in which attending Princeton affected black alumni's sense of connection to the black community. At Obama's request, the thesis was embargoed until November 5, 2008. Last month, amid charges of hypocrisy—the Obama campaign has congratulated itself on transparency—Obama finally released the document to the Web site Politico. A sample passage: "Unfortunately there are very few adequate support groups which provide some form of guidance and counsel for black students having difficulty making the transition from their home environments to Princeton's environment. Most students are dependent upon the use of their own faculties to carry them through Princeton." She dedicated the project to "Mom, Dad, Craig and all of my special friends. Thank you for loving me and always making me feel good about myself."

Obama went straight from Princeton to Harvard Law School. After graduating, she became a junior associate, specializing in intellectual property law, at the Chicago firm of Sidley & Austin. She worked there for three years, eventually becoming, as she says in her stump speech, disenchanted with "corporate America." Valerie Jarrett hired her as an assistant to the mayor, Richard Daley. "In the planning department, part of her job was to help businesses solve problems," Jarrett told me. Sort of like a one-woman 311? "No, a 911," Jarrett responded. "She made problems go away just that fast." In 1993, she was appointed the founding director of the Chicago office of a public-service program called Public Allies, which places young adults from diverse backgrounds in paid internships with nonprofit organizations. An early appearance in the *Chicago Tribune* was in an article about Gen X-ers. Obama told the reporter, "I wear jeans, and I'm the director."

Michelle and Barack met at Sidley & Austin, when she was assigned to advise him during a summer job. Michelle's co-workers warned her that the summer associate was cute. "I figured that they were just impressed with any black man with a suit and a job," she later told Barack. Over her protestations—she felt that dating someone she worked with would be "tacky," her brother recalls—Barack began to court his boss. "She took me to one or two parties," Barack writes, "tactfully overlooking my limited wardrobe, and she even tried to set me up with a couple of her friends." Before the end of the summer, he'd got her to agree to go out for a movie—Spike Lee's *Do the Right Thing*—and an ice-cream cone at Baskin-Robbins. Vacationing on Martha's Vineyard in 2004, Barack met Spike Lee at a reception. As Michelle has recalled, he told Lee, "I owe you a lot," because, during the movie, Michelle had allowed him to touch her knee.

Barack had a more bohemian attitude toward romance. "We would have this running debate throughout our relationship about whether marriage was necessary," Obama told me. "It was sort of a bone of contention, because I was, like, 'Look, buddy, I'm not one of these who'll just hang out forever.' You know, that's just not who I am. He was, like"—she broke into a wishy-washy voice—" 'Marriage, it doesn't mean anything, it's really how you feel.' And I was, like, 'Yeah, right.' " Eventually, he proposed to her over dinner at Gordon, a restaurant in Chicago. "He took me out to a nice dinner under the guise of celebrating the fact that he had finished the bar," Obama recalled. "And he got me into one of these discussions again, where, you know, he sort of just led me down there and got fired up and it's like you've got blah blah blah blah, and then dessert comes out, the tray comes out, and there's a ring!"

The couple married in 1992, and moved into a condominium in a walkup building in Hyde Park. Cindy Moelis recalled a dinner party the Obamas gave when they were newlyweds: shrimp and pasta, inexpensive art on the walls from their travels to Hawaii and Kenya. Barack was not the life of the party. "Because Barack was so smart, he was pretty serious when we were in our thirties. I'd poke him and say, 'Come on, let's talk about the last movie you saw,'" Moelis said. "At some point in our forties, I said to Michelle, 'You know, I think he's so much grown into who he is now. He's so much more lighthearted.' Because he became a senator and he had this wonderful outlet to be a policy person and to be intense, and when he got home he could relax and laugh and just have dinner with friends and talk about movies and basketball."

Parenthood, far more than politics, has been the catalytic force in Michelle's adult life. She is passionate about being a mother, and about confronting the problems that working women face in making time for both their families and their professions. When I asked if there was an issue she has worked particularly hard to bring to her husband's attention, she replied, "The attention that he's focused on work–family balance. . . . That is our life. To the extent that we have challenges, and struggles, headaches that everybody else is going through . . . those are our conversations." (Barack has candidly chronicled their struggle "to balance work and family in a way that's equitable to Michelle and good for our children," and its toll on their marriage.) Her frame of reference can seem narrow. When she talks about wanting "my girls to travel the world with pride" and the decline of America "over my lifetime," you wonder why her default pronoun is singular if the message is meant to be concern for others and inclusiveness.

Last summer, Obama's mother retired from her job as a bank secretary in order to look after Malia and Sasha when Barack and Michelle are on the road. (The Obamas employ a full-time housekeeper, and Michelle tries to see a personal trainer four times a week, but they do not have a nanny.) Obama speaks frequently of her reliance on a network of female relatives, friends, and co-workers. Her staff comprises a collection of mostly young women, practical yet fashionable, like their leader, efficient but not effusive. On Super Tuesday, before the triumphant couple took the stage in the ballroom of the Chicago Hyatt, one of Obama's aides leaned over and whispered in my ear, "Tonight, she's wearing red."

When Barack was elected to the United States Senate, the Obamas decided that Michelle and the girls would remain in Chicago rather than leave behind what she refers to as her "support base." A local mother told the *Tribune,* of their chore-swapping, "This weekend was Hannah Montana, next weekend Michelle has soccer-skills practice."

One morning, during a roundtable at Ma Fischer's, a diner in Milwaukee, Elizabeth Crawford, a recently divorced caterer with two children, brought up the subject of the eating habits of American families. "I really, really hope that Barack will jump on that," she said.

Then, having given thoughtful but boilerplate responses most of the morning, Obama suddenly departed from her script. It was the most animated I saw her on the campaign trail. "You know," she said, "in my household, over the last year we have just shifted to organic for this very reason. I mean, I saw just a moment in my nine-year-old's life—we have a good pediatrician, who is very focused on childhood obesity, and there was a period where he was, like, 'Mmm, she's tipping the scale.' So we started looking through our cabinets. . . . You know, you've got fast food on Saturday, a couple days a week you don't get home. The leftovers, good, not the third day! . . . So that whole notion of cooking on Sunday is out. . . . And the notion of trying to think about a lunch every day! . . . So you grab the Lunchables, right? And the fruit-juice-box thing, and we think—we think—that's juice. And you start reading the labels and you realize there's high-fructose corn syrup in everything we're eating. Every jelly, every juice. Everything that's in a bottle or a package is like poison in a way that most people don't even know. . . . Now we're keeping, like, a bowl of fresh fruit in the house. But you have to go to the fruit stand a couple of times a week to keep that fruit fresh enough that a six-year-old—she's not gonna eat the pruney grape, you know. At that point it's, like, 'Eww!' She's not gonna eat the brown banana or the shrivelledy-up things. It's got to be fresh for them to want it. Who's got time to go to the fruit stand? Who can afford it, first of all?"

The Obamas are fixtures of Chicago's philanthro-social scene: there they are, waving from a silver Mustang at the annual Bud Billiken Parade and Picnic; there's Michelle delivering remarks at the Alpha Kappa Alpha Sorority's Seventy-second Central Regional Conference; there she is arriving at the Black Creativity Gala with a shopping bag full of "Obama for Senator" buttons. Cindy Moelis recalls being shocked, after agreeing to host Obama's baby shower, that the guest list included fifty people. "Hmmm," Michael Sneed, the *Sun-Times* columnist, reported in 2006. "Sneed hears rumbles a mink coat reportedly belonging to Michelle Obama, wife of Sen. Barack Obama, may have gone missing following the Rev. Jesse Jackson's birthday bash at the South Shore Cultural Center."

The Obamas' financial standing has risen sharply in the past three years, largely as a result of the money Barack earned from writing *The Audacity of Hope*. In 2005, their income was $1.67 million, which was more than they had earned in the previous seven years combined. "Our lives are so close to normal, if there is such a thing when you're running for president," Michelle has said. "When I'm off the road, I'm going to Target to get the toilet paper, I'm standing on soccer fields, and I think there's just a level of connection that gets lost the further you get into being a candidate."

Just after Barack was elected to the United States Senate, Michelle received a large pay increase—from $121,910 in 2004 to $316,962 in 2005. "Mrs. Obama is extremely overpaid," one citizen wrote in a letter to the editor of the *Tribune*, after the paper published a story questioning the timing of the award. "Now, what is the real reason behind such an inflated salary?" Her bosses at the University of Chicago Hospitals vigorously defended the raise, pointing out that it put her salary on a par with that of other vice-presidents at the hospital. (As it happens, Obama has spent most of her life working within the two institutions for which she most frequently claims a populist disdain: government and the health-care system.)

Michelle's roots in the community predate her involvement with Barack; in fact, he has written that it was one of the things that attracted him to her, awakening, after years of peripatetic soul-searching, "a longing for stability and a sense of place that I had not realized was there." Barbara Pace-Moody, the development director of Muntu, an African-dance company on whose board Obama serves, recalls meeting her, in the early nineties, when they were both volunteers for a mentoring program: "We spent every Saturday with young women from the Chicago Housing Authority. We had a big gala, and she and her sister-in-law took their own money and paid for the girls to get their hair done and set them up in a hotel downtown. I remember thinking, Who is this Michelle Robinson?"

More troubling to the Obamas' image of civic rectitude is their entanglèment with a campaign contributor named Antoin (Tony) Rezko in a 2005 real-estate deal. (Rezko is now awaiting trial on corruption charges.) That year, as the *Tribune* reported, the Obamas moved to a $1.65 million Georgian Revival mansion in Hyde Park, which features a thousand-bottle wine cellar and bookcases made of Honduran mahogany. On the day they bought the house, Rita Rezko, Tony's wife, purchased the adjacent lot, which was wooded and empty, for $625,000. After the deal went through, Michelle contacted the city's landmarks commission, which she had served on, and received an e-mail from a deputy commissioner with suggestions for obtaining permits to erect a fence between the parcels. The Obamas paid for legal, architectural, and landscaping work, while Rezko got the bill for the fence's construction, for fourteen thousand dollars. (Obama paid the proper fraction of the purchase price for a sliver of land that he bought from the Rezkos as a buffer.)

The other Chicago connection that dogs the Obamas is Dr. Jeremiah A. Wright, Jr., their pastor at Trinity United Church of Christ. Wright, who drives a Porsche and references Bernie Mac and Terry McMillan in his unorthodox sermons ("Take what God gave you and say, 'In your face, mediocrity, I'm a bad mamma jamma!' "), officiated at Michelle and Barack's wedding and baptized their two daughters. Barack took the title *The Audacity of Hope* from a sermon that Wright preached. In 2006, the Obamas gave $22,500 to the church.

Wright espouses a theology that seeks to reconcile African American Christianity with, as he has written, "the raw data of our racist existence in this strange land." The historical accuracy of that claim is incontestable. But his message is more confrontational than may be palatable to some white voters. In his book *Africans Who Shaped Our Faith*—an extended refutation of the Western Christianity that gave rise to "the European Jesus . . . the blesser of the slave trade, the defender of racism and apartheid"—he says, "In this country, racism is as natural as motherhood, apple pie, and the fourth of July. Many black people have been deluded into thinking that our BMWs, Lexuses, Porsches, Benzes, titles, heavily mortgaged condos and living environments can influence people who are fundamentally immoral."

In portraying America as "a Eurocentric wasteland of lily-white lies and outright distortions," Wright promulgates a theory of congenital separatism that is deeply at odds with Obama's professed belief in the possibilities of unity and change. Last year, *Trumpet* newsmagazine, which was launched by Trinity United and is run by Wright's daughter, gave the Dr. Jeremiah A. Wright Jr. Trumpeter Award to Louis Far-rakhan, leading to accusations that Wright was anti-Semitic.

Barack's advisers have tried to dismiss the criticisms of his association with Wright as a witch hunt by conservative blogs and talk-show hosts. The candidate disinvited Wright from giving the convocation when he announced his presidential bid. Last month, I attended an Ash Wednesday service at the church. When it was over, I approached Wright and asked him to tell me about Michelle Obama. "She's from the 'hood," he said. Within seconds, a minder rushed over to say that I was forbidden to conduct any interviews on the premises.

"We don't want our church to receive the brunt of this notoriety," Obama told me. I asked her whether Wright's statements presented a problem for her or for Barack. "You know, your pastor is like your grand-father, right?" she said. "There are plenty of things he says that I don't agree with, that Barack doesn't agree with." When it comes to absolute doctrinal adherence, she said, "I don't know that there would be a church in this country that I would be involved in. So, you know, you make choices, and you sort of—you can't disown yourself from your family because they've got things wrong. You try to be a part of expanding the conversation." (She made a similar argument when I asked if she agreed with her husband in opposing gay marriage. "It's like you gotta do the baby steps. . . . You don't start with the hardest, toughest issues when you're trying to unite a group.")

Obama does not avoid blunt discussions about race. One year, she and Cindy Moelis, who is white, went to a spa in Utah to celebrate their birth-days. "We were in the cafeteria, getting healthy food for breakfast," Moelis recalled. "Everybody was, like, 'Hey, Michelle!'" Moelis won-dered aloud why nobody remembered her name. "See any more six-foot-tall African American women?" Obama replied. "I didn't think so. So stop taking it personally."

Michelle's perceived authenticity has been an asset to Barack. Ron Carter, a former associate of the Black Panther Party who is the publisher of the *South Street Journal,* told me that he was impressed by her handling of a combustible situation that arose during Barack's senatorial cam-paign, following a speech that he gave at Liberty Baptist Church, on Chicago's South Side. "There were lots of radicals protesting, calling into question his loyalty to the community," Carter recalled. "She came out the back door, and there were a bunch of hoodlum thugs ready to do a full-blast demonstration. She put on her street sense and asked all the guys, 'Y'all got a problem or something?' They all froze, guys who would slap the mayor, who would slap Jesse Jackson in the face, even."

Barack has written eloquently about the pressure of assimilation for members of minority groups. When I asked Michelle if she had felt that sort of pressure, she replied, "What minority communities go through still represents the challenges, the legacies, of oppression and racism. You know, when you have cultures who feel like second-class citizens at some level . . . there's this natural feeling within the community that we're not good enough . . . we can't be as smart as or as prepared—and it's that internal struggle that is always the battle." She talked about her first trip to Africa—Barack took her to Kenya to meet his father's family—and the realization that, as much as white society fails to account for the African American experience, so does any conception of pan-blackness. "There's also the view among many black Americans that Africa is home," she said. "But when you're a black American you're very much an American first."

Marian Robinson told me that she did not know that Barack's mother was white until long after she met him. "He never talked about himself," she said. The Obamas' partnership has been a source of great pride among African American women. In an essay on *TheRoot.com*, Kim McLarin writes that Obama reminds her of Ntozake Shange's play *For Colored Girls Who Have Considered Suicide When the Rainbow Is Enuf:* "ordinary / brown braided woman / with big legs and full lips / reglar." For her, the Obamas' relationship is a public validation of the worthiness of dark-skinned women. "He chose one of us, and I am thrilled," McLarin writes. "She loves, respects, and adores Barack, but she is the prize and she damn well knows it. He better know it, too."

In Chicago, Barbara Pace-Moody opened her e-mail to show me a JPEG of Barack and Michelle that she had been forwarded as an exemplar of a strong marriage. In it, Michelle stands behind Barack, her arms clasped around his waist, while he leans back, his hands over hers, closing his eyes ever so slightly. The picture was taken at a rally in New Hampshire, but they could have been on a beach in Hawaii. *Ebony* named "Barack & Michelle" to its "10 Hottest Couples" list this year, in the company of Beyoncé and Jay-Z. An aide, referring to their "kissy" backstage displays, told me, "They're, like, 'We don't care who's standing by.' "

Some observers have detected in Obama an air of entitlement. Her defenders attribute these charges of arrogance to racist fears about uppity black women. While it's a stretch to call the suggestion that Obama projects an air of self-satisfaction bigoted, it may at least reflect a culture gap: last April, after Maureen Dowd wrote a column criticizing Obama for undermining her husband's mystique, a blog riposte, circulated widely on the Internet, was titled "The White Lady Just Doesn't Get It."

Things had been going remarkably smoothly for Michelle Obama until mid-February. Campaigning four days a week, she was drawing crowds in the thousands. According to David Axelrod, she had urged the campaign to be aggressive in its outreach to female voters, and her husband had made significant inroads with a demographic that had been a Clinton stronghold. "She's pivoted her language to 'See how far we've come' as opposed to 'Don't we have a long way to go,' " one of Obama's advisers told me, in Sheboygan. "It's weird," Craig Robinson said, at the beginning of the month. "It's like if your sister's a budding actress, and all of a sudden she's Julia Roberts."

Speaking at a rally in Wisconsin on February 18, Obama remarked, "For the first time in my adult lifetime, I am really proud of my country, and not just because Barack has done well, but because I think people are hungry for change." The sentiment—that America was in a mess, and Mrs. Obama was not happy about it—was not a new one, but her unfortunate formulation instantly drew charges that she was unpatriotic. Bill O'Reilly spawned his own scandalette, remarking, "I don't want to go on a lynching party against Michelle Obama unless there's evidence, hard facts, that say this is how the woman really feels." Victor Maltsev, of Rego Park, wrote to the *Post*, "Obama wants to be our next first lady? Watch out, America!" Cindy McCain seized the opportunity to draw a sniffy contrast between the Obamas and her and her war-hero husband, telling a cheering crowd, "I don't know about you—if you heard those words earlier—I'm very proud of my country."

It was a manufactured controversy, but it reflected a real cavalierness on Obama's part—not toward the Blue Angels and 9/11 and the Berlin Wall and America's armed forces, as her various critics had it, but toward the reality that it might be wise for a person whose spouse is running for President not to say something that could be construed that way. The controversy over her brand of household humor may have been a matter of cultural misinterpretation. But Obama's blitheness about politics may have less to do with race than it does with class—conservative commentators pegged her as a paragon of élitist leftism—or, more likely, for a daughter of blue-collar Chicago, with personal disposition. In our conversation, she came across as almost apolitical. I asked her about the first time she voted. "Oh, God, um, I've voted every time that I could vote, but I don't—it doesn't stand out," she said. "You know, that was just something you did. You know, you didn't not vote. . . . But I, you know, it wasn't like this moving experience for me"—she breathed in dramatically—" 'I cast my first vote!' " ("I feel kind of bad about it," she once told a reporter, unconvincingly, who asked whether she participated in the Senate spouses' club.)

The self-assurance that colors Obama's assumption that her personal feelings are some bellwether of American achievement is also palpable in her forceful declarations that her husband is the only person who can solve the country's problems. "I tell people I am married to the answer," she said, in a speech in Harlem. "The man . . . who I am willing to sacrifice," she called her husband, in Iowa. In November, on MSNBC: "Black voters will wake up and get it." There is a hectoring, buy-one-while-supplies-last quality to Obama's frequent admonitions that Americans will have only one chance to elect her husband president. Someone who has spent a good portion of her life gaining purchase has suddenly been asked to sell something, and she seems to find it slightly beneath her.

Perhaps Obama's high-handedness is preemptive, her way of "claiming a seat at the table"—as she is fond of calling enfranchisement in the power-brokering structure—rather than waiting to be offered one. It's as though she figures she might as well say that she and her husband are all that before someone can say that they aren't. And there's a sort of strategic genius to her presentation of campaigning as grinding work that takes her away from her family, rather than a glorious tour of the world's greatest country that she would be thrilled to be undertaking even if she didn't have to. She frequently tells her audiences, "I don't care where I am, the first question is 'How are you managing it all? How are you holding up?' " The effect, of course, is to set up an expectation of tribute, like those hairdressers who display all their gifts in the days leading up to Christmas. By loudly voicing her distaste for retail politicking, Obama makes people feel as though, by showing up, she were doing them a favor.

One on one, Obama is gracious. A week before the Wisconsin primary, she made an appearance at the Hops Haven Brew Haus, in Sheboygan. When it was over, I joined her in the back seat of a Ford Explorer for part of the ride to Green Bay. Space was tight, and I couldn't find anywhere to put my sludgy boots except practically on top of her black leather pocketbook. (If a woman's handbag is a window onto her soul, Obama really is normal: hers had an empty M&M's wrapper and an iPod sticking out of an unzipped compartment.) "You know what, let me move it because I can put it out of your way," she said. Someone was trying to put something in the trunk, which was locked. "Oh, they're trying to get in the back," she said, and moved to help, like a mother packing her charges into the station wagon.

The acrimony between the Obamas and the Clintons had been intensifying in the days leading up to the Wisconsin primary. I asked Obama if she was worried about negative attacks on her husband. She was diplomatic. "We've pretty much heard it all," she said.

"She's very competitive, and she believes deeply in him and in what we're doing," David Axelrod said later. "I don't think she's a pacifist—if she thinks we're being treated unfairly or doesn't think we're being aggressive enough in debunking attacks, she will say so. She does not fold up into the lotus position and start chanting 'kumbaya.' She's against gratuitous attacks but she's not against defending our position and making sure we don't get punked."

Others in the Obama camp were less circumspect. "I'm telling you, she's not faking the funk, that's for sure. Neither is he," Craig Robinson said, over lunch in Providence. "And that's why it's working. That's why people are connecting. Cause you can't B.S. that good. Even if you're Bill Clinton you can't, because he's getting called on it."

I asked Robinson about Bill Clinton's "fairy tale" comment. "He's straight up saying things that aren't true," Robinson responded. "And it was great, because Barack didn't go crazy. He just said, 'Hey, we just have to say something when somebody says something that's blatantly not true.' No one's ever called those people on it." He went on, "Michelle and Barack's plan is to win this election. They can't be worried about what he says. I mean, you know, sometimes you get angry. But it's so ludicrous that it's almost comical. It really is. It really is. And the whole crying now before every primary? You've got to be kidding me. If I was a woman, I'd be embarrassed for her," he said of Hillary Clinton.

The competition between the two couples, and specifically between Michelle Obama and Bill Clinton, became explicit later when one of Michelle's advisers pulled me aside and pointed out that Michelle had recently been given Secret Service protection. "So that's both spouses on both sides," the aide pointed out.

Back in the Explorer, I asked Obama if she thought that her husband, as the Democratic nominee, could take John McCain. "Oh, yeah. We got him," she replied.

When the conversation turned to the broader significance of Obama's candidacy, I wondered if the burden of history weighed upon her. "No, I just don't think in those terms," Obama said. "I'm very much one foot in front of the other. You know, we're not there. We've got to win a bunch of states and delegates and, you know, this is a messy process. And then there's still a general election. So I am so far away from history right now that it's like, 'Why get caught up in that emotionally when there's so much stuff in front of us that we have to do?' Plus, I've got kids, and, you know, what are we doing for spring break, and their birthdays are coming up. I've got plenty of stuff to worry about before my legacy in history and all that."

In *The Audacity of Hope*, Barack Obama perceives a vulnerability in his wife, one so closely guarded that even her brother professed to me never to have noticed it. There was "a glimmer that danced across her round, dark eyes whenever I looked at her," he writes, "the slightest hint of uncertainty, as if, deep inside, she knew how fragile things really were, and that if she ever let go, even for a moment, all her plans might quickly unravel." The Explorer rolled on to Green Bay.

Reverend
Wright
Revisited

———————— ✳ ————————

Project Trinity: The Perilous Mission of Obama's Church

Kelefa Sanneh

"I have never seen so many white people here in my life!" It was Good Friday on the South Side of Chicago, at Trinity United Church of Christ, which has been Senator Barack Obama's church for about twenty years and the most notorious congregation in America for about three and a half weeks. The preacher was in the pulpit, recalling a scene outside the church earlier in the week. He gestured at the reporters who had come to take notes. "I hope you're tithing," he said.

As millions of people with no particular interest in African American religious institutions now know, Trinity is home to the Reverend Jeremiah A. Wright, Jr. Since March 13, when *Good Morning America* broadcast clips of Wright at his most incendiary, he has been an unlikely political celebrity, half of an American odd couple: the fiery, noisy, sixties-influenced spiritual adviser to a presidential candidate who is supposed to be cool, quiet, and new. Wright's greatest hits found a home on the Internet and on cable news. There are those seven words he uttered, days after September 11: "America's chickens? Are coming home! To roost." And there's the way he rewrote a classic Irving Berlin lyric: "Not

'God bless America.' 'God damn America!' " But by the time the scandal broke, Wright was already gone. He had announced his retirement at the age of sixty-six, preaching his last sermon at Trinity on February 10, and he kept out of sight while the controversy deepened.

On Good Friday, the church held its annual "Seven Last Words of Christ" service, featuring seven sermons from as many guest preachers. Trinity calls itself "unashamedly black and unapologetically Christian," but the preacher who was marvelling at all those white people was himself white: Father Michael Pfleger, the leader of the Faith Community of St. Sabina, also on Chicago's South Side, which proclaims itself to be an "African American Catholic church." For one of the historic African American churches, such a proclamation would be gratuitous, but Pfleger's church, like Wright's, belongs to a denomination in which African Americans are a small minority. The insistence on race is, in part, an assertion of self-determination, a declaration that no church is culturally neutral.

Seven preachers, seven sermons: that's either a celebration or an endurance test. Inevitably, it's a competition. The first at the pulpit, the Reverend Dr. Eugene L. Gibson, Jr., from Olivet Fellowship Baptist Church, in Memphis, set the bar high. His sermon came from Luke 23:34, which records the first words of Christ during the crucifixion: "Then said Jesus, 'Father, forgive them; for they know not what they do.' " It's one of the best-known lines in the New Testament, an eloquent expression of grace in extremis. But Gibson added his own rejoinder: "Yes, they do!" And, in case anyone missed the heresy, he spelled it out: "I. Dis-a-gree. With Jesus."

The momentum was building. Gibson talked about tormentors who knew exactly what they were doing, making implicit reference to Wright's detractors and explicit reference to the petty naysayers of everyday life. Only near the end did he draw back, admitting that—as usual—Jesus was right and he was wrong. "It's not what they were doing," he said. "It's who they were doing the what to." They knew exactly what a crucifixion was; they just didn't know who Jesus was. Even so, his caustic reproach hung in the air all afternoon: "Yes, they do!"

The Reverend Dr. E. Dewey Smith, from the Greater Travelers Rest Baptist Church, in Decatur, Georgia, based his sermon on Jesus' dying words, as recorded in John 19:30: "He said, 'It is finished.' " Smith urged the congregation to be strong and smart in the face of the onslaught, and his sermon built to an exuberant, sung finale: worshippers cried out, re-

joicing in their own fortitude. Pfleger, taking up the question that is Jesus'
last utterance during the crucifixion in the Gospel of Mark ("My God, my
God, why hast thou forsaken me?"), inveighed against BET, "prosperity-
pimping preachers," and rappers. He also delivered one of the day's most
impassioned calls to arms: "I'll be damned if I'm gonna sit back while you
tear down Farrakhan and Jeremiah Wright. How dare you!" During each
sermon, the non-preaching preachers lounged on pews next to the pulpit,
joined by the Reverend Otis Moss III, a thirty-seven-year-old Yale Di-
vinity School graduate who will succeed Wright as Trinity's senior pastor. Moss and others sometimes swarmed the pulpit when they heard a
particularly heated cadence, pantomiming gestures of restraint that came
to seem indistinguishable from encouragement.

You could hear Wright's influence in every sermon. His life and work
can't be accurately extrapolated from a few video clips, and, at the church
now, "sound bite" is uttered like a curse word. But there's nothing on
YouTube that seems likely to scandalize anyone who has spent time at
Trinity. Even Obama does not claim to be surprised by what he called, in
his "A More Perfect Union" speech, which he gave on March 18, Wright's
"profoundly distorted view of this country." (Despite such disavowals,
there is no evident resentment toward Obama at the church; on Good Friday, every mention of his name and reference to his candidacy was
greeted with applause.) Few of the preachers resisted the temptation to
draw parallels between the man on the Cross and the man on the news,
though most of them found ways to do so indirectly. The Reverend Dr.
Rudolph W. McKissick, Jr., from Bethel Baptist Institutional Church, in
Jacksonville, Florida, looked suggestively around the room as he described the last days of Jesus: "He does not retire in celebration, but he re-
tires with a crucifixion." Worshippers were free to think about any retiree
they liked.

The hints of modern-day crucifixion may have been, in part, Holy
Week hyperbole, designed to rouse the indignation of congregants who
dislike hearing their church criticized. But there's no denying the intensity of the media barrage. In a bipartisan display of umbrage, commentators on television and online have largely agreed that Wright is nutty, or
insane, or worse. And because the Democratic primary schedule has a big
hole in it—six weeks separate Pennsylvania from Mississippi—the tale of
the Chicago pastor who said "God damn America" was for an excruciat-
ingly long time the biggest political story in the country. While Good Friday worshippers were making their way out of the marathon service, Bill

O'Reilly was preparing his seventh straight television program devoted, at least in part, to the Wright affair.

"Christianity is the white man's religion." That was Malcolm X's verdict, and though he meant it to be final, a generation of black Christian leaders decided to treat it as provisional. In 1969, a thirty-one-year-old theologian named James H. Cone published *Black Theology & Black Power*, a short, astringent book that Wright would use as a blueprint for Trinity. Cone proposed a reciprocal arrangement: just as the Black Power movement could find redemption in the Church, so the Church—dominated and distorted by generations of white men—could find redemption in the Black Power movement. He wrote that there was "a need for a theology whose sole purpose is to emancipate the gospel from its 'whiteness' so that blacks may be capable of making an honest self-affirmation through Jesus Christ." And he argued that, since African American suffering was such a powerful metaphor for the suffering of Christ, color-blind Christianity was a contradiction in terms. "To be Christian is to be one of those whom God has chosen," he wrote. "God has chosen black people!"

Like many brash-sounding manifestos of the era, this one came with fine-print qualifications. Throughout the book, Cone was careful to explain that a black-centered Church need not be a black-separatist Church. And even the simplest phrases—"black people," for instance—turned out to be slippery. It wasn't about being "physically black," he wrote. "To be black means that your heart, your soul, your mind, and your body are where the dispossessed are." In his view, blackness was as radically inclusive as Christianity itself, and just as demanding.

Cone, now sixty-nine, is a professor at Union Theological Seminary, in New York; he has a high, emphatic voice and a tendency to slide to the edge of his seat when he's about to make a point. On a recent afternoon at his faculty apartment in Morningside Heights, which is decorated with African art, he explained the genesis of black liberation theology. He was following the lead of the National Committee of Negro Churchmen, a group that in 1966 had purchased a full-page advertisement in the *Times* which endorsed—and, in a sense, tried to co-opt—the goals of the Black Power movement. Cone wasn't among the signatories; his formative experience came the next year.

"It was the riots in Detroit, in Newark, both in '67—that was what shook me," he recounted. "I said to myself, 'I have to have a theology that speaks to the hurt in my community. I want a theology that would empower people to be more creative. To be just as aggressive as they are in the riots, but more constructive.' "

The doctrine he laid out was a response, too, to the paradox at the heart of black Christianity: the new religion of enslaved Africans was also the old religion of the American enslavers. In abolitionist tracts (like David Walker's *Appeal*) and slave narratives, black writers struggled to find a way to distinguish between righteous Christianity and its monstrous opposite. Frederick Douglass, in an appendix to his *Narrative,* earnestly assures readers that he is not an atheist, then redoubles his attack on the theology of slaveholding America: "Between the Christianity of this land, and the Christianity of Christ, I recognize the widest possible difference—so wide, that to receive the one as good, pure, and holy, is of necessity to reject the other as bad, corrupt, and wicked." (Or, rendered into cable-news crawl: CONTROVERSIAL MEMOIRIST ATTACKS RELIGION. DOUGLASS: AMERICAN VALUES "WICKED.")

There was, for Cone, another motivating force in the rise of black liberation theology. In black neighborhoods across America, the spiritual marketplace was getting crowded, and churches seemed in danger of being edged out. Politically inclined young people who wanted no part of "the white man's religion" could turn instead to Marxism, or to various strains of black-nationalist thought, or to Elijah Muhammad's Nation of Islam, the group that groomed Malcolm X. Cone found himself on the wrong side of a growing divide—as he puts it, "We were Martin Luther King, Jr., people"—and he realized that not just the sales pitch but the product had to be changed; the urgency in his prose reflected his anger but also his fear that the black Church was becoming obsolete. Preachers who had helped lead the civil-rights movement were being outflanked by black nationalists who mistrusted any belief system that claimed to be universal. The historian and theologian Gayraud Wilmore contends that the Nation of Islam "kept fire at the feet of the historic black churches." It's no coincidence, he observes, that the black liberation–theology movement cooled after 1975, the year Elijah Muhammad died. But the effect lingered. In a study published in 1990, C. Eric Lincoln and Lawrence Mamiya found that about a third of urban pastors cited black liberation theology as an influence.

When Wright began his tenure at Trinity United Church of Christ, in 1972, it had fewer than a hundred worshippers. His ministry thrived: through sermons and protests and an ever-expanding list of support groups and workshops, Wright turned it into a megachurch with eight thousand members. Cone calls Trinity "the best representation" of black liberation theology. "It's offensive, because it speaks the truth in harsh, blunt terms," he says. Yet, after all those years of talking and organizing and agitating, Wright became black liberation theology's most famous exponent a few weeks after he stepped aside, during a period when, for perhaps the first time in his adult life, he wasn't holding forth on anything at all.

Wright was born into the pulpit. His father, Jeremiah A. Wright, Sr., was a preacher, the leader of the Grace Baptist Church of Germantown, in Philadelphia. The younger Wright started his undergraduate career at Virginia Union University, his father's alma mater, and, after a few years in the Marines and the Navy (he was a medical technician), he graduated from Howard University in 1968, with a degree in English. Seven years later, he earned a master's degree from the University of Chicago. Even during Wright's early years at Trinity, political provocation was part of his approach, although some of his gestures—like the "Free South Africa" banner he hung across the old church building in 1977—don't seem terribly controversial now. On Chicago's South Side, they probably never did.

Although Cone's work had a major influence on him, Wright was carried along, too, by his own research and inclinations. He criticized Cone's assertion that blacks "were completely stripped of their African heritage as they were enslaved," and argued that the black Church should engage more with the African roots of its worshippers: he defined Trinity as "a congregation with a non-negotiable commitment to Africa." That much is evident in the African patterns on the church robes, and in the names of the various ministries and associations; the bookshop, for example, is called Akiba, the Swahili word for "savings."

In his sermons, Wright loves to amplify Bible passages by translating them into the black vernacular. Matthew 19:27 describes Peter's impatience and exasperation with Jesus: "Behold, we have forsaken all, and followed thee; what shall we have therefore?" Wright's rendering is expansive, both informal and intimate:

> *The Samaritans don't want us. The Galileans asked us to leave their territory. They were more interested in saving pigs than saving people. The Pharisees don't like us. The Sadducees ain't too happy about us. The scribes are hot under the collar. Herod is mad at you, and your own family thinks you're kind of touched in the head.*

Similarly, his insistence on the presence of Africa in the Bible makes Scripture seem slightly less exotic while getting worshippers to think of themselves as slightly more exotic. When he discusses Esther 2:17, for example, he turns Mordecai's decision to adopt his cousin Esther into a testament to black family values: "Operating on the African principle of extended family, Mordecai took her in, adopted her, and reared her."

The rise of Jeremiah Wright, in the seventies and eighties, coincided with the rebirth of the Nation of Islam under Minister Louis Farrakhan. In fact, the uproar over Obama and Wright has been, in part, an uproar over Farrakhan, who keeps sneaking into the frame. He and Wright were twinned at the Democratic Presidential debate in Cleveland, on February 26, when Tim Russert of NBC, ascribed to Wright the claim that Farrakhan "epitomizes greatness." (Actually, the statement came from an article by Rhoda McKinney-Jones in *Trumpet*, a Trinity-associated magazine published by Wright's daughter Jeri L. Wright; as has been widely noted since then, Farrakhan was given a lifetime-achievement award at a *Trumpet* banquet in November.) Last summer, the *Trinity Bulletin* reprinted an open letter by a Farrakhan ally convinced that Israel and apartheid South Africa had "worked on an ethnic bomb that kills blacks and Arabs." Yet Wright seems to have a complicated relationship with Farrakhan, whose national headquarters are in the South Shore neighborhood, a few miles from Trinity. His remarks about Farrakhan veer from the fulsome (the minister's analysis of America's racial ills is "astounding and eye opening") to the equivocal (he is "sincere about his faith and his purpose"), but for the most part Wright chooses his words with tactical care, the way Cone did when he wrote about Elijah Muhammad. It is the language of a respectful, and possibly anxious, rival. Like Cone in the 1960s, Wright may have worried that he would be judged, and found wanting, by purer and less forgiving forms of black nationalism. Farrakhan represented the threat; his followers—particularly the young black men whom churches sometimes had trouble reaching—represented the prize.

Wright attended (but didn't address) the Million Man March, the 1995 gathering in Washington that Farrakhan convened to promote self-reliance and "spiritual renewal" among black men. In the months afterward, Wright delivered a series of sermons that were reprinted in a book, *When Black Men Stand Up for God*, which presents a Christian response to the challenge posed by the Nation of Islam. In it, he lambastes the preachers who opposed the march on political or religious grounds: they had missed a prime opportunity to present their case to African American men. And, by way of establishing his bona fides, he reminds readers that he studied Islam at the University of Chicago. "I have a different perspective on Islam than the average preacher," he writes. "Islam and Christianity are a whole lot closer than you may realize. Islam comes out of Christianity." That's interfaith dialogue, served with a hint of one-upmanship.

It seems apt that an American pastor who was eager to discover his African past should have crossed paths with a community organizer of Kenyan (and Kansan) descent, who was eager to discover his American future. If Obama felt attacked by Wright's stormy sermons and prickly politics, he may also have felt flattered to be part of a congregation rooted in the righteous history of a civil-rights struggle that he himself had missed, except as a beneficiary. Nor was the decision to join innocent of strategic calculation. In *Dreams from My Father*, Obama seems to worry that the church's reputation could be a professional liability. "Some people say that the church is too upwardly mobile," he told Wright during their first meeting. (These days, that charge doesn't seem to be foremost in people's minds.)

Eventually, Obama came to see the church as a "redistributor of values," helping congregants like him to navigate tricky social and economic divisions:

> *Only now the redistribution didn't run in just a single direction from the schoolteacher or the physician who saw it as a Christian duty to help the sharecropper or the young man fresh from the South adapt to big-city life. The flow of culture now ran in reverse as well; the former gang-banger, the teenage mother, had their own forms of validation—claims of greater deprivation, and hence authenticity, their presence in the church providing the lawyer or doctor with an education from the streets. By widening its doors to allow all who would enter, a church like Trinity assured its members that their fates remained inseparably bound, that an intelligible "us" still remained.*

In order to serve the black community, the church also had to create one.

Still, the worry that Trinity might be "too upwardly mobile" says something about the challenges facing a black preacher trying to hold together an economically disparate congregation. It also helps explain the church's famous "disavowal of the pursuit of middleclassness," and

Wright's focus, in his sermons, on poverty and oppression. To speak of the "pursuit of middleclassness" as something shameful would seem to imply that moving up means selling out. Yet the credo might also have reassured well-to-do worshippers trying to negotiate the crosshatched lines of race and class: their presence at Trinity was proof that they hadn't, after all, been swallowed by "middleclassness."

Certainly, Wright's avidity for such provocations served to distance him from other black megachurch leaders, many of whom give their congregations—and, of course, themselves—dispensation to celebrate the trappings of worldly success. (On Easter Sunday, for instance, Bishop Eddie Long, of the New Birth Missionary Baptist Church, held his annual Georgia Dome service; the rapper T.I. was released from house arrest for the occasion, and the *Atlanta Journal-Constitution* reported that some thirty thousand people attended. "Jesus wasn't poor," Long has said.) Similarly, Wright's rawer imprecations separated him from the respectable mainstream of black clergy. ("You just can't cuss like that from the pulpit," Calvin O. Butts, of Harlem's Abyssinian Baptist Church, said during his Easter sermon.) But mainstream acceptance is what Wright has volubly disdained; he prefers to cast himself as a rebel preacher, telling the hard truths that most black churches avoid.

Wright's successor, Otis Moss III, seems to acknowledge that some of Wright's claims were best heard as mere "barbershop" talk. But, when Wright is in full prophetic mode, he can make it difficult for listeners to separate metaphorical claims from literal ones, visions from explanations, urban legend from history. He has propounded dubious theories about how Africans and African Americans are "right-brain people." And, like many preachers who see biblical parables in contemporary politics, he has a weakness for theories that match his sense of outrage but not the facts, as when he repeated the popular conspiracy theory that "the government lied about inventing the H.I.V. virus as a means of genocide against people of color." His forays into electoral politics—"Hillary ain't never been called a nigger!"—can come off as simply churlish. At the same time, the sometimes outlandish rhetoric remains tethered to his practical, social-mission side; one YouTube clip, posted by Trinity, shows Wright, at the pulpit, having his mouth swabbed for an H.I.V. test, in the hope of persuading worshippers to follow his example.

Obama, in his speech, refused to dissociate himself from Wright (at this late date, to do so would have been futile anyway), but he sought to draw a distinction between his world view and his pastor's. He said that

Wright's error was to talk about race in America "as if no progress has been made"; he contrasted Wright's perspective with his own "audacity to hope for what we can and must achieve tomorrow." This was itself an audacious move, because "the audacity to hope" was a coinage of Wright's. Audacious hopefulness is sometimes said to be the thing that separates Obama from more conventional politicians, but it is also what separates him from the radicals who have given it up. (The Back to Africa movement—echoed in Wright's Afrocentric approach to Christianity—was, in part, a politics of resignation, fueled by a sense that America would never be truly hospitable to blacks.) Hope is proof that Obama believes in the system, after all. And it is what helps him appeal to swing voters with fond memories of Bill Clinton, who never tired of reminding voters that he was born in a town called Hope.

Wright's hope is a different thing. His 1991 "Audacity to Hope" sermon was based on 1 Samuel 1:1–18, which tells the story of a woman, Hannah, childless and bereft, who prays for a son. Wright isn't interested in the happy ending, so he doesn't mention 1 Samuel 1:20, in which Hannah finally gives birth. Instead, he dwells on her torment, comparing her to Martin Luther King, Jr., in his last years, when the civil-rights coalition seemed to be crumbling and his old allies were criticizing his increasingly comprehensive political program. "There was nothing on the horizon to say that he should keep on hoping, but he kept on hoping anyhow," Wright said. For Wright, earthly adversity and the struggle against it are existential. If he thinks that things haven't changed much in the past hundred years, it's because he thinks that things haven't changed much in the past two thousand years. You don't hope because the odds look good. You hope because they don't.

It was almost six o'clock on Easter morning, but on Ninety-fifth Street in Chicago it looked more like Saturday night. Sunrise was more than half an hour away, and worshippers were converging on Trinity for the first of the day's five services (six, eight, ten, noon, and six), stepping carefully over snow and mud, looking like smartly dressed revellers headed for an after-hours party. It was still too dark to see the steeple, which is about as tall, and as ornate, as the cell-phone tower across the street.

A satellite truck was parked near the church entrance, and when its proprietors were asked where they came from they gamely replied, "Fox News." On the church door, signs offered a stern reminder: "No cameras & no recording devices allowed in the building." Trinity has been through this before: last year, after the *Times* reported that Obama had disinvited Wright from speaking at the announcement of his presidential candidacy, Wright responded with an open letter to the reporter, which took up three pages in the bulletin. (It began, "Thank you for engaging in one of the biggest misrepresentations of the truth I have ever seen in sixty-five years," though Wright never cited any errors of fact.) Recent events have heightened the church's bunker mentality, and people attending services have received "The Truth About Trinity," a flyer listing some of the church's good works and urging worshippers to send e-mails in support of Trinity to Fox News and other media outlets.

The Wright controversy has shifted the balance between the public church (a place to proclaim God's love) and the private church (a place to receive it). Trinity still distributes its services on cable television, on radio, and on the Internet. And, despite the no-recording policy, the church takes it for granted that there are spies in the house, and that any controversial statement will be flashed around the world. Though preachers might be more careful now, the dominant rhetorical mode is defiance: Moss and the other preachers cannot afford to be seen as capitulators. During the Good Friday marathon, Reverend Gibson had declared Wright to be "one of the most generous men you will ever meet." Then he said, "Print that! Put that on the blog!"

Near the end of Good Friday's service, Moss ordered that the church's video cameras be shut off. What followed wasn't particularly exciting: he plugged a pro-Trinity blog (truthabouttrinity.blogspot.com) and the church's official YouTube channel, inviting church members to flood both with positive comments. "We want you to be our foot soldiers in cyberspace," he said. Then he said, "You can turn the video back on," and the pews erupted. After weeks of scrutiny, the church members seemed thrilled to have had a semi-private moment, however inconsequential and illusory.

Moss was to deliver the six-o'clock Sunday-morning sermon, and it bore a provocative title: "How to Handle a Public Lynching." Moss is the son of the preacher and civil-rights activist Otis Moss, Jr., and likes to remind listeners that he is part of the hip-hop generation, calling himself "a theological d.j." He came to Trinity two years ago, lured away from Tabernacle Baptist Church, in Augusta, where, for nine years, he had, in the manner of Wright, turned a few hundred worshippers into a few thousand. He is fully devoted to Trinity's program of black liberation theology, but he's a more restrained, less spontaneous-sounding speaker than his predecessor. His youth and easy confidence and self-control can make him seem closer in temperament to Obama than to Wright.

Moss is also given to rambling displays of erudition, sometimes with an ironic flourish; he'll choose big words to make the congregation chuckle at his sesquipedalian flair. He started with a long riff on his love of literature—he emphasized all four syllables of the word—and, after listing favorite authors ranging from Wole Soyinka to Colson Whitehead, found his way to William Faulkner's short story about a lynch mob, "Dry September," which he called "a mythic but truthful novel of American life in the South." Then, paying tribute to McKissick's Good Friday sermon, he talked about how the ministry of Jesus ended not with a celebration but with a crucifixion—a lynching, in other words. And he paid particular attention to the plight of the apostles, who knew that this grisly spectacle was only the beginning. "No one should start their ministry with a lynching," he said, drawing cheers of agreement and encouragement and maybe also sympathy.

As the church band started to stir, Moss's voice became more fervent and more musical, even as his homily became more abstract. He underscored the link between Easter and the vernal equinox, he talked about the metaphorical importance of the moment when day starts to outlast night, and he noted that "Easter will never come this early for another hundred and fifty-two years." He moved nimbly, flexing his knees or leaning over the lectern to emphasize a point, but he sometimes tripped over the words when he was perorating at full speed and volume. And his pew-pummelling, raw-throated climaxes seemed slightly mannered; you got the feeling that his matter-of-fact business announcements came closer to capturing his true personality. (On Sunday, he announced the creation of a "Resurrection Fund" to combat negative perceptions of Trinity, and he named a number. "I'm gonna just put it out there," he said: a supplementary contribution of a hundred dollars a month would help a lot.) A gifted preacher like Wright can convey the thrilling sensation that rhetoric and rhythm are pulling him along; Moss, instead, often seems to be pushing.

Of course, leading a church, especially this one, isn't just a matter of preaching. Wright inherited a small congregation in need of a spark; Moss has inherited a sprawling corporate labyrinth that includes dozens of subassociations (the Drug & Alcohol Recovery Ministry, the Career Development Ministry, the Diabetes Support Group) and initiatives, including an "African-centered" grade school, Kwame Nkrumah Academy, which is scheduled to open in September. Jeremiah Wright, scholar and preacher and political activist, was also a successful entrepreneur, with a knack for figuring out his congregants' needs, both pastoral and rhetorical, and meeting them, though not always in expected ways. (His post-9/11 fulminations, for example, were undoubtedly less startling to some members than his support for gays and lesbians.) Motivated and emboldened by the decline of the politically engaged black Church and, perhaps, by the rise of Farrakhan, he built an empire and a community in his own image, and in his congregants'. Now it is Moss's turn.

Across the street from Trinity's main entrance is a small building with a sign that says, *St. Matthew Gordon AME Zion*. Its presence, for anyone who notices it, is a reminder of the scrappy little church that Trinity used to be, and of the scrappy little churches all over the city, each harboring dreams of fruitful multiplication. For Wright, black Chicago's highly competitive religious market was a challenge and a spur; for a different preacher, in a different era, it could be a threat. The media frenzy has obscured, and postponed, the real test facing the church. Bad press does no real harm to a church that relishes an air of opposition and that relies on cheerful givers, not on mainstream sponsors. (On the contrary, Moss told NPR, the controversy "has brought the entire church together.") But the next challenge will become increasingly clear. After thirty-six years with Wright at the helm, an idiosyncratic megachurch is trying to change its leadership without changing its identity. Once Wright's moment in the media spotlight is over, his church will have to figure out how to get along without him.

Rev. Jeremiah Wright Isn't the Problem

Gary Kamiya

Maybe we really are doomed to elect John McCain, remain in Iraq forever and nuke Iran. Nations that forget history may not be doomed to repeat it, but those that never even recognize reality in the first place definitely are. Last week's ridiculous uproar over Rev. Jeremiah Wright's sermons proves yet again that America has still not come to terms with the most rudimentary facts about race, 9/11—or itself.

The great shock so many people claim to be feeling over Wright's sermons is preposterous. Anyone who is surprised and horrified that some black people feel anger at white people, and America, is living in a racial never-never land. Wright has called the U.S. "the United States of White America," talks about the "oppression" of black people and says, "White America got their wake-up call after 9/11." Gosh, who could have dreamed that angry racial grievances and left-wing political views are sometimes expressed in black churches?

It's not surprising that the right is using Wright to paint Barack Obama as a closet Farrakhan, trying to let the air out of his trans-racial balloon by insinuating that he's a dogmatic race man. But beyond the fake shock and the all-too-familiar racial politics, what the whole episode reveals is how narrow the range of acceptable discourse remains in this country. This is especially true of anything having to do with patriotism or 9/11—which have become virtually interchangeable. Wright's unforgivable sin was that he violated our rigid code of national etiquette. Instead of the requisite "God bless America," he said "God damn America." He said 9/11 was a case of chickens coming home to roost. Now we must all furrow our brows and agree that such dreadful words are anathema and that no presidential candidate can ever have been within earshot of them.

This is absurd. We're worrying about someone in Row 245 who refuses to stand up for "The Star Spangled Banner," while the people who are singing loudest and waving the biggest flags are the ones who got us into the mess we're in today.

Wright isn't the problem. Stupid patriotism is the problem.

We are now five years into a war that may outrank Vietnam as the most pointless and disastrous one in our history. George W. Bush and his neoconservative brain trust conceived that war, but they were only able to push it through because the American people, their political leaders and the mainstream media signed off on it. And they did so because they were in the grip of the fearful, vengeful, patriotic frenzy that swept the nation after 9/11. Without 9/11 and America's fateful reaction to it, there would be no Iraq War. Every day that the war drags on is yet another indictment of that self-righteous, unthinking "patriotism."

Bill Clinton's line that McCain and Hillary are "two people who love their country" may or may not have been intended to subtly denigrate Obama's patriotism. But whatever it meant, it didn't have anything to do with the actual problems facing the country. Loving America more than your opponent does is not a qualification for higher office.

In fact, the same all-American flag-wavers who called loudest for war against Iraq are now denouncing Wright as a hate-monger and a traitor, and attacking Michelle Obama for saying that only recently has she had reason to feel proud of her country. They insist that anyone who is not permanently proud of the United States, whose patriotism isn't plastered on his or her face like the frozen smile of a beauty queen waving from a Fourth of July float, is beyond the pale. Never mind that the glorious results of their debased version of patriotism—four thousand American troops dead, a wrecked Iraq, and a greatly strengthened terrorist enemy—are plain for all to see.

You wouldn't expect the Republican Party, Fox News, Bill Kristol or the readers of *FreeRepublic* to issue any mea culpas—they don't acknowledge that they've done anything wrong. But the mainstream media's pious tut-tutting over the Wright affair shows that it, too, has learned nothing from its disgraceful post-9/11 performance. The worst excesses of media groveling—the flag pins, the instructions not to run anti-U.S. stories—may be history, but the timorous mind-set remains the same.

Its reaction to Wright shows that the American establishment still cowers before the patriotic idol. It cited the "God damn America" sermon again and again, like the Spanish Inquisition ritually intoning the words of some heretic before drawing and quartering him. It didn't matter that Wright uttered his curse in the context of demanding that America live up to its ideals—all that mattered were those three talismanic words. Anyone this angry, our media gatekeepers solemnly informed us, must be rejected. The only question was whether Obama was irrevocably tainted by his association with the evildoer. Wright's "chickens coming home to roost" line about 9/11 produced the same unthinking, reflexive reaction. How dare this apostate suggest that America might not be blameless, that its actions could have had anything to do with the 9/11 attacks?

This isn't a brief for Wright. I'm not a fan of Sharpton-style black demagoguery, with its knee-jerk grievance and identity politics. I don't know Wright's political philosophy or racial views well enough to place him on the vast spectrum of black leaders. Based on the few clips I've seen and the excerpts I've read, Wright certainly has his shortcomings. His preaching can be over-the-top, crude and ludicrous. His assertion that the U.S. government spread AIDS in the black population is a caricature of paranoid black demagoguery. In his "chickens coming home to roost" sermon, when he thundered that America's sins were being revisited upon us, he failed to make the essential distinction between saying U.S. actions were partly *responsible* for the attacks and saying that we *deserved* the attacks. At times his aggressive, almost gloating tone and delivery made it seem like that's exactly what he was saying.

But if Wright's "chickens" sermon was unpleasant, the fact is that it was also largely right. He had the bad taste, and the courage, to say exactly what America did not want to hear at that moment. He said that although those who were murdered by terrorists were innocent, America itself was far from innocent. He placed 9/11 in a historical context, instead of pretending that it emerged out of nowhere. Critically, he said that lashing out in vengeful anger, however tempting, was not a wise or just response. To make this point, he used the Bible against itself, citing the terrible Verse 9 of Psalm 137, in which David, speaking in imagination to his Babylonian captors, gives voice to his people's desire for vengeance: "Happy shall he be, that taketh and dasheth thy little ones against the stones." This path, Wright pointed out, had biblical sanction. But it was not the right one.

Yes, Wright was angry, shrill and one-sided. But America would have been better off if his uncomfortable sermon had echoed through every church in the country after 9/11, instead of the patriotic, ahistorical pablum that did.

What's strange, and depressing, is that all this has happened before— and we've learned nothing. In the days after 9/11, the nation whipped itself up into an ecstasy of moral sanctimony. Among the few who dared to resist the groupthink was Susan Sontag, who in a brief *New Yorker* piece wrote, "The disconnect between last Tuesday's monstrous dose of reality and the self-righteous drivel and outright deceptions being peddled by public figures and TV commentators is startling, depressing. The voices licensed to follow the event seem to have joined together in a campaign to infantilize the public. Where is the acknowledgment that this was not a 'cowardly' attack on 'civilization' or 'liberty' or 'humanity' or 'the free world' but an attack on the world's self-proclaimed super-power, undertaken as a consequence of specific American alliances and actions?" Sontag was saying the same things Wright did. Like him, she was instantly pilloried. She was called a traitor, an enemy of the state, an appeaser, a supporter of Osama bin Laden. But she was right.

Today, after five years of a catastrophic war driven by patriotic vengeance, it's still not acceptable to disturb the myth of eternal American innocence. As David Bromwich wrote in a recent piece in the *New York Review of Books*, "the uniformity of the presentation by the mass media after 2001, to the effect that the United States now faced threats arising from a fanaticism with religious roots unconnected to anything America had done or could do, betrayed a stupefying abdication of judgment." Stupefying indeed: Patriotism has proved to be a stronger opiate of the people than religion.

The taboo against any critical national self-examination has always existed here. But 9/11 sealed it in blood and made it virtually untouchable. Only a few academics, Middle East specialists and outspoken journalists have dared to suggest that U.S. foreign policies played a role in the 9/11 attacks. The Democrats, terrified of being called unpatriotic and "weak on national security," won't go there. Which is a big reason that the desperately needed national discussion over how to deal with the Arab/Muslim world after Bush leaves office still hasn't started.

Turkey has a notorious law, Article 301, that makes "insulting Turkishness" a crime. We're a lot closer to this than we like to think. In fact, we can expect John McCain's entire campaign to basically be an American version of Article 301.

Our currently mandated version of patriotism is banal and genteel, as if we are afraid to dig beneath the surface of America and find out what's really there. But there is another tradition of patriotism—a prophetic one. It is dark, angry, disturbing, even terrifying. And it cannot be dismissed, for its exponents include figures who exist at the very heart of the way Americans define themselves and their nation. Wright was vilified for saying "God damn America." But it turns out that the words are inscribed in our national charter.

In *The Shape of Things to Come: Prophecy and the American Voice*, the culture critic Greil Marcus looks at the dark visions articulated and made manifest by John Winthrop, Abraham Lincoln and Martin Luther King, Jr. Like Wright, these three figures did more than demand that America live up to its ideals. Whether in their rhetoric or by the example of their lives, they held a prophetic sword over it.

In 1630, Winthrop delivered a sermon to his fellow members of the Massachusetts Bay Company. The line that has gone down in history, oft cited by Ronald Reagan, is "wee shall be as a Citty upon a Hill." But Reagan, eager to present America as perfect, omitted the passage that followed. Winthrop warned that if the community of Puritans dealt falsely with their God, they would be cursed "till wee be consumed out of the good land whether wee are goeing." Marcus describes this terrible image as "the replacement of God by a demon who, as citizens went about their work or leisure, would suddenly devour them."

In his Second Inaugural Address, delivered near the end of the Civil War, Abraham Lincoln issued an equally terrifying warning—one also largely erased from the national memory. "Fondly do we hope—fervently do we pray that this mighty scourge of war may speedily pass away," Lincoln said. But then he added, "Yet, if God wills that it continue, until all the wealth piled by the bond-man's two hundred and fifty years of unrequited toil shall be sunk, and until every drop of blood drawn with the lash, shall be paid by another drawn with the sword, as was said three thousand years ago, so still it must be said 'the judgments of the Lord, are true and righteous altogether.' " Of this horrific vision, Marcus comments that it is "a call for a reenactment, on a national scale, of an Old Testament sacrifice."

Finally, there is Martin Luther King's "I have a dream" speech, delivered in 1963 in Washington. "I have a dream that my four little children will one day live in a nation where they will be judged not by the color of their skin but by the content of their character," King thundered. Time has smoothed and sentimentalized King's soaring rhetoric; the sheer force of his language has allowed us to convince ourselves that his words came true. But as Marcus points out, they have still not come true—a fact that makes his great speech both inspiring and unbearably painful.

I am not comparing Jeremiah Wright to these towering figures. My point is that his angry claims that his nation has betrayed its promises of racial equality and a just foreign policy are part of a long and honorable prophetic tradition. It was not critics like Wright who got us into the bloody mess we're in today. That honor belongs to the flag-wavers, the patriots—"the real Americans."

The
United States,
Past and Present

America's Greatest Hits

Lolis Eric Elie

Dear Mr. Jones:

You can stop looking; I have found you.

Word has reached me down in the nation's nether regions that you are putting together a collection of America's Greatest Hits. *Such a simple-sounding task. You take Nathan Hale's "One Life to Give," and FDR's "Fear Itself," add Abe Lincoln's "House Divided," and John F. Kennedy's "Ask Not," and,* voilà!, *you have the perfect package to sell alongside the commemorative coin collections on the late-night infomercials. Or is your project intended for international distribution? Perhaps you will ship it off to Zimbabwe or Sri Lanka so they can learn to play our liberated music and dance our freedom dances.*

I can tell you this: You ship such a willfully bland collection overseas, or even to the hipper pockets of America, and hardly a hip will be moved.

Yes, it is a simple-sounding task, and if you do it that way, it will be simplicity itself. For simple, you don't need me. But is that really what you want? A collection of songs calibrated to appeal to the warm-weather patriot in all of us?

If you're really going to anthologize America's Greatest Hits—*your title, certainly not mine—you're going to need someone who has seen a lot more of the world than the Ivy-League American-Studies major I assume you think you're looking for. I've spun records for every occasion from Manhattan champagne soirees to Maringouin, Louisiana, ice-water parties; red-hot stomps to blue-light-in-the-basement grinds; waist-line parties to sock hops; house-rent happenings to country barn raisings; bar mitzvahs to Cinco de Mayo celebrations. I've been paid in everything from gold bullion to fresh yard eggs. I've arrived by horse-drawn carriage and also on the bare, bleeding leather of my own callused feet.*

You see where this is going, don't you?

If there is to be any greatness in this collection, it'll need to include more America than can easily fit in that cloistered space between the ears of the average American.

First of all, you need a new title. The United Hits of America. *Something that's big enough for all the national moods and grooves.*

Can you get to that? Are you willing to include those moments in our national music that may hardly have qualified as moments in your own private America? There are great hits that may have escaped your memory, but trust me, they rest cherished in other recesses of our national consciousness. And they rest uneasy in certain repositories of our national conscience.

I know how the crowds react to the old standards. There are some tunes all Americans have been taught to love. When "Boston Tea Party" dropped, the Mount Vernon crew was doing polite minuets to it. Some of the help got so swept up in the promise of change that they were chanting, "The British Are Coming," right alongside the folks who actually had something at stake. When Patrick Henry came out with "Give Me Liberty or Give Me Death," you couldn't tune in to underground radio without hearing its strains. But don't forget that Crispus Attucks song, "Give Me Or!" That man might have been a one-hit wonder, but he rocked everything from the big house to the slave quarters when he came out with that one. They were still playing it all the way until the 1960s. (Shame he never got to perform it live.)

I know that George Washington's biggest hit was "Cherry Tree." But, truth be told, that's not the song that made his career. If it weren't for 1779's "Lay Waste All the Settlements Around," his name would be virtually unknown outside Virginia. Hardly anybody remembers it now, but the Iroquois sure do. How did it go again?

"Lay waste all the settlements around/That the country may not be merely overrun, but destroyed. . . . /[Don't] listen to any overture of peace/Before the total ruin of their settlements is effected."

I know their music can be a bit cerebral, but is there any group in American history with more hits than the Supremes? Even with all the personnel changes? I like those early albums, when Chief Justice John Marshall was still the lead singer. Remember "Johnson v. McIntosh, 1823"? *The Indiana Indians (some of whom were from Illinois) had just released "Free Enterprise" on their* What Freedom Means to Me *album: "It's my land/I'll sell if I want to." But Big John had an answer song for them. They could live on their land, but they couldn't own it because the white people had discovered it. Has there ever been a more subtle logic expressed in pop music than the one Big John penned? The "right of occupancy" is subordinate to the "right of discovery."*

Of course, the Supremes being old-fashioned, their music tended to be polite and understated. Andrew Jackson was straight-up raw. Some of his lyrics might have been legalistic: "To provide for an exchange of lands with the Indians/Residing in any of the states or territories/And for their removal west of the river Mississippi." But his titles were straight-up gangsta: Not until Hitler came on the scene in the 1930s did anybody have the balls to release anything on vinyl as bold as Jackson's "Indian Removal Act."

The Indians remember lots of songs like that. Ballads, mostly. Songs of lust and yearning about what could have been and maybe what ought to have been, but what ultimately wasn't. My favorite is still "Trail of Tears." Whenever I hear it, I grow nostalgic over my own lost loves: "Every step another tear drop/Forms frozen on my cheek."

People forget now that Indian singers actually ruled the pop charts for centuries. Then they just disappeared. Nowadays, people don't even remember that Indians once could sing. But I still play old Indian records when the mood is right. When I got back with my third wife for the fourth time, I got on my knees and I played a song by that last great Indian singer, Chief Joseph, "I Will Fight No More Forever." (We played it again at the wedding reception when I married my fourth wife.)

But has there been any taproot of inspiration for American music that has run deeper or been sustained longer than the American Negro?

Jeremiah Guttman—Jewish American foot soldier in World War II, shipper of arms to the Zionist cause, and hero of the ACLU—remembers a certain ditty that was all the rage in Florida when his family used to vacation there in the 1930s. "No Niggers, Dogs, Gypsies, or Jews," the song went. The SPCA got its knickers in a twist about the discrimination in that one, but it was the niggers who felt the bulk of American hits. (Who ever heard of a Gypsy water fountain?)

"I Tremble for My Country," Thomas Jefferson crooned at the height of his career. And if God is just, as Jefferson claimed he was, then some songs about the Negro must yet squeeze their way into this anthology. I know you're going to include Abe Lincoln's "If Slavery Is Not Wrong, Nothing Is Wrong." But don't forget, Lincoln was only a star in the North. When Andrew Johnson's "This Is a Country for White Men" came out, it played on every station across the nation. You mention Theodore Roosevelt, and "San Juan Hill" comes immediately to mind. But don't forget, old Teddy created his own genre of protest song with "All Coons Do Not Look Alike to Me!"

Even now, you can hear echoes of Woodrow Wilson's "Making the World Safe for Democracy" in songs about American foreign policy. But is its message more enduring or more worthy than "Why Not Make Us Safe?," Monroe Trotter's forgotten hit? (I know, I know. Trotter was a protectionist. But there is a proper place for such sentiments, is there not?)

The curious thing about Negro-themed material is it induces whiplash on the dance floor. Every time the pace of progress picks up, there's a frenzy of feet. Then a tuneful rebuttal ascends even higher on the charts than its inspiration. Harry Truman's "Executive Order 9981" might have desegregated the armed forces, but his sister, Mary Jane, wrote the song that reassured a fearful nation. "Harry Is No More for Nigger Equality (Than Any of Us)," she sang. When Earl Warren and the Supremes released their desegregation anthem "With All Deliberate Speed," the dance floors were awash with frenetic gyration. But the tempo reverted to its natural crawl when Ike Eisenhower put out "Make Haste Slowly." John F. Kennedy's fusion number, "What Can We Do to Help (But Without Getting Too Far Out Front)?," melded the fast and slow tempos into a seamlessly tuneful hypocrisy.

But was there any performer who had more of an affinity for the ways and rhythms of the Negro than Richard Nixon? Remember, he's the one who produced Earl Butz's song "Tight Pussy, Comfortable Shoes, and a

Warm Place to Shit." But he was working solo when he composed that great gift to black dancers, "Make Sure There's Something in It for the Jigs."

I wish we could include videos. Do you remember John Lewis dancing on the "Edmund Pettus Bridge" video with Sheriff Jim Clark and the Deputies? When it really got good and hot, the sheriff looked over at the Deputies like James Brown looking over at the J.B.s. Then he hollered, "Hit him!" And the whole band, all dressed in their official uniforms, came down with their billy clubs, Whump!

Then the sheriff looked over again and hollered, "Hit him two times!" Whump! Whump!

World War II was The Great War, and the most popular songs from its sound track still warm the hearts that pump American blood. But does anybody ever play Admiral William Halsey's "Kill Japs, Kill Japs, Kill More Japs"? Sunada Toshu was virtually unknown at the time. But in this more enlightened era, I think we could safely include one of his songs in the collection. (You know, the Japanese are very in now.) Why not include "Loyalty, Disloyalty"?

"If asked, what should I answer?" he sang.

✳

Mr. Jones, this has taken up more time—yours and mine—than either of us expected. For that, I apologize. It's your anthology, and you should be proud of it in every particular. Mine is merely the vision of an old American, a student of this place and its less-studied particulars. I fervently believe that this vast nation—yours and mine—is big enough to contain both our selections, though perhaps not in any officially sanctioned capacity. I kid myself into thinking that my collection could ever rise to the level of popularity and acceptance to which you no doubt aspire. My discourse, taking place as it does on the lower frequencies, might better be called Greater Causes, Lesser Hits, or some such couplet that would only be in with the out-crowd.

You have indulged me this long, and for that I owe you a bit of gratitude. But I am not so thankful as to be above begging another indulgence. I have penned my own rejection letter; enclosed it in a self-addressed, stamped envelope. Please, if you would, place it in a mailbox. It will save you the trouble of writing the explanation of how "the caliber *of candidates was unforeseeably high,"* etc., etc. *And it would save me the trouble of wondering whether you had ever even considered that other Americans have felt the beats and hits of this nation not only in their hearts but on their heads as well.*

✳

Sincerely,
Your impertinent servant

The End of the Black American Narrative

Charles Johnson

It is ambition enough to be employed as an under-labourer in clearing the ground a little, and removing some of the rubbish that lies in the way of knowledge.
—*John Locke,* An Essay Concerning Human Understanding

Back to the things themselves!

—*Edmund Husserl*

As a writer, philosopher, artist, and black American, I've devoted more than forty years of my life to trying to understand and express intellectually and artistically different aspects of the black American narrative. At times during my life, especially when I was young, it was a story that engaged me emotionally and consumed my imagination. I've produced novels, short stories, essays, critical articles, drawings, and PBS dramas based on what we call the black American story. To a certain degree, teaching the literature of black America has been my bread and butter as a college professor. It is a very old narrative, one we all know quite well, and it is a tool we use, consciously or unconsciously, to interpret or to make sense of everything that has happened to black people in this country since the arrival of the first twenty Africans at the Jamestown colony in 1619. A good story always has a meaning (and sometimes layers of meaning); it also has an epistemological mission: namely, to show us something. It is an effort to make the best sense we can of the human experience, and I believe that we base our lives, actions, and judgments as often on the stories we tell ourselves about ourselves (even when they are less than empirically sound or verifiable) as we do on the severe rigor of reason. This unique black American narrative, which emphasizes the experience of victimization, is quietly in the background of every conversation we have about black people, even when it is not fully articulated or expressed. It is our starting point, our agreed-upon premise, our most important presupposition for dialogues about black America. We teach it in our classes, and it is the foundation for both our scholarship and our popular entertainment as they relate to black Americans. Frequently it is the way we approach each other as individuals.

As a writer and a teacher of writing, I have to ask myself over and over again, just what *is* a story. How do we shape one? How many different forms can it take? What do stories tell us about our world? What details are necessary, and which ones are unimportant for telling it well? I constantly ask my creative writing students two questions: Does the story work, technically? And, if so, then, what does it *say*? I tell them that, like a work of philosophy (which is the sister discipline to storytelling among the interpretive arts), a narrative vision must have the qualities of coherence, consistency, and completeness. The plot of a modern story must be streamlined and efficient if it is to be easily understood. And, like Edgar Allan Poe in his 1842 essay "On the Aim and the Technique of the Short Story," I argue that a dramatic narrative should leave the listener with "a certain unique or single effect" that has emotional power. For the last thirty-two years, I've stressed to my students that a story must have a conflict that is clearly presented, one that we care about, a dilemma or disequilibrium for the protagonist that we, as readers, emotionally identify with. The black American story, as we tell it to ourselves, beautifully embodies all these narrative virtues.

The story begins with violence in the seventeenth-century slave forts sprinkled along the west coast of Africa, where debtors, thieves, war prisoners, and those who would not convert to Islam were separated from their families, branded, and sold to Europeans who packed them into the pestilential ships that cargoed twenty million human beings (a conservative estimate) to the New World.

As has been documented time and again, the life of a slave—our not-so-distant ancestors—was one of thinghood. Former languages, religions, and cultures were erased, replaced by the Peculiar Institution, in which the person of African descent was property, and systematically—legally, physically, and culturally—denied all sense of self-worth. A slave owns nothing, least of all himself. He desires and dreams at the risk of his life, which is best described as relative to (white) others, a reaction to their deeds, judgments, and definitions of the world. And these definitions, applied to blacks, were not kind. For 244 years (from 1619 to 1863), America was a slave state with a guilty conscience: two and a half centuries scarred by slave revolts, heroic black (and abolitionist) resistance to oppression, and, more than anything else, physical, spiritual, and psychological suffering so staggering it silences the mind when we study the classic slave narratives of Equiano or Frederick Douglass. Legal bondage, the peculiar antebellum world, ended during the Civil War, but the Emancipation Proclamation did not bring liberation.

Legal freedom instead gradually brought segregation, America's version of apartheid. But "separate" clearly was not "equal." Black Americans were not simply segregated; they were methodically disenfranchised, stripped of their rights as citizens. From the 1890s through the 1950s, the law of black life was experienced as second-class citizenship. In the century after the Emancipation Proclamation, members of each generation of black Americans saw their lives disrupted by race riots, lynchings, and the destruction of towns and communities, such as the Greenwood district of black homes, businesses, and churches in Tulsa, Oklahoma, on May 31, 1921. The challenge for black America and the conflict for its story, then, was how to force a nation that excluded black people from its promise of "Life, liberty and the pursuit of happiness" after the Revolutionary War, and failed to redress this grievance after Reconstruction, to honor these principles enshrined in its most sacred documents.

What I have described defines the general shape of the black American group narrative before the beginning of the Civil Rights Movement, the most important and transformative domestic event in American history after the War Between the States. The conflict of this story is first slavery, then segregation and legal disenfranchisement. The meaning of the story is group victimization, and every black person is the story's protagonist. This specific story was not about ending racism, which would be a wonderful thing; but ending racism entirely is probably as impossible for human beings as ending crime, or as quixotic as President Bush's "war on terror." No, the black American story was not as vague as that. It had a clearly defined conflict. And our ancestors fought *daily* for generations, with courage and dignity, to change this narrative. That was the *point* of their lives, their sacrifices, each and every day they were on this earth. We cannot praise enough the miracle they achieved, the lifelong efforts of our leaders and the anonymous men and women who kept the faith, demonstrated, went to jail, registered black people to vote in the Deep South, changed unjust laws, and died in order that Americans of all backgrounds might be free. I have always seen their fight for us as noble.

Among those I pay special tribute to is W. E. B. Du Bois, one of the founders of the NAACP, who deeply understood the logic and structure of this narrative as it unfolded from Reconstruction through the 1950s. It was a sign of his prescience that he also could see *beyond* this ancient story while still in the midst of it and fighting mightily to change it.

In 1926, Du Bois delivered an address titled "Criteria of Negro Art" at the Chicago Conference for the NAACP. His lecture, which was later published in *The Crisis,* the official publication of the NAACP, which Du Bois himself edited, took place during the most entrenched period of segregation, when the opportunities for black people were so painfully circumscribed. "What do we want?" he asked his audience. "What is the thing we are after?"

Listen to Du Bois eighty-two years ago:

> *What do we want? What is the thing we are after? As it was phrased last night it had a certain truth: We want to be Americans, full-fledged Americans, with all the rights of American citizens. But is that all? Do we want simply to be Americans? Once in a while through all of us there flashes some clairvoyance, some clear idea, of what America really is. We who are dark can see America in a way that white Americans cannot. And seeing our country thus, are we satisfied with its present goals and ideals? . . .*
>
> *If you tonight suddenly should become full-fledged Americans; if your color faded, or the color line here in Chicago was miraculously forgotten; suppose, too, you became at the same time rich and powerful;—what is it that you would want? What would you immediately seek? Would you buy the most powerful of motor cars and outrace Cook County? Would you buy the most elaborate estate on the North Shore? Would you be a Rotarian or a Lion or a What-not of the very last degree? Would you wear the most striking clothes, give the richest dinners, and buy the longest press notices?*

Even as you visualize such ideals you know in your heart that these are not the things you really want. You realize this sooner than the average white American because, pushed aside as we have been in America, there has come to us not only a certain distaste for the tawdry and flamboyant but a vision of what the world could be if it were really a beautiful world; if we had the true spirit; if we had the Seeing Eye, the Cunning Hand, the Feeling Heart; if we had, to be sure, not perfect happiness, but plenty of good hard work, the inevitable suffering that comes with life; sacrifice and waiting, all that—but, nevertheless, lived in a world where men know, where men create, where they realize themselves and where they enjoy life. It is that sort of world we want to create for ourselves and for all America.

This provocative passage is, in part, the foundation for my questioning the truth and usefulness of the traditional black American narrative of victimization. When compared with black lives at the dawn of the twenty-first century, and forty years after the watershed events of the Civil Rights Movement, many of Du Bois' remarks now sound ironic, for all the impossible things he spoke of in 1926 are realities today. We are "full-fledged Americans, with the rights of American citizens." We *do* have "plenty of good hard work" and live in a society where "men create, where they realize themselves and where they enjoy life." Even more ironic is the fact that some of our famous rappers and athletes who like "living large," as they say, seem obsessed with what Du Bois derisively called "the tawdry and flamboyant" (they call it "bling"). Furthermore, some of us *do* use the freedom paid for with the blood of our ancestors to pursue conspicuous consumption in the form of "powerful motor cars," "elaborate estates," "striking clothes," and "the richest dinners."

To put this another way, we can say that forty years after the epic battles for specific civil rights in Montgomery, Birmingham, and Selma, after two monumental and historic legislative triumphs—the Civil Rights Act of 1964 and the Voting Rights Act of 1965—and after three decades of affirmative action that led to the creation of a true black middle class (and not the false one E. Franklin Frazier described in his classic 1957 study, *Black Bourgeoisie*), a people oppressed for so long have finally become, as writer Reginald McKnight once put it, "as polymorphous as the dance of Shiva." Black Americans have been CEOs at AOL Time Warner, American Express, and Merrill Lynch; we have served as secretary of state and White House national security adviser. Well over ten thousand black

Americans have been elected to offices around the country, and at this moment Senator Barack Obama holds us in suspense with the possibility that he may be selected as the Democratic Party's first biracial, black American candidate for president. We have been mayors, police chiefs, best-selling authors, MacArthur fellows, Nobel laureates, Ivy League professors, billionaires, scientists, stockbrokers, engineers, theoretical physicists, toy makers, inventors, astronauts, chess grandmasters, dot-com millionaires, actors, Hollywood film directors, and talk show hosts (the most prominent among them being Oprah Winfrey, who recently signed a deal to acquire her own network); we are Protestants, Catholics, Muslims, Jews, and Buddhists (as I am). And we are not culturally homogeneous. When I last looked, West Indians constituted forty-eight percent of the "black" population in Miami. In America's major cities, fifteen percent of the black American population is foreign born—Haitian, Jamaican, Senegalese, Nigerian, Cape Verdean, Ethiopian, Eritrean, and Somalian—a rich tapestry of brown-skinned people as culturally complex in their differences, backgrounds, and outlooks as those people lumped together under the all too convenient labels of "Asian" or "European." Many of them are doing better—in school and business—than native-born black Americans. I think often of something said by Mary Andom, an Eritrean student at Western Washington University, and quoted in an article published in 2003 in *The Seattle Times:* "I don't know about 'chitlings' or 'grits.' I don't listen to soul music artists such as Marvin Gaye or Aretha Franklin. . . . I grew up eating *injera* and listening to *Tigrinya* music. . . . After school, I cook the traditional coffee, called boun, by hand for my mother. It is a tradition shared amongst mother and daughter."

No matter which angle we use to view black people in America today, we find them to be a complex and multifaceted people who defy easy categorization. We challenge, culturally and politically, an old group narrative that fails at the beginning of this new century to capture even a fraction of our rich diversity and heterogeneity. My point is not that black Americans don't have social and cultural problems in 2008. We have several nagging problems, among them poor schools and far too many black men in prison and too few in college. But these are problems based more on the inequities of class, and they appear in other groups as well. It simply is no longer the case that the essence of black American life is racial victimization and disenfranchisement, a curse and a condemnation, a destiny based on color in which the meaning of one's life is thinghood, created even before one is born. This is not something we can assume. The specific conflict of this narrative reached its dramatic climax in 1963 in Birmingham, Alabama, and at the breathtaking March on Washington; its resolution arrived in 1965, the year before I graduated from high school, with the Voting Rights Act. Everything since then has been a coda for almost half a century. We call this long-extended and still ongoing anticlimax the post-civil-rights period. If the NAACP is struggling these days to recruit members of the younger generation and to redefine its mission in the twenty-first century—and it *is* struggling to do that—I think it is a good sign that the organization Du Bois led for so long is now a casualty of its own successes in the 1960s.

Yet, despite being an antique, the old black American narrative of pervasive victimization persists, denying the overwhelming evidence of change since the time of my parents and grandparents, refusing to die as doggedly as the Ptolemaic vision before Copernicus or the notion of phlogiston in the nineteenth century, or the deductive reasoning of the medieval schoolmen. It has become ahistorical. For a time it served us well and powerfully, yes, reminding each generation of black Americans of the historic obligations and duties and dangers they inherited and faced, but the problem with any story or idea or interpretation is that it can soon fail to fit the facts and becomes an ideology, even kitsch.

This point is expressed eloquently by Susan Griffin in her 1982 essay "The Way of All Ideology," where she says, "When a theory is transformed into an ideology, it begins to destroy the self and self-knowledge. . . . No one can tell it anything new. It is annoyed by any detail which does not fit its worldview. . . . Begun as a way to restore one's sense of reality, now it attempts to discipline real people, to remake natural beings after its own image."

In his superb book *In My Father's House*, philosopher Kwame Anthony Appiah writes, "There is nothing in the world that can do all we ask race to do for us." We can easily amend or revise this insight and apply it to the pre-twenty-first-century black American narrative, which can do very little of the things we need for it to do today.

But this is an enduring human problem, isn't it? As phenomenologist Edmund Husserl revealed a hundred years ago, we almost always perceive and understand the new in terms of the old—or, more precisely, we experience events through our ideas, and frequently those are ideas that bring us comfort, ideas *received* from our parents, teachers, the schools we attend, and the enveloping culture, rather than original ones of our own.

While a story or model may disclose a particular meaning for an experience, it also forces into the background or conceals other possible meanings. Think of this in light of novelist Ralph Ellison's brilliant notion of "invisibility," where—in his classic *Invisible Man*—the characters encountered by his nameless protagonist all impose their ideologies (explanations and ideas) on the chaos of experience, on the mysterious, untamed life that forever churns beneath widely accepted interpretations and explanations of "history" and "culture," which in our social world, for Ellison, are the *seen*. I know, personally, there is value in this Ellisonian idea because in the historical fictions I've been privileged to publish, like "Martha's Dilemma" in my second collection, *Soulcatcher and Other Stories,* I discovered that the most intriguing, ambiguous, and revealing material for stories can often be found in the margins of the codified and often repeated narrative about slavery. In this case, I dramatized a delicious anecdote about what happened to Martha and her slaves right after the death of George.

What I am saying is that "official" stories and explanations and endlessly repeated interpretations of black American life over decades can short-circuit direct perception of the specific phenomenon before us. The idea of something—an intellectual construct—is often more appealing and perfect (in a Platonic sense) than the thing itself, which always remains mysterious and ambiguous and messy, by which I mean that its sense is open-ended, never fixed. It is always wise, I believe, to see all our propositions (and stories) as provisional, partial, incomplete, and subject to revision on the basis of new evidence, which we can be sure *is* just around the corner.

Nevertheless, we have heavily and often uncritically invested for most of our lives in the pre-twenty-first-century black American narrative. In fact, some of us depend upon it for our livelihood, so it is *not* easy to let go, or to revise this story. Last October, Nation of Islam minister Louis Farrakhan spoke for two and a half hours at the Atlanta Civic Center. He and his mentor, black separatist Elijah Muhammad, provided black Americans with what is probably the most extreme, Manichean, and mythological version of the black American narrative, one that was anti-integrationist. In this incomplete and misleading rendition of the black American story, the races are locked in eternal struggle. As a story, this narrative fails because it is conceived as melodrama, a form of storytelling in which the characters are flat, lack complexity, are either all good or all bad, and the plot involves malicious villains and violent actions.

Back in the 1930s when Elijah Muhammad shaped his myth of Yacub, which explained the origins of the white race as "devils," he sacrificed the credibility of both character and plot for the most simplistic kind of dramatic narrative. Farrakhan covered many subjects that day last October, but what I found most interesting is that he said successful black people like Oprah Winfrey, Senator Obama, Colin Powell, and Condoleezza Rice give black Americans a false impression of progress. In other words, their highly visible successes do not change the old narrative of group victimization. Minister Farrakhan seems unwilling to accept their success as evidence that the lives of black Americans have improved. He seems unwilling to accept the inevitability of change. He was quoted in the press as saying, "A life of ease sometimes makes you forget the struggle." And despite the battles for affirmative action that created a new middle class, he added, "It's becoming a plantation again, but you can't fight that because you want to keep your little job."

I beg to differ with Farrakhan, with his misuse of language, his loose, imprecise diction, because we obviously do *not* live on plantations. And wasn't job opportunity one of the explicit goals of the black American narrative? Farrakhan's entire life has been an investment in a story that changed as he was chasing it. So, we can understand his fierce, personal, and even tragic attachment to dusty, antebellum concepts when looking at the uncharted phenomena in the early twenty-first century that outstrip his concepts and language.

However, it is precisely because Farrakhan cannot progress beyond an oversimplified caricature of a storyline for racial phenomena that the suddenly notorious Rev. Jeremiah Wright praises him, saying "His depth of analysis . . . when it comes to the racial ills of this nation is astounding and eye-opening," and, "He brings a perspective that is helpful and honest." Recently Wright called the Nation of Islam leader, "one of the most important voices in the twentieth and twenty-first centur[ies]." I do not doubt that Wright and Farrakhan are men who have experienced the evil of racism and want to see the conditions of our people improve, or that both have records of community service. But it is the emotional attachment to a dated narrative, one leavened with the 1960s-era liberation theology of James Cone, that predictably leads Wright to proclaim that the U.S. government created the AIDS virus to destroy blacks (he invokes the old and proven, the ghastly Tuskegee syphilis experiment, in an effort to understand a new affliction devastating black people, and thus commits the logical fallacy known as misuse of analogy); that Jesus was "a black man"; and that the brains of blacks and whites operate differently. The former pastor of Trinity United Church of Christ in Chicago has made these paranoid and irresponsible statements publicly again and again without offering the slightest shred of evidence for these claims. "A bunch of rants that aren't grounded in truth" was how Barack Obama described his former minister's incendiary oratory, which is clearly antithetical not only to the postracial spirit of the Illinois senator's own speeches but also to his very racially and geographically mixed background. For in the realm of ideological thinking, especially from the pulpit, feeling and faith trump fact, and passion (as well as beliefs based on scripture) replaces fidelity to the empirical and painstaking logical demonstration.

Furthermore, such obsolete stories can also lead to serious mistakes in scholarship. I'm thinking now of Henry Louis Gates, Jr., who in 1988 directed the publication of Oxford University Press's forty-volume Schomburg Library of Nineteenth-Century Black Women Writers. In his foreword, Gates praised the lost works of these black women writers as being the literary ancestors of Zora Neale Hurston, Toni Morrison, and Alice Walker. Furthermore, he said it was the discovery of a particular lost black novel, called *Four Girls at Cottage City*, published in 1895 by Emma Dunham Kelley-Hawkins, that inspired him to direct this Schomburg series in the first place so, he said, "I can read them myself."

Okay, so far so good.

But in 2005, Holly Jackson, then a doctoral student of English at Brandeis University, was given the academically pedestrian, grunt-work assignment of writing an entry about Kelley-Hawkins for the *African American National Biography*. At the time very little was known about Kelley-Hawkins. After checking birth records in the Massachusetts Vital Records, and other documents, Jackson realized that Kelley-Hawkins was not black—as five decades of scholars had assumed—but white. Yet all the evidence to suggest her whiteness was clearly present in the books she wrote. Something that had always puzzled scholars, Jackson said, was "the apparent whiteness of her characters, who are repeatedly described with blue eyes and skin as white as 'pure' or 'driven' snow." Even more fantastic are the theories that literary scholars came up with to explain why Kelley-Hawkins, supposedly a black woman, made no references to race or blackness in her two novels written in the 1890s. Jackson says, "Scholars have explained this away by arguing that the abundance of white signifiers is actually politically radical, with some even going so far as to argue that this extremely white world depicts a kind of post-racial utopia," a modern world where, according to critic Carla L. Peterson, "racial difference no longer existed."

Obviously, all these explanations are hogwash. Fifty years of scholarship based on these mistakes—articles, dissertations, courses in African American women's writing that include the work of Kelley-Hawkins—turns out to be an illusion created by the blinding intentionality of those who wrote about this white author based on a tangled knot of beliefs and prejudices, their concept of her completely distorting the facts.

Once Gates learned of this research by Jackson and also investigations by Katherine Flynn, a genealogist, he immediately went into the mode of damage control. He told a reporter that the work of Kelley-Hawkins would at least be removed from future editions of the Schomburg series, and he downplayed the significance of these discoveries by Jackson and Flynn. But Jackson, being a true scholar, would not allow this intellectual scandal to be swept under the rug. Of this "enormous historical misconception," she said, "there is so much at stake here, because of all the writing that has been done based on a false assumption about race." She asks us to wonder, "How have her [Kelley-Hawkins's] overwhelmingly 'white' texts successfully passed as black for so long in the absence of any corroborating historical data? How does this discovery change our understanding of African American literary history?" Finally, she said, "We have stretched our understanding of how black women have written in America to incorporate texts that do not fit."

I've gone into great detail about the Kelley-Hawkins story because it is a cautionary tale for scholars and an example of how our theories, our explanatory models, and the stories we tell ourselves can blind us to the obvious, leading us to see in matters of race only what we want to see based on our desires and political agendas. When we confront phenomena of any kind, we are wise if we assume the position phenomenologist Herbert Spiegelberg called epistemological humility, which is a healthy skepticism about what we think we already know. When constructing our narratives, it would also help if we remember a famous and often-quoted statement by C. S. Lewis on the characteristics of the human mind: "Five senses; an incurably abstract intellect; a haphazardly selective memory; a set of preconceptions and assumptions so numerous that I can never examine more than a minority of them—never become conscious of them all. How much of total reality can such an apparatus let through?"

How much, indeed.

But if the old black American narrative has outlived its usefulness as a tool of interpretation, then what should we do? The answer, I think, is obvious. In the twenty-first century, we need new and better stories, new concepts, and new vocabularies and grammar based not on the past but on the dangerous, exciting, and unexplored present, with the understanding that each is, at best, a provisional reading of reality, a single phenomeno-logical profile that one day is likely to be revised, if not completely over-turned. These will be narratives that do not claim to be absolute truth, but instead more humbly present themselves as a very tentative thesis that must be tested every day in the depths of our own experience and by all the reliable evidence we have available, as limited as that might be. For as Bertrand Russell told us, what we know is always "vanishingly small." These will be narratives of individuals, not groups. And is this not exactly what Martin Luther King, Jr., dreamed of when he hoped a day would come when men and women were judged not by the color of their skin, but instead by their individual deeds and actions, and the content of their character?

I believe this *was* what King dreamed and, whether we like it or not, that moment is now.

In Defense of George Bush

Jelani Cobb

I. Anatomy of a Conflict

On January 20, 2009, former President George W. Bush and his wife Laura boarded a United States Marine Corps helicopter. For the first time in eight years he entered a vehicle that did not carry the presidential seal of the United States. The thrum of the engines likely spared the ex-president the sound of the boos and hisses emanating from some of the two million citizens gathered on the national mall to watch his departure.

I was there that afternoon, frozen nearly solid, but still able to recognize the magnitude of the moment. A former commander in chief was exiting the nation's capital while beneath him hundreds of thousands chanted

Na-na-na-na
Hey, Hey, Hey
Goodbye

Nearly three months have passed since then, hardly enough time to establish final conclusions but certainly enough to begin asking important questions. It would be easy to dismiss Bush, as many of us have, as the "worst president in history," because it offers us a simple answer, a clean resolution to an era of nightmares. But in some way Bush has become, perhaps, the most powerful fall guy in American history.

His administration was horribly flawed; they committed acts that I believe warrant prosecution and incarceration. But as the old saying goes, in a democracy people get the leaders they deserve. It is difficult to say that anyone deserved George W. Bush and Dick Cheney.

We will, no doubt, devote many years to wondering why Bush did what he has done, but we will generally avoid the most difficult question—why did we allow him to?

Presidents have been impeached for lesser offenses than many that occurred during Bush's tenure. We saw comparatively little protest and anemic offerings of public dissent. The reasonable conclusion is that in pointing toward Bush we shift blame away from ourselves, away from the bitter, difficult, profane answers to those questions: He did what many of us wanted him to do; we allowed him to do it because we were afraid.

The presidency of George W. Bush began on September 11, 2001. The images are carved into our memory: the airplanes accelerating into the World Trade Center, the people falling from the towers like charred confetti, the clouds of dust that settled over lower Manhattan. The South Tower collapsed at 9:58 a.m.; the North Tower fell precisely thirty minutes later. What began the morning as a symbol of American might had now become an abstract crematorium, the first American ruin. We saw the Pentagon with its gaping fiery abscess and the scorched crater in Pennsylvania where United flight 93 went down.

We were all shaken from our isolation, what some would call our self-absorption. I remember walking into my African American history class at Spelman College that morning, a new professor with just two weeks of time at my first academic job. I recall being told that a plane had hit the World Trade Center and believing it to be simply a massively tragic accident. I taught about W. E. B. Du Bois that day. When I left the classroom I saw a colleague who told me that a second plane had struck the towers and that the United States was under attack.

There is a belief deeply rooted in this nation's history called American Exceptionalism. It is the idea that America stands apart from other nations, that its ideals are a model for the rest of the world. The Exceptionalist believes that, while most nations believe themselves to be unique and favored, it really is the case with the United States. That, in short, we are to the world what the New York Yankees are to baseball. As a historian I know that this creed undergirded manifest destiny and the inhumanity of Indian removal. It gave substance to the Monroe Doctrine and sanctioned the U.S. interventions throughout this hemisphere for nearly two centuries. History shows us that national hubris and the belief that God favors one nation can provide cover for the most brutal of undertakings.

As an African American I see this story from a different perspective. My ancestors understood themselves not as proponents of American Exceptionalism but as exceptions to America. An accumulated brutality of slavery, Jim Crow, sharecropping, mob violence, lynching, disfranchisement, rape, economic exploitation, forced sterilization and the incalculable tally of racial insults define black–white relations in this country.

The end result is a sort of jaded black perspective on America's claims to greatness. Frederick Douglass expressed this best in 1852 when he asked "What to the slave is the Fourth of July" and answered "a day that reveals to him more than all other days in the year the gross injustice and cruelty to which he is the constant victim."

Ultimately our very history has made African Americans immune to this creed of American Exceptionalism. Or has it?

On September 11, 2001, I stood in the history department and refused to believe that the World Trade Center had simply ceased to exist. I saw the horrid details on television as did billions of others; I understand the simple facts of physics that superheated metal loses its integrity and that even that grandest feat of modern engineering was not capable of holding the weight of a burning 747.

I am a native New Yorker. I have the missing consonants and concave vowels to prove it. I know that the place spelled M-A-N-H-A-T-T-A-N is pronounced *Manha-an*, not *Manhattan*. I grew up in the shadow of the Twin Towers and took innocent pride in the fact that the tallest structures in the world existed in my home city. My home city existed in the United States, and these things made America somehow greater than its peer nations. By way of degrees I converted to the faith called American Exceptionalism, a belief system that, among other things, holds that burning skyscrapers do not collapse, that passenger jets do not tear through steel and glass and that America is like base in a child's game of tag. People here do not die at the hands of foreign assault.

If nothing else, 9/11 revealed the common assumptions that lay beneath our diverse and fractured citizenship. Seven years later it reveals our common complicity in the conflicted history that has transpired since then.

We have witnessed more history than most in these past seven years. We history professors tend to divide our American history courses into halves: from Colonialism to the Civil War and from the Civil War to present. It is not hard to imagine some future point where American history courses are divided into thirds, with a new heading: 9/11 to present. This much is clear: The past seven and a half years contain enough history to be a course in itself.

We live in a time when, as they say, "change is the only constant." We use terms like "communicate in real-time" as if the older, slower forms of communication were "false time." We dole out micro-fragments of history via Twitter and alter the term "friend" from an ally, colleague or associate with whom we share regular contact to mean persons whose digital profiles we have read and with whom we exchange occasional electronic one-liners. The result is that we expect change. But one side effect is that tremendous changes and minute ones tend to run together.

This is a problem. The country we live in now is not the country we were born into, not the one many of us grew to middle age in. The culture of this country continues to reverberate with the ghost echoes of its monuments crumbling into dust. The saying is wrong: Change is not our only constant. Conflict is.

Here is what future historians will point out about the period between 2001 and 2008: The United States launched an attack in Afghanistan designed to bring down the Taliban regime led by Mullah Omar. On September 20, 2001, in a speech to a joint session of Congress, President George W. Bush announced that the country had adopted a policy of preemptive war. During this era, the U.S. government effectively suspended the Constitution, created secret military tribunals, engaged in torture, contracted with other governments to facilitate torture, secretly wiretapped its own citizens, revealed the identity of a CIA agent, misled the public regarding an international threat, launched a war in Iraq based upon false information, deposed a head of state and turned him over to rivals for a public execution.

These things have happened incrementally, so jammed into a frantic context and the general blur of events that we could forget what they are in totality. But we should reflect upon this: We have been at war longer than World War II, longer than the Civil War, longer than the American Revolution, the Mexican–American War or any other conflict with the exception of Vietnam.

We have also witnessed the most massive transfer of power to the executive branch in any time since Abraham Lincoln suspended habeas corpus during the Civil War and declared that he had the right to arrest those who simply spoke against the war effort.

In a numb sequence we saw a president with a bullhorn, three days after the attack, standing at Ground Zero and declaring that there would be retribution. Nine days after the attack he told the world that they were either with us or with the terrorists. Twenty-six days later the United States began bombing Afghanistan. Forty-five days later Congress passed the Patriot Act, vastly expanding the federal government's powers of surveillance and interdiction. One year and six months later the United States invaded Iraq in pursuit of "weapons of mass destruction." One year and ten months later, Valerie Plame's identity as a CIA agent was revealed—following an editorial her husband wrote criticizing the Bush administration's rationale for the war.

Two years and six months later an investigation revealed that United States forces conducted torture at Abu Ghraib prison. The actions and excesses echo with clockwork regularity, counting down toward March 2009, when the now former Vice President Dick Cheney, who stood accused of commanding secret assassination squads abroad, told the nation that the country was "less safe" in the hands of Barack Obama.

The official estimate of the 9/11 Commission holds that 2,983 Americans died that day. The horror refuses to recede into history: In October 2006, body parts and bone fragments were discovered by construction crews beneath a manhole at Ground Zero. In July 2008 a judge rejected a request from families wishing to sift through the Fresh Kills landfill in search of human remains. During the week of the attack, as the first estimates rolled in, I recall thinking that nearly as many were lost on a single day as died during the entire course of the American Revolution. At this point, however, I look at them—the Revolutionary War dead and the 9/11 dead—as occupying two difficult poles in American history: the blood lost in the pursuit of liberty and the liberty lost in the pursuit of blood.

II. Of Evildoers and Freedom-Seekers

These are political acts. But it is also clear that they have profoundly shaped—and been shaped by—our cultural values. The so-deemed "War on Terror" is a geopolitical affair—a conflict resulting directly from the

United States' position in the world and the actions of its leaders to preserve, indeed to expand, that position and ensure the safety of its citizenry, as they understand it. The war has been prosecuted by military
commanders and political figures; it has brought the collapse of governments and the establishment of new ones. There are policy prerogatives
at the cornerstone of this war.

When Osama Bin Laden declared jihad on the United States in 1998,
he said it was the religious duty of Muslims across the world to kill Americans, not because of any cultural concerns but because he found three elements of American foreign policy to be intolerable. First, he argued, the
United States' steadfast support for Israel amounted to an ongoing,
decades-long assault upon the Palestinian people. Second, he pointed out
that the U.S. embargo on Iraq between 1993 and 2001 had prevented the
country from receiving much-needed medical supplies and resulted in
deaths of children conservatively estimated at 500,000 even by aid agencies in the West. Finally, and perhaps most central to his declaration of
jihad, the presence of U.S. military bases in Saudi Arabia was, in Bin
Laden's estimation, an unforgivable intrusion upon the sacred home of
Islam. The presence of soldiers from what is at best a "Christian" state
and at worst a godless secular one was seen as a profanity, a persistent poi-
soning of the soil upon which the Prophet Muhammad was born. It was
for this reason that suicide bombers attacked the U.S. base in Riyadh,
Saudi Arabia, on May 12, 2003. We should note that the increase in terrorist attacks targeting the United States—from the bombings of the em-
bassies in Kenya and Tanzania through the assault on the USS
Cole—came after the first Iraq War and gradually increased in intensity,
culminating in 9/11.

In the days and weeks after the towers fell, we heard a single question
echoed in conversations across the country: *Why do they hate us?* In response, George W. Bush offered a one-line reply—*They hate us for our
freedom*. Critics on the left and some on the right howled their protests
that a complex global affair, one that required years to plan and execute,
one with roots deeply planted in decades of American foreign policy,
could be reduced to a simple six-word answer. For many it was further evidence of the reductive reasoning of the commander in chief, yet more
ballast for the conclusion that he saw the world in stark binaries that
would invariably preserve all virtue for his own motivations and malice as
the only engine for the actions of his counterparts. His insistent tendency
to refer to the authors of 9/11 as "the evildoers" suggested that the

United States was involved in a neo-crusade led by a president whose views of human motivation were somewhat less complex than the average *X-Men* comic book. Moreover, by attributing this "unprovoked attack" to a simple contempt for freedom, it dismissed any possibility that the United States could bear any responsibility for the conflict. We are, after all, an exceptional nation. The comedian Bill Maher summed up this sentiment when he said, "They don't hate us for our freedom, they hate us for our air strikes."

But there was something else involved in this calculation. The subtle reality was that, in offering a reductive response to Bush's reductive statement, we found ourselves battling with dueling simplicities.

Years before the Taliban became synonymous with 9/11, Amnesty International and other international human-rights organizations had cited the regime for its repressive behavior toward women. The reports from the late 1990s highlight instances in which women had acid thrown in their faces for failing to wear what the regime deemed proper Islamic dress. Videotape smuggled out of the country during that period shows a man accused of being a homosexual being brought into a stadium. He is forced to kneel and then is swiftly decapitated. The crowd cheers. His severed head falls to the dirt in front of his lifeless body.

In the United States we have ongoing problems with sexism, as the backlash against Hillary Clinton during last year's presidential election made clear. And no one could look at the recent battles over Proposition 8 in California and similar battles across the country and conclude that the position of gays and lesbians in this society has reached a level of democratic equality. But at the same time, few of us subscribe to the belief that a woman wearing revealing clothing should be subject to arbitrary mutilation; few of us would support the public execution of an individual based upon their sexual preference. Abortion is the most divisive domestic issue in American society, one that goes to the roots of religious belief and secular rights, yet there is comparatively little violence between pro-choice and pro-life groups. And the reason for this boils down to a single, sometimes oversimplified term: *freedom.*

There is an uneasy, conflicted but nonetheless vital recognition of the individual freedom to make decisions, even ones that we disagree with. Or, as we tend to say in the language of multiculturalism, "tolerance."

The place where Bush's idea finds some redemption is this: When viewed by hostile eyes, tolerance appears indistinguishable from endorsement. America is not a society that "tolerates" homosexuality, alcohol consumption and miniskirts; it is a haven for such godless behaviors. What looks like liberty to one set of eyes appears to be libertine to another.

The immediate aftermath of 9/11 saw an upsurge of suspicion, hostility and outright assault upon Muslim Americans. Yet any reasonable evaluation would indicate that the United States has generally been far less concerned with the issue of "homegrown terrorists" than other nations with Muslim populations. This is perhaps because of the size of the population—by some estimates Muslims constitute less than one percent of the U.S. population, compared with eight percent in France, 5.6 percent in the Netherlands and just over three percent in Germany. Some observers have theorized that it is precisely because of the general tolerance of religion in the United States that this has been the case. The heyday of religious intolerance in the United States saw Jews and Catholics excluded from society, but in the post–World War II era the concern with religious identity has generally been replaced by other aspects—sexual orientation and, in the case of recent immigrants, language and ethnic background. Another study showed some forty percent of American Muslims to be African American—heirs to the centuries-long struggle to reshape the country in a more humane direction.

Among the many subtleties lost in the toxic clouds of 9/11 was this one: Terrorists overwhelmingly attack democratic societies. This is partially due to logistics: Open societies provide more abundant and easier targets than repressive ones do. There is the sidewalk café, the nightclub, a government office open to the public, the library. But this is also for more substantial reasons: Terrorism seeks to undermine the will of its primary victims—the public. In a democratic society the will of the public actually carries some importance. Bombing a café in North Korea will bring you to the attention of the government, but it can't be said to produce a noticeable effect on popular will, since popular will is all but invisible. Compare that to the decades of bombing the IRA directed at the British and you can see a clear line of distinction: The goal was simply to make the public grow weary and demand that the government meet the IRA's terms.

This means that culture—how people understand and interpret their experiences—becomes vitally important in these circumstances. The threat is not that liberty will be seized by tyrants so much as ceded by citizens. Democracies can only be undermined from within, and culture is the glue holding people to their belief in democracy.

And here is the central irony of the past seven years of our history: We responded to a conflict centering on freedom by curtailing that very freedom.

In the wake of the Soviet Union's collapse and the victory of the mujahideen fighters in Afghanistan, Osama Bin Laden is said to have remarked that the United States could be defeated too, that the country was too vast to be invaded but through proper provocation it could be lured into fighting the same war in the same place where the ashes of the Soviet Union were interred. Five weeks after 9/11, the United States invaded Afghanistan, and in the ensuing years American society became progressively less Constitutional and therefore less free. This tells me that by any measure other than body count, Osama Bin Laden has won the War on Terror—at least as it has been waged for the past seven years.

III. Cowboys in the Path of History

I suspect that these future historians will begin the class on "America and the Culture of 9/11" by tracing the history of previous conflict in this country and the way in which the society reacted to it. In essence, delving into our cultural DNA. The syllabus for that class will, no doubt, include readings from Richard Slotkin and Richard Hofstadter.

In 1964 Hofstadter published a book titled *The Paranoid Style in American Politics;* twenty-eight years later, Slotkin published a book titled *Gunfighter Nation.* Together they provide two strands in the helix and explain a great deal about how we process conflict in this society. They provide something of a guideline to how the nation with these particular political genes would see and interpret 9/11.

Slotkin points out that the nation was born on the frontier, that our core values were influenced by that terrain. The frontier is a lawless territory, one where self-preservation is the ultimate concern and rugged individualism is the highest virtue. It is also the birthplace of the American ideal of the cowboy and his theme of regeneration through violence. The frontier has a law of its own, one much closer to the law of nature than the soft principles of civilization. That frontier legacy is the reason why our heroes, from Dirty Harry to Jack Bauer, kill bad guys and worry about the ACLU later.

Hofstadter wrote about the way in which America has always been insecure and unconfident in its liberty. It is on this level that the conspiracy theory is a fundamentally American undertaking. Across time and political affiliation they share a common thread: a secret force that is quietly subverting the public will, surreptitiously seizing control of the levers of government or posing a foreign threat to freedom. At varying times these have been Tories, Freemasons, Catholics, Socialists, anarchists, Communists, and—forty-five years after Hofstadter wrote his book—Islamic terrorists.

Most of these surges of popular fear have coincided with expansions of federal authority, with the supposed aim of protecting us from the threat. We see this in the Alien and Sedition Acts of 1798, the Chinese Exclusion Act of 1882, the Sedition and Subversion Acts of 1917 and 1918, the Smith and McCarran Acts of the Cold War era and, on October 27, 2003, the Patriot Act.

These moments are generally concerned with some foreign evil that stands in contrast to American values. But not always. During the Civil Rights era, the paranoid style and conspiracy theories of J. Edgar Hoover led to the wiretapping of Martin Luther King's phones and the bugging of his hotel rooms. It led to the harassment of Malcolm X and the possible involvement in his assassination. It led to the illegal surveillance and assault program called COINTELPRO, in which federal law enforcement, like the cowboys of old, figuratively took off their badges to bring down the Black Panther Party. It explains why Southern politicians and law enforcement blame sit-ins and freedom marches on "outside agitators."

It is not surprising, then, that a president who styled himself a cowboy, who claimed to hunt down and smoke out America's enemies, would preside over a paranoid contraction of the United States Constitution. The cowboy must always step outside the effete barriers of the law to bring down the bandits that have blown into town and terrorized its citizens. The Constitution is not equipped for this dark business of self-preservation. Vice President Dick Cheney essentially gave the blueprint for what was to come just five days after the towers fell. Appearing on *Meet the Press*, he told Tim Russert:

> *We also have to work, though, sort of the dark side, if you will. We've got to spend time in the shadows in the intelligence world. A lot of what needs to be done here will have to be done quietly, without any discussion, using sources and methods that are available to our intelligence agencies, if we're going to be successful. That's the world these folks op-*

erate in, and so it's going to be vital for us to use any means at our disposal, basically, to achieve our objective.

In literature, statements like this are called foreshadowing. In life, it is called advance warning. In history, it is called a missed opportunity.

It is our largest grace that these times have commonly brought together people of democratic conscience to challenge this aggregation of power, people who subscribed to Benjamin Franklin's dictum that those who would trade liberty for security deserve neither. History also shows us Thomas Jefferson's and James Madison's protests against the Acts of 1798, of reformers and advocates who founded the ACLU to guard against the excesses of the attorney general A. Mitchell Palmer during the first Red Scare.

The lesson here is that history is on the side of the fearless. War is an ugly but tragically recurrent and sometimes unavoidable aspect of human existence. The task of humanity as we move forward is to find rational ways of resolving human conflict. But I would not deny a nation its capacity to defend itself any more than I would have denied my own ancestors the right to violent revolt against those who had stolen their freedom.

But the cornerstone lesson is that "fighting terror" means combating the wrongs perpetrated by madmen abroad *and* those done by your own government in the name of bringing them to justice. Mark Twain wrote that patriotism means supporting your country always and your government when it deserves it. This means that our culture has to resist the temptation toward seeking endless vengeance against nameless enemies, that we must respond to external threats in ways that affirm democratic traditions, not curtail them.

And in the end, if they truly hate you for your freedom, you cannot solve the problem by simply getting rid of it.

The End of White America?

Hua Hsu

"Civilization's going to pieces," he remarks. He is in polite company, gathered with friends around a bottle of wine in the late-afternoon sun, chatting and gossiping. "I've gotten to be a terrible pessimist about things. Have you read *The Rise of the Colored Empires* by this man Goddard?" They hadn't. "Well, it's a fine book, and everybody ought to read it. The idea is if we don't look out the white race will be—will be utterly submerged. It's all scientific stuff; it's been proved."

He is Tom Buchanan, a character in F. Scott Fitzgerald's *The Great Gatsby*, a book that nearly everyone who passes through the American education system is compelled to read at least once. Although *Gatsby* doesn't gloss as a book on racial anxiety—it's too busy exploring a different set of anxieties entirely—Buchanan was hardly alone in feeling besieged. The book by "this man Goddard" had a real-world analogue: Lothrop Stoddard's *The Rising Tide of Color Against White World-Supremacy*, published in 1920, five years before *Gatsby*. Nine decades later, Stoddard's polemic remains oddly engrossing. He refers to World War I as the "White Civil War" and laments the "cycle of ruin" that may result if the "white world" continues its infighting. The book features a series of foldout maps depicting the distribution of "color" throughout the world and warns, "Colored migration is a universal peril, menacing every part of the white world."

As briefs for racial supremacy go, *The Rising Tide of Color* is eerily serene. Its tone is scholarly and gentlemanly, its hatred rationalized and, in Buchanan's term, "scientific." And the book was hardly a fringe phenomenon. It was published by Scribner, also Fitzgerald's publisher, and Stoddard, who received a doctorate in history from Harvard, was a member of many professional academic associations. It was precisely the kind of book that a 1920s man of Buchanan's profile—wealthy, Ivy League–educated, at once pretentious and intellectually insecure—might have been expected to bring up in casual conversation.

As white men of comfort and privilege living in an age of limited social mobility, of course, Stoddard and the Buchanans in his audience had nothing literal to fear. Their sense of dread hovered somewhere above the concerns of everyday life. It was linked less to any immediate danger to their class's political and cultural power than to the perceived fraying of the fixed, monolithic identity of whiteness that sewed together the fortunes of the fair-skinned.

From the hysteria over Eastern European immigration to the vibrant cultural miscegenation of the Harlem Renaissance, it is easy to see how this imagined worldwide white kinship might have seemed imperiled in the 1920s. There's no better example of the era's insecurities than the 1923 Supreme Court case *United States v. Bhagat Singh Thind,* in which an Indian American veteran of World War I sought to become a naturalized citizen by proving that he was Caucasian. The Court considered new anthropological studies that expanded the definition of the Caucasian race to include Indians, and the justices even agreed that traces of "Aryan blood" coursed through Thind's body. But these technicalities availed him little. The Court determined that Thind was not white "in accordance with the understanding of the common man" and therefore could be excluded from the "statutory category" of whiteness. Put another way: Thind was white, in that he was Caucasian and even Aryan. But he was not *white* in the way Stoddard or Buchanan were white.

The twenties' debate over the definition of whiteness—a legal category? a commonsense understanding? a worldwide civilization?—took place in a society gripped by an acute sense of racial paranoia, and it is easy to regard these episodes as evidence of how far we have come. But consider that these anxieties surfaced when whiteness was synonymous with the American mainstream, when threats to its status were largely imaginary. What happens once this is no longer the case—when the fears of Lothrop Stoddard and Tom Buchanan are realized, and white people actually become an American minority?

Whether you describe it as the dawning of a post-racial age or just the end of white America, we're approaching a profound demographic tipping point. According to an August 2008 report by the U.S. Census Bureau, those groups currently categorized as racial minorities—blacks and Hispanics, East Asians and South Asians—will account for a majority of the U.S. population by the year 2042. Among Americans under the age of eighteen, this shift is projected to take place in 2023, which means that every child born in the United States from here on out will belong to the first post-white generation.

Obviously, steadily ascending rates of interracial marriage complicate this picture, pointing toward what Michael Lind has described as the "beiging" of America. And it's possible that "beige Americans" will self-identify as "white" in sufficient numbers to push the tipping point further into the future than the Census Bureau projects. But even if they do, whiteness will be a label adopted out of convenience and even indifference, rather than aspiration and necessity. For an earlier generation of minorities and immigrants, to be recognized as a "white American," whether you were an Italian or a Pole or a Hungarian, was to enter the mainstream of American life; to be recognized as something else, as the *Thind* case suggests, was to be permanently excluded. As Bill Imada, head of the IW Group, a prominent Asian American communications and marketing company, puts it: "I think in the 1920s, 1930s, and 1940s, [for] anyone who immigrated, the aspiration was to blend in and be as American as possible so that white America wouldn't be intimidated by them. They wanted to imitate white America as much as possible: learn English, go to church, go to the same schools."

Today, the picture is far more complex. To take the most obvious example, whiteness is no longer a precondition for entry into the highest levels of public office. The son of Indian immigrants doesn't have to become "white" in order to be elected governor of Louisiana. A half-Kenyan, half-Kansan politician can self-identify as black and be elected president of the United States.

As a purely demographic matter, then, the "white America" that Lothrop Stoddard believed in so fervently may cease to exist in 2040, 2050, or 2060, or later still. But where the culture is concerned, it's already all but finished. Instead of the long-standing model of assimilation toward a common center, the culture is being remade in the image of white America's multiethnic, multicolored heirs.

For some, the disappearance of this centrifugal core heralds a future rich with promise: In 1998, President Bill Clinton, in a now-famous address to students at Portland State University, remarked:

> *Today, largely because of immigration, there is no majority race in Hawaii or Houston or New York City. Within five years, there will be no majority race in our largest state, California. In a little more than fifty years, there will be no majority race in the United States. No other nation in history has gone through demographic change of this magnitude in so short a time . . . [These immigrants] are energizing our culture and broadening our vision of the world. They are renewing our most basic values and reminding us all of what it truly means to be American.*

Not everyone was so enthused. Clinton's remarks caught the attention of another anxious Buchanan—Pat Buchanan, the conservative thinker. Revisiting the president's speech in his 2001 book, *The Death of the West*, Buchanan wrote: "Mr. Clinton assured us that it will be a better America when we are all minorities and realize true 'diversity.' Well, those students [at Portland State] are going to find out, for they will spend their golden years in a Third World America."

Today, the arrival of what Buchanan derided as "Third World America" is all but inevitable. What will the new mainstream of America look like, and what ideas or values might it rally around? What will it mean to be white after "whiteness" no longer defines the mainstream? Will anyone mourn the end of white America? Will anyone try to preserve it?

✳

Another moment from *The Great Gatsby*: as Fitzgerald's narrator and Gatsby drive across the Queensboro Bridge into Manhattan, a car passes them, and Nick Carraway notices that it is a limousine "driven by a white chauffeur, in which sat three modish negroes, two bucks and a girl." The novelty of this topsy-turvy arrangement inspires Carraway to laugh aloud and think to himself, "Anything can happen now that we've slid over this bridge, anything at all . . ."

For a contemporary embodiment of the upheaval that this scene portended, consider Sean Combs, a hip-hop mogul and one of the most famous African Americans on the planet. Combs grew up during hip-hop's late-1970s rise, and he belongs to the first generation that could safely make a living working in the industry—as a plucky young promoter and record-label intern in the late 1980s and early 1990s, and as a fashion designer, artist, and music executive worth hundreds of millions of dollars a brief decade later.

In the late 1990s, Combs made a fascinating gesture toward New York's high society. He announced his arrival into the circles of the rich and powerful not by crashing their parties, but by inviting them into his own spectacularly over-the-top world. Combs began to stage elaborate annual parties in the Hamptons, not far from where Fitzgerald's novel takes place. These "white parties"—attendees are required to wear white—quickly became legendary for their opulence (in 2004, Combs showcased a 1776 copy of the Declaration of Independence) as well as for the cultures-colliding quality of Hamptons elites paying their respects to someone so comfortably nouveau riche. Prospective business partners angled to get close to him and praised him as a guru of the lucrative "urban" market, while grateful partygoers hailed him as a modern-day Gatsby.

"Have I read *The Great Gatsby*?" Combs said to a London newspaper in 2001. "I am the Great Gatsby."

Yet whereas Gatsby felt pressure to hide his status as an arriviste, Combs celebrated his position as an outsider-insider—someone who appropriates elements of the culture he seeks to join without attempting to assimilate outright. In a sense, Combs was imitating the old WASP establishment; in another sense, he was subtly provoking it, by over-enunciating its formality and never letting his guests forget that there was something slightly off about his presence. There's a silent power to throwing parties where the best-dressed man in the room is also the one whose public profile once consisted primarily of dancing in the background of Biggie Smalls videos. ("No one would ever expect a young black man to be coming to a party with the Declaration of Independence, but I got it, and it's coming with me," Combs joked at his 2004 party, as he made the rounds with the document, promising not to spill champagne on it.)

In this regard, Combs is both a product and a hero of the new cultural mainstream, which prizes diversity above all else, and whose ultimate goal is some vague notion of racial transcendence, rather than subversion or assimilation. Although Combs's vision is far from representative—not many hip-hop stars vacation in St. Tropez with a parasol-toting manservant shading their every step—his industry lies at the heart of this new mainstream. Over the past thirty years, few changes in American culture have been as significant as the rise of hip-hop. The genre has radically reshaped the way we listen to and consume music, first by opposing the pop mainstream and then by becoming it. From its constant sampling of past styles and eras—old records, fashions, slang, anything—to its mythologization of the self-made black antihero, hip-hop is more than a musical genre: it's a philosophy, a political statement, a way of approaching and remaking culture. It's a lingua franca not just among kids in America, but also among young people worldwide. And its economic impact extends beyond the music industry, to fashion, advertising, and film. (Consider the producer Russell Simmons—the ur-Combs and a music, fashion, and television mogul—or the rapper 50 Cent, who has parlayed his rags-to-riches storyline into extracurricular successes that include a clothing line; book, video-game, and film deals; and a startlingly lucrative partnership with the makers of Vitamin Water.)

But hip-hop's deepest impact is symbolic. During popular music's rise in the twentieth century, white artists and producers consistently "mainstreamed" African American innovations. Hip-hop's ascension has been different. Eminem notwithstanding, hip-hop never suffered through anything like an Elvis Presley moment, in which a white artist made a musical form safe for white America. This is no dig at Elvis—the constrictive racial logic of the 1950s demanded the erasure of rock and roll's black roots, and if it hadn't been him, it would have been someone else. But hip-hop—the sound of the post-civil-rights, post-soul generation—found a global audience on its own terms.

Today, hip-hop's colonization of the global imagination, from fashion runways in Europe to dance competitions in Asia, is Disney-esque. This transformation has bred an unprecedented cultural confidence in its black originators. Whiteness is no longer a threat, or an ideal: it's kitsch to be appropriated, whether with gestures like Combs's "white parties" or the trickle-down epidemic of collared shirts and cuff links currently afflicting rappers. And an expansive multiculturalism is replacing the us-against-the-world bunker mentality that lent a thrilling edge to hip-hop's mid-1990s rise.

Peter Rosenberg, a self-proclaimed "nerdy Jewish kid" and radio personality on New York's Hot 97 FM—and a living example of how hip-hop has created new identities for its listeners that don't fall neatly along lines of black and white—shares another example: "I interviewed [the St. Louis rapper] Nelly this morning, and he said it's now very cool and *in* to have multicultural friends. Like you're not really considered hip or 'you've made it' if you're rolling with all the same people."

Just as Tiger Woods forever changed the country-club culture of golf, and Will Smith confounded stereotypes about the ideal Hollywood leading man, hip-hop's rise is helping redefine the American mainstream, which no longer aspires toward a single iconic image of style or class. Successful network-television shows like *Lost, Heroes,* and *Grey's Anatomy* feature wildly diverse casts, and an entire genre of half-hour comedy, from *The Colbert Report* to *The Office,* seems dedicated to having fun with the persona of the clueless white male. The youth market is following the same pattern: consider the Cheetah Girls, a multicultural, multiplatinum, multiplatform trio of teenyboppers who recently starred in their third movie, or Dora the Explorer, the precocious bilingual seven-year-old Latina adventurer who is arguably the most successful animated character on children's television today. In a recent address to the Association of Hispanic Advertising Agencies, Brown Johnson, the Nickelodeon executive who has overseen Dora's rise, explained the importance of creating a character who does not conform to "the white, middle-class mold." When Johnson pointed out that Dora's wares were outselling Barbie's in France, the crowd hooted in delight.

Pop culture today rallies around an ethic of multicultural inclusion that seems to value every identity—except whiteness. "It's become harder for the blond-haired, blue-eyed commercial actor," remarks Rochelle Newman-Carrasco, of the Hispanic marketing firm Enlace. "You read casting notices, and they like to cast people with brown hair because they could be Hispanic. The language of casting notices is pretty shocking because it's so specific: 'Brown hair, brown eyes, could look Hispanic.' Or, as one notice put it: 'Ethnically ambiguous.'"

"I think white people feel like they're under siege right now—like it's not okay to be white right now, especially if you're a white male," laughs Bill Imada, of the IW Group. Imada and Newman-Carrasco are part of a movement within advertising, marketing, and communications firms to reimagine the profile of the typical American consumer. (Tellingly, every person I spoke with from these industries knew the Census Bureau's projections by heart.)

"There's a lot of fear and a lot of resentment," Newman-Carrasco observes, describing the flak she caught after writing an article for a trade publication on the need for more-diverse hiring practices. "I got a response from a friend—he's, like, a sixty-something white male, and he's been involved with multicultural recruiting," she recalls. "And he said, 'I really feel like the hunted. It's a hard time to be a white man in America right now, because I feel like I'm being lumped in with all white males in America, and I've tried to do stuff, but it's a tough time.' "

"I always tell the white men in the room, 'We need you,' " Imada says. "We cannot talk about diversity and inclusion and engagement without you at the table. It's okay to be white!

"But people are stressed-out about it. 'We used to be in control! We're losing control!' "

✳

If they're right—if white America is indeed "losing control," and if the future will belong to people who can successfully navigate a post-racial, multicultural landscape—then it's no surprise that many white Americans are eager to divest themselves of their whiteness entirely.

For some, this renunciation can take a radical form. In 1994, a young graffiti artist and activist named William "Upski" Wimsatt, the son of a university professor, published *Bomb the Suburbs*, the spiritual heir to Norman Mailer's celebratory 1957 essay, "The White Negro." Wimsatt was deeply committed to hip-hop's transformative powers, going so far as to embrace the status of the lowly "wigger," a pejorative term popularized in the early 1990s to describe white kids who steep themselves in black culture. Wimsatt viewed the wigger's immersion in two cultures as an engine for change. "If channeled in the right way," he wrote, "the wigger can go a long way toward repairing the sickness of race in America."

Wimsatt's painfully earnest attempts to put his own relationship with whiteness under the microscope coincided with the emergence of an academic discipline known as "whiteness studies." In colleges and universities across the country, scholars began examining the history of "whiteness" and unpacking its contradictions. Why, for example, had the Irish and the Italians fallen beyond the pale at different moments in our history? Were Jewish Americans *white*? And, as the historian Matthew Frye Jacobson asked, "Why is it that in the United States, a white woman can have black children but a black woman cannot have white children?"

Much like Wimsatt, the whiteness-studies academics—figures such as Jacobson, David Roediger, Eric Lott, and Noel Ignatiev—were attempting to come to terms with their own relationships with whiteness, in its past and present forms. In the early 1990s, Ignatiev, a former labor activist and the author of *How the Irish Became White,* set out to "abolish" the idea of the white race by starting the New Abolitionist Movement and founding a journal titled *Race Traitor.* "There is nothing positive about white identity," he wrote in 1998. "As James Baldwin said, 'As long as you think you're white, there's no hope for you.' "

Although most white Americans haven't read *Bomb the Suburbs* or *Race Traitor,* this view of whiteness as something to be interrogated, if not shrugged off completely, has migrated to less academic spheres. The perspective of the whiteness-studies academics is commonplace now, even if the language used to express it is different.

"I get it: as a straight white male, I'm the worst thing on Earth," Christian Lander says. Lander is a Canadian-born, Los Angeles–based satirist who in January 2008 started a blog called *Stuff White People Like* (stuffwhitepeoplelike.com), which pokes fun at the manners and mores of a specific species of young, hip, upwardly mobile whites. (He has written more than one hundred entries about whites' passion for things like bottled water, "the idea of soccer," and "being the only white person around.") At its best, Lander's site—which formed the basis for a recently published book of the same name (reviewed in the October 2008 *Atlantic*)—is a cunningly precise distillation of the identity crisis plaguing well-meaning, well-off white kids in a post-white world.

"Like, I'm aware of all the horrible crimes that my demographic has done in the world," Lander says. "And there's a bunch of white people who are desperate—*desperate*—to say, 'You know what? My skin's white, but I'm not one of the white people who's destroying the world.' "

For Lander, whiteness has become a vacuum. The "white identity" he limns on his blog is predicated on the quest for authenticity—usually other people's authenticity. "As a white person, you're just desperate to find something else to grab onto. You're jealous! Pretty much every white person I grew up with wished they'd grown up in, you know, an ethnic home that gave them a second language. White culture is *Family Ties* and Led Zeppelin and Guns N' Roses—like, this is white culture. This is all we have."

Lander's "white people" are products of a very specific historical moment, raised by well-meaning Baby Boomers to reject the old ideal of white American gentility and to embrace diversity and fluidity instead. ("It's strange that we are the kids of Baby Boomers, right? How the hell do you rebel against that? Like, your parents will march against the World Trade Organization next to you. They'll have bigger white dreadlocks than you. What do you do?") But his lighthearted anthropology suggests that the multicultural harmony they were raised to worship has bred a kind of self-denial.

Matt Wray, a sociologist at Temple University who is a fan of Lander's humor, has observed that many of his white students are plagued by a racial-identity crisis: "They don't care about socioeconomics; they care about culture. And to be white is to be culturally broke. The classic thing white students say when you ask them to talk about who they are is, 'I don't have a culture.' They might be privileged, they might be loaded socio-economically, but they feel bankrupt when it comes to culture . . . They feel disadvantaged, and they feel marginalized. They don't have a culture that's cool or oppositional." Wray says that this feeling of being culturally bereft often prevents students from recognizing what it means to be a child of privilege—a strange irony that the first wave of whiteness-studies scholars, in the 1990s, failed to anticipate.

Of course, the obvious material advantages that come with being born white—lower infant-mortality rates and easier-to-acquire bank loans, for example—tend to undercut any sympathy that this sense of marginalization might generate. And in the right context, cultural-identity crises can turn well-meaning whites into instant punch lines. Consider *ego trip's The (White) Rapper Show,* a brilliant and critically acclaimed reality show that VH1 debuted in 2007. It depicted ten (mostly hapless) white rappers living together in a dilapidated house—dubbed "Tha White House"—in the South Bronx. Despite the contestants' best intentions, each one seemed like a profoundly confused caricature, whether it was the solemn graduate student committed to fighting racism or the ghetto-obsessed suburbanite who had, seemingly by accident, named himself after the abolitionist John Brown.

Similarly, Smirnoff struck marketing gold in 2006 with a viral music video titled "Tea Partay," featuring a trio of strikingly bad, V-neck-sweater-clad white rappers called the Prep Unit. "Haters like to clown our Ivy League educations / But they're just jealous 'cause our families run the nation," the trio brayed, as a pair of bottle-blond women in spiffy tennis whites shimmied behind them. There was no nonironic way to enjoy the video; its entire appeal was in its self-aware lampooning of WASP culture: verdant country clubs, "old money," croquet, popped collars, and the like.

"The best defense is to be constantly pulling the rug out from underneath yourself," Wray remarks, describing the way self-aware whites contend with their complicated identity. "Beat people to the punch. You're forced as a white person into a sense of ironic detachment. Irony is what fuels a lot of white subcultures. You also see things like Burning Man, when a lot of white people are going into the desert and trying to invent something that is entirely new and not a form of racial mimicry. That's its own kind of flight from whiteness. We're going through a period where whites are really trying to figure out: Who are we?"

✳

The "Flight from Whiteness" of urban, college-educated, liberal whites isn't the only attempt to answer this question. You can flee *into* whiteness as well. This can mean pursuing the authenticity of an imagined past: think of the deliberately white-bread world of Mormon America, where the fifties never ended, or the anachronistic WASP entitlement flaunted in books like last year's *A Privileged Life: Celebrating WASP Style*, a handsome coffee-table book compiled by Susanna Salk, depicting a world of seersucker blazers, whale pants, and deck shoes. (What the book celebrates is the "inability to be outdone," and the "self-confidence and security that comes with it," Salk tells me. "That's why I call it 'privilege.' It's this privilege of time, of heritage, of being in a place longer than anybody else.") But these enclaves of preserved-in-amber whiteness are likely to be less important to the American future than the construction of whiteness as a somewhat pissed-off minority culture.

This notion of a self-consciously white expression of minority empowerment will be familiar to anyone who has come across the comedian Larry the Cable Guy—he of "Farting Jingle Bells"—or witnessed the transformation of Detroit-born-and-bred Kid Rock from teenage rapper into "American Bad Ass" southern-style rocker. The 1990s may have been a decade when multiculturalism advanced dramatically—when American culture became "colorized," as the critic Jeff Chang put it—but it was also an era when a very different form of identity politics crystallized. Hip-hop may have provided the decade's soundtrack, but the highest-selling artist of the nineties was Garth Brooks. Michael Jordan and Tiger Woods may have been the faces of athletic superstardom, but it was NASCAR that emerged as professional sports' fastest-growing institution, with ratings second only to the NFL's.

As with the unexpected success of the apocalyptic Left Behind novels, or the Jeff Foxworthy–organized Blue Collar Comedy Tour, the rise of country music and auto racing took place well off the American elite's radar screen. (None of Christian Lander's white people would be caught dead at a NASCAR race.) These phenomena reflected a growing sense of cultural solidarity among lower-middle-class whites—a solidarity defined by a yearning for American "authenticity," a folksy realness that rejects the global, the urban, and the effete in favor of nostalgia for "the way things used to be."

Like other forms of identity politics, white solidarity comes complete with its own folk heroes, conspiracy theories (Barack Obama is a secret Muslim! The United States is going to merge with Canada and Mexico!), and laundry lists of injustices. The targets and scapegoats vary—from multiculturalism and affirmative action to a loss of moral values, from immigration to an economy that no longer guarantees the American worker a fair chance—and so do the political programs they inspire. (Ross Perot and Pat Buchanan both tapped into this white identity politics in the 1990s; today, its tribunes run the ideological gamut, from Jim Webb to Ron Paul to Mike Huckabee to Sarah Palin.) But the core grievance, in each case, has to do with cultural and socioeconomic dislocation—the sense that the system that used to guarantee the white working class some stability has gone off-kilter.

Wray is one of the founders of what has been called "white-trash studies," a field conceived as a response to the perceived elite-liberal marginalization of the white working class. He argues that the economic downturn of the 1970s was the precondition for the formation of an "oppositional" and "defiant" white-working-class sensibility—think of the rugged, anti-everything individualism of 1977's *Smokey and the Bandit*. But those anxieties took their shape from the aftershocks of the identity-based movements of the 1960s. "I think that the political space that the civil-rights movement opens up in the mid-1950s and '60s is the transformative thing," Wray observes. "Following the black-power movement, all of the other minority groups that followed took up various forms of activism, including brown power and yellow power and red power. Of course the problem is, if you try and have a 'white power' movement, it doesn't sound good."

The result is a racial pride that dares not speak its name and that defines itself through cultural cues instead—a suspicion of intellectual elites and city dwellers, a preference for folksiness and plainness of speech (whether real or feigned), and the association of a working-class white minority with "the real America." (In the Scots–Irish belt that runs from Arkansas up through West Virginia, the most common ethnic label offered to census takers is "American.") Arguably, this white identity politics helped swing the 2000 and 2004 elections, serving as the powerful counterpunch to urban white liberals, and the McCain–Palin campaign relied on it almost to the point of absurdity (as when a McCain surrogate dismissed Northern Virginia as somehow not part of "the real Virginia") as a bulwark against the threatening multiculturalism of Barack Obama. Their strategy failed, of course, but it's possible to imagine white identity politics growing more potent and more forthright in its racial identifications in the future, as "the real America" becomes an ever-smaller portion of, well, the real America, and as the soon-to-be white minority's sense of being besieged and disdained by a multicultural majority grows apace.

This vision of the aggrieved white man lost in a world that no longer values him was given its most vivid expression in the 1993 film *Falling Down*. Michael Douglas plays Bill Foster, a downsized defense worker with a buzz cut and a pocket protector who rampages through a Los Angeles overrun by greedy Korean shop-owners and Hispanic gangsters, railing against the eclipse of the America he used to know. (The film came out just eight years before California became the nation's first majority-minority state.) *Falling Down* ends with a soulful police officer apprehending Foster on the Santa Monica Pier, at which point the middle-class vigilante asks, almost innocently: "*I'm* the bad guy?"

✳

But this is a nightmare vision. Of course most of America's Bill Fosters aren't the bad guys—just as civilization is not, in the words of Tom Buchanan, "going to pieces" and America is not, in the phrasing of Pat Buchanan, going "Third World." The coming white minority does not mean that the racial hierarchy of American culture will suddenly become inverted, as in 1995's *White Man's Burden*, an awful thought experiment of a film, starring John Travolta, that envisions an upside-down world in which whites are subjugated to their high-class black oppressors. There will be dislocations and resentments along the way, but the demographic shifts of the next forty years are likely to reduce the power of racial hierarchies over everyone's lives, producing a culture that's more likely than any before to treat its inhabitants as individuals, rather than members of a caste or identity group.

Consider the world of advertising and marketing, industries that set out to mold our desires at a subconscious level. Advertising strategy once assumed a "general market"—"a code word for 'white people,' " jokes one ad executive—and smaller, mutually exclusive, satellite "ethnic markets." In recent years, though, advertisers have begun revising their assumptions and strategies in anticipation of profound demographic shifts. Instead of herding consumers toward a discrete center, the goal today is to create versatile images and campaigns that can be adapted to highly individualized tastes. (Think of the dancing silhouettes in Apple's iPod campaign, which emphasizes individuality and diversity without privileging—or even representing—any specific group.)

At the moment, we can call this the triumph of multiculturalism, or post-racialism. But just as *whiteness* has no inherent meaning—it is a vessel we fill with our hopes and anxieties—these terms may prove equally empty in the long run. Does being post-racial mean that we are past race completely, or merely that race is no longer essential to how we identify ourselves? Karl Carter, of Atlanta's youth-oriented GTM Inc. (Guerrilla Tactics Media), suggests that marketers and advertisers would be better off focusing on matrices like "lifestyle" or "culture" rather than race or ethnicity. "You'll have crazy in-depth studies of the white consumer or the Latino consumer," he complains. "But how do skaters feel? How do hip-hoppers feel?"

The logic of online social networking points in a similar direction. The New York University sociologist Dalton Conley has written of a "network nation," in which applications like Facebook and MySpace create "crosscutting social groups" and new, flexible identities that only vaguely overlap with racial identities. Perhaps this is where the future of identity after whiteness lies—in a dramatic departure from the racial logic that has defined American culture from the very beginning. What Conley, Carter, and others are describing isn't merely the displacement of whiteness from our cultural center; they're describing a social structure that treats race as just one of a seemingly infinite number of possible self-identifications.

The problem of the twentieth century, W. E. B. Du Bois famously predicted, would be the problem of the color line. Will this continue to be the case in the twenty-first century, when a black president will govern a country whose social networks increasingly cut across every conceivable line of identification? The ruling of *United States v. Bhagat Singh Thind* no longer holds weight, but its echoes have been inescapable: we aspire to be post-racial, but we still live within the structures of privilege, injustice, and racial categorization that we inherited from an older order. We can talk about defining ourselves by lifestyle rather than skin color, but our lifestyle choices are still racially coded. We know, more or less, that race is a fiction that often does more harm than good, and yet it is something we cling to without fully understanding why—as a social and legal fact, a vague sense of belonging and place that we make solid through culture and speech.

But maybe this is merely how it used to be—maybe this is already an outdated way of looking at things. "You have a lot of young adults going into a more diverse world," Carter remarks. For the young Americans born in the 1980s and 1990s, culture is something to be taken apart and remade in their own image. "We came along in a generation that didn't have to follow that path of race," he goes on. "We saw something *different*." This moment was not the end of white America; it was not the end of anything. It was a bridge, and we crossed it.

Personalities

Amy Winehouse and the (Black) Art of Appropriation

Daphne A. Brooks

London's Victoria and Albert Museum is currently paying tribute to the Supremes, the queen mother of all "girl groups," in a colorful exhibit that celebrates the more-than-passing connections between the Motown trio's rise to pop prominence and the 1960s struggle for civil rights. Featuring a luminous array of vintage glitter gowns and go-go petal dresses donated by original Supreme Mary Wilson, "The Story of the Supremes" highlights the link between the groundbreaking group's consistent execution of refined elegance and what you might call the civil right to black glamour that was dominant for much of twentieth-century black music history.

English pop phenom and London native Amy Winehouse is a singer who owes as much to the sound and look of the Supremes, the Ronettes and other pioneering girl groups as she does to the vocal stylings of bygone jazz and R&B greats like Dinah Washington, Sarah Vaughan and Afro-Scottish pop legend Dame Shirley Bassey. On second thought, "owing" is putting it nicely. Winehouse's Tower of Pisa beehive, satin gowns and little black gloves invoke the styles of everyone from Lena

Horne to the Shirelles, and her frothy brew of Motown girl-group melodies crossed with Etta James–era rock and blues riffs and silky-smooth 1970s soul arrangements are textbook BET lifetime achievement material. Just about the only thing Winehouse hasn't repackaged from the black music archives is the one thing she could use: a lesson from Motown's legendary etiquette coach Maxine Powell, who taught her charges to exude grace and a classic Hollywood glow. The mannered, elegant look that Winehouse pairs with a shot glass was, for Diana Ross, Mary Wilson and Florence Ballard, about more than Cleopatra eyeliner. It was about affirming black dignity and humanity amid the battle to end American apartheid.

Winehouse's infamous image, as anyone who has looked on the Internet lately knows, is less about dignity and more about a march toward Sid Vicious–style self-immolation—a No Future punk-degeneration dream-girl chic, with a dash of *Funny Girl* Babs thrown in for good measure. What makes this act slightly less than amusing is the fact that Winehouse has built her stardom on recycling the looks and sounds—the Wurlitzer, hand claps and upright bass—of Freedom Ride–era pop music to sell her tale of rapidly unfolding decline. It's one thing in our celebreality culture of scandals and bad behavior to garner attention by singing a pop anthem about resisting rehab. It's quite another to set these finely crafted tales from the "gritty" English 'hood to doo-wop hopefulness and buoyant, "Dancing in the Streets" percussive melodies that recall the upbeat tenor of King-era activism. This summer, the dissonance grew deafening when Winehouse was caught on video singing slurs about blacks and Asians—not to mention gays and disabled folk—to the tune of "Head, Shoulders, Knees and Toes" while hanging out in what looked like a crack den. A few weeks later, after issuing the requisite public apology, she slurred her way through the lead vocals of the Special AKA's New Wave radio classic "Free Nelson Mandela" in the presence of the man himself, on the occasion of his ninetieth-birthday celebration in Hyde Park.

It's been a whirlwind year and a half for the twenty-five-year-old Winehouse, whose second album, *Back to Black*, has sold ten million copies worldwide and who, in February, won five Grammys, including Best New Artist, Record of the Year and Song of the Year. But for every polite critic who cites her work as another example of cultural "borrowing," there are others who would argue that she is another version of Colonel Tom Parker's white chocolate dream—Elvis reincarnated as a white woman who can "sing like a Negress." And while some might get caught up in debating whether Winehouse is merely a hack black-music ventriloquist, the most troubling aspect of her routine is rarely discussed. The real travesty of Winehouse's work is the way that her retro-soul draws from and yet effaces those black women—from Diana Ross to Aretha Franklin to Tina Turner—whose experiences helped to ignite the rock and soul revolution of our contemporary era.

Black women are everywhere and nowhere in Winehouse's work. Their extraordinary craft as virtuosic vocalists is the pulse of *Back to Black,* an album on which Winehouse mixes and matches the vocalizing of 1940s jazz divas and 1990s neo-soul queens in equal measure. Piling on a motley array of personas, she summons the elegance of Etta "At Last" James alongside roughneck, round-the-way allusions to pub crawls and Brixton nightlife, as well as standard pop women's melancholic confessionals about the evils of "stupid men." What holds it all together is her slinky contralto and shrewd ability to cut and mix sixties R&B and Ronnie Spector Wall of Sound "blues pop" vocals with the ghostly remnants of hip-hop neo-soul's last great hope, Lauryn Hill. Who needs black female singers in the flesh when Winehouse can crank out their sound at the drop of a hat?

Winehouse wouldn't be anywhere, though, without a few crackerjack handlers. Key among them is hipster-producer DJ Mark Ronson, the central creative engine behind the *Black* album concept and the figure who united Winehouse and the Dap-Kings. Considered by some listeners to be the heartbeat of the current retro-soul revival, Brooklyn's Dap-Kings emerged in 2000 as the house band at Daptone Records with an analog sound in an increasingly digital world. Heavy on brass and a crisp, early funk-and-soul percussive beat, the band developed a nostalgia-hungry indie following by reproducing note for note the compositional style of a bygone era. (A word of advice to hipster strivers: leapfrogging backward over hip-hop will always get you cred.) It was music that resuscitated the sound as well as the aura of black culture circa 1964—yet it was played by a predominantly white group of musicians.

Winehouse is something of a departure for the Dap-Kings, who are regularly fronted by fifty-two-year-old African American vocalist Sharon Jones, perhaps the true heir apparent to James and Ruth Brown alike. With a deeper and more powerful range than Winehouse, Jones has recorded three full-length albums with the Dap-Kings, none of which have moved anywhere near the number of units that Winehouse has. It would be easy to suggest that Winehouse "hijacked" Jones's retro-soul soundtrack, but Winehouse doesn't sound all that much like Jones, whose raw power and propulsive energy is more Godfather of Soul and less girl-group demure. Far removed from Jones's infectious spirit, Winehouse's pseudo-inebriated singing is more like a caricature of *Amos 'n' Andy* meets one of Billie Holiday on heroin.

Last March, *New Yorker* pop critic Sasha Frere-Jones wrote that Wine-house's "inflections and phonemes don't add up to any known style." Her "mush-mouthed" phrasings on tracks such as "You Know I'm No Good" are, he wrote, her "real innovation," a "Winehouse signature" that stresses linguistic distortion and sounds heavy on the wine. This, to some, is the sonic allure of Amy Winehouse: her absolutely inscrutable delivery seemingly sets her apart from the legions of white artists who've hopped on the Don Cornelius soul train to find their niche.

Let's be real. These "mush-mouthed" phrasings are anything but new. Winehouse is drawing on a known style that's a hundred years old, rooted in a tradition of female minstrelsy. Think of the oft-overlooked blues recording pioneer Mamie Smith, the artist who, with songwriter Perry Bradford, laid down the first-ever blues recording by an African American vocalist, "Crazy Blues," in 1920. Mamie Smith is hardly an iconic figure like Ma Rainey and Bessie Smith. Her rep as "a vaudeville chanteuse" rather than a juke-joint vet all but guarantees her exclusion from the traditional blues canon. But it's this background that enabled Smith to draw on a range of styles crafted in part from watching and listening to white female performers like Sophie Tucker and, eventually, Mae West—white women who, as theater scholar Jayna Brown has written, often learned to "perform blackness" from the women who worked for them. It goes to show that there were plenty of women, black and white, who benefited from the minstrel craze.

So Frere-Jones is right on one count: Winehouse is indeed creating a pastiche of sounds. But this pastiche is a homage to old-school musical traditions, gone but not forgotten. Her rich combination of split vocal stylings recalls Mamie Smith's sly and oscillating phrasings—moving from Northeastern vaudeville intonations in one note to early Southern blues in the next. She's as much a modern-day Billie Holiday as a contemporary Sophie Tucker, the self-proclaimed "Last of the Red Hot Mamas" and an original Jewish "coon-shouter" who borrowed liberally from the singing style of blues pioneer Alberta Hunter and others. Smith and Tucker were women of the theater who dressed elegantly, fronted brass bands and performed lavish numbers. Though a century removed from Winehouse, these women clearly set a precedent for her high drama on and off the stage.

What, then, is real pop "innovation"? Winehouse has been lauded for essentially throwing Holiday along with Foster Brooks, Louis Armstrong, Wesley Willis, Megan Mullally's Karen on *Will and Grace,* Moms Mabley and Courtney Love into a blender and pressing pulse. And her ability to bring that tricked-out mix of characters to life has made for some eyebrow-raising, highly orchestrated stage shows. Curious to many is Winehouse's use of black male backup dancers and singers, brothers with skinny ties, black mod suits and hats who hustle to choreographed moves, conjuring up images of a bygone era of black male "coolness": Belafonte and Poitier, Nkrumah and Lumumba. Putting this "coolness" in the service of backing up a "ruint" white retro femme figure seems laughable in one sense and egregiously patronizing in another. In either case this sight-gag gimmick is perhaps the key to the obsessions of *Back to Black.*

Whether letting her man know that she'd "rather be at home with Ray" (Charles) than in rehab; hatin' on a suitor for having gotten in the way of her and her "man, Mr. Jones" (*aka* the New York rapper Nas, Nasir Jones); spitting remorse for having "missed the Slick Rick gig"; or, perhaps most cryptically, telling a confidant that "'side from Sammy, you're my best black Jew," Winehouse may be belting it out like a black woman, but her references and posturings are so, so def, pop-ya-collar, hip-hop machismo, all the way down to her weirdly inverted "you my nigga" bonding reference to Sammy Davis, Jr. Witness too how, in her videos, Winehouse rehearses the lowdown "junkie jazz musician" caricature, idling in the bar long after closing time when he should be home with his woman.

To borrow a question from Winehouse herself, "What kind of fuckery is this?" Well beyond merely singing, as a white woman, about her desire for black men, Winehouse, in what is perhaps her real innovation, has created a record about a white woman wanting to be a black man—and an imaginary one at that, stitched together from hip-hop and bebop and juke-joint mythologies. She's a "ride or die chick" from another era, the Jewish English lass who's rolling with the boys, who morphs into the J. Hova gangsta driving the Jag herself. All hail the retro-soul Jolson in a dress who, it seems, is really our first hip-hop drag king, a thug for life indeed, and who clearly, oh, so clearly, these days, seems frighteningly ready to die.

"This Is How We Lost to the White Man"

Ta-Nehisi Coates

Last summer, in Detroit's St. Paul Church of God in Christ, I watched Bill Cosby summon his inner Malcolm X. It was a hot July evening. Cosby was speaking to an audience of black men dressed in everything from Enyce T-shirts or polos to blazers and ties. Some were there with their sons. Some were there in wheelchairs. The audience was packed tight, rows of folding chairs extended beyond the wooden pews to capture the overflow. But the chairs were not enough, and late arrivals stood against the long shotgun walls, or out in the small lobby, where they hoped to catch a snatch of Cosby's oratory. Clutching a cordless mic, Cosby paced the front of the church, shifting between prepared remarks and comic ad-libs. A row of old black men, community elders, sat behind him, nodding and grunting throaty affirmations. The rest of the church was in full call-and-response mode, punctuating Cosby's punch lines with laughter, applause, or cries of "Teach, black man! Teach!"

He began with the story of a black girl who'd risen to become valedictorian of his old high school, despite having been abandoned by her father. "She spoke to the graduating class and her speech started like this,"

Cosby said. " 'I was five years old. It was Saturday and I stood looking out the window, waiting for him.' She never said what helped turn her around. She never mentioned her mother, grandmother, or great-grandmother.

"Understand me," Cosby said, his face contorted and clenched like a fist. "Men? Men? Men! Where are you, men?"

Audience: "Right here!"

Cosby had come to Detroit aiming to grab the city's black men by their collars and shake them out of the torpor that has left so many of them—like so many of their peers across the country—undereducated, over-incarcerated, and underrepresented in the ranks of active fathers. No women were in the audience. No reporters were allowed, for fear that their presence might frighten off fathers behind on their child-support payments. But I was there, trading on race, gender, and a promise not to interview any of the allegedly skittish participants.

"Men, if you want to win, we can win," Cosby said. "We are not a piti-ful race of people. We are a bright race, who can move with the best. But we are in a new time, where people are behaving in abnormal ways and calling it normal . . . When they used to come into our neighborhoods, we put the kids in the basement, grabbed a rifle, and said, 'By any means necessary.'

"I don't want to talk about hatred of these people," he continued. "I'm talking about a time when we protected our women and protected our children. Now I got people in wheelchairs, paralyzed. A little girl in Cam-den, jumping rope, shot through the mouth. Grandmother saw it out the window. And people are waiting around for Jesus to come, when Jesus is already within you."

Cosby was wearing his standard uniform—dark sunglasses, loafers, a sweat suit emblazoned with the seal of an institution of higher learning. That night it was the University of Massachusetts, where he'd gotten his doctorate in education thirty years ago. He was preaching from the book of black self-reliance, a gospel that he has spent the past four years carry-ing across the country in a series of events that he bills as "call-outs." "My problem," Cosby told the audience, "is I'm tired of losing to white people. When I say I don't care about white people, I mean let them say what they want to say. What can they say to me that's worse than what their grandfather said?"

From Birmingham to Cleveland and Baltimore, at churches and col-leges, Cosby has been telling thousands of black Americans that racism in

America is omnipresent but that it can't be an excuse to stop striving. As Cosby sees it, the antidote to racism is not rallies, protests, or pleas, but strong families and communities. Instead of focusing on some abstract notion of equality, he argues, blacks need to cleanse their culture, embrace personal responsibility, and reclaim the traditions that fortified them in the past. Driving Cosby's tough talk about values and responsibility is a vision starkly different from Martin Luther King's gauzy, all-inclusive dream: it's an America of competing powers, and a black America that is no longer content to be the weakest of the lot.

It's heady stuff, especially coming from the man white America remembers as a sitcom star and affable pitchman for E. F. Hutton, Kodak, and Jell-O Pudding Pops. And Cosby's race-based crusade is particularly jarring now. Across the country, as black politics has become more professionalized, the rhetoric of race is giving way to the rhetoric of standards and results. Newark's young Ivy League–educated mayor, Cory Booker, ran for office promising competence and crime reduction, as did Washington's mayor, Adrian Fenty. Indeed, we are now enjoying a moment of national self-congratulation over racial progress, with a black man running for president as the very realization of King's dream. Barack Obama defied efforts by the Clinton campaign to pigeonhole him as a "black" candidate, casting himself instead as the symbol of a society that has moved beyond lazy categories of race.

Black America does not entirely share the euphoria, though. The civil-rights generation is exiting the American stage—not in a haze of nostalgia but in a cloud of gloom, troubled by the persistence of racism, the apparent weaknesses of the generation following in its wake, and the seeming indifference of much of the country to black America's fate. In that climate, Cosby's gospel of discipline, moral reform, and self-reliance offers a way out—a promise that one need not cure America of its original sin in order to succeed. Racism may not be extinguished, but it can be beaten.

Has Dr. Huxtable, the head of one of America's most beloved television households, seen the truth: that the dream of integration should never supplant the pursuit of self-respect; that blacks should worry more about judging themselves and less about whether whites are judging them on the content of their character? Or has he lost his mind?

✳

From the moment he registered in the American popular consciousness, as the Oxford-educated Alexander Scott in the NBC adventure series *I Spy*, Cosby proffered the idea of an America that transcended race. The series, which started in 1965, was the first weekly show to feature an African American in a lead role, but it rarely factored race into dialogue or plots. Race was also mostly inconspicuous in Cosby's performances as a hugely popular stand-up comedian. "I don't spend my hours worrying how to slip a social message into my act," Cosby told *Playboy* in 1969. He also said that he didn't "have time to sit around and worry whether all the black people of the world make it because of me. I have my own gig to worry about." His crowning artistic and commercial achievement—*The Cosby Show*, which ran from 1984 to 1992—was seemingly a monument to that understated sensibility.

In fact, blackness was never absent from the show or from Bill Cosby. Plots involved black artists like Stevie Wonder or Dizzy Gillespie. The Huxtables' home was decorated with the works of black artists like Annie Lee, and the show featured black theater veterans such as Roscoe Lee Brown and Moses Gunn. Behind the scenes, Cosby hired the Harvard psychiatrist Alvin Poussaint to make sure that the show never trafficked in stereotypes and that it depicted blacks in a dignified light. Picking up Cosby's fixation on education, Poussaint had writers insert references to black schools. "If the script mentioned Oberlin, Texas Tech, or Yale, we'd circle it and tell them to mention a black college," Poussaint told me in a phone interview last year. "I remember going to work the next day and white people saying, 'What's the school called Morehouse?' " In 1985, Cosby riled NBC by placing an anti-apartheid sign in his Huxtable son's bedroom. The network wanted no part of the debate. "There may be two sides to apartheid in Archie Bunker's house," the *Toronto Star* quoted Cosby as saying. "But it's impossible that the Huxtables would be on any side but one. That sign will stay on that door. And I've told NBC that if they still want it down, or if they try to edit it out, there will be no show." The sign stayed.

Offstage, Cosby's philanthropy won him support among the civil-rights crowd. He made his biggest splash in 1988, when he and his wife gave $20 million to Spelman College, the largest individual donation ever given to a black college. "Two million would have been fantastic; twenty million, to use the language of the hip-hop generation, was off the chain," says Johnnetta Cole, who was then president of Spelman. Race again came to the fore in 1997, when Cosby's son was randomly shot and killed while fixing a flat on a Los Angeles freeway. His wife wrote an op-ed in *USA Today* arguing that white racism lay behind her son's death. "All African Americans, regardless of their educational and economic accomplishments, have been and are at risk in America simply because of their skin colors," she wrote. "Most people know that facing the truth brings about healing and growth. When is America going to face its historical and current racial realities so it can be what it says it is?"

The column caused a minor row, but most of white America took little notice. To them, Cosby was still America's Dad. But those close to Cosby were not surprised. Cosby was an avowed race man, who, like much of his generation, had come to feel that black America had lost its way. The crisis of absentee fathers, the rise of black-on-black crime, and the spread of hip-hop all led Cosby to believe that, after the achievements of the 1960s, the black community was committing cultural suicide.

His anger and frustration erupted into public view during an NAACP awards ceremony in Washington in 2004 commemorating the fiftieth anniversary of *Brown v. Board of Education*. At that moment, the shades of mortality and irrelevance seemed to be drawing over the civil-rights generation. Its matriarchs, Rosa Parks and Coretta Scott King, would be dead within two years. The NAACP's membership rolls had been shrinking; within months, its president, Kweisi Mfume, would resign (it was later revealed that he was under investigation by the NAACP for sexual harassment and nepotism—allegations that he denied). Other movement leaders were drifting into self-parody: Al Sharpton would soon be hosting a reality show and, a year later, would be doing ads for a predatory loan company; Sharpton and Jesse Jackson had recently asked MGM to issue an apology for the hit movie *Barbershop*.

That night, Cosby was one of the last honorees to take the podium. He began by noting that although civil-rights activists had opened the door for black America, young people today, instead of stepping through, were stepping backward. "No longer is a person embarrassed because they're pregnant without a husband," he told the crowd. "No longer is a boy considered an embarrassment if he tries to run away from being the father of the unmarried child."

There was cheering as Cosby went on. Perhaps sensing that he had the crowd, he grew looser. "The lower-economic and lower-middle-economic people are not holding their end in this deal," he told the audience.

Cosby disparaged activists who charge the criminal-justice system with racism. "These are people going around stealing Coca-Cola. People getting shot in the back of the head over a piece of pound cake," Cosby said. "Then we all run out and are outraged: 'The cops shouldn't have shot him.' What the hell was he doing with the pound cake in his hand? I wanted a piece of pound cake just as bad as anybody else. And I looked at it and I had no money. And something called parenting said, 'If you get caught with it, you're going to embarrass your mother.' "

Then he attacked African American naming traditions, and the style of dress among young blacks: "Ladies and gentlemen, listen to these people. They are showing you what's wrong . . . What part of Africa did this come from? We are not Africans. Those people are not Africans. They don't know a damned thing about Africa—with names like Shaniqua, Shaligua, Mohammed, and all that crap, and all of them are in jail." About then, people began to walk out of the auditorium and cluster in the lobby. There was still cheering, but some guests milled around and wondered what had happened. Some thought old age had gotten the best of Cosby. The mood was one of shock.

✳

After what has come to be known as "the Pound Cake speech"—it has its own Wikipedia entry—Cosby came under attack from various quarters of the black establishment. The playwright August Wilson commented, "A billionaire attacking poor people for being poor. Bill Cosby is a clown. What do you expect?" One of the gala's hosts, Ted Shaw, the director-counsel of the NAACP Legal Defense and Education Fund, called his comments "a harsh attack on poor black people in particular." Dubbing Cosby an "Afristocrat in winter," the Georgetown University professor Michael Eric Dyson came out with a book, *Is Bill Cosby Right? Or Has the Black Middle Class Lost Its Mind?*, that took issue with Cosby's bleak assessment of black progress and belittled his transformation from vanilla humorist to social critic and moral arbiter. "While Cosby took full advantage of the civil rights struggle," argued Dyson, "he resolutely denied it a seat at his artistic table."

But Cosby's rhetoric played well in black barbershops, churches, and backyard barbecues, where a unique brand of conservatism still runs strong. Outsiders may have heard haranguing in Cosby's language and tone. But much of black America heard instead the possibility of changing their communities without having to wait on the consciences and attention spans of policy makers who might not have their interests at heart. Shortly after Cosby took his Pound Cake message on the road, I wrote an article denouncing him as an elitist. When my father, a former Black Panther, read it, he upbraided me for attacking what he saw as a message of black empowerment. Cosby's argument has resonated with the black mainstream for just that reason.

✳

The split between Cosby and critics such as Dyson mirrors not only America's broader conservative/liberal split but black America's own historic intellectual divide. Cosby's most obvious antecedent is Booker T. Washington.

At the turn of the twentieth century, Washington married a defense of the white South with a call for black self-reliance and became the most prominent black leader of his day. He argued that southern whites should be given time to adjust to emancipation; in the meantime, blacks should advance themselves not by voting and running for office but by working, and ultimately owning, the land.

W. E. B. Du Bois, the integrationist model for the Dysons of our day, saw Washington as an apologist for white racism and thought that his willingness to sacrifice the black vote was heretical. History ultimately rendered half of Washington's argument moot. His famous Atlanta Compromise—in which he endorsed segregation as a temporary means of making peace with southerners—was answered by lynchings, land theft, and general racial terrorism. But Washington's appeal to black self-sufficiency endured.

After Washington's death, in 1915, the black conservative tradition he had fathered found a permanent and natural home in the emerging ideology of Black Nationalism. Marcus Garvey, its patron saint, turned the Atlanta Compromise on its head, implicitly endorsing segregation not as an olive branch to whites but as a statement of black supremacy. Black Nationalists scorned the Du Boisian integrationists as stooges or traitors, content to beg for help from people who hated them.

Garvey argued that blacks had rendered themselves unworthy of the white man's respect. "The greatest stumbling block in the way of progress in the race has invariably come from within the race itself," wrote Garvey. "The monkey wrench of destruction as thrown into the cog of Negro Progress, is not thrown so much by the outsider as by the very fellow who is in our fold, and who should be the first to grease the wheel of progress rather than seeking to impede." Decades later, Malcolm X echoed that sentiment, faulting blacks for failing to take charge of their destinies. "The white man is too intelligent to let someone else come and gain control of the economy of his community," Malcolm said. "But you will let anybody come in and take control of the economy of your community, control the housing, control the education, control the jobs, control the businesses, under the pretext that you want to integrate. No, you're out of your mind."

Black conservatives like Malcolm X and Louis Farrakhan, the leader of the Nation of Islam, have at times allied themselves with black liberals. But in general, they have upheld a core of beliefs laid out by Garvey almost a century ago: a skepticism of (white) government as a mediating force in the "Negro problem," a strong belief in the singular will of black people, and a fixation on a supposedly glorious black past.

Those beliefs also animate *Come On People*, the manifesto that Cosby and Poussaint published last fall. Although it does not totally dismiss government programs, the book mostly advocates solutions from within as a cure for black America's dismal vital statistics. "Once we find our bearings," they write, "we can move forward, as we have always done, on the path from victims to victors." *Come On People* is heavy on black pride ("no group of people has had the impact on the culture of the whole world that African Americans have had, and much of that impact has been for the good"), and heavier on the idea of the Great Fall—the theory, in this case, that post–Jim Crow blacks have lost touch with the cultural traditions that enabled them to persevere through centuries of oppression.

"For all the woes of segregation, there were some good things to come out of it," Cosby and Poussaint write. "One was that it forced us to take care of ourselves. When restaurants, laundries, hotels, theaters, groceries, and clothing stores were segregated, black people opened and ran their own. Black life insurance companies and banks thrived, as well as black funeral homes . . . Such successes provided jobs and strength to black economic well-being. They also gave black people that gratifying sense of an interdependent community." Although the authors take pains to put some distance between themselves and the Nation of Islam, they approvingly quote one of its ministers who spoke at a call-out in Compton, California: "I went to Koreatown today and I met with the Korean merchants," the minister told the crowd. "I love them. You know why? They got a place called what? Koreatown. When I left them, I went to Chinatown. They got a place called what? Chinatown. Where is your town?"

The notion of the Great Fall, and the attendant theory that segregation gave rise to some "good things," are the stock-in-trade of what Christopher Alan Bracey, a law professor at Washington University, calls (in his book, *Saviors or Sellouts*) the "organic" black conservative tradition: conservatives who favor hard work and moral reform over protests and government intervention, but whose black-nationalist leanings make them anathema to the Heritage Foundation and Rush Limbaugh. When political strategists argue that the Republican Party is missing a huge chance to court the black community, they are thinking of this mostly male bloc— the old guy in the barbershop, the grizzled Pop Warner coach, the retired Vietnam vet, the drunk uncle at the family reunion. He votes Democratic, not out of any love for abortion rights or progressive taxation, but because he feels—in fact, he knows—that the modern-day GOP draws on the support of people who hate him. This is the audience that flocks to Cosby: culturally conservative black Americans who are convinced that integration, and to some extent the entire liberal dream, robbed them of their natural defenses.

"There are things that we did not see coming," Cosby told me over lunch in Manhattan last year. "Like, you could see the Klan, but because these things were not on a horse, because there was no white sheet, and the people doing the deed were not white, we saw things in the light of family and forgiveness . . . We didn't pay attention to the dropout rate. We didn't pay attention to the fathers, to the self-esteem of our boys."

Given the state of black America, it is hard to quarrel with that analysis. Blacks are thirteen percent of the population, yet black men account for forty-nine percent of America's murder victims and forty-one percent of the prison population. The teen birth rate for blacks is 63 per 1,000, more than double the rate for whites. In 2005, black families had the lowest median income of any ethnic group measured by the Census, making only sixty-one percent of the median income of white families.

Most troubling is a recent study released by the Pew Charitable Trusts, which concluded that the rate at which blacks born into the middle class in the 1960s backslid into poverty or near-poverty (forty-five percent) was three times that of whites—suggesting that the advances of even some of the most successful cohorts of black America remain tenuous at best. Another Pew survey, released last November, found that blacks were "less upbeat about the state of black progress now than at any time since 1983."

The rise of the organic black conservative tradition is also a response to America's retreat from its second attempt at Reconstruction. Blacks have watched as the courts have weakened affirmative action, arguably the country's greatest symbol of state-sponsored inclusion. They've seen a fraudulent war on drugs that, judging by the casualties, looks like a war on black people. They've seen themselves bandied about as playthings in the presidential campaigns of Ronald Reagan (with his 1980 invocation of "states' rights" in Mississippi), George Bush (Willie Horton), Bill Clinton (Sister Souljah), and George W. Bush (McCain's fabled black love-child). They've seen the utter failures of school busing, and housing desegregation, as well as the horrors of Katrina. The result is a broad distrust of government as the primary tool for black progress.

In May 2004, just one day before Cosby's Pound Cake speech, *The New York Times* visited Louisville, Kentucky, once ground zero in the fight to integrate schools. But *The Times* found that sides had switched, and that black parents were more interested in educational progress than in racial parity. "Integration? What was it good for?" one parent asked. "They were just setting up our babies to fail."

In response to these perceived failures, many black activists have turned their efforts inward. Geoffrey Canada's ambitious Harlem Children's Zone project pushes black students to change their study habits and improve their home life. In cities like Baltimore and New York, community groups are focusing on turning black men into active fathers. In Philadelphia last October, thousands of black men packed the Liacouras Center, pledging to patrol their neighborhoods and help combat the rising murder rate. When Cosby came to St. Paul Church in Detroit, one local judge got up and urged Cosby and other black celebrities to donate more money to advance the cause. "I didn't fly out here to write a check," Cosby retorted. "I'm not writing a check in Houston, Detroit, or Philadelphia. Leave these athletes alone. All you know is Oprah Winfrey and Michael Jackson. Forget about a check . . . This is how we lost to the white man. 'Judge said Bill Cosby is gonna write a check, but until then . . .' "

Instead of waiting for handouts or outside help, Cosby argues, disadvantaged blacks should start by purging their own culture of noxious elements like gangsta rap, a favorite target. "What do record producers think when they churn out that gangsta rap with antisocial, women-hating messages?," Cosby and Poussaint ask in their book. "Do they think that black male youth won't act out what they have repeated since they were old enough to listen?" Cosby's rhetoric on culture echoes—and amplifies—a swelling strain of black opinion: last November's Pew study reported that seventy-one percent of blacks feel that rap is a bad influence.

The strain of black conservatism that Cosby evokes has also surfaced in the presidential campaign of Barack Obama. Early on, some commentators speculated that Obama's Cosby-esque appeals to personal responsibility would cost him black votes. But if his admonishments for black kids to turn off the PlayStation and for black fathers to do their jobs did him any damage, it was not reflected at the polls. In fact, this sort of rhetoric amounts to something of a racial double play, allowing Obama and Cosby to cater both to culturally conservative blacks and to whites who are convinced that black America is a bastion of decadence. (Curiously, Cosby is noncommittal verging on prickly when it comes to Obama. When Larry King asked him whether he supported Obama, he bristled: "Do you ask white people this question? . . . I want to know why this fellow especially is brought up in such a special way. How many Americans in the media really take him seriously, or do they look at him like some prize brown baby?" The exchange ended with Cosby professing admiration for Dennis Kucinich. Months later, he rebuffed my requests for his views on Obama's candidacy.)

※

The shift in focus from white racism to black culture is not as new as some social commentators make it out to be. Standing in St. Paul Church on that July evening listening to Cosby, I remembered the last time The Street felt like this: in the summer of 1994, after Louis Farrakhan announced the Million Man March. Farrakhan barnstormed the country holding "men only" meetings (but much larger). I saw him in my native Baltimore, while home from Howard University on vacation. The march itself was cathartic. I walked with four or five other black men, and all along the way black women stood on porches or out on the street, shouting, clapping, cheering. For us, Farrakhan's opinions on the Jews mostly seemed beside the point; what stuck was the chance to assert our humanity and our manhood by marching on the Mall, and not acting like we were all fresh out of San Quentin. We lived in the shadow of the eighties crack era. So many of us had been jailed or were on our way. So many of us were fathers in biology only. We believed ourselves disgraced and clung to the march as a public statement: the time had come to grow up.

Black conservatives have been dipping into this well of lost black honor since the turn of the twentieth century. On the one hand, vintage black nationalists have harked back to a golden age of black Africa, where mighty empires sprawled and everyone was a king. Meanwhile, populist black conservatives like Cosby point to pre-1968 black America as an era when blacks were united in the struggle: men were men, and a girl who got pregnant without getting married would find herself bundled off to Grandpa's farm.

What both visions share is a sense that black culture in its present form is bastardized and pathological. What they also share is a foundation in myth. Black people are not the descendants of kings. We are—and I say this with big pride—the progeny of slaves. If there's any majesty in our struggle, it lies not in fairy tales but in those humble origins and the great distance we've traveled since. Ditto for the dreams of a separate but noble past. Cosby's, and much of black America's, conservative analysis flattens history and smooths over the wrinkles that have characterized black America since its inception.

Indeed, a century ago, the black brain trust was pushing the same rhetoric that Cosby is pushing today. It was concerned that slavery had essentially destroyed the black family and was obsessed with seemingly the same issues—crime, wanton sexuality, and general moral turpitude—that Cosby claims are recent developments. "The early effort of middle-class blacks to respond to segregation was, aside from a political agenda, focused on a social-reform agenda," says Khalil G. Muhammad, a professor of American history at Indiana University. "The National Association of Colored Women, Du Bois in *The Philadelphia Negro,* all shared a sense of anxiety that African Americans were not presenting their best selves to the world. There was the sense that they were committing crimes and needed to keep their sexuality in check." Adds William Jelani Cobb, a professor of American history at Spelman College: "The same kind of people who were advocating for social reform were denigrating people because they didn't play piano. They often saw themselves as reluctant caretakers of the less enlightened."

In particular, Cosby's argument—that much of what haunts young black men originates in post-segregation black culture—doesn't square with history. As early as the 1930s, sociologists were concerned that black men were falling behind black women. In his classic study, *The Negro Family in the United States*, published in 1939, E. Franklin Frazier argued that urbanization was undermining the ability of men to provide for their families. In 1965—at the height of the civil-rights movement—Daniel Patrick Moynihan's milestone report, "The Negro Family: The Case for National Action," picked up the same theme.

At times, Cosby seems willfully blind to the parallels between his arguments and those made in the presumably glorious past. Consider his problems with rap. How could an avowed jazz fanatic be oblivious to the similar plaints once sparked by the music of his youth? "The tired longshoreman, the porter, the housemaid and the poor elevator boy in search of recreation, seeking in jazz the tonic for weary nerves and muscles," wrote the lay historian J. A. Rogers, "are only too apt to find the bootlegger, the gambler and the demi-monde who have come there for victims and to escape the eyes of the police."

Beyond the apocryphal notion that black culture was once a fount of virtue, there's still the charge that culture is indeed the problem. But to reach that conclusion, you'd have to stand on some rickety legs. The hip-hop argument, again, is particularly creaky. Ronald Ferguson, a Harvard social scientist, has highlighted that an increase in hip-hop's popularity during the early 1990s corresponded with a declining amount of time spent reading among black kids. But gangsta rap can be correlated with other phenomena, too—many of them positive. During the 1990s, as gangsta rap exploded, teen pregnancy and the murder rate among black men declined. Should we give the blue ribbon in citizenship to Dr. Dre?

"I don't know how to measure culture. I don't know how to test its effects, and I'm not sure anyone else does," says the Georgetown economist Harry Holzer. "There's a liberal story that limited opportunities, and barriers, lead to employment problems and criminal records, but then there's another story that has to do with norms, behaviors, and oppositional culture. You can't prove the latter statistically, but it still might be true." Holzer thinks that both arguments contain truth and that one doesn't preclude the other. Fair enough. Suffice it to say, though, that the evidence supporting structural inequality is compelling. In 2001, a researcher sent out black and white job applicants in Milwaukee, randomly assigning them a criminal record. The researcher concluded that a white man with a criminal record had about the same chance of getting a job as a black man without one. Three years later, researchers produced the same results in New York under more-rigorous conditions.

The accepted wisdom is that such studies are a comfort to black people, allowing them to wallow in their misery. In fact, the opposite is true—the liberal notion that blacks are still, after a century of struggle, victims of pervasive discrimination is the ultimate collective buzz-kill. It effectively means that African Americans must, on some level, accept that their children will be "less than" until some point in the future when white racism miraculously abates. That's not the sort of future that any black person eagerly awaits, nor does it make for particularly motivating talking points.

Last summer, I watched Cosby give a moving commencement speech to a group of Connecticut inmates who'd just received their GEDs. Before the speech, at eight in the morning, Cosby quizzed correctional officials on the conditions and characteristics of their inmate population. I wished, then, that my seven-year-old son could have seen Cosby there, to take in the same basic message that I endeavor to serve him every day— that manhood means more than virility and strut, that it calls for discipline and dutiful stewardship. That the ultimate fate of black people lies in their own hands, not in the hands of their antagonists. That as an African American, he has a duty to his family, his community, and his ancestors.

If Cosby's call-outs simply ended at that—a personal and communal creed—there'd be little to oppose. But Cosby often pits the rhetoric of personal responsibility against the legitimate claims of American citizens for their rights. He chides activists for pushing to reform the criminal-justice system, despite solid evidence that the criminal-justice system needs reform. His historical amnesia—his assertion that many of the problems that pervade black America are of a recent vintage—is simply wrong, as is his contention that today's young African Americans are somehow weaker, that they've dropped the ball. And for all its positive energy, his language of uplift has its limitations. After the Million Man March, black men embraced a sense of hope and promise. We were supposed to return to our communities and families inspired by a new feeling of responsibility. Yet here we are again, almost fifteen years later, with seemingly little tangible change. I'd take my son to see Bill Cosby, to hear his message, to revel in its promise and optimism. But afterward, he and I would have a very long talk.

✳

On the day last summer when Cosby met me for lunch in the West Village, it was raining, as it had been all week, and New York was experiencing a record-cold August. Cosby had just come from Max Roach's funeral and was dressed in a natty three-piece suit. Despite the weather, the occasion, and the oddly empty dining room, Cosby was energized. He had spent the previous day in Philadelphia, where he spoke to a group in a housing project, met with state health officials, and participated in a community march against crime. Grassroots black activists in his hometown were embracing his call. He planned, over the coming year, to continue his call-outs and release a hip-hop album. (He has also noted, however, that there won't be any profanity on it.)

Cosby was feeling warm and nostalgic. He asked why I had not brought my son, and I instantly regretted dropping him off at my partner's workplace for a couple of hours. He talked about breaking his shoulder playing school football, after his grandfather had tried to get him to quit. "Granddad Cosby got on the trolley and came over to the apartment," he recalled. "I was so embarrassed. I was laid out on the sofa. He was talking to my parents, and I was waiting for the moment when he would say, 'See, I told you, Junior.' He came back and reached in his pocket and gave me a quarter. He said, 'Go to the corner and get some ice cream. It has calcium in it.' "

Much pop psychology has been devoted to Cosby's transformation into such a high-octane, high-profile activist. His nemesis Dyson says that Cosby, in his later years, is following in the dishonorable tradition of upper-class African Americans who denounce their less fortunate brethren. Others have suggested more-sinister motivations—that Cosby is covering for his own alleged transgressions. (In 2006, Cosby settled a civil lawsuit filed by a woman who claimed that he had sexually assaulted her; other women have come forward with similar allegations that have not gone to court.) But the depth of his commitment would seem to belie such suspicions, and in any case, they do not seem to have affected his hold on his audience: in the November Pew survey, eighty-five percent of all African American respondents considered him a "good influence" on the black community, above Obama (seventy-six percent) and second only to Oprah Winfrey (eighty-seven percent).

Part of what drives Cosby's activism, and reinforces his message, is the rage that lives in all African Americans, a collective feeling of disgrace that borders on self-hatred. As the comedian Chris Rock put it in one of his infamous routines, "Everything white people don't like about black people, black people really don't like about black people . . . It's like a civil war going on with black people, and it's two sides—there's black people and there's niggas, and niggas have got to go . . . Boy, I wish they'd let me join the Ku Klux Klan. Shit, I'd do a drive-by from here to Brooklyn." (Rock stopped performing the routine when he noticed that his white fans were laughing a little too hard.) Liberalism, with its pat logic and focus on structural inequities, offers no balm for this sort of raw pain. Like the people he preaches to, Cosby has grown tired of hanging his head.

This disquiet spans generations, but it is most acute among those of the civil-rights era. "I don't know a better term than *angst*," says Johnnetta Cole. "I refuse to categorize every young African American with the same language, but there are some 'young'uns'—and some of us who are not 'young'uns'—who must turn around and look at where we are, because where we're headed isn't pretty." Like many of the stars of the civil-rights movement, Cole has gifts that go beyond social activism. She rose out of the segregated South and went to college at age fifteen, eventually earning a bachelor's from Oberlin and a doctorate in anthropology from Northwestern. That same sort of dynamism exists today among many younger blacks, but what troubles the older generation is that their energy seems directed at other pursuits besides social uplift.

Cosby is fond of saying that sacrifices of the sixties weren't made so that rappers and young people could repeatedly use the word *nigger*. But that's exactly why they were made. After all, chief among all individual rights awarded Americans is the right to be mediocre, crass, and juvenile—in other words, the right to be human. But Cosby is aiming for something superhuman—twice as good, as the elders used to say—and his homily to a hazy black past seems like an effort to redeem something more than the present.

When people hear Bill Cosby's message, many assume that he is the product of the sort of family he's promoting—two caring parents, a stable home life, a working father. In fact, like many of the men he admonishes, Cosby was born into a troubled home. He was raised by his mother because his father, who joined the Navy, abandoned the family when Cosby was a child. Speaking to me of his youth, Cosby said, "People told me I was bright, but nobody stayed on me. My mother was too busy trying to feed and clothe us." He was smart enough to be admitted to Central High

School, a magnet school in Philadelphia, but transferred and then dropped out in tenth grade and followed his father into the service.

But the twists and turns of that reality seem secondary to the tidier, more appealing world that Cosby is trying to create. Toward the end of our lunch, in a long, rambling monologue, Cosby told me, "If you looked at me and said, 'Why is he doing this? Why right now?,' you could probably say, 'He's having a resurgence of his childhood.' What do I need if I am a child today? I need people to guide me. I need the possibility of change. I need people to stop saying I can't pull myself up by my own bootstraps. They say that's a myth. But these other people have their mythical stories—why can't we have our own?"

Before Grief

Jerald Walker

This is one of a handful of essays that I added to Best African American Essays 2010 after Randall Kennedy made his selections and the book was well into production. Events happen, as a famous British Prime Minister once said, and some important occurrences in 2009 that occurred after the book was in production needed to be acknowledged and written about for this volume. Pop star Michael Jackson's untimely death in June was one such occurrence. I was not especially taken with any of the voluminous published commentary on Jackson that appeared in the days and weeks following his death. Jerald is a fine writer, having had an essay in the 2009 Best African American Essays, and he really wanted to write something about Jackson, who, as you can tell from the essay, meant a great deal to him. This was just the sort of essay I was looking for. I am much in his debt for having produced such a fine piece on such short notice.

—Gerald Early

✳

Before the glove; before the anorexia and addictions; before the moonwalk and crotch grabs and Fred Astaire's admiration and envy; before his color faded and his nose shriveled; before he stunned and confused me, entwining one arm with Brooke Shields's and nestling Emmanuel Lewis with the other; before he was said to be spending some nights with Lisa Marie and other nights alone in an oxygen chamber; before Bubbles and the boa constrictor and the rest of the menagerie that he'd come to trust more than people; before the people he *did* finally trust mentioned "Jesus juice" and sleepovers and gave me reason not to trust *him,* another reason to wonder if now was the time for my disavowal, the moment when I'd say, at last, I've had enough, even though I knew I never could, because yes, before all of this there was the dazzling child vocalist with a pink gangster hat slicing toward one eye, his four brothers dancing at his side, while the Walker Six—that's what we called ourselves—mimicked their act, imagined that it was us up on Ed Sullivan's stage, blowing people's minds.

Though my siblings and I were only having fun, just messing around, for Michael this was serious business, this was *work*—like performing was work for James Brown, the man whose style he had already mastered, like performing was work for Smokey Robinson, the man whose soul he had already cloned. The fact that Michael was less than half their age was part of his appeal, because implicit in his youth was the promise of more, the hope that there'd be years and then decades of watching his legend unfold. But for now it was still 1969, a blustery December evening, bringing to a close a blustery American decade, assassinations and race riots at our heels, and the Walker Six, dumbstruck to see a black family on TV, was bantering over who should sing lead.

Jimmy's case was strong. Like Michael, he was the youngest of the group, having departed our mother's womb a full twelve minutes after me. But I owned a pink gangster hat (really a brown skullcap, but still . . .), Mary could reach those high notes, Linda could carry a tune, Tommy was the best dancer, while Timmy, by his own estimation, was the cutest. All of these points were argued compellingly but a little too loudly, prompting our father to threaten corporal punishment, ending a debate that would erupt again the next morning when we heard "I Want You Back" on the living-room console. I don't remember how or if the matter was resolved—perhaps we were *all* Michael—only that the volume was cranked up and we fell into our clumsy choreography, dipping in time to our off-key voices, our arms open wide as we implored six loves to return.

Meanwhile, just as we were being Michael, our parents were being his parents—stern, loving, optimistic, highly religious, and always on the lookout for an escape hatch, some elusive portal that would lead us to better opportunities. They would find that portal in 1970, issuing out into a middle-class community on Chicago's South Side. Until then we lived in a ghetto not unlike the Jacksons' in Gary, Indiana, a mere thirty miles away. But that night in 1969, it was clear that their family would be leaving soon, carried off to the good life—not by talent, our parents stressed, but by the values that had seen it to fruition. No loitering in the streets for Michael and his brothers, no slacking in school, no messing around with drugs and gangs, and certainly no being spared the rod, because this was before belts and the backs of hands were considered cruel weapons, before parents' desire to instill discipline and respect in their children by any means necessary was considered wrong. "Hard *work*," our father said that night, over the applause of the Ed Sullivan studio audience, "is what got those boys to where they are." To which our mother added, "Hard work *and*, of course, God."

Theirs was named Jehovah. In the eyes of some black folk, that made the Jacksons a little strange. But at least most people had *heard* of the Jehovah's Witnesses, whereas very few had heard of our religion, the Worldwide Church of God, and that made the Walkers even stranger. Like the Jacksons' faith, ours forbade celebrating Christmas, Halloween, birthdays, and Easter, and we were also discouraged from socializing with nonmembers, resulting in siblings being not just siblings but also best friends. And so I understood that the childhood bond between Michael and his brothers and sisters was both strong and vital, exactly like the bond between my brothers and sisters and me. But this was before the Walker Six grew up and then apart, slowly establishing and tending to separate lives, just as the Jackson Five became the Jacksons, and then the Jacksons became Michael Jackson, and then Michael Jackson became the King.

Now the King is dead. I write this more than three weeks after he passed away, at a time when the media's preoccupation with him is still going strong. Many feel this is justified, a sensible response to his unparalleled fame. Others disagree. "I've seen so many good people the last few days," said one New York politician, "who aren't going to get credit for anything, and then I see this guy, who's really a lowlife, and he's being treated like a hero of civilization." A reporter at *The Washington Post* echoed this theme: "The coverage is out of control, and it's becoming an embarrassment to the news business." Another reporter commented in his blog, "This country has misplaced priorities and a lack of moral values. We celebrate the lives of freaks, yet neglect real heroes."

But back in 1971, no one held this view; that was the year the Walker Six was allowed to turn on the television on a Saturday, our Sabbath, because the first episode of the *Jackson 5ive* cartoon was on. Breaking the Sabbath was a violation of God's law, pretty significant stuff, but then so, too, was an all-Negro cartoon. Something important was happening in our country, our parents understood, a new level of racial tolerance and acceptance, being brought about by a family that looked and behaved like our own. And so my parents sanctioned those Saturday morning viewings, and it was okay for us to spend our allowances on the Jackson Five albums, T-shirts, and posters. It was okay to stay up late after their television specials in 1971 and 1972 to practice our routine. And in 1976, when the Jacksons launched their variety show, the first black family to have one, it was okay to say that Donny and Marie Osmond were lame.

Two years later, the Jacksons were also lame. Michael must have thought so too, because he was already busy on his first solo album, *Off the Wall*, which debuted in 1979, when I was fifteen and seeking, like Michael, my own way. I'd found it by 1982 when *Thriller* was released, and by some bizarre fate it was as if the portal I'd entered this time led me directly to the music video of his title song, a world of ghouls and goblins, otherwise known as pushers and pimps. This was during a terrible period of chaos and wrong choices for me, when the only family I was close to was two of my brothers, who'd climbed through portals similar to mine. While I do not know if this is true, I have a vague memory that the three of us, in 1983, watched the *Motown 25* television special together, and maybe we rose at some point to attempt Michael's moonwalk before collapsing back into our seats, succumbing to the dope coursing through our veins, much as dope would course through Michael's, nearly three decades later, and stop his heart.

Mine stopped, for a moment, when I heard the news. And in that pause before grief, I had a vision of the Walker Six, dancing and singing . . . and then it was gone.

Profiles

---　✳　---

The Other Black President

Adam Serwer

Ben Jealous steps through the metal detector in the Hart Senate Office building on Capitol Hill. He removes his black baseball cap and jacket, hunching over as he affixes a gold NAACP pin to his lapel before entering a press conference in support of Attorney General nominee Eric Holder. It's January, and the thirty-five-year-old Jealous has been president of the National Association for the Advancement of Colored People for a mere four months.

As he stands behind the podium, rubbing shoulders with senators and other civil-rights leaders, his gaze drifts to the space between his shoes. After a few moments, he realizes he's on camera, and his chin jerks up as he rocks back on his heels a bit. When he takes the mic, he puts aside his prepared remarks and in a soft voice reminds the assembled crowd of reporters about the many civil-rights violations under the Bush administration. "With the Bill of Rights in tatters, with the Department of Justice in tatters, we need a man who can hold it together, and Holder is that man," Jealous says confidently. He halts and squints for a moment. "We need a *person* who can hold it together. Holder is that person."

The NAACP had only recently decided that Jealous was the man—er, person—who could hold it together. On the eve of its centennial year, the organization risks becoming a victim of its own success. The leader of the Western world is a black man named Barack Obama, and even Bill Cosby sounds optimistic about the future of black America. The organization that publicized lynching and awakened the conscience of the nation, litigated against segregation all over the country, and helped organize the 1964 March on Washington now finds itself suffering from dwindling membership and an inability to connect to youth. Where once the visible realities of segregation and discrimination either forced or inspired the best and brightest African Americans to join the NAACP, the civil-rights victories of the last century have given them other choices and opportunities.

"Even the so-called 'new black politics,' people who are Ivy League educated and all this, who want to transcend race, people like [D.C. Mayor Adrian] Fenty and [Philadelphia Mayor] Michael Nutter, have aligned themselves with forces that are not really connected to the old civil-rights guard," says Peniel Joseph, a professor of African and Afro-American studies at Brandeis University. "They're building on the legacy of civil rights and black power, but they portray themselves as pragmatists rather than ideologically inclined."

While Jealous possesses much of the "new black politics" pedigree— an Ivy League degree, a Rhodes scholarship, an ease with business interests, and a professional demeanor that allows him to speak about issues of race to broad audiences—he chose to be an activist rather than a politician. "I think like everybody in my generation, we were encouraged to see it as all the great battles had been won," Jealous says. "But at the same time we were growing up in a period of increasing violence in the black community, in the Latino community. So the older we got, the more reality conflicted with the stories we were being told." Obama may be president, but black men are also incarcerated in record numbers, public schools remain segregated, the wealth of the middle class is tumbling, and AIDS is the No. 1 killer of black women ages twenty-four to thirty-five.

Jealous is part community organizer, part savvy financial operator, and part tech geek. In less than a year as president, he has made converts out of his critics both within the NAACP and outside it, and he has modernized the organization by drawing young, gifted and black talent. In advance of the presidential election, Jealous developed a new online system to help the NAACP register thousands of voters. And he has used his fundraising connections to resolve the fiscal crisis left by his predecessor. "He knows just about everyone," says Tammy Tanner, an administrative assistant at the Rosenberg Foundation, the philanthropic organization Jealous ran before leaving for the NAACP. "He says, let's have wine and sit down and talk, and people are writing ten-thousand-dollar checks for him." When several donors pulled out of an NAACP fundraiser in San Francisco over the chapter president's opposition to the Proposition 8 gay-marriage ban, Jealous jumped on a plane to California and raised $19,000 to fill the gap.

But before he could do any of this, Jealous had to convince the NAACP's board that he could keep the organization relevant in an era when many people are asking, does America still need a National Association for the Advancement of Colored People when colored people have advanced further than any of us ever dreamed?

Last May, the board of the NAACP huddled into a Marriott Hotel in Baltimore to select its new president. The sixty-four members were sharply divided between two candidates: Benjamin Todd Jealous and the Rev. Frederick Douglass Haynes III. The board's choice was stark. Haynes fit the mold of previous NAACP leaders, a pastor turned civil-rights crusader. An accomplished orator who turned a small Dallas congregation into an eight-thousand-member megachurch, he combined a charismatic presence with a business savvy the financially troubled NAACP desperately needed. Jealous, on the other hand, came from a tradition of mixing journalism with advocacy. He developed a strong reputation as a manager during stints as head of the National Newspaper Publishers Association (NNPA), an association of black newspapers, and as president of the Rosenberg Foundation.

In recent years, the NAACP brand had been badly tarnished. After the Rev. Ben Hooks, a movement veteran, resigned as president in the early 1990s, the organization's next two leaders were tainted by sex scandals and fiscal mismanagement. In 2005, the NAACP elected Bruce Gordon, a former Verizon executive, who was considered a more business-friendly face for a more conservative time. But he too proved a poor financial manager, leaving the NAACP almost $4 million in debt. Gordon, who spoke openly about America being in a "post-civil-rights era," also clashed ideologically with longtime Chairman Julian Bond and other board members. He resigned after less than two years.

This time, the board needed to pick a president who could handle vast fundraising responsibilities, manage its 300,000 members, restore fiscal prudence, and attract new blood. And the new president would have to do these things without, you know, embarrassing the NAACP. Supporters of

Haynes argued that he was the safer bet. "Anyone who can build a church of four, five, six thousand members clearly shows he can bring people together and run a multimillion-dollar organization," said Pennsylvania Conference President Jerry Monedesire, who originally supported Haynes. But Bond threw his support behind Jealous, whose experience as a community organizer brought him closer to Bond's vision for the NAACP as a social-justice organization.

The board's marathon eight-hour debate session lasted until 2:00 a.m., when Jealous was finally selected by a vote of 34–21. Grumpy board members shuffled out of the meeting to air their objections to the press—a marked contrast from just two years prior, when the newly elected Gordon strolled triumphantly into a room full of reporters. Many of the board members' complaints—that Jealous was inexperienced, dismissive of established leaders like Al Sharpton and Jesse Jackson, or simply not an active enough member of the NAACP—were published by NNPA columnist George Curry, who despite being Jealous' longtime friend and colleague, disagreed with the board's decision. In a column he wrote about the increasing number of biracial blacks in leadership positions, Curry obliquely referenced Jealous' light skin tone, recalling a time when access to social gatherings of the black elite was often dependent on whether or not one was "light, bright, and damn near white."

Bond says that the issue also came up in private. During a closed-door meeting of the presidential search committee, one member questioned whether the light-skinned Jealous was a good choice for the voice of the NAACP. Bond was incensed. ("It would be beneath us to consider it," he says.) The next meeting, he brought in a copy of *Time* magazine from 1938 featuring famed NAACP leader Walter White, who was light enough to pass as white. The subject was never brought up again.

✳

It was a typical 1960s love story: Jealous' parents met while battling Jim Crow laws. Fred Jealous was used to being the only white guy thrown in jail for integrating lunch counters, and Ann Todd was active with the Student Nonviolent Coordinating Committee. After Fred was disowned by his family for marrying a black woman, he and Ann left their families on the East Coast to settle in Monterey County, California, which Ben Jealous describes as a community of disaffected activists of all stripes. Jealous was born in 1973, and by age fourteen he was hitting the streets to register voters in anticipation of Jesse Jackson's presidential run. "It was a compelling ask," Jealous recalls. "If you were forty years old and you had a fourteen-year-old on your doorstep asking you to vote, how could you say no?"

When Jealous enrolled at Columbia University in 1990, he began working as an organizer with the NAACP Legal Defense Fund. On campus, his activist streak got him in trouble. Protesting a plan to turn the site of Malcolm X's assassination into a research facility, Jealous was suspended for "aiding and abetting the obstruction of an entrance to a university facility for more than a very short period of time," he says, citing the charge from memory. So he made a pilgrimage to the South to join a struggle similar to the one that drew his parents together. Mississippi's three black colleges were slated to be closed, and Jealous organized with the local NAACP chapter to keep them open and fully funded.

While in Mississippi, he began working as a reporter for a weekly black newspaper called *The Jackson Advocate,* where his journalism training consisted of "reading *The Guardian* and getting [my] ass kicked by [publisher Charles Tisdale's] red pen." Tisdale viewed journalism as not just a way to provide information but also as a commitment to the black community, and working with him was a formative experience for Jealous. Tisdale's widow, Alice Thomas-Tisdale, who is now publisher of the *Advocate,* explains, "The black press believes that as long as one [person] is held back, we all are. So it's more of an institution than just a source of information."

After cutting his teeth at the *Advocate* and then becoming its managing editor, Jealous returned to Columbia in 1997. With most of his friends gone and the struggle for apartheid finally over, Jealous was able to bring his grades up and win a Rhodes Scholarship. When he returned from Oxford in 1999, his experience at the *Advocate* led to a job as head of the NNPA. As president, Jealous struck a deal with Microsoft to finance the relocation of the organization's office to Howard University in Washington, D.C. He also set up a Web site that syndicates articles from all of its member papers. The NNPA now functions not only as an association of black newspapers but also as an online wire service and a training ground for journalism students.

Jealous' experiences are anchored in the struggle for civil rights, but he is perhaps the first NAACP president to have a background in human rights as well. In 2002, he left the NNPA to become the director of Amnesty International's American human-rights program, where he lobbied against racial profiling, particularly of Arab Americans and Muslims after September 11. When discussing civil-rights issues, Jealous frequently refers to other ethnic groups affected by discrimination or poverty, although his emphasis is on the community that raised him, that made him who he is. While previous generations of civil-rights leaders no doubt believed that the struggle for black civil rights was part of a struggle for the rights of all people, Jealous is keenly affected by that view, and it deeply informs his leadership of the NAACP. "For a hundred years [the NAACP has] consistently transformed this country for the better," Jealous says. "Not just for black people or some people but for all people."

Only a few years out of college, Jealous quickly climbed the ranks of the nonprofit world. In 2005, he was named president of the Los Angeles–based Rosenberg Foundation, which grants money to groups working in low-income communities. Jealous whipped the foundation into fiscal and managerial shape and directed its money toward an emerging method of dealing with mass incarceration: reentry programs that help former inmates readjust to society and find work. Jealous plans to prioritize these issues as president of the NAACP. "A hundred years from now we're going to be judged by our grandchildren," he says. "They're going to look back, and they're going to say this country had the most incarcerated on Earth. Young black people were the most incarcerated in modern history. What did you do about it?"

But Jealous got tired of simply funding activism. He wanted to return to the front lines. When friends in the civil-rights community started floating his name to the NAACP search committee, Jealous was interested. But he realized that he would have to move across the country to Baltimore in order to take the job.

Ultimately, it was the birth of his daughter that would make the decision for him. Jealous had met fellow activist and lawyer Lia Beth Epperson at a Hungarian pastry shop during his first stint at Columbia University, and although they had fallen in love, work had kept them apart. But by the summer of 2002, they had reunited and married. As Jealous contemplated the move from Rosenberg, their newborn child was his primary consideration. He explains, "Being a young black parent in this country leaves you with an urgent desire to improve the world quickly." He decided the move was worth it.

✳

For decades, the NAACP was the first responder against injustices like segregation, discrimination, and brutality against blacks because the United States government refused to act on their behalf. But as progress was made and barriers fell, critics began to argue that the NAACP was merely a reactionary organization, stuck in the past and unsuited to the new era.

In August 2007, when influential black blogger Gina McCauley first heard about a woman and her son who were gang-raped in the Dunbar Village housing project in Florida, she called the NAACP. She says the organization told her that responding to the crime "wasn't in their mission." But while the national office declined to take a position either way, the local NAACP chapter in Boca Raton eventually did speak out—on behalf of the suspected perpetrators, alleging that they had been treated unfairly by the courts. For McCauley and others, the experience proved that the NAACP was out of touch: it responded to racism but not to broader social issues that affect the community, such as black-on-black crime.

Even when it has been proactive, the NAACP has had trouble connecting with young black Americans. When the organization held a ritual "burial of the N-word" two years ago, it seemed comically tone-deaf to the word's frequent use among young blacks, Latinos, and even some whites. To young people, "the NAACP is a relic of another age," says author and journalist Juan Williams. "When I was covering the NAACP . . . I wrote they were a bunch of gray-haired revolutionaries. And that was in the eighties."

The NAACP has faced generational conflicts since the 1960s, when young activists broke off and formed or joined organizations like the Student Nonviolent Coordinating Committee and the Southern Christian Leadership Conference, but it has always persevered, possibly due to the strength of its history and brand. Today, the NAACP sometimes finds itself outmaneuvered by grass-roots groups like James Rucker's Color of Change, an online activist network whose quick rise to prominence suggests there is a space for advocacy the NAACP simply isn't taking advantage of. "The NAACP has had difficulty demonstrating its relevance to people who weren't already true believers," Rucker says.

Still, he emphasizes, even the most effective new civil-rights groups don't have the infrastructure to compete with the NAACP, with its hundreds of chapters and vast lobbying experience. "We're not trying to beat the NAACP," Rucker says. "My goal is to amplify each other's efforts.

Given the issues that we face, we need everything that we got to make change happen."

But the fact is many civil-rights-minded youth are coming to activism through groups like Rucker's, not the NAACP. The struggle that originally brought young people to the NAACP is over. There are no segregated lunch counters, no poll taxes, no lynching epidemic. After years of fighting for equal rights through organizing, litigation, and lobbying, the barriers to the most powerful positions in the land have been breached.

Jealous sees these successes—and the challenges they bring—as an opportunity rather than a death knell. "Our founders said we were going to eradicate lynch mobs; thirty years later we did it. In 1918, we said we were going to desegregate the military; thirty years later we did it. In 1932, we said we were going to outlaw Jim Crow; twenty-two years later we did it. In 1954, we said we were going to desegregate every institution in this country, from the local school to the global corporation. . . . It took forty years, but we succeeded. In 1960, we said we were going to level the political playing field; we've done it," Jealous says. "It's okay in our mind to pick not a three-year goal but a thirty-year goal, because that's how we've succeeded consistently."

For Jealous, mass incarceration is the civil-rights challenge of this generation. Addressing it, he says, requires more than just changing draconian drug laws; it also requires confronting poverty and a failing public-education system. Young black folks, particularly the urban poor who most need an organization like the NAACP to look out for them, are facing problems of violence, drugs, AIDS, and unequal education.

Most civil-rights activists, and even their critics, agree with Jealous that this is the biggest civil-rights challenge of the modern era—they just disagree on how to meet it. John McWhorter of the conservative Manhattan Institute says that a dysfunctional black culture, not racism, is the issue, and it can only be addressed internally. "The proper thing for a civil-rights organization to do today is to go into services," McWhorter says.

Jealous, however, argues that the NAACP needs to stick to its roots—advocating for better public policy. Providing services isn't the NAACP's role, he argues. "Some people would like to see us be an alternative government infrastructure for black people," Jealous says. "I understand where that comes from; the reality is that's what we've been fighting against for a hundred years. What we've been fighting for is for the government that we already have to respond to the needs of all people. Our focus is on the needs of black America; that's what we do best; that's where we're known best. But our goal is a fully functioning democracy."

✳

During the 2004 Democratic National Convention speech that made him a star, Barack Obama invoked the idea of a nation where the inner-city resident and the rural factory worker are equally American. Fulfilling this promise is why the NAACP was created. There could not be a Barack Obama without the NAACP, and yet the organization faces particular challenges in lobbying this president—the most popular black political figure in history.

Some people have learned the hard way just how tricky it can be. During the campaign, when media personality Tavis Smiley criticized Obama for not paying enough attention to black problems, the ensuing uproar caused Smiley to cancel upcoming media appearances. Radio host Tom Joyner told his listeners that Smiley "couldn't take the hate."

Jealous must figure out how to hold Obama accountable without drawing "the hate." Melissa Harris-Lacewell, a professor of politics and African American studies at Princeton, is optimistic. The NAACP "could become the authentic supportive and yet challenging voice to the Obama administration," she says.

This is the role Jealous envisions. "It would be disrespectful not to criticize [Obama]," he says. "If we don't let the brother know when he's not living up to people's expectations, he's only going to be there four years."

Whether Jealous can restore the NAACP to its former glory and help the organization hold its own in the crowd of special interests jockeying for the president's attention is an open question. While Obama may be uniquely sympathetic to the NAACP's agenda, his popularity among black folks and ephemeral personal connections to the organization might limit their influence. Jealous needs to do more than remind young people that the NAACP is fighting for them; he needs to convince them that the NAACP has their interests in mind even when the president doesn't.

On the day before Obama's inauguration, Jealous spoke to a small gathering of reporters at an NAACP reception in Washington. When asked what Obama's rise meant for the NAACP, Jealous simply said, "History has proven the fallacy of the Moses archetype for black leadership."

One person, even the president, is no substitute for a movement.

Family Matters

Henry Louis Gates, Jr.

My father's father, Edward St. Lawrence Gates—known to his children and his grandchildren as Pop—had two hobbies. He was renowned for one of them in and around his hometown of Cumberland, Maryland: he grew tulips, "like a Dutchman," people said. He looked like a Dutchman, too—"light and bright and damned near white," as my father used to say. I learned about my grandfather's second hobby only after his death, in 1960, when he was eighty-one and I was nine.

Pop Gates was buried at the Rose Hill Cemetery, where our forebears were among the very few Negroes allowed to disturb the eternal sleep of Cumberland's élite white Episcopal citizenry. The town's Episcopal churches had been segregated at least since the black St. Philips offered its first Communion, on June 19, 1910. That day, the church's records show, Pop, his mother, Maud, his wife, Gertrude Helen Redman, and about half a dozen other Gateses took the Sacrament, which was offered by the Diocese of Maryland's white bishop.

I was struck by how different Rose Hill was from Thorn Rose, the all-colored cemetery in Keyser, West Virginia, where my mother's relatives had been buried. The effect was one of unkempt, chaotic modesty, each plot separately maintained by the family of the deceased. The dead at

Rose Hill, by contrast, looked almost prosperous, their graves immaculate, some even regnant, crowned with ornate granite memorials. Rose Hill had a full-time groundskeeper and a stone-clad gatehouse, where records of the dead were kept. It was locked at night, unlike Thorn Rose, where just about everyone went to make out. At Thorn Rose, records of the dead seemed to exist only in the collective memory of the families whose ancestors were buried there.

My brother and I had been made keenly aware, early in our childhood, that the Gateses had a certain status in Cumberland. No one ever explained whether this was because they had owned property for a very long time in what is still a mostly white neighborhood, or because of light-skin privilege, or some combination of both. Being a Gates was somehow special, and not just within the black community in Cumberland.

After Pop's burial, my father took us back to the Gates family home, at 505 Greene Street, a two-family house that my great-grandfather had bought in 1882. My brother and I followed my father up stairs that I had never climbed. As we walked in single file behind my dad, I noticed that the walls of the living room and staircase of my grandparents' house were lined with framed sets of blue, red, and yellow ribbons, which Pop had won for his tulips. My grandparents' bedroom was a cabinet of wonders, its walls decorated with only blue ribbons, along with photographs of family members I would never meet. My dad led my brother and me past the bedroom and onto a sun porch adjoining it. On the right was a trunk that was brimming with toys; it reminded me of something I'd recently seen in a Disney movie. My father turned left, though. Opening a closet door, he pulled out dozens of musty leather books: partially used bank ledgers. (Pop had once been a janitor at the First National Bank on Baltimore Street.) The books were about an inch thick, with big blue- and red-lined pages. A few had been tied with string where the red leather binding had lost its strength. Slowly and silently, he turned glue-stiffened pages that were covered, front and back, with newspaper clippings. So— Pop Gates had kept scrapbooks! That was his second hobby.

The clippings covered various news stories and human-interest items. There were hundreds of them, seemingly random, sharing only a macabre tenor: headlines about injuries and death, especially murders and fatal accidents; articles about war casualties, robberies, automobile accidents, and even plane crashes. Nestled among them were obituaries, funeral notices, funeral programs, and those laminated bookmarks noting the passing of the dead, complete with a bit of religious verse, a passage from the Bible, birth and death dates, and sometimes a photograph of the deceased. Those scrapbooks were like an archive, decade by decade, of Cumberland's colored dead, although plenty of dead white people poked their pale visages out of those pages as well, fighting for air among all those Negroes.

After a while, it occurred to me that the white and the colored denizens of the obituary notices were dressed alike, their sartorial equality reflecting the shared aesthetic of an Olan Mills photography parlor: three-piece suits and white starched collars, hair slicked down or pressed. I felt as if those scrapbooks were a portal into a world I did not know. I began to wonder: Who were these people?

"Look here, boy," Daddy said, startling me as he broke the silence. There, deep in those yellowing pages of newsprint, were two obituaries. One, dated Saturday, January 7, 1888, was from the Cumberland *Evening Times*. The headline read DEATH OF "AUNT JANE GATES":

> *Last night at 11 o'clock "Aunt Jane Gates," colored, a family servant of the Stover's died in the 75th year of her age. She has lived for a long time on Green Street where her death occurred. Her remains will be interred at Rose Hill Cemetery tomorrow afternoon at 3 o'clock. Services will be held at her residence on Green Street.*

I especially remember another article that called her "an estimable colored woman." Daddy then retrieved a framed photograph of this woman, who had lived just up the street from where we sat, and was buried steps away from Pop Gates's newly dug grave. "That woman was Pop's grandmother," Daddy said. "She is your great-great-grandmother. And she is the oldest Gates."

I stared at the picture until I had that face memorized, an image of the oldest colored woman I'd ever seen, etched indelibly into my nine-year-old head. In 1979, my great-aunt Pansy made a present to me of the original, which now hangs in my kitchen. What was most striking about the woman in the photograph, apart from the white nurse's hat and uniform she wore, was that she didn't look like a Gates. She was much darker than her grandson. I would have guessed that she was about my color, although the sepia patina that the photograph has acquired over a century and a quarter makes it hard to tell. But she had a long, straight nose, light eyes, high cheekbones, and an austere countenance. Her hair, poking out from under her nurse's bonnet, appeared to be a curly wave. She didn't look especially feminine; in fact, she could have been a man in drag, as my father pointed out years later with irreverent glee.

Finally, Daddy shut the album and slowly stood up. By the time we made our way downstairs, the house was teeming with family. Enough food to start a restaurant had been crowded onto the oak dining table. I headed for the fried chicken and the potato salad, hungry all of a sudden, not sure what had taken place upstairs. When I got home, I looked up the word "estimable."

※

My career as a historian began that afternoon in 1960. Soon after the funeral, I became obsessed with my family tree. I peppered my mother and father with questions about the names of their ancestors, their birthplaces and birthdays, their occupations, the places and dates of their deaths. My father was the storyteller of the family, and most of my conversations about our ancestors ended up being with him.

And, besides, I was far more concerned with my Gates lineage than I was with my mother's ancestors, as I was convinced that if any distinction was to be found on my family tree it would be through the Gates branches, given the family members' skin color and the texture of their hair, and the fact that they had owned so much property for so long, including a two-hundred-acre farm, where my father was born, in 1913, at Patterson Creek, just across the West Virginia border. On more than one occasion, my father tried to tell me that my mother's family was more distinguished than his, but I thought that he was being modest. He never seemed to tire of these interrogations, even when I repeated questions that I had asked a year or two earlier. I dutifully began to write it all down, in a brown spiral notebook.

Sometimes I would grow bored and put the notebook away; then, after a few days or weeks had passed, I would be seized with a desire to learn more. Once, I took my notebook for a presentation before my fifth-grade class but found myself embarrassed that I was unable to explain, when asked, how my ancestors had come to be slaves, or where in Africa they had come from. The girl who asked was, like most of my classmates, white. As far as I knew, the only way to explore a black family's history was through family stories.

Eventually, as glossy magazines began to advertise that they could send you your family's "coat of arms," I longed to possess the knowledge that would allow me to claim one of these. What I really wanted, as much as the family tree detailing the identity of my African American ancestors, was a family crest that would tie us to our white ancestors. History had allowed them to hide, to avoid responsibility for their progeny. Perhaps that crest could lead to a new set of ancestors and cousins whose identities had been reduced to whispers, gossip, and wishful thinking—the speculation, sometimes playful and sometimes maddened, that fuelled so many discussions among my father and his siblings.

When we studied American Colonial history in fourth grade, we learned that the first black slaves arrived on the James River in 1619, two hundred years before Jane Gates was born. Were there black people who could trace their families that far back? I couldn't bring myself to order the family tree of some other Gates line, though I did relish the idea that we were related, somehow, to Horatio Gates, the Revolutionary War general whom we had studied at school.

✳

I was searching not just for the names of my ancestors to fill out my family tree but also for stories about them. Each new name that I was able to find and print in my notebook was another link to the colored past that had produced, by fits and starts, but also, inevitably, the person I had become and was becoming. On my mother's side, J. R. Clifford, my great-uncle, was, I learned, the first black man to be admitted to the bar in the state of West Virginia. Far more thrilling to me was the fact that, during the Civil War, he had served in the U.S. Colored Troops. He had also published his own newspaper, the *Pioneer Press*, in Martinsburg, West Virginia. Later, I learned that, in 1905, he had cofounded the Niagara Movement—the forerunner of the NAACP—with W. E. B. Du Bois. On my father's side, three generations of Jane Gates's descendants had graduated from Howard University, starting with my great-aunt Pansy, in 1910, and including two generations of dentists. My father's first cousin had graduated from Harvard Law School in 1949; there he had met his wife, who, in 1955, was the first black woman to earn a Ph.D. in comparative literature at Harvard. Kind of hard to top that, my father would argue, but J. R. Clifford knew Du Bois, and Du Bois was the ultimate trump card, black history's ace of spades.

With just a little effort, most African Americans can trace at least one line of their family back to the 1870 federal census, which was the first taken after the Civil War and is therefore the first in which all our ancestors appear as citizens with two names, rather than as property. In the 1850 and 1860 censuses, there is a list of "Slave Inhabitants" held by each owner, recorded by age, gender, and color (black or mulatto) but not by name. Since many freedmen took their surnames from their masters, one part of the pre-1870 puzzle can sometimes be solved through a simple comparison: once you have found your ancestor in the 1870 census, you can examine the "Slave Inhabitants" list from the 1850 and 1860 censuses to see if a white person with the same surname and in the same geographical area owned a slave; then see whether a slave ten or twenty years younger than your ancestor is identified on those lists. Estate papers and property records can also be used to cobble together a history of slave ancestors. The 1870 census, which relied on the same door-to-door information gathering used when I was a boy, lists all the members of a particular household, by their full names, birth places, ages, and occupations.

Census data, despite their simplicity, can be surprisingly revealing. The entry for Jane Gates, for example, says the following, if I summarize the relevant columns: "Jane Gates, age fifty-one, female, mulatto, laundress and nurse, owns real estate valued at $1,400, born in Maryland, cannot read or write." A mulatto? An illiterate mulatto at that? Nothing in the oral lore of the Gates family had prepared me for either of these facts. Who was Jane's father? And who was the father of her children? With her in the house are her daughter Alice, age twenty-two; her son, Edward, age twelve; and two grandchildren (Jennie, age five, and David, age nine, both children of her daughter Laura). Edward and David are in school and can read and write. Alice can read but not write; she also works as a laundress and nurse.

As a child, I had been told with absolute certainty that the Gateses were descended from an Irishman named Samuel Brady, who supposedly owned Jane, fathered her children, and gave her the money to purchase her home. Jane's son (and Pop's father), Edward, my great-grandfather, who was born into slavery in 1857, on Brady's farm, would, when questioned by his children, respond only that he and his siblings all shared the same father. It was his children—my grandfather's generation—who were the source of the Brady rumor. Had Jane given her son some clue that this was so? Did Edward the elder whisper it to Pop in a moment of speculation or confessional intimacy? Whatever the source of the rumor, it had become canon law by the time I was born.

The more I learned about Brady and the Gateses, the more likely it seemed that he had known Jane and, indeed, slept with her, as family lore held. Edward Gates was born—I learned from his obituary, of 1945— "on the Brady Farm near Cresaptown." According to extensive research by Jane Ailes, a genealogist (and Brady's third-great-granddaughter), Samuel Brady had a farm just outside Cresaptown, exactly as family legend had it. And between 1828 and 1865 Samuel Brady owned slaves, starting with one, and reaching a high point of forty-two, in 1850, according to the federal census. Brady was a study in contradictions: three of his sons fought for the Confederacy, and one of them spent eighteen months in a Union prison; nevertheless, a year before the war ended, Brady signed deeds of manumission for four of his slaves so that they could enlist in the 30th Regiment of the U.S. Colored Troops and fight for the North.

Emboldened by these findings, I set out to prove or disprove the family story about the supposed father of Jane's children. In the past decade, developments in DNA testing and the retrieval and digitization of archival records have made it possible for black families to begin to trace their ancestry further back through American history and, ultimately, even across the Atlantic. In 2005, I placed an advertisement in the Cumberland *Times* and posted a message on a Brady-family online forum asking for male descendants of Samuel Brady to identify themselves, hoping that one of them would submit a DNA sample for a belated paternity test.

One of Brady's direct male descendants and a direct male descendant of Brady's brother William agreed to take a DNA test. The tests established, without a doubt, that Samuel Brady was not the father of Jane Gates's children. When I told my father and his sister, Helen, what the tests had revealed, Aunt Helen summed up the reaction of just about all the Gates family members: "I've been a Brady eighty-nine years, and I am still a Brady, no matter what that test says."

I found myself pleased by Aunt Helen's defiance, as irrational as it might seem; I guess I had always thought of myself as a Brady, too. Being told that we weren't Bradys was a bit like being orphaned. For my cousin John Gates, there will always be two stories about our ancestry: the story that our genes tell, and the story that our ancestors told. And he wants both to be in play for his three sons and his grandchildren. The challenge of genealogy used to be the reconciliation of a family's oral memories with public written records, and in the search for one's ancestors nothing is as pleasing as having these two streams of testimony confirm each other. But genetics can now demolish or affirm a family's most cherished beliefs and stories with just a bit of saliva and a cotton swab.

What about the father of Jane's children, then? Well, given that all males with my Y-DNA marker (it's known as the Ui Neill haplotype) bear one of a few dozen surnames, a team of genealogists and I have begun to compile a list of all the men with those names in the 1850 and 1860 censuses for Allegany County, Maryland. We are advertising for their male descendants, and asking them to take a DNA test. With a little patience, and a lot of luck, perhaps DNA can solve the last remaining mystery in the Gates family line, the secret that Jane Gates took with her to her grave.

African American history is a young discipline; restoring the branches of even one black-family tree can profoundly change our understanding of the larger story of who the African American people really are. By telling and retelling the stories of our ancestors, we can move that history from our kitchens and parlors into the textbooks, ultimately changing the official narrative of American history itself.

My family tree hangs in my kitchen, just across from the photograph of Jane Gates. But the graphic record of the entangled blood lines, impressive and gratifying though it is, does not fulfill my boyhood longing for a coat of arms. Of the scores of names neatly arrayed in those boxes, only one is that of a white ancestor, even though a "genetic admixture" test reveals me to be fifty percent "European." Until the family crest of the Irishman who fathered Jane Gates's children graces my family tree, along with his name and the names of his ancestors, my family story will remain a tale only half told.

Then again, I'm still amazed by the ancestral additions I've already gained. The genealogists, in the process of researching my family tree, found three sets of my fourth-great-grandparents, all free Negroes, including, on my mother's side, John Redman, who enlisted in the Continental Army, at Winchester, Virginia, in 1778, and served until 1782, seeing combat near Savannah, Georgia. So we had a patriot ancestor after all, even if his name wasn't Horatio and even if he wasn't a Gates. When I discovered that my mother had descended from seven lines of Negroes who had been freed by the 1830s—three of them by 1776—I felt chagrined that I hadn't spent more time interviewing her. She had an enigmatic reserve when it came to her family's past, an attitude that was in stark contrast to my father's fondness for vivid narratives. "We come from people," she liked to say.

✳

I had long assumed that Pop Gates's scrapbooks had been discarded, perhaps after a spring cleaning, by someone who wasn't aware of their value or by someone who didn't wish to revisit the past. As part of the celebration of my father's ninety-fifth birthday, last summer, I decided to scan the photographs owned by the far-flung Gates family members, so that we could collect them in a book and present it to him. Amid my aunt Helen's possessions, my cousin Bette found a red-and-black bank ledger, full of old news clippings and stamped with the logo of Cumberland's First National Bank. My grandfather was such a shadowy figure in my life that I can't even remember the sound of his voice. But the discovery of this scrapbook, covering the years 1943–46, allowed me to take a stroll through his mind.

I am tempted to call the scrapbook Pop Gates's Book of the Dead, just as I might have been when I was nine. Its interpretation of this grim theme is even more all-encompassing than I had remembered, though. The book is full of statistics about war casualties but also contains intimate stories about the individual dead. And tallies of Cumberland's wartime losses are mixed in with articles cataloguing the massacre of thousands of Jews and Serbs and reports about the starving population of India.

On April 5, 1943, an article reports that the governor of Alabama "Calls for Full Racial Segregation": "The two races are distinct. They occupy spheres in life that began in different origins, have continued in diverging channels and should remain separate, as they have always been since the creation. No influences from outside should or can change these fundamental safety principles." But the war was bringing hope for race relations, and Pop recorded that, too. While, early in the scrapbook, an A.P. article applauds "the first all-Negro division activated by the United States Army" because "at the outbreak of war, the American Negro clamored for an active part in the nation's war effort," a feature near the book's end, datelined Paris, March 20, 1945, announces, "Negroes and Whites . . . Go Into Battle Side by Side for First Times in U.S. Army History." The pages of Pop's chronicle celebrate the appointment of Francis

Ellis Rivers as a City Court judge in New York, as well as the first nine months of service of Hugh Mulzac, the "First Negro Captain of an American Ship."

Pop compiled these clippings about the wartime heroics of black servicemen while working as a janitor at the First National Bank. At sixty-three, he was too old to serve but was required to register. Pop's draft-registration card from 1942 contains the fullest description of him that has ever come to my attention: his height is five feet eight inches, his eyes are hazel, his weight is a hundred and sixty-two pounds, his hair is gray, and his complexion is "ruddy." (The choices for complexion were "sallow," "light," "ruddy," "dark," "freckled," "light brown," "dark brown," and "black.") Under the column for "Race," the "White" box had initially been checked; evidently, the registrar had taken him for a white man. In decisive black ink, the check mark was crossed out. The registrant must have demurred. (By contrast, Pop's brother Roscoe chose to take advantage of a similar error that year and pass for white.) Identity wasn't merely a matter of skin color; it was a matter of history. Pop knew himself to be an estimable colored man. A new check mark appeared beside "Negro."

The Purrrfect Diva:
Eartha Kitt Had a Taste
for the Best Things in Life

Wil Haygood

In her fantastical life, Eartha Kitt came to like a great many things. Men, sex, bawdy songs. I personally know about the lemon sorbet, the mango sorbet and the strawberry sorbet.

I found myself dining with Kitt—who died of cancer at the age of eighty-one yesterday—at the swanky Café Carlyle in Manhattan several years ago. I was working on a book about Sammy Davis, Jr., once a romantic interest of Kitt's. Kitt's office suggested the Carlyle. Being on book leave, without a steady income and counting pennies, I gulped: The Carlyle wasn't the place for a penny-pincher. But I needed the interview, so I dared not back out of the chance to talk with her. Kitt had known Davis when both were very young and both were hanging out at the Fairmont Hotel in San Francisco.

Arriving early on the day of our meeting, I was led to a table. There was fine sunlight, lovely wood and an attentive waiter. I looked at the prices on the menu and wanted to scram. Kitt was late—first ten minutes, then twenty. She may have been born poor, but she traveled through life with the blood of a true diva. So, of course, she'd be late. But I fretted she might have forgotten, or changed her mind. Then I noticed heads swiveling toward the entrance—and there stood Eartha Kitt, wearing a short, bone-white fur coat, white slacks and a canary yellow turban atop her head. She had a white poodle cupped in each arm. I gave a wave, and she strode over, the poodles twisting in her arms.

"Let's order!" she demanded. She said she didn't care to remove her sunglasses because it was still early in the day. It was around one-thirty in the afternoon.

A waiter came over and took the poodles away, delivering them to Kitt's suite upstairs. She had a gig going at the Carlyle, and most of the shows were sold out.

The next ninety minutes were unforgettable. There were stories of men she had conquered (Sammy Davis, Jr., among them), foreign lands she had traveled to, songs she had sung. I remember what she ordered because I held on to the receipt for years to show to people: salmon, asparagus, white wine, two glasses, which turned into three glasses. I wanted to cry every time I saw her motioning for the waiter: "Water, please, and bottled." But every other minute brought forth some delicious revelation, a tale of a child born in South Carolina to sharecropper parents and who forced the entertainment world to take notice of her.

Consider the era she thrived in—and the competition she faced. Kitt came of age when a bevy of sepia beauties were just starting to strut their stuff from Broadway to Hollywood. It was the 1950s, and Madison Avenue may have ignored these women, but they were seen now and then in the pages of *Life* and *Holiday* magazines.

Lena Horne, Dorothy Dandridge, Hazel Scott, Joe Lewis's wife, Marva, Sugar Ray Robinson's wife, Edna Mae, and Kitt were different from the darkly hued and heavy-set black women of 1940s Hollywood, women like Hattie McDaniel, Ethel Waters, Butterfly McQueen and Louise Beavers. Those women were known mostly for playing maid roles in cinema.

This new group of beauties changed the way that America looked at the black woman. They went to parties hosted by Joe Louis in Chicago or Manhattan; they hung out at Sugar Ray's nightclub in Harlem, their images reflected in the long mirror behind the bar. They all came to admire themselves in some of those old Negro periodicals—*Sepia, Ebony* and *Brown*. Their pictures hung in hair salons in black communities throughout America. They competed against one another for movie roles: Kitt got *Anna Lucasta* alongside Davis, among other roles. And she had to sweat her way through the *Anna* auditions.

"The camera couldn't conceal the fact that Eartha was not a beautiful woman," Philip Yordan, the writer of *Anna*, told me.

But no one, absolutely no one, could have told Eartha Kitt she was not beautiful. She refused to be in the shadow of Horne or Dandridge. Kitt had a repertoire that ranged from nightclubs to Broadway to dramatic roles in movies and TV.

Maybe it was because she was born poor, and maybe that birthright either scars you or propels you into other dimensions, but Kitt fought harder than Horne, Dandridge and Scott for recognition. She took risks, kept an edge about her, singing sexually suggestive songs and parading her body onstage in a way that some thought was too provocative. Her rendition of "Santa Baby," for instance, could be described as For Adults Only. She wore her political beliefs out in the open, too, and was on Richard Nixon's enemies list. She was ashamed of Davis when he supported Nixon and told him so to his face.

I wrote furiously during our interview. I laughed—loud—when Kitt told me she had flipped Davis over her shoulder one day when he came to see her after one of her stage shows. Davis grimaced, but "I was just fooling around!" she said.

Lunch finished, I tensed as I got ready to ask for the bill. But Kitt wanted dessert. She tried a scoop of the mango sorbet. She loved it, so much so that she now wanted a scoop of the lemon sorbet. I wanted to cry. Sorbet at the Carlyle is not cheap.

She did not detect from my body movements that I was quite ready to go. "Let me try that strawberry sorbet, please," she said in that famously Kitt-enish voice. I smiled as my shoulders sagged.

But there were more stories! About her and Orson Welles, her and Sidney Poitier, her and Sammy when he tried to take back the engagement ring he had given her. There was more laughter.

Then the bill came: $138.06.

It remains, to this day, the most expensive lunch I have ever paid for. But it was Eartha Kitt, in white fur, with poodles. It was worth every penny.

Miriam Makeba:
In Troubled Times, She Was
the Voice of a Country

Wil Haygood

It was a time of ghosts in South Africa. Men and women who were heroes in the anti-apartheid movement were banned. No pictures anywhere of Nelson Mandela, Hugh Masekela, Miriam Makeba. You could be jailed for the offense. Children had to imagine them from stories told by their parents.

But you could hear the ghosts, especially Masekela and Makeba, one-time husband and wife—powerful, jazzy, trilling, syncopated music—if you got to some out-of-the-way shebeen, which was what they call the little watering holes in Soweto, or into some brave soul's home. There was something sweet and dangerous about listening to banned music. It was an act of rebellion.

Miriam Makeba, who died last Sunday in Italy of a heart attack while performing onstage, seemed to be everywhere she wasn't supposed to be when I landed in South Africa in 1990. You could hear her in a park, some family with a cassette player lying atop a blanket, her voice rising and falling and rising. You could hear her just beyond the kick of a soccer ball at a neighborhood field. (The volume was never too high out in public. Those big yellow tanks with South African soldiers could roar into view out of nowhere.) You could always hear her at funerals, someone's boombox set on the back of a pickup truck. Miriam over there, and over there, and right there. It was as if she were hiding in the trees.

The lady famous for "Pata Pata," "Kilimanjaro," "The Click Song" and so many others performed around the world, with Paul Simon, Nina Simone and Harry Belafonte, who helped introduce her to American audiences.

But you never heard her voice in South Africa's office buildings or police stations. Her music wasn't piped into the sound system in stores. Family members kept their Makeba in shoe boxes, in tin tubs in the backyard, anyplace save out in the open.

Alf Kumalo, a great Johannesburg photographer, and Jovial Rantao, a local reporter, gave me some of her tapes shortly after my arrival. "You must listen to Makeba, man," Rantao said. The tape that stood out was an underground compilation of music she had performed with the Skylarks and the Manhattan Brothers. That was before her passport had been revoked in 1960 while she was out of the country. She'd been palling around with human rights activists in America and Europe, and the South African government didn't appreciate it.

Even if some of the selections on the tapes were in Xhosa and Zulu and beyond me, it sounded lyrical, a tender blending of gospel and jazz. Kumalo and Rantao warned me that I must take the tape out of the car's cassette player whenever approaching a military police roadblock. I was fast on the yank. Then, pulling away, there was Miriam, filling the car again.

On my first visit to a Soweto shebeen, I skipped the homemade brew, but the fried potatoes were quite tasty. It was dark outside, as if the dark had doubled over on itself. Everyone worried about soldiers, but I relaxed knowing Rantao had my back. Then came Makeba's lovely voice. There were other voices, too, but you listened for Makeba. She was the voice of a country, achieving a one-name appellation like de Klerk or Mandela. That's a big chunk of the country's identity right there—the Afrikaans president who made the important overtures to Mandela; the freedom fighter imprisoned twenty-seven years; and the lady who was the international voice for the townships.

She'd found her way but lost her homeland. Blood spilled in South Africa—Sharpeville, Soweto—and they sang her music in the jail cells.

Isaac Hayes: Unshackled by History's Chains

Wil Haygood

Somehow, the little country boy grew up to rattle chains.

Isaac Hayes made music, of course, and plenty of it—soulful and gritty ballads and that disco-heaving soundtrack *Shaft*—but there was nothing like those chains. They adorned his chest onstage like thick jewels. He wouldn't run from history.

Hayes was a black man born in the South in 1942. And that, of course, is a birth and time period that gives a black man some extra challenges: He has to pick up things along the way; he has to look beyond the cotton fields and the Memphis docks and all the hauling of furniture that so many of his high school friends had to do.

Hayes, who died yesterday at sixty-five, rolled himself out as a musical personification of black manhood. If the sixties shook the nation up—musically and politically—the seventies represented a deeper digging in. There were more black fashion models on Madison Avenue. There were more black actors on television. Black was beautiful and cool and defiant.

Music was everywhere and seemingly everything—at least to the young minds trooping in and out of the record stores, watching *American*

Bandstand and *Soul Train,* listening to black radio in those convertible Mustangs.

If the north—Detroit—had Motown, the South—Memphis—had Stax Records, where a whole bevy of songwriters and artists, Otis Redding, David Porter, Isaac Hayes, were cats in the summer heat making their music. They'd write on sketch pads; they'd wolf down fried fish sandwiches between sessions; they'd roll over to the Lorraine Motel to see who was in town; they'd chat about women and love and heartache. And they'd watch that poor child, Isaac, now a man, hone his own image.

Elvis had white satin.

Isaac had those chains.

His *Black Moses* album, released in 1971, got alarming stares from plenty of folks—especially whites—but blacks considered it an instant revelation. It was, in one flourish, a kind of iconic art: a muscular black man in flowing robe. The religious merged with the political, all coming alive against a backdrop of thumping music. "People were probably saying to themselves, 'Here is Memphis, the buckle on the Bible Belt, and Isaac Hayes is coming out onstage dressed as black Moses,' " Jim Spake, a Memphis-based sax player who played with Hayes over the years, recalled yesterday. "If you notice, that album opened out [with flaps] kind of like a crucifix. That was seen as pretty heavy for those times. And that was the mystique about him, wearing those chains."

And when he cut the movie soundtrack for *Shaft,* the Gordon Parks–directed movie that starred Richard Roundtree and garnered Hayes his Oscar, it seemed as if he had crashed through the strange and Byzantine gates of Hollywood and its racial history. It seemed as if John Shaft was Cagney and Bogart all rolled out from behind a sepia-tinged curtain. The soundtrack had such a propulsive and aggressive beat that it seemed like something ripped from both the urban and rural parts of the Earth—domains that Isaac Hayes certainly came to know throughout his life.

Michael Toles, a guitarist and Memphis musician, first met Hayes in the 1960s and would later play concerts with him. He remembers the evolution of the chains. "The first few shows I did with him, he didn't wear the chains," Toles says.

Many of the musicians who knew Hayes were aware of how the assassination of Martin Luther King, Jr., on the balcony at the Lorraine Motel in 1968 affected him. Toles goes on: "But then he started wearing them and I think it represented to him the coming freedom of the black man."

Hayes insisted on traveling with a large number of musicians. Bobby Manuel, also a guitarist, began traveling with Hayes in 1969. "His music represented an identity of what it meant to be black," he says. "It was exciting, in a kind of strength. Of course it all coincided with the civil rights movement. And for a musician, his was a different image, coming out there onstage with no shirt and those chains. Man, it was a whole other world."

Manuel was aghast at the crowds that swooped around Hayes when he left the stage. "I remember we had been on the road and he came offstage and people were howling and grabbing for him. And one of the musicians said, 'Man, you are the black Moses. People will follow you anywhere.' It was really radical."

A whole generation came to know Hayes through his more recent role as the deep-voiced cartoon character on *South Park* and for his continued coast-to-coast live musical appearances. But to his musician friends in and around Tennessee, he remained the soulful cat from the 1960s who was always trying to help them get gigs and always looking forward to his next show.

Sometimes, Manuel says, he and Hayes would go fishing on the Mississippi. Matter of fact, they had a fishing outing scheduled for next week. "He used to hum all of his tunes first," Manuel says. "So everything you hear on his albums, he had hummed to himself first."

And so, he was a musician who liked to fish, who wore chains, who was aware of the politics around him, and who also gave off a menacing image that those who knew him say was quite ironic. "He was such a sweet guy," says Manuel. "And I don't know if people quite realized what he really did."

Pig Candy

Lise Funderburg

I knew my father's father, Frederick Douglas Funderburg, in the last two decades of his life. He was already seventy when I was born, a distinguished but shrinking man. Pictures indicate that in his prime he was robust, arguably obese, but in my time his button-down shirts hung loosely from his frame, tucked into perma-press double-knit pants held up by suspenders he referred to as "galluses."

When I knew him he ate a banana every morning and checked his blood pressure each day with a kit left over from his days as a practicing physician. When he came to visit, or, later, when I visited him, he turned his entire attention toward me, undistracted by other cares or obligations. He taught me how to play cards: pinochle, casino, and gin. He was patient when I forgot a rule or flubbed an attempt to bridge while I shuffled, but he could not give away a great hand. As he threw down his victorious last card, he'd offer a sympathetic shake of the head and drawl, "Sad and touching. Sad and touching." In the time it took him to pick up the winning trick, he'd paraphrase a poem by Frank Lebby Stanton, the southern homilist:

This old world we're a-livin' in
Is mighty hard to beat;
With every rose you get a thorn
But ain't the roses sweet?

Once in a while, pretending sympathy, Granddaddy employed the expression that I thought for a long time had originated in my family, a locution that conveyed disappointment or bore witness to tragedy or simply asked, *Can you beat that?*, its accent laid heavily onto the first syllable, the next two descending in equal measure, like steps down a staircase:

"Mm-mm-mm."

He lived to be ninety-seven. In the 1980s, five of his last birthday dinners were held at my father's house in Philadelphia, where Grandfather cooked or supervised the cooking of one of his specialties, roast leg of lamb. The keys to the dish's success were slivers of garlic slipped into deep cuts made across the surface of the meat, Campbell's cream of mushroom soup stirred into the drippings to render a gravy, and plenty of mashed potatoes.

Lois, back then a zealous family archivist, conscientiously attempted to make recordings of my grandfather, using a low-fidelity cassette recorder from an office supply store. The "on" button was pushed and left alone until tapes ran out, so there was as much of the business of eating—at one point, my father turned the pepper grinder twenty-five consecutive times—as there was of my grandfather's life story.

There was also a lot of my father. Although no one seemed to dispute his position as host, master of ceremonies, and general shot caller, he reasserted it constantly. He cut off Granddaddy's reminiscences: "Hey, Dad, we went over that. . . . That was not the story I was trying to prompt. . . . I think we've imposed upon you enough."

He challenged his father on points ranging from what year something happened to how to pronounce *irrefutable:*

"Think so, Dad? . . . Are you sure about that, Dad? . . . You want to defend that position you're taking?" At times, he was cloyingly solicitous. "Say something for posterity, Granddad . . . Tell me, what do you think young folk ought to do today?"

And he regularly interrupted whoever was speaking, no matter what the topic, to offer more food. "Is there anyone else that I can cut just a sliver of lamb for? Just a sliver? It's mighty, mighty good."

Despite his tendency to challenge in the name of accuracy, my father did not tolerate correction well. At one point, he was describing how Granddaddy's patients paid him during the Great Depression. "There used to be four and five wagons lined up in our driveway on Saturday," Dad said. "Two chickens. A bushel of corn."

"Not a bushel," Granddaddy said. "*Bushels* of corn."

"Well, whatever. Your fees weren't that high, so what the hell are you talking about?"

In the last recording, taped just months before Grandfather died, my father's slurring suggests more wine than usual. Grandfather was delighting the married couple who had come for dinner, the center of their attention for a time. Perhaps too much time. My father said to the woman, "My father has a photographic memory, and he bores you with it sometimes, reciting chapter and verse. My father can recite to you every door number, every birthday, everything that went on in the city of Monticello since nineteen hundred and twenty-two."

The guest seemed impressed. "Write it down," she encouraged my father. "Do you get him to write?"

"I don't get him to do a damn thing," my father said, " 'cause it bores the hell out of me. I don't want to hear it."

Despite the limited technology of these recordings, not to mention the obliterating clatter of plates and cross-talk and my father, I can still piece together twenty years later the texture of my grandfather's life and the world into which my father was born—so fittingly a breech baby, a newly minted nonconformist determined to hit the ground running.

✳

Grandfather was born in Anniston, Alabama, in 1889, thirty-three years after the United States abolished slavery. Anniston was a town of ten thousand, hugged up along the Alabama–Georgia border. Grandfather was the first of four boys. His father, George Washington Funderburg, was a foreman at Anniston's soil pipe foundry and a bootlegger on the side. His mother, Ophelia Blassingame Funderburg, was a homemaker known for her nonstop cooking ("That's what killed her," one of her in-laws once told me, "too much cooking.") and a forceful personality attributed, both disparagingly and admiringly, to her being half Creek.

As a child, Grandfather attended school sporadically. When he finished the equivalent of seventh grade, he went to teach in a one-room country school, then tried working in Alabama's coal mines. But he didn't want to end up like the undereducated, struggling blacks who dominated his community in Anniston's Furnace Hill section, where the shotgun shacks lacked even the basic southern amenity of a front porch. "The intellectual and cultural and social environment did not magnetize me in any sense of the word," he declared in one birthday dinner recording. "I left. I did not want any more life in Anniston or the coal mine. I moved to Atlanta. I went there a stranger."

It was 1906 when he made the ninety-one-mile trip. He was seventeen years old and nearly penniless, asking a cab driver to suggest a place where he might stay.

His first job was as a bellhop. He detested it. "I hated for the man in charge of the front office to tell me I had to clean the cuspidor. Damn it, I just didn't like it. I resented it like hell." When an acquaintance opened the Silver Moon Barber Shop and offered to teach Granddaddy how to barber, he didn't hesitate to make the move.

"That was 1911, and I worked there 'twelve, 'thirteen, and 'fourteen. The happiest years of my life I lived in Atlanta. There was a bridge club in the vacant room upstairs over the barber shop. There was a poolroom on the corner. I could go when business got dull to the matinees in the afternoon. When the grand opera came, I got employment up at the auditorium in the hat check concession so that I could hear [Enrico] Caruso, Frieda Hempel, *Lucretia Borgia,* and [Antonio] Scotti."

The Silver Moon was on Auburn Avenue, which guaranteed a passerby clientele of professional black men. Around the time my grandfather came to the city, one-third of Atlanta's 155,000 inhabitants were African American, and Auburn served as their professional and commercial center. Several institutions on the street anchored black Atlanta's life: Big Bethel A.M.E. Church, the Odd Fellows building and auditorium, and Ebenezer Baptist Church, in which both Martin Luther Kings, father and son, preached. The entire street smacked of firsts: the first black-owned office building, the office of Atlanta's first black optometrist, the first black-owned drugstore, and the first black life insurance company. "Sweet Auburn," as it was known, was the "richest Negro street in the world," according to the civic leader John Wesley Dobbs, who lived in Atlanta from 1897 until his death in 1961.

The social structure in black Atlanta was said to be like a pie with no filling: there was an upper crust and a bottom, but no middle class. As a barber, my grandfather befriended railway workers, postal clerks, and doctors. He partnered in bridge games with a West Indian statistician who worked for the life insurance company, shot pool with Auburn Avenue habitués, went to house parties with college graduates, and played tennis with young men and women of whom much was expected. Even though he presided over the Silver Moon's prestigious first chair, Grandfather grew dissatisfied with his prospects amid the strops and razors, the witch hazel and bay rum.

"In the spring of nineteen hundred and fourteen," Granddaddy said on his ninety-second birthday as the rest of us ate lamb and potatoes smothered in gravy, and pressure-cooked green beans seasoned with cubes of fatback, "a friend came into the shop. He was bell captain at the Alabama Hotel. He had gotten married, saved enough money to make a down payment on a house, and moved his bride into it."

The news pushed my grandfather into a funk. When, he wondered, would he ever be able to do the same on the wages of a barber? He ruminated for days on end.

"I sat down and assessed my assets. I never had a hundred dollars above my needs. I lived and moved in the upper echelon, but I saw no potential there to acquire what I would need to have in order to live and interact on that plateau of society. I decided, finally, that I would strive for the attainment of my first love. Whatever the cost, I would tie up the broken threads of my aspiration and do what I saw a black man doing in my home when I was a child: practice medicine. Barbering was not my realm. I was going back to school and whatever the price, I was going to pay it to become a doctor."

A fine plan, but Granddaddy hadn't finished high school. A doctor friend helped him solve the problem: they manufactured a résumé that included a high school degree. His deceit, told to me not by Grandfather himself but by my father after Granddaddy's death, won him admission to a two-year premedical program at Raleigh, North Carolina's Shaw University, the oldest black college in the South. He paid his way through, barbering over the holidays and working for the railroad in the summers. He graduated and applied to Columbia University's College of Physicians and Surgeons in New York. Again he was accepted. Eleven years after leaving Alabama, he joined Columbia's incoming class of 1917, the first to admit women and in which he was most likely the only African American, a point of information he may have hidden from the school.

He managed Columbia's coursework through the fall term but ran into trouble with chemistry in the spring. He worried that he would fail the course and be expelled, so he weighed his other options. World War I was still on. Grandfather knew that there were advantages to joining up rather than being drafted: as a volunteer, he could specify in which branch he'd serve. He headed for a recruitment office on Manhattan's lower Broadway. The U.S. military was and would remain segregated for another three decades. Pay scales were set accordingly, so it mattered that the recruitment officer never asked my fair-skinned grandfather his race. The recruiter did say, at one point, referring to the wiry texture of my grandfather's hair, "I've never seen a white man with black hair." My grandfather said nothing. Later on in the interview, the recruiter repeated his comment. Again, Grandfather said nothing.

Granddaddy shipped out as part of an all-white medical corps stationed in rural France. He saw no battlefields, and the armistice was signed shortly after his arrival, so his enduring memories were of Gallic cooking and gardening techniques.

When he mustered out, he transferred to a black medical school, Meharry Medical College in Nashville, Tennessee. He also proposed to Ethel Maude Westmoreland, a woman six years his junior. They met while Fred, working at the Silver Moon, was renting a room in the house of Ethel's sister Mamie. Ethel, the tenth of eleven children from a top-crust Atlanta family, had lost her mother at the age of twelve. She was raised by another beloved sister, Eva, and watched over by siblings in between. Ethel continued to live with Eva while waiting for Fred to finish his studies, even after the couple married.

In June of 1922, my grandfather's fate, and thus my father's, and thus mine, was cast. Four years before my father's birth, my grandfather stood on a corner of Auburn Avenue, having just stepped off a train from Nashville. With a diploma he'd received at the end of May, he was freshly graduated from Meharry with, as he would point out even seventy years later, the second-highest average in his class.

He was thirty-two years old and ready to begin a residency that would equip him to carry out the school's mission, which was to care for underserved minority populations. His career stood ready to take off, and his personal life held equal promise. Ethel had given birth to their first child, Frederick Jr., on the thirteenth of March. My grandfather couldn't attend the birth. He pawned his gold watch to pay the obstetrician's fifteen-dollar delivery fee, and the last of his funds were reserved for paying off school accounts, a prerequisite for receiving one's diploma.

He had planned this June stopover between graduation and another summer of railroading, but the visit could not last long. Like many pre-professional African Americans of the time, my grandfather earned relatively good wages as a Pullman porter, carrying luggage, cleaning shoes, and making beds for well-to-do white passengers on their way to summer retreats in the Adirondack Mountains. He performed the tasks well enough to make ends meet during medical school, and in fact well enough to curry the favor of one passenger, a Mrs. Chase of the Manhattan banking family, who gave him a small subsidy for school expenses. School was now over, his professional life was about to commence, but the income from railroading was too certain to ignore.

My grandfather started across Auburn Avenue, but a landau blocked his path. The horse-drawn carriage held four doctors, men my grandfather knew, some whose hair he'd cut. The men exchanged amenities with the young graduate, then invited him to climb up into the carriage.

"Get in and go with us!" one doctor entreated. "We're going out to the cemetery to bury Turner." The deceased was a black doctor who had practiced in a rural town sixty-five miles south of Atlanta.

Grandfather had heard of Turner: the nation's entire pool of black doctors consisted of fewer than thirty-five hundred people. But Granddaddy knew him only by reputation, that Turner was from an island in the Caribbean and had graduated from McGill University Medical School in Canada. Because Grandfather was going to meet his wife and new baby, he declined the carriage-borne doctor's invitation. Some days later, Grandfather again stood on Auburn Avenue. This time, he ran into his old bridge partner, the statistician.

"Funderburg," the man asked, "what are you gonna do this summer?"

"I'm going to New York and railroad, to work for the Pullman Company as I've done in past years. Then I've got an internship coming up in October," Granddaddy told his friend, "on the basis of the second-highest average in my class."

"Awww," the bridge partner said, "your days for railroading are over. What you ought to do is to go down to Jasper County and break into the practice of medicine. You've taken the board already. Break into the practice of medicine and acquire Turner's library and office equipment.

"I'm co-executor, with his wife, of his estate," continued the partner, who, like Turner, was West Indian. "I'm going down this weekend, and I'll make arrangements for you to stay with her." And so my grandfather went.

✳

Monticello, in the center of Jasper County, was a bustling farm town of 1,900 people, even though the county itself ranked as the state's poorest and most rural. On the ride down, my grandfather would have passed lush fields of spring wheat, acres of cotton planted by farmers who still hoped for profit despite the boll weevil's recent devastations, and orchard after orchard of peach trees, leafed out and verdant. The land was neither mountainous, like the Appalachian and Blue Ridge sections of north Georgia, nor flat, like the gulf and coastal plains further south and east. Instead, it was fertile, rolling piedmont, and it boasted several waterways. The Ocmulgee River, to the west, served as the area's major trade route until railroads came along. Murder Creek ran to the east, and the 4,700-acre Jackson Lake, created by a dam built in 1910, anchored the northwest corner of the county.

Monticello formed around the intersection of several highways. Routes 16 and 212 ran east-west, and Routes 11 and 83 were roughly north-south, creating a spider with the town square as its belly. A hotel, drugstores, groceries, banks, and the large department store, Benton Supply Company, framed the square. In the center stood a statue paying tribute to the Confederate fallen. Numerous memorials had been erected since the Civil War, but this particular style, a spiking obelisk topped by a lone soldier, had close likenesses in town squares across the South. All were erected around 1910 and funded by their local branch of the United Daughters of the Confederacy. The impetus was most likely no particular anniversary of a battle or invasion but rather the desire to pay homage while one or two of those being honored might still be alive to receive it.

Turner's widow had a house on Colored Folks Hill, at the top of Warren Street. The neighborhood was next to a well-to-do white section, physically separated by the rail line that angled into town from the city of Macon, forty miles away. Upon his arrival, my grandfather had to assess not only what the Turner estate had to offer, but also what kind of life Monticello would provide. He walked the town's streets, introducing himself first to the white leadership.

"I went to see the lawyer, the leading physician, and then the sheriff," he remembered. The lawyer was pleasant enough and the town's gregarious white physician, Francis Belcher, urged Grandfather to fill Turner's shoes.

"Funderburg," Belcher said, "your people need you. I hope you come."

Grandfather finally got to the sheriff, Will Persons, a man who was at that point only halfway through thirty-three years of holding his position. Grandfather spoke first.

"Sheriff," he said, "my name is Funderburg. I'm down here looking over Turner's field with the idea of coming to practice medicine."

Sheriff Persons wore a broad-brimmed black Stetson on his head and a six-shooter in his holster. Over six feet tall, he towered above my grandfather, who was only five feet eight inches. Persons responded to my grandfather's introduction by launching into a story of his various political contests.

"I ran for sheriff two terms and won," he told my grandfather. "The third term I lost. The fourth term I won. And the morning after the election, I met Turner on the street, and Turner said to me, 'Sir, I wanna congratulate you on your victory,' and shook his own hand. He was a good nigger. He knew his place."

※

When he took leave of Persons, Grandfather wandered off the square and into the black neighborhoods.

"I went among the black people, and they were most importunate. I can see the old lady rocking on her front porch . . ."

At this point in the tape, he switches into an unschooled country dialect, a way of speaking he resolutely avoided in the twenty-eight years I knew him, except for when he recited the sly vernacular poems of Paul Laurence Dunbar. Otherwise, Granddaddy veered in the opposite direction, toward a painstaking and baroque articulation. He was the king of the dependent clause, and he never, according to all available records, dangled a preposition.

"I jes' don' know whud I'm gon' do fuh a doctah," the woman said to him.

My grandfather took over Turner's practice. It was to be temporary, a way to get his feet on the ground. Then he'd move Ethel and baby Fred up to West Virginia, where a fellow doctor promised there was money to be made by the baleful, where Granddaddy could be worth a hundred thousand dollars in just ten years, for him a fortune almost beyond imagining. But that's not how it turned out. As he built his practice and responded to the call of the destitute, trampled population around him, Monticello became home. And the family grew. Ilon Owen and Mary

Hannah Howe Chase were born in the first two years. Two years after that, in the spring of 1926, my father arrived. The last child, Charles Edward, came along in 1930.

My grandfather held the curious position of heading up black Monticello's leading family. For many years he was the only black resident with either a college or postgraduate degree. He held one of the only jobs besides undertaking with a guaranteed income stream. Actually, since patients were often too poor to pay at the time of service, or in cash, or ever, it would be more accurate to say he had a guaranteed clientele. Still, the Funderburg house was two and three times the size of most neighbors' shotgun shacks. My father and his siblings never went hungry, and throughout my father's childhood my grandparents hired a neighbor named Annie Chapman to assist with the washing and cooking and cleaning that filled each day.

But the family's affluence was relative. In the separate-but-equal world of Jim Crow, the leading black family was still a black family. My grandfather received some privileged treatment. He was light-skinned and educated; he paid his bills and bank notes early rather than on time; and he made a point of conducting himself in a manner beyond reproach. As he said on one birthday, "I practiced medicine for fifty years in a rural community and boasted of the fact that no one had ever smelled liquor on my breath, and no one had had a drink of liquor with me. I had a bar in my house. Self-discipline."

His self-discipline would have meant little if a conflict were to arise or a spiteful accusation made. He was still the "nigger doctor" and therefore without recourse. As a consequence, he strove to protect his family from exposure. He forbade his wife to enter white-owned stores for fear of what could happen. It was bad enough that the youngest stock clerk would call her Ethel, not Mrs. Funderburg, but if she were insulted or threatened, Grandfather would have had to retaliate. If that happened, the family would have to leave town. Immediately.

He had to negotiate his own safety as well. In one incident, as he backed his sedan out of an angled parking space on the square, a white woman rear-ended him. She was in the midst of apologizing when a white policeman came along.

"Not so fast," the policeman said, and he began to recraft the incident with the fault falling to my grandfather. While my aunt Chase watched from the front seat, her father stood silent as the policeman carried on, insulting and threatening, finally permitting him to leave. He drove home humiliated, only to be greeted by a ringing telephone. It was a different white man, the manager of a store on the square who had seen the interchange. The manager had talked the policeman into backing off the threatened charges, and now worked to mollify Grandfather so that he wouldn't pack up the family and leave.

Whites had a vested interest in having a black doctor around to keep their labor pool healthy, and some benefited directly from his expertise. For many years, Granddaddy's only white patients were men who came knocking on the kitchen door, late at night, seeking treatment for venereal diseases. But when a flu epidemic hit the region in 1938 and temporarily put the white doctor out of commission, white citizens had no choice but to come to Dr. Funderburg for help. He built a reputation as a skilled diagnostician, and not all the white patients wanted to leave him after the flu crisis subsided.

Fitting an integrated patient roster into a segregated world was no small challenge. He devised a strategy that he first tried out in the town of Eatonton, which was thought to be somewhat less racist. When it worked, he brought it to his Monticello office, the former Odd Fellows' lodge he'd bought a block south of the square. In the front portion of the small building, its footprint no more than forty feet square, he made a rectangular waiting room, each half a mirror image of the other. Same art, same chairs, same flowers in the same vases. Mrs. Freeman, the office manager who kept the room spotlessly clean, made sure each day that even the ashtrays were positioned correspondingly. Grandfather put up no signs designating which race should sit on which side. He didn't have to. When patients came through the door, they segregated themselves. The left half would be white one day and black the next.

Grandfather took an active civic role, which included serving on the school board for decades, in both its segregated and integrated versions. Early on, he and his cohorts attracted well-trained teachers from Atlanta by reducing living costs. An empty building on Warren Street was converted into a dormitory, furnished with beds and cooking utensils, and offered free to the new hires, all young women. Beyond such efforts, Granddaddy also lent his reputation. In a town where blacks were expected to clear the sidewalk whenever a white person approached, where a black man had been shot for waiting outside a store for his wife longer than the proprietor appreciated, and where a black woman was slapped in the face for not calling the butcher "Sir," the simple act of buying provisions could be perilous as many of his postprandial stories showed.

None of the girls had any money when they came down to start teaching school. I would take them to Benton's Supply and ask the manager to open an account for them and make myself responsible for the paying. Well, bringing in five schoolteachers was giving them some business.

Benton's had a country boy clerking in dry goods. One new teacher went in and she bought this and that and the clerk said to her, "Anything else?"

She said, "No." And then she reflected a moment, "Oh, yes. I want some kerosene."

"Have you got the can?"

"No. I haven't."

He said to her, "I'm a white man. Don't you say yes and no to me. You say 'Yessuh.'"

Well, he frightened the girl. She came to the house and told my wife. My wife told me. I didn't want a community affair over it. I didn't want anybody taking revenge on her or on me. I finally evolved an approach. The man that ran the store was a very fair-minded Christian man. On a certain day, as he stepped up on the sidewalk out of the intersection, I stepped up on the sidewalk. Spoke to him. I said, "Mr. Malone, I have come to believe that hate is a destructive force. Destructive not only of the person towards whom it is directed, but also for the person who feels it." Now, that was the introduction. I said, "Your young man in the grocery department hates black people."

He looked at me superciliously. I recited the incident. He said, "Well, now, I'm surprised, Doctor. What happened to him over the counter is nothing more than what happens to me back at the office. I'll handle that."

Ten days later, I went in the store and he said, "Doctor, I looked on the books to see if that boy was selling those girls as much merchandise as he'd been selling them in the past, and I've sat here in the office and watched him when your teachers came in to see if he tried to avoid them. And I haven't seen any change in him."

Well, I wasn't quite satisfied with that. The girls got their paychecks. I went to them and said, "I want you to pay your bill, ask for receipts, ask that it be marked paid in full, and then when you get your bill, ask the clerk to close your account." All hell broke loose then.

That was, say, Thursday. Saturday I was in the store. The manager of the dry goods department was there. He stopped selling merchandise, came over to me, and said, "Doctor, I've been here X number of years and I've never lost any business." He said, "This boy was wrong. 'Yes' and 'no' is the English language. If you'll help me get that business back, I'll wait on your teachers myself."

What went around, came around. When Will Persons, the unwelcoming sheriff, grew too old to run for office, the alcohol control board threw a patronage job his way, a position with the office that tracked down moonshiners. Persons was breaking up a still one day and stepped on a tenpenny nail. "The irony of fate came into play," my grandfather exulted. "He had to come to me for treatment."

Because my grandfather never left, practicing medicine in Monticello for fifty years "to the day," as he would say, the place incorporated itself into his blood and the personal histories of his children and the two generations that have followed. Years after Granddaddy retired, after old age and frailty took him away—reluctantly, by then, because his memories lived there, the path and pace of life worn and familiar—he still marveled at how he had ended up with that town as his geography, how he had struggled to fulfill dreams and feed his family when the patients he treated earned no more than a dollar a day.

"When I found that I had let down roots," he said on his ninety-second birthday, "I often wondered what I had done to displease Almighty God to cause him to locate me in this godforsaken place."

Race Talk

Talking About Not Talking About Race

Patricia J. Williams

On a short flight to New York recently, I was sitting behind two white, well-dressed twentysomethings chattering loudly and uninhibitedly about going to clubs and travel plans and the possibility of living in New Jersey. Then came the question: "So who are you voting for?"

"I was for Hillary, but now . . . I'm kind of undecided," volunteered the first woman.

"Are you a Democrat?" asked the second.

"Yeah. But I think I might go with McCain. It's just that, well, I don't know. You know." Her voice dropped. I leaned forward to hear better. "You kind of hate to say it aloud, but . . ." Here her voice dropped again, to a murmur lost in the roar of the jet engines, and I missed whatever came next.

Let's start with this concession: I have no idea what that young woman actually said. In a perfect world, I suppose that would be the end of the story and I would go back to minding my own business. In the context of contemporary political discourse, however, it did cross my mind that if this conversation were presented on one of those "finish the sentence" cultural-literacy tests, then pretty much every American, of whatever creed, color, or class, would have exactly the same guess as to how the woman completed her thought.

I think there's some consensus, in other words, about the one thing in America we really "hate to say" aloud. Yet by refraining from saying audibly that-which-must-not-be-spoken, was the young woman's political choice rendered rational, neutral, pure? Conversely, if I were to spell it out here, would I be the one accused of "playing the race card"?

This is a complicated monkey wrench in our supposedly post-race society. On the one hand, everyone knows that race matters to a greater or lesser degree; on the other, few of us want to admit it. Indeed, race is the one topic that's probably even more taboo in polite company than sex. Yet in the absence of fact or frank conversation, grown people get buried in the kind of whispered fear, fantasy, and ignorant mistake that a five-year-old makes when explaining how icky it was when Daddy got Mommy pregnant using the garden hose and a large bowl of avocados. Is this misinformation really so different from when Fox News and Karl Rove fill in the blanks of those awkward silences with images of the perpetually pantyless Paris Hilton rocking the foundations of our civilization on the same stage as Barack *Hussein* Osama, oops, I mean Obama. This is racial pornography that exploits the barely suppressed caverns of imagined horrors that have haunted us since D.W. Griffith's *The Birth of a Nation*.

Obama predicted this phenomenon and attempted to expose it to the anodyne of common sense: "They're going to try to make you afraid of me. 'He's young and inexperienced and he's got a funny name. And did I mention he's black?' " The not-altogether-surprising backlash from McCain's campaign is a deflection, an expression of deep discomfort. The reflexive accusation that Obama was playing the race card has a certain resemblance to the juvenile retort one gets when the science teacher tries to explain the human reproductive system: "Ooooh! He said a dirty word!" In this way, the opportunity for thoughtful public analysis sinks, once again, below the sound of the audible. Yet the fear of race rolls on, pantomimed in palpably influential and consequential ways.

At the same time, the civil-rights movement has given us a moral conscience that was not as prevalent when *The Birth of a Nation* was made. Today, it's fair to say that the overwhelming majority of white Americans "hate to say it aloud" because they also hate to think of themselves as racists. But blacks and whites tend to differ in their very definition of racism. Some years ago, researchers conducting a study for the Diversity Project, at UC Berkeley's Institute for the Study of Social Change, asked black and white college students about their perceptions of racism on a given campus. White students tended to say there was none, but blacks and Native Americans said it was everywhere. In fact, the study documented an interesting phenomenon: As Diversity Project sociologist Troy Duster put it, "White students see diversity as a potential source of 'individual enhancement,' " while African American students were more likely to see the goal as "institutional change."

When the white students were asked to give illustrations that substantiated their positions, they spoke of their own experiences and of personal intentions. "Last night, I had dinner with a black friend," they might offer. Or, "I have a black roommate, and we get along"; "I play basketball with a couple of black guys"; "I've never used a racist epithet"; "I treat everyone the same."

On Black History Month

Eric Holder

Every year, in February, we attempt to recognize and to appreciate black history. It is a worthwhile endeavor, for the contributions of African Americans to this great nation are numerous and significant. Even as we fight a war against terrorism, deal with the reality of electing an African American as our president for the first time and deal with the other significant issues of the day, the need to confront our racial past, and our racial present, and to understand the history of African people in this country, endures. One cannot truly understand America without understanding the historical experience of black people in this nation. Simply put, to get to the heart of this country one must examine its racial soul.

Though this nation has proudly thought of itself as an ethnic melting pot, in things racial we have always been and continue to be, in too many ways, essentially a nation of cowards. Though race-related issues continue to occupy a significant portion of our political discussion, and though there remain many unresolved racial issues in this nation, we, average Americans, simply do not talk enough with each other about race. It is an issue we have never been at ease with, and given our nation's history, this is in some ways understandable. And yet, if we are to make progress in this area, we must feel comfortable enough with one another, and tolerant enough of each other, to have frank conversations about the racial matters that continue to divide us. But we must do more—and we in this room bear a special responsibility. Through its work and through its example this Department of Justice, as long as I am here, must—and will—lead the nation to the "new birth of freedom" so long ago promised by our greatest president. This is our duty and our solemn obligation.

We commemorated five years ago the fiftieth anniversary of the landmark *Brown v. Board of Education* decision. And though the world in which we now live is fundamentally different than that which existed then, this nation has still not come to grips with its racial past nor has it been willing to contemplate, in a truly meaningful way, the diverse future it is fated to have. To our detriment, this is typical of the way in which this nation deals with issues of race. And so I would suggest that we use February of every year to not only commemorate black history but also to foster a period of dialogue among the races. This is admittedly an artificial device to generate discussion that should come more naturally, but our history is such that we must find ways to force ourselves to confront that which we have become expert at avoiding.

As a nation we have done a pretty good job in melding the races in the workplace. We work with one another, lunch together and, when the event is at the workplace during work hours or shortly thereafter, we socialize with one another fairly well, irrespective of race. And yet even this interaction operates within certain limitations. We know, by "American instinct" and by learned behavior, that certain subjects are off limits and that to explore them risks, at best, embarrassment and, at worst, the questioning of one's character. And outside the workplace the situation is even more bleak in that there is almost no significant interaction between us. On Saturdays and Sundays America in the year 2009 does not, in some ways, differ significantly from the country that existed some fifty years ago. This is truly sad. Given all that we as a nation went through during the civil rights struggle, it is hard for me to accept that the result of those efforts was to create an America that is more prosperous, more positively race conscious and yet is voluntarily socially segregated.

As a nation we should use Black History Month as a means to deal with this continuing problem. By creating what will admittedly be, at first, artificial opportunities to engage one another, we can hasten the day when the dream of individual, character-based acceptance can actually be realized. To respect one another we must have a basic understanding of one another. And so we should use events such as this to not only learn more about the facts of black history but also to learn more about each other. This will be, at first, a process that is both awkward and painful but the rewards are potentially great. The alternative is to allow to continue the polite, restrained mixing that now passes as meaningful interaction but that accomplishes little. Imagine if you will situations where people—regardless of their skin color—could confront racial issues freely and without fear. The potential of this country, which is becoming increasingly diverse, would be greatly enhanced. I fear, however, that we are taking steps that, rather than advancing us as a nation, are actually dividing us even further. We still speak too much of "them" and not "us." There can, for instance, be very legitimate debate about the question of affirmative action. This debate can, and should, be nuanced, principled and spirited. But the conversation that we now engage in as a nation on this and other racial subjects is too often simplistic and left to those on the extremes who are not hesitant to use these issues to advance nothing more than their own, narrow self-interest. Our history has demonstrated that the vast majority of Americans are uncomfortable with, and would like to not have to deal with, racial matters, and that is why those, black or white, elected or self-appointed, who promise relief in easy, quick solutions, no matter how divisive, are embraced. We are then free to retreat to our race-protected cocoons, where much is comfortable and where progress is not really made. If we allow this attitude to persist in the face of the most significant demographic changes that this nation has ever confronted—and remember, there will be no majority race in America in about fifty years—the coming diversity that could be such a powerful, positive force will, instead, become a reason for stagnation and polarization. We cannot allow this to happen and one way to prevent such an unwelcome outcome is to engage one another more routinely—and to do so now.

As I indicated before, the artificial device that is Black History Month is a perfect vehicle for the beginnings of such a dialogue. And so I urge all of you to use the opportunity of this month to talk with your friends and co-workers on the other side of the divide about racial matters. In this way we can hasten the day when we truly become one America.

It is also clear that if we are to better understand one another, the study of black history is essential because the history of black America and the history of this nation are inextricably tied to each other. It is for this reason that the study of black history is important to everyone—black or white. For example, the history of the United States in the nineteenth century revolves around a resolution of the question of how America was going to deal with its black inhabitants. The great debates of that era and the war that was ultimately fought are all centered around the issue of, initially, slavery and then the reconstruction of the vanquished region. A dominant domestic issue throughout the twentieth century was, again, America's treatment of its black citizens. The civil rights movement of the 1950s and 1960s changed America in truly fundamental ways. Americans of all colors were forced to examine basic beliefs and long-held views. Even so, most people who are not conversant with history still do not really comprehend the way in which that movement transformed America. In racial terms the country that existed before the civil rights struggle is almost unrecognizable to us today. Separate public facilities, separate entrances, poll taxes, legal discrimination, forced labor, in essence an American apartheid, all were part of an America that the movement destroyed. To attend her state's taxpayer-supported college in 1963 my late sister-in-law had to be escorted to class by United States Marshals and past the state's governor, George Wallace. That frightening reality seems almost unthinkable to us now. The civil rights movement made America, if not perfect, better.

In addition, the other major social movements of the latter half of the twentieth century—feminism, the nation's treatment of other minority groups, even the anti-war effort—were all tied in some way to the spirit that was set free by the quest for African American equality. Those other movements may have occurred in the absence of the civil rights struggle, but the fight for black equality came first and helped to shape the way in which other groups of people came to think of themselves and to raise their desire for equal treatment. Further, many of the tactics that were used by these other groups were developed in the civil rights movement.

And today the link between the black experience and this country is still evident. While the problems that continue to afflict the black community may be more severe, they are an indication of where the rest of the nation may be if corrective measures are not taken. Our inner cities are still too conversant with crime, but the level of fear generated by that crime, now found in once quiet, and now electronically padlocked, suburbs, is alarming and further demonstrates that our past, present and future are linked. It is not safe for this nation to assume that the unaddressed social problems in the poorest parts of our country can be isolated and will not ultimately affect the larger society.

Black history is extremely important because it is American history. Given this, it is in some ways sad that there is a need for a Black History

Month. Though we are all enlarged by our study and knowledge of the roles played by blacks in American history, and though there is a crying need for all of us to know and acknowledge the contributions of black America, a Black History Month is a testament to the problem that has afflicted blacks throughout our stay in this country. Black history is given a separate, and clearly not equal, treatment by our society in general and by our educational institutions in particular. As a former American history major I am struck by the fact that such a major part of our national story has been divorced from the whole. In law, culture, science, athletics, industry and other fields, knowledge of the roles played by blacks is critical to an understanding of the American experiment. For too long we have been too willing to segregate the study of black history. There is clearly a need at present for a device that focuses the attention of the country on the study of the history of its black citizens. But we must endeavor to integrate black history into our culture and into our curriculums in ways in which it has never occurred before so that the study of black history, and a recognition of the contributions of black Americans, become commonplace. Until that time, Black History Month must remain an important, vital concept. But we have to recognize that until black history is included in the standard curriculum in our schools and becomes a regular part of all our lives, it will be viewed as a novelty, relatively unimportant and not as weighty as so-called real American history.

I, like many in my generation, have been fortunate in my life and have had a great number of wonderful opportunities. Some may consider me to be a part of black history. But we do a great disservice to the concept of black history recognition if we fail to understand that any success that I have had cannot be viewed in isolation. I stood, and stand, on the shoulders of many other black Americans. Admittedly, the identities of some of these people, through the passage of time, have become lost to us—the men, and women, who labored long in fields, who were later legally and systemically discriminated against, who were lynched by the hundreds in the century just past and those others who have been too long denied the fruits of our great American culture. The names of too many of these people, these heroes and heroines, are lost to us. But the names of others of these people should strike a resonant chord in the historical ear of all in our nation: Frederick Douglass, W. E. B. Du Bois, Walter White, Langston Hughes, Marcus Garvey, Martin Luther King, Malcolm X, Joe Louis, Jackie Robinson, Charles Drew, Paul Robeson, Ralph Ellison, James Baldwin, Toni Morrison, Vivian Malone, Rosa Parks, Marian Anderson, Emmet Till. These are just some of the people who should be generally recognized and are just some of the people to whom all of us, black and white, owe such a debt of gratitude. It is on their broad shoulders that I stand as I hope that others will some day stand on my more narrow ones.

Black history is a subject worthy of study by all our nation's people. Blacks have played a unique, productive role in the development of America. Perhaps the greatest strength of the United States is the diversity of its people, and to truly understand this country one must have knowledge of its constituent parts. But an unstudied, not discussed and ultimately misunderstood diversity can become a divisive force. An appreciation of the unique black past, acquired through the study of black history, will help lead to understanding and true compassion in the present, where it is still so sorely needed, and to a future where all of our people are truly valued.

Thank you.

On Race, Blacks Are Cowards, Too

Bill Maxwell

U.S. Attorney General Eric Holder is catching flak for saying during Black History Month that on matters of race, the United States is "essentially a nation of cowards" in too many ways. Holder, the first black to head the Justice Department, is absolutely right.

Based on responses to his remarks, most people assume that the "cowards" Holder refers to are white Americans. Most blacks are cheering the attorney general for his forthrightness, and many whites, especially conservatives, are angry and resentful. Still others are just plain surprised by the audacity of the observation after millions of white people voted to elect the nation's first black president.

I do not have a problem with what Holder said. I do have a problem, however, with what is not being publicly talked about in this controversy: On matters of race, blacks are cowards, too. We may be the worst cowards of all. First, we have perfected the crude art of controlling the terms of race talk. Second, we have developed various ways of avoiding and squashing the truth about our complicity in matters of race that are self-destructive.

I cannot count the times I have participated in or attended events on race that devolved into acrimony and shouting because blacks attacked whites who said "insensitive things," often meaning that the whites expressed their true feelings and thoughts about blacks.

Seeing themselves as victims of racism, most blacks reject raw race talk from whites. After all, whites are viewed as being the perpetrators of racism. The perpetrator, therefore, should confess, shut up and listen. Because of this dynamic, far too many whites have learned to avoid direct matters of race.

Holder recognizes this problem. During his now-infamous speech, he said: "If we're going to ever make progress, we're going to have to have the guts, we have to have the determination, to be honest with each other. It also means we have to be able to accept criticism where that is justified."

Although black attacks against whites are harsh, our attacks against other blacks who tell the truth are downright vicious. I know from personal experience. You are tar-brushed with the stain of Uncle Tomism, and it sticks to you forever.

You are ostracized and given the silent treatment. Your mistake is not that you told the truth but that you told the truth in public, thereby giving the enemy valuable ammunition. (Here, think of comedian Bill Cosby, who is castigated for saying that too many low-income blacks have not held up their end of the nation's civil rights gains.) In short, you committed the unforgivable sin of "airing dirty laundry."

Your achievements and good deeds are never recognized. You simply do not exist, unless you put yourself in people's faces to have your say.

On matters of race, most blacks run away from introspection, and we do not like to hear others publicly remind us of our responsibilities to ourselves. One problem we should openly talk about, but run from, is the high number of black children born out of wedlock. Depending on whose numbers we use, between seventy percent and eighty percent of black children are born to single mothers.

Some black neighborhoods do not have any two-parent families. I know dozens of black kids who do not know who their biological fathers are, and most of their friends are in the same fix. We need to remind ourselves, which we rarely do, that having a child is a choice we make.

Out-of-wedlock births may not be a problem unto themselves, but evidence shows that this factor alone can initiate a chain of self-destruction. The overwhelming majority of black children growing up without fathers are poor, and the chances of large numbers of them escaping poverty are remote. Studies show that they are less likely to perform well in school, making them a major part of the achievement gap, suspensions and expulsions—flashpoints for whites with hostility toward blacks. Graduation among these students is low, and few of them attend college, factors that eventually lead to high unemployment and underemployment.

We also run away from discussing crime, especially horrific cases of black-on-black crime that capture headlines and lead nightly news reports. We try to rationalize the high numbers of blacks in prison by blaming everyone except ourselves. Many whites, especially racists, use these phenomena to bash us. We leave ourselves open as targets for such attacks by refusing to confront crime honestly and openly.

To mention the deleterious effects of hip-hop is to be attacked. The ugly truth is that this outlaw culture, with its anti-intellectualism, antiauthoritarianism and nihilism, will do more harm than virtually anything else to a generation of blacks. Fearing attack, too many blacks remain silent on this issue, and when whites bring it up, they are shouted down as racists.

Holder should make a second speech on race, this time specifically taking blacks to task for keeping silent on the abandonment of their personal responsibilities.

What Is the Race Card?

Richard Thompson Ford

In 1903 the black sociologist W. E. B. Du Bois opined that "the problem of the twentieth century is the color line." In the twenty-first century, will the problem be that everyone talks a good line about color?

Playing the race card is not new. Tom Wolfe called it "mau-mauing" back in 1970. Ever since the civil rights movement convinced the majority of Americans that racial prejudice is petty and contemptible, people have complained of racism loud and long, for good reasons and, sometimes, for bad ones. But when Wolfe coined the term, mau-mauing was the exclusive tactic of underprivileged minorities: people with legitimate complaints of discrimination, if occasionally excessive modes of expressing those complaints. Today the rhetoric of racism is a national patois, spoken fluently by ghetto hustlers and Wall Street stockbrokers, civil rights agitators and Republican Party hacks, criminal defense attorneys and Supreme Court nominees. Lawyers and judges and parishioners and priests have mastered the sleight of hand required to play the race card.

Superstar entertainers complain of racism when negotiating, renewing, or breaching their multimillion-dollar contracts; liberal and conservative politicians alike play subtle race politics to win elections or secure the confirmation of nominees: wealth and privilege are no impediments to deploying the race card. Nor, for that matter, is race. Upper-class WASPs complain of "reverse racism"—a melodramatic description of integrationist policies that no one believes are motivated by racial animus or bigotry. And if race isn't directly involved, you can always insist that whatever's eating you is like racism. Opponents of same-sex marriage aren't just narrow-minded religious zealots; they're the moral equivalent of the KKK. A rule that requires obese passengers to buy the number of seats they occupy—which in crowded coach class may be *two*—isn't a way to ensure that other customers get their share of scarce elbow room; it's like making Rosa Parks stand in the back of the bus. A dress code against tattoos, body piercings, funky haircuts, or cutoff shorts isn't just uptight; it's a new Jim Crow. Smoking bans consign nicotine addicts to "ghettos" or "concentration camps." Gripes are as common as face cards in a pinochle deck. The race card may turn yours into a winning hand.

Playing the race card is wrong and troubling for several reasons. Most obviously, it's dishonest. When people transgress or just screw up, they should take their lumps—not try to wriggle out of them with tactics of distraction or blame shifting. When people face disappointments, they should forbear graciously, not try to wheedle a more favorable outcome through false accusation. Playing the race card is also dangerous and shortsighted. Like the boy who cried wolf, people who too frequently cry racism are unlikely to be taken seriously when a predator actually emerges from the woods. Playing the race card places all claims of racism—valid and phony—under a cloud of suspicion. Finally, playing the race card is mean-spirited. Racism is a serious charge—it ruins careers and destroys reputations. When warranted, it should. But when trumped up, the charge of racism is a particularly vicious slander.

But the race card is not a simple matter of opportunism and deception. It is a by-product of deep ideological conflict in our society over how to describe and deal with questions of social justice. When bigotry was openly tolerated, people often announced it or did nothing to conceal it. Therefore, many of the earliest struggles for civil rights aimed at some conspicuous targets: Jim Crow laws, blatantly discriminatory practices, out-and-out race-based exclusion. But today most people try to hide their prejudices. As a result, a lot of time and energy must be spent just trying to determine whether bigotry is in play or not. Everyone involved—accuser and accused alike—has an incentive to lie and dissemble, to downplay or to exaggerate. And as overt prejudice has receded, we've developed new theories of prejudice designed to tease out hidden or repressed motivations and to identify inadvertent forms of wrongful discrimination.

This has given rise to a great deal of conflict over how to define bigotry and how to decide whether it's at work. Some of this conflict is necessary and healthy. We should refine and revisit our understanding of wrongful discrimination as part of an ongoing struggle for social justice. And we should debate and argue over civil rights, which reflect some of our society's most profound moral commitments. If no one ever pressed novel or controversial civil rights claims, we could never expand our conception of justice.

But there are also costs to more ambitious applications of civil rights. The extraordinary social and legal condemnation of racism and other social prejudices encourages people to recast what are basically run-of-the-mill social conflicts as cases of bigotry. Overuse and abuse of the claim of bias is bad for society and bad for social justice. When a conflict really does involve hatred or deep-seated irrational prejudice, dialogue is pointless and condemnation is appropriate. But the emotionally charged accusation of bigotry is counterproductive when a conflict involves questions on which reasonable people can differ. Playing the race card makes it too easy to dismiss rather than address the legitimate concerns of others. And the accusation of bigotry inevitably provokes defensiveness and resentment rather than thoughtful reaction. The resulting interactions usually don't qualify as speech, much less dialogue. They're generally closer to mud wrestling. No one gets away clean.

When does a grievance deserve the special and unequivocal condemnation reserved for racism? Despite more than a century of litigation under the Constitution and federal civil rights laws, we still don't have a straightforward answer to that question. In fact, in some ways the answer is getting more convoluted and confusing, and the resulting conflicts more numerous and frustrating.

Some people are convinced that most accusations of bias are disingenuous. There are plenty of pundits, politicians, and bloggers ready to dismiss any accusation of bias as calculating and self-serving. One Internet blog posted this parody: "Is the society not giving you what you think it owes you? Then it's time to get yourself the Race Card . . . It's like a 'Get Out of Jail Free' card, but much, much more. Losing an argument in a debate? Throw down your Race Card and quickly hush your opponent . . ." Clever, but this perspective suffers from a toxic cynicism and a blissed-out naïveté all at once. On the one hand, it implies that racism is not a real social problem, that less than a generation after federal troops were required to integrate schools and court orders were needed to integrate lunch counters, there's no racial bias left. Anyone who suggests otherwise is playing the race card. On the other hand, it presumes that racial minorities are so devious as to consistently make claims they know to be false, and that many people are credulous enough to believe them, despite the fact that racism has long since gone the way of wooden shoes.

At the same time, many people—and not only the credulous and the opportunistic—believe such accusations as Clarence Thomas's shrill complaint of a high-tech lynching and Brawley/Sharpton's apparently staged and obviously managed racial assault, and they rally to the causes of some unlikely victims. Many blacks rallied to Thomas after his notorious exclamation, and the conflict between those who wanted to support a beleaguered victim of racism and those opposed to Thomas on ideological grounds split major black organizations. Law professor Patricia Williams, one of academia's more nuanced and astute commentators on issues of race and gender, struggled to find in Tawana Brawley's story evidence of her victimization rather than her duplicity: "Even if she did it to herself . . . Her condition was . . . the expression of some crime against her, some tremendous violence, some great violation that challenges comprehension."

Indeed, some people object to the idea that anyone might ever "play the race card." For instance, Professor Michael Eric Dyson argues, "There's no such thing as a race card being played by black people not already dealing with the race deck that white America has put on the table." This is true enough as far as it goes. Playing the race card is an effective tactic because accusations of racism are plausible, and they're plausible because there are in fact a lot of instances of racism. But don't some people take advantage of this real social evil for unearned advantage? And don't people, even with good intentions, occasionally misapprehend their plight, complaining of prejudice when other factors are to blame? What accounts for such disagreements? Why do some reasonable people see evidence of racism where others see only the smirking one-eyed jack of the race card?

Creature Features:
A Two-Part Invention on
Racial Profiling

By Gerald Early

Randall Kennedy had wanted to include an essay I wrote for the Chronicle of Higher Education about race and Obama that was published in the early fall of 2008. I nixed that idea because I did not want readers of the Best African American Essays series to think I was using the books for self-promotion. Debra Dickerson had included an essay of mine in the 2009 volume and that was more than enough for me. Then, the dust-up between Harvard professor Henry Louis Gates and a Cambridge police officer became national news for nearly a week in the month of July 2009 and something about it had to appear in the book. I chose to write about it because a somewhat similar incident had happened to me many years earlier that I had, in fact, written about in a book I published back in 1994. I was driven to write this new essay more for personal reasons than for purely intellectual ones, because I was curious to know how my feelings might have changed in the eighteen years that had passed since the original event. Both of my daughters, one of whom played a rather prominent role in my first telling of the story, asked me about it after the Gates incident was reported. They are adults now and live on their own, and I found their perspective interesting, although they were quite detached and in fact quite brief in their comments. I think they thought it would pain or irritate me to talk about it for very long. I also knew I did not like to talk about it and had not spoken about it at all to them for years. So, this essay was a bit of necessary sorting out for me, and although my daughters are hardly mentioned in the new piece, my relationship with them, my memory of having experienced the incident with them, was far more important to me in writing this essay than any sense of identification with Gates, which in fact was quite minimal.

✳

1. It Takes a Lot to Laugh

In early June, while I was attending a conference in Seoul, South Korea, my wife emailed me with the news that, during a brief but vicious storm, a huge old tree on our property had been blown over by fierce winds. Fortunately, it did not hurt anyone or strike our house or our neighbor's house. But it damaged another tree in its fall, wrecked our front lawn, and destroyed many of my wife's flower beds, which distressed her greatly. It took more than a month for the tree to be removed, by not-so-easy stages. There was the usual delay over the insurance claim and the site survey and the like. And then it rained for several days, which caused a further delay. When the weather finally turned hot and dry, the tree-removal company showed up and set to work, first laying down some boards on a patch of public grass connected to the property of my next-door neighbor in order to avoid trampling the undamaged flower beds that surround the street side of my front lawn as they fed chunks of the fallen tree into the chipper. But something strange happened next.

My neighbor is an ill-tempered man, who has had run-ins with several of the people in the vicinity, including the family who owned my house before my wife and I bought it. Let us say that he aggressively, sometimes harshly and rudely, protects the sanctity of his property. I am not sure if the men from the removal service asked his permission to use the patch of grass adjoining his property before placing the boards on it, which they should have, for simple courtesy. But it does belong to the city and is therefore available for public use, even though he must maintain it. In any case, on this very hot day, I found the men in a dispute with my neighbor, and he ordered them off his property in no uncertain terms.

My neighbor's pettiness annoyed me greatly, and the workmen's insistence on drawing me into the matter irritated me as well. I thought I was paying them to handle this. At any rate, I asked my neighbor to clarify the situation for me. He told me in a very nasty tone of voice that this was the way it was going to be and that no one was going to put anything on his property. As I walked away, he continued to talk loudly to one of the workmen, suggesting that they just go through the undamaged flower beds on the front of my property, in effect destroying them as well, saying gruffly, "Their lawn's already messed up anyway." I was incensed at this remark and told him to mind his own business and not offer advice about what the men should do on my property. He simply waved his hand at me and began to walk away. In my anger and in my immature need to wound him in some way, I called him a name, the most severe name I could think of at the moment. I called him a racist.

I might have called him many things: a fool, an ass, a dog, the waste matter of a horse, a cranky son of a bitch, a selfish jerk, a misanthrope, a mistake his mother would have done well to have aborted. But I chose to highlight our racial differences and called him a racist, on no other grounds than that he was irascible and that he was causing me a lot of trouble by making the removal of this tree much more difficult than it needed to be. I sensed that that was giving him a perverse sort of pleasure that made me all the angrier. He had given several of the white neighbors who lived around him a hard time for years, so I had absolutely no reason to call him a racist. But I wanted to insult him, to lower him, to show my contempt for him, and the most immediate way for me to do this in my anger was to mindlessly racialize him. I suppose it was one of those wild moments of lack of control when if all else fails you accuse someone who did something you don't like of committing a political crime, which, in essence, is what my name-calling amounted to. I knew, even at the instance that I said it, I should not have called him this and that I should apologize. Instead, I repeated the name, hoping, I suppose, as children do, that if you work your incantation enough, the person will become, before your eyes, the very thing you have named him.

He responded by calling me a racist, saying that in all the years I lived next door to him I had never spoken to him. This is true. He is an unfriendly man, and I had decided to return the favor by being as demonstrably unfriendly as I could. (Should I therefore have been surprised that he would not let the tree company use his patch of public grass!) What struck me most forcibly about this was the fact that he had *noticed* it. He was quite aware that I was unfriendly to him, that I did not like him, felt grandly superior to him. Of course, I had wanted my antipathy to be noticed, hoped that it was, but was nonetheless surprised to hear him acknowledge it as something manifest in the world. But for him to call me a racist for my pronounced display of dislike toward him struck me as ludicrous. After all, I got along well with the whites around me. In fact, earlier in the year, my white neighbors gave me the lifetime achievement award in the arts. I am a well-known Washington University professor, my wife the secretary of the Washington University board of trustees; the community thinks we are a wonderful couple. How could this idiot say something like that? Calling me a racist—merely repeating my own charge against him in a kind of dumb mimicry as some kind of defense? I would dislike him no matter what color he was. I almost wanted to protest when he said it. But I suppose his calling me a racist was no more ludicrous than my calling him one, and I must have sensed that, even at the moment. I walked away. He should have called me a snob, for that more accurately describes the attitude I exhibited toward him. But isn't racism, in fact, a form of snobbery?

We both called the cops and made identical charges: We each accused the other of being uncooperative and foul-tempered. We are more alike, I guess, than we know.

I thought about this a few weeks later when the dustup between Harvard professor Henry Louis Gates and the Cambridge police happened at Gates's home. Calling a white person a racist because he is being, by your standards at least, disagreeable, is a complex and perhaps pernicious, though understandable, display of minority self-consciousness, of minority profiling or stereotyping of the majority, if you will; but it is a weakness and an overwrought politicized arrogance to think that some of the bad things that happen to everyone in this world are happening to you because you are black. I wonder if blacks who are successful—tenured university professors and the like—are so used to being petted and praised by the whites who surround us in our professional bubble that it distorts our sense of worth or how we think whites in general should see us. I wonder, too, if successful blacks feel our success is so precarious that the whites around us might sabotage it at any minute. After all, we are not likely to forget that we are where we are as some manifestation of "diversity," a so-called social and political good only because we have brainwashed ourselves into thinking that it is. In a society that prizes "diversity," whatever it is that makes you "diverse"—and this, for a minority, is everything—is essentially the only product you have to sell. It's your pedigree, your cocoon, your political shtick, your trap, your protection, and ultimately your tiny piece of an absurd reality that everyone should recognize as a form of collective madness: where your social category substitutes for your humanity and your individuality and most people think that that is a significant advance over the past.

Ironically, my neighbor may have had much more of a reason to call me a racist, if only because I called him one first, so race had to be on my mind. It may never have been on his until I gave him the suggestion. Race was on Gates's mind in his encounter with the white police officer. We have no idea if it was on the cop's mind at all.

The Gates incident also brought to mind something similar that happened to me many years earlier.

2. The Myth of Kodachrome

In November 1991, I was impatiently walking around a small upscale mall called Le Chateau in the white suburban town of Frontenac, waiting for my wife and children to leave a Junior League Christmas bazaar, so we could go home. At the time, my wife was quite active in the St. Louis Junior League; she would in fact eventually become its first African American president. After having walked through the mall, I went outside and was waiting at the entrance when a police officer drove up, got out of his car, and approached me, wanting to know what I was doing there and asking to see some identification. At the time the officer arrived, in response to a complaint from one of the shop owners about a suspicious-looking black man prowling the mall—"casing the joint," in his phrase—I was the only black man there. Our encounter occurred as people were leaving the bazaar, including my wife, Ida, with the kids in tow. (At the time, our children were ten and twelve.) So I felt particularly humiliated to have been singled out for questioning by a police officer in front of all the whites who had been attending this Junior League function, as well as my own family. (I wrote a full account of this event and the distress it caused me and my family in "This Machine Kills Fascists," a chapter in my book about being a parent, entitled *Daughters: On Family and Fatherhood*, which was published in 1994. I append the chapter to this essay for those who want a fuller account of the incident and its aftermath.)

The differences between what happened to me and what happened to Henry Louis Gates are: What I was doing could not remotely be construed as a crime, nor did the shop owner call and report a crime, only a vague fear he had that a strange black man—he identified me by race—was walking in the mall and might be there to commit a crime; the incident happened during the day; it happened in front of my family; I was not arrested. Although I was certainly belligerent with the police officer, I did obey him, and he did exhibit patience and professionalism. Similar to what Gates did, my wife and I (she was more outraged about it than I was; I had never seen her so upset about anything or so determined to get justice) demanded an apology from the city of Frontenac for what had happened to me, or rather to us. This led to a protracted struggle over the following two weeks that was even written about in *The New York Times* (with a nice picture of Ida and me, arm in arm) and finally came to an end with a lame victory as the mayor reluctantly issued a halfhearted missive of regret. My wife and I never sued the city of Frontenac. We never felt we really had a case. Moreover, we never wanted to, because we were never interested in money. In fact, the idea of taking money for what happened was unseemly to us. It would have cheapened us. It is remarkable how many people in St. Louis think we received some sort of cash settlement for our pains.

I think on the whole the public, certainly the liberal white public of St. Louis, saw Ida and me as highly dignified people—Sidney Poitier and Ruby Dee–type characters in some production about racial injustice. We were the ideal victims—educated, well spoken in interviews, polite, clean-cut, bourgeois, Christian, courageous in the face of hate mail, in a word, assimilated, the romanticized personification of middle-class black life. *How could something that was so clearly racially motivated happen to these people!* The incident seemed such a sharp, clear snapshot of racial persecution, it was as if it had been shot in the brilliant colors of Kodachrome film. There was nothing ambiguous about it, because the good guys and bad guys were so clearly etched. And that has always been the aspect of it that most bothered me: that the whole incident became a big deal only because of the people to whom it happened, rather than the fact that it happened at all. If I had been a custodian rather than a university professor, and Ida had been a beautician, say, rather than an officer of the Junior League, the local media and the national press would never have taken it up, no matter how much Ida and I protested.

I rehash this story not out of any fondness for reliving it. I was so adamant for so many years in my refusal to discuss the matter, after having written *Daughters,* that I suppose the local media took me at my word, and I heard nary a peep from them when the Gates story broke. Or perhaps the locals have forgotten it, at last. (I was certainly more famous among many St. Louisans for having been "arrested" in Frontenac—I had to keep reminding people I was never arrested—than for any books I wrote or any awards I won. That fact itself is enormously humbling; it is good to be reminded of the distance between how you see yourself and how others see you.) I am grateful to have become not even a footnote in St. Louis history in this regard. But I dredge it up again because Gates's arrest underscores how complicated racial profiling is, politically and culturally, and how dishonest we in the United States have been about it.

Even as I was living through the Frontenac affair, I felt uneasy about pressing for an apology, especially because the demand had become focused on the police, which was not where the focus should have been. The police officer never hurt, abused, or disrespected me. He himself hadn't racially profiled me. He was simply doing his job. Some would argue that he was a tool in a larger mechanism of race profiling or, better put, racial tracking. I would not disagree with that, but focusing on the police was still beside the point. I tried to rationalize this at the time by saying publicly that I was exposing a serious problem and that I was speaking out for all black men who have been stopped by the police for no reason. But was I really? Or was it really only about me, about my own humiliation and shame? How could I possibly be speaking for or representing all black men in such situations? No two situations are exactly the same. No two black persons are exactly the same. Surely I would never have had the temerity to say such a thing, except that I desperately wanted to make some appeal to racial solidarity. But hadn't blacks like myself spent our lives trying to show how different we were from other blacks, those poor blacks who always got arrested, had poor work habits, no respect for education, and the like? We weren't like the kind of people that the cop who stopped me may have thought I was. We have cried solidarity only when it was convenient for us to do so as part of the "diversity" we were meant to represent for the whites in whose world we worked or when we wanted political concessions from whites.

I wondered at the time if perhaps my whole gesture of protest was nothing more than an appeal to lower-class blacks to say that I had not forgotten what it was like to be black, that I, heaven forbid the cliché, felt their pain, that I was one of the group, despite working at the great "white" university on the hill. During the entire episode there was something about what I was doing that made me feel like a fake. Wasn't I just being a whiner? Wasn't I just saying that I was too good, too exceptional, to be stopped by the cops? What complaint had I against the police then or now? In the thirty-plus years I have lived in St. Louis, the police have stopped me four times: three times for speeding, of which I was guilty, and once for having brake lights that didn't work, which was true. I was never stopped for being black, except this one time in Frontenac. I am sure now and was sure even then that there are many black people who have suffered indignities far greater and far more often than I ever have or ever will and who have a much greater right to complain or at least to not take my complaint very seriously. I did not want this to become some sort of trumped-up trauma, for I have always wanted to believe that I was never traumatized by it. Perhaps I was but cannot bring myself to accept trauma as a fact because I feel unworthy of it. It is always difficult, especially when there is so much at stake emotionally, to separate what you feel from what you think you feel or what you think you ought to feel. Only the truly aggrieved feelings of my wife kept me going in pursuit of the apology. It pained me deeply that Ida was so wounded by this. (Why she felt this way is more fully explained in the appended chapter from *Daughters*.)

And what about the shop owner who called the police in the first place? Blacks had robbed and killed his father, a jewelry store owner, some years before. From his perspective, it made perfect sense to call the police when he saw a lone black man walking around a lily-white mall in the late afternoon in a city where violent crime is prevalent. (Although I am sure he would have taken my money if I had walked into his store and bought something. Money legitimizes you as nothing else can.) And that is the huge elephant in the room that no one wishes to acknowledge: Black men commit an enormous number of the violent crimes in America, a percentage far in excess of the black proportion of the general population (13.5 percent). According to the Justice Department statistics, blacks are both seven times more likely to commit a violent crime than whites, and six times more likely to be a victim of a violent crime than whites. Between 1976 and 2005, blacks constituted 52 percent of the perpetrators of homicides in the United States, an astonishing number. (In fact, overall, according to BlackDemographics.com, there are more black men in prison than white men.) Blacks committed 56 percent of gun homicides between 1976 and 2005. And on and on the dreary figures go. Even though most violent crimes are intra-racial—meaning that whites commit their crimes mainly against other whites, and blacks commit their crimes mainly against other blacks—whites are still twice as likely to be the victim of a violent black perpetrator as my wife or I am to be the victim of a white perpetrator.

So, the assumptions underlying racial profiling are not merely the fictional products of the bigoted white mind. Why blacks are so overrepresented in violent-crime statistics is, of course, another story or set of disputed stories for another day, but the fact is that, after reviewing these statistics, only a fool would not take some caution around blacks, especially black men, which is a kind of national shame and ought to be a cause of despair. I suppose the white shop owner was granting me a kind of racial solidarity that I did not particularly care to have, not in the way he wished to bestow it upon me.

In the end, what happened to me in 1991 could not be captured by a photo shot in the clarity of Kodachrome but only by a grainy black-and-white picture, a sort of miniature film noir about race in America, where the good have mixed motives and the bad aren't entirely or even mostly bad, but certainly privileged and clearly opportunistic, and the world, finally, is what it is. Maybe, as the leftists would say, it was all about institutions and structures, about one of those inevitable moments when the power and intentions of white hegemony came into conflict with a member of the stigmatized minority and created the clashing drama in which I became helplessly enmeshed. I know how to do that close reading. And I know how to do the close reading of the right that says that blacks are self-destructive, need to acquire better cultural habits and stop being so damn racial, and that when that day comes, I and other black men will not be stigmatized. But, as I used to say to my children when they were young, I sometimes wonder what might happen in this world if more adults simply acted like grown-up people. But as the priest in Malraux's *Anti-Memoirs* said, people are more unhappy than you think.

"This Machine Kills Fascists"

Gerald Early

. . . in this white-man world you got to take yuh mouth and make a gun.
    —*Florrie in Paule Marshall's* Brown Girl, Brownstones

It might be said that I ran the risk of living a completely uneventful life, of being able to avoid even the most remote possibility of ever being notorious or an object of scrutiny. But the town of Frontenac, a suburb of St. Louis, saved me from such a fate, and for two weeks in November in 1991, I was probably the most talked-about man in St. Louis.

The cause of this was simple enough: Ida, an officer in the Junior League, took me and the children to a Junior League Christmas bazaar at Le Chateau Mall, which was where the Junior League headquarters was located then. While she and the girls looked at the Christmas displays, I, bored and restless, walked around the mall for a bit, then went back to our van and sat there for a time and read. After twenty or thirty minutes, I went back through the mall to get them. I walked past a jewelry store. A man and a woman stood in front of it, talking. I didn't say anything to them, never stopped to look at anything in the jewelry store, barely even glanced at them. I simply wanted to get home. None of us had eaten dinner. I was fairly hungry by this point, and we had promised the kids their favorite: pizza.

When I arrived back at the Junior League headquarters, I couldn't find Ida or the kids. Once again, I went down the front steps of the Junior

League and stood there, waiting for them to come out. Then the adventure began. A young police officer named Mayer drove up and asked me what I was doing there. He told me that he had received a call with a description of someone who looked like me "lurking" in the mall. Something in me snapped. There I was, I immediately thought, about to be humiliated before the whites coming in and out of the building (and there were a good many of them doing so, through the front entrance), being reminded that I was a nigger, that I had no business being where I was, that I was a "threat" to the good white folk of Frontenac.

"You want identification," I said, flinging my wallet at him. "Here's mountains of identification. Take your pick."

He refused to pick it up, so I bent over, picked it up, and put it on the hood of his car.

"What's in your pocket?" he asked ominously. I had been holding one hand in my pocket since his arrival. I took off my jacket, flung it on the car, dumped the contents of my pocket on the hood of his car, and spread-eagled for him.

"I don't want you to have any reason to kill me," I said. "Besides, we all know that we're going through this little drama because of my race."

"Your race has nothing to do with this," Officer Mayer told me.

"Well, there are plenty of white guys 'lurking' around here and nobody's stopping them."

At that point both Ida and the kids came out.

"Come on, Jer, let's go," she called.

"I can't go anywhere," I said. "This police officer is trying to see if I am a dangerous criminal."

Ida dropped her purchases on the front steps of the league, left the children, and ran over to Officer Mayer.

"What are you doing?" she shouted. "What are you doing? This is my husband. He hasn't done anything. What the hell are you doing?"

"We got a call about a person lurking in the mall who fit your husband's description . . ." Officer Mayer began.

"What call?" Ida asked frantically. "Who called? Who made that call?"

By this time, Officer Mayer had finished running my driver's license through the computer check and had given it back to me. I picked up my jacket and belongings and walked back to the kids, who were completely nonplussed about what was going on. I picked up Ida's purchases, took the kids by the arm, and we sat on the steps in front of the league, waiting while Ida angrily argued with the officer, who kept insisting that he was merely doing his job.

"What's going on, Daddy?" Linnet asked.

"The police stopped me for questioning and an I.D. check," I said.

"But why? You hadn't done anything."

"I guess because I looked like somebody who might do something," I said, holding my head in my hands.

"I can't believe this," Ida said as we were driving home. "I can't believe this. Who would call the cops? I don't understand this."

"Maybe one of your Junior Leaguers who was scared by the big bad Negro man," I said.

"They wouldn't do that. They wouldn't do something like that. I just can't believe one of them would do something like that."

"Well, somebody did," I said, "and that's that. Let's just chalk this up as an inevitable embarrassment you experience from time to time being black and call it a day. I just want to forget the whole business."

No one ate much dinner that night.

Although I was ready to forget the whole affair, Ida was not. The next morning she told me she wanted to see the chief of police in Frontenac and get an apology for what happened.

"Just forget about it," I said. "They aren't going to give you an apology. For what? A guy who didn't get arrested and who didn't get his head beaten in? Why, that chief of police is just going to look at you and say, 'Why, your husband is one lucky nigger as far as I can tell. He ain't in jail and he's still in one piece.' "

"No," Ida said adamantly. "This wasn't right, and I'm going to see somebody about it."

"Okay, okay, listen. Since I can't talk you out of it, don't go see anybody without calling me first. I'll go with you."

When I arrived at school that day, I ran into my friend Wayne Fields, then the chair of the English department, and I told him the story, almost jocularly now. I had gotten over the whole business. It seemed a small thing to worry about.

"Listen," Wayne said, "I'm going to call the *Post-Dispatch*. I know a guy down there and I'm going to have this written up. This stuff has got to stop."

I was almost instantly sorry I had told Wayne. I'm not telling a reporter about this, I thought. This is too ridiculous for words. It's no big deal. I just won't call him back and he'll forget about it by this afternoon. I also thought that by the time Ida was on the job, busy with the day-to-day stuff at the office, she, too, would forget about it.

At around four in the afternoon, I finally reached Ida. I had tried her several times earlier in the day without success. Since she hadn't called me, I figured that she had simply changed her mind about seeing the police chief of Frontenac.

"Where have you been?" I asked. "I've been trying you all day."

"Oh, out driving," she said thickly. Her voice sounded tight and strange, as if she had been crying.

"Out driving where?" I asked.

"I don't know, Gerald, just anywhere. I don't know. I don't know where I've been. I've just been driving." She started crying into the phone.

"Ida, what happened?" I asked. "Were you hurt or injured or something?"

"No, I went to see . . . the chief of police of Frontenac. Some guy named, named, I think, Ben Branch," she said, trying to control her sobbing.

"I told you not to go out there unless you called me first. I told you not to go see those people without me," I said angrily.

"No, Gerald, it was better this way. It was safer for you. That's why I went by myself. It was better that way. I thought they wouldn't feel as threatened just facing a woman."

"Well, what happened?" I asked anxiously.

"Oh, Gerald, it was awful. He just sat there defending his police officer. He didn't care. To him, you were just a nigger who was in the wrong place at the wrong time. I was just sitting there listening to all this. I just started crying and crying. I couldn't control myself and I was so ashamed because I didn't want to cry in front of this man. But I couldn't help it. He was killing me, Gerald. Everything he was saying. The way he acted. He was just killing me as if he were shooting me with bullets. They don't see us as human beings. We're just, I don't know, just some kind of animal or something. He kept saying that the officer followed procedure. I told him the officer humiliated you in front of all those people, all those white people, in front of your own children. But he didn't care. Then, finally, he played the tape of the call they received. It was the jeweler in the mall, and you should have heard the way he described you. He said you were 'casing the joint' and that it was obvious you were planning a robbery. He said the white woman who was there was afraid to go to her car after seeing you. I just started crying all over again.

"Well, I left there and decided to see this jeweler. I just couldn't believe he would make this call and say those awful things about you. And I went to see him and he was worse than Branch. He said, 'Your husband must not be much of a man, sending you out to get his apologies. And what's so special about your husband anyway? I've been stopped before. If he hadn't done anything, why should he mind? Maybe you guys were afraid because you were trying to hide something.' I just couldn't believe the ugly things he said. But I wouldn't cry in front of him. No, not him. But he was killing me too. But I wouldn't cry.

"Then, I left his store and I don't know what I did. I was crying in the car for I don't know how long. I couldn't go back to work because I couldn't stop crying. Then, I started driving, just anywhere. Just driving and crying. I'm surprised I wasn't killed in an accident. Finally, I got back to work just a few minutes ago.

"I'm sorry I didn't tell you. But it was better this way. Especially with that jeweler. He was so hateful and racist."

I was quiet for so long that Ida had to ask to see if I was still on the line.

"I'll call you back," I said.

I called Wayne and told him what Ida had said. As I talked I was finding it harder and harder to control my voice. I could feel myself breaking down.

"And she was crying, Wayne, crying so much. She was crying more about this than over anything I've ever done to her," I said, trying to make a joke but failing miserably.

"They think I'm some kind of animal, that they can do whatever they want to me," I said, and now to my astonishment, I was crying too. "They think I'm an animal and that Ida is nothing more than the wife of an animal. *I am not an animal!*" I shouted. *"I am not an animal. I am not an animal."* My head was on the desk and I was crying to one of my colleagues. Wayne was trying to calm me down. I was silent for a time, pulling myself together. I said at last:

"If you can get hold of that reporter, I'm willing to talk."

✳

Once the story broke, the next two weeks were the most stressful and trying of my life. At first, Ida and I considered the story minor, just a bit of publicity to embarrass Frontenac, the jeweler, and the police. But the local press decided the story about a black professor versus the lily-white, affluent town of Frontenac was too rich to let go. Bigger stories followed. Interviews on the television news. "Will the W.U. Professor Stopped and Questioned by Frontenac Police Get His Apology?" I hadn't been aware that that was even what I was after until the news stories told me. The jeweler tried to put a different spin on things by saying that I was actually standing in front of his store, looking at his merchandise.

"That's a damn lie," I told Ida. "Anybody who knows me knows I don't like jewelry, never wear it, and would never be caught dead in a jewelry store or even window-shopping for jewelry. Remember how mad you were when I lost our wedding ring two weeks after we were married? That's how much I dislike jewelry."

"Forget it, Gerald. Don't get into a fight about whether you were actually standing in front of the store. That's what he would want. That would play to his advantage. We both know it's a lie but it doesn't matter."

Ida and I began to receive hate mail. This too made her cry. We were attacked on the editorial page by a variety of police officers who said I was "arrogant" and the like. The *Post-Dispatch* countered by running an editorial supporting us. But after about a week or so, I felt I had to issue some sort of statement and take some sort of definitional control over the matter. One Friday, I taped to my PC the words "This Machine Kills Fascists" and started writing my own op-ed piece.

"What does that mean, Daddy?" Rosalind asked. " 'This Machine Kills Fascists.' "

"It is something that the great folksinger Woody Guthrie used to write on his guitar. It means that I am going to use my words to slay all fascist and fascist-thinking people."

"Are fascists white people?"

"No," I said, "fascists are bad people. They can be any color and they have screwy ideas about race and blood. And when I get finished killing these white racist dogs, there are plenty of black fascists that need killing through words too." The piece that ran in the *Post-Dispatch* told readers that my stepfather was a retired police officer, that I was well aware of the hazards of the profession and was certainly not antipolice. But I went on to remind readers that despite my black skin, I was allowed free and equal access to all public places without compromise and without suspicion unless my actions clearly warranted such. Mere walking did not justify my having to give an account of myself to the police.

Some people at my church and at school started a letter-writing campaign on my behalf. I was on talk radio. The dean of the college, the provost, and the chancellor all called me to express concern about what happened. The Junior League rallied to my defense. I never knew I had so many friends, so many white friends at that. Many of the people who knew me and Ida were genuinely and deeply upset about what had happened. A white woman at my church came up to me after service one Sunday, rubbed my back tenderly, and said, her eyes welling with tears, "I'm so sorry about what happened to you. It's a disgrace to every white person in St. Louis." And, of course, I heard from black folk. Many called me at my office, often to recite more horrible encounters with the police than I had had. The local black newspaper did a big story about the incident. Yet I felt strange and uncomfortable, especially talking about it with blacks. I discovered, surprisingly, that the entire racial aspect of the incident embarrassed me, the call for racial solidarity, the demand for it, in effect, because of the incident, made me uneasy. I did not feel as though I was my brother's brother, truly, and becoming a racial firebrand or at least a symbol for racial justice made me often see myself, frankly, as a hypocrite. For many blacks, I was demanding an apology for the race itself, for all the untold number of times white police stopped and humiliated some poor black soul who had not done anything except live and be black. But at least a few saw through me as a race hero or made me feel more richly the alienation from my brothers and sisters that my education and my temperament had engendered. And their reactions made me feel my ambivalence about racial solidarity more acutely, for there was nothing I wanted more, nothing I yearned for more deeply, than to be taken into the fold of blackness, and yet at the same time nothing that more appalled me, made me feel more imprisoned than the security blanket of racial isolation. O, to be a hero of the race for a mere hour! O, to be burdened by race at all!

"You know I appreciate what you're doing," a black male caller told me one afternoon. "But you know you can take the stand that you're taking because you won't lose your job. In fact, the white folks on your job see you as some kind of hero or symbol. And you have the backing of rich white folks. Because you know and I know that you could have the backing of every black person in this city, and the white press and the white media wouldn't even be taking you seriously. I'm not trying to belittle what you're doing, but you're not a race man. You're just a black man with powerful white connections."

"I'm sorry if I've disappointed you," I told the caller, "but I'm not a race hero. And I'm not trying to be one." Yet the call wounded me deeply, stung me to the quick, for I had wanted to be seen in a bit better light than that.

On the other hand, Vernon, a black man who happens to be the custodian at my church, would just beam every time he saw me. "Yeah, Doc," he would say, "them folks out in Frontenac knowin' now you ain't a black man to mess around with. All the black folks I know are one hundred percent behind you. Especially because you ain't one of them big rabble-rousing race guys. Folks are proud 'cause you got a lot of education and you and your wife are doing this with a lot of dignity and not just callin' people racist. You a real role model, Doc."

※

"My teachers were talking about you at school today," Linnet told me one afternoon when she came home from school. "They think you're a hero and they hope you make Frontenac apologize."

"Do you think I'm a hero?" I asked.

"I don't know," she said somewhat distractedly, "I guess you're doing what you think you've got to do."

"I'm tired of the teachers asking me about you at school, Daddy," Rosalind said on another day. "I want to tell them that this is something you're doing, not me. I want to tell them that if they want to know about it, they should talk to you."

"Do you think I'm a hero?" I asked, with true anxiety in my voice.

"Do *you* think you're one, Daddy?" Rosalind shot back incredulously.

What I learned from this incident was this: that blackness has something to do with solidarity, with a sense of connection with other people who share your condition and with other people who could not possibly share your condition; and that blackness has nothing to do with solidarity, nothing to do with some idea we call race and is, finally, the exploration of the night within you, what Céline called "the depths of the night themselves," and that all other conceptions of blackness are merely distractions. This is what I hated about the Frontenac incident, not its punishing reality, but its unrelenting unreality. It was a brutalizing fantasy, a distraction of the most unrewarding kind. I was neither hero nor opportunist. I was simply a man caught up in some bemusing circumstances, "getting my head rubbed against a hard, grainy wall," someone once put it. For I should not have wanted the approval of black people, nor should I have seen myself as a pet of the whites and reveled in that privilege. I should have wanted justice simply for the sake of justice and because it would have pleased God for me to seek this on His behalf and in His name.

It was at this time, during the Frontenac trial, that I, worst card player in the world, tried to teach Linnet and Rosalind some card games, with indifferent success. Linnet kept insisting that she wanted to learn how to play Pinochle because it was "a cool game with a cool name."

"I can't teach you that game," I said.

"Why not?" Linnet insisted. "Can't you just look up the rules in a card game book?"

"It's not that simple," I said. "I mean, the game is not that simple. When I was a boy, the guys would try to teach it to me. But they would be talking so fast and showing me all the stuff so quickly that I could never catch on. So, I kept getting my head rubbed. At first, they were amused by this but then they got bored and irritated. After a while, they said, 'We're dealing you out of this. You keep getting your head rubbed. You can't play. You just a chump, Jerry. You can't play.' It's just a game I could never understand. So, it doesn't matter about reading the rules. I just can't play that game."

✳

At last, there was a meeting set up for me and Ida and the mayor of Frontenac, Newell Baker, to settle the matter. I knew this gathering was not likely to go well when he started the meeting with some bad, anti-Catholic jokes about pigeons. Oh God, I thought, some white people truly have one type of mentality and that is idiocy. It never got any better as the mayor and his aide simply tried to tell me that nothing bad had happened to me. The police stop white people every day for the same sort of stuff. The mayor's position was that the police had acted properly, and this was true: the true culprit in this was the jeweler. But of course his action was understandable because it was reasonable for him to fear robbery. The jeweler's father had been, apparently, injured or killed in a holdup. But the jeweler's fears or the police officer's conduct was not, at last, the issue. The fact of the matter was that there were plenty of white men walking around that mall that night just as I was, and they weren't stopped in front of their families and questioned as suspicious characters. If they were good enough to pass muster as law-abiding citizens, then so was I. And the town of Frontenac owed me an apology on that basis: for not having treated me as it treats white men (and if we profess to live in a color-blind society, that is precisely the treatment I want, the same that is accorded to white men). The mayor refused to see any aspect of the larger picture, of the significance of what had happened, perhaps afraid that any concession on his part would instigate a lawsuit. I felt like just walking out, telling the good mayor and his henchman that they could take their bullshit and shove it back up their asses. Finally, after about forty-five minutes of getting nowhere, Ida rose and said that since the mayor was not willing to apologize, we might as well leave as this was a waste of everybody's time. It was then that the mayor, obviously not wishing for us to go out to reporters (a group of whom were waiting outside the door) and tell them of the city officials' intransigence in this regard, came up suddenly with a letter that said that Frontenac, well, sort of apologized to those exceptional Negroes Ida and Gerald Early, for making them feel uncomfortable and unwanted. It wasn't much, but it was the most we were going to get.

But this small victory was not without its considerable price. Ida and I were afraid to drive anywhere in St. Louis for a time because we felt we would be harassed by police officers sympathetic to Frontenac. We were afraid to open our mail because of the hate mail we were receiving. We were afraid to answer the phone because of the crank calls. I was so tense that I could scarcely sleep. I had little appetite. For Ida it was much the same. But more than anything else, these two weeks nearly wrecked my relationship with my children.

✳

On the night the incident happened, Linnet was so upset that she went straight to bed.

"I think I'm getting a cold," she said.

And neither Linnet nor Rosalind wanted to talk about it. Every time it was broached to them, they wanted to change the subject, or they would simply listen quietly.

"I'll be glad when this is over," Rosalind said.

"Why?" I asked. "Because it is too stressful for you?"

"No," she said. "Because I'm tired of hearing about race."

Once, while she was lying in bed, still sick from something, I tried patiently to explain it all to Linnet.

"Do you know why I was stopped?" I asked.

"No, Daddy," she moaned, "I don't know. I mean, I don't understand."

"Well, because I'm a black man," I said, as if that made everything clear and self-evident.

"Oh," she said. "Do we have to talk about it? I don't feel that well."

"Yes," I said emphatically, "yes, we have to talk about it. You're used to being around these white folks and you think they mean you some good. But they don't mean you any good."

"Daddy, I'm tired, do we have to talk about it now?"

"Yes," I said, feeling myself becoming slowly, more hysterically angry, "yes, right now. Because I have to get these nutty notions out of your head about white folks."

"Daddy, I don't want to hear it," she said, her voice rising.

"I don't care what you want to hear. You're going to hear this now. Don't you know race runs this world?" I threw the blankets from her. I was losing control of myself entirely.

"Do you see this?" I grabbed her arm and held it. "This skin color? This is what determines what goes on in this world. This, and only this. Nothing but this. Has never been anything but this."

"Daddy, stop this!"

"I'm your father and you're going to listen. You've gotten too cozy with these white folks, but I'm going to get you out of that. It's time you understood about race, about being black. Your mother and I made a mistake trying to be nice, good Negroes, striving Negroes, liberal Negroes who were going to try to accept these white folk. Why, we thought we were too good to talk about race in this house like the common, complaining niggers do. No sir, we were enlightened Negroes and we were going to raise our children with none of this race consciousness stuff. Well, that was just nonsense! We're not avoiding race anymore and I'm tired of trying to accommodate myself to these whites. Do you hear? I'm tired. Do you know what they did?" I was shouting uncontrollably now.

"Daddy, stop it. Please stop it. I don't want to hear this."

"Well, I'm going to tell you. They humiliated me in front of you. Can you understand that? Those bastards humiliated me in front of you! *Can you understand?* They think I'm an animal. I am not an animal. This is what they think of your father. That he is an animal! That he can be humiliated! That he can be . . ."

"Daddy!" Rosalind burst into the room. "Stop it! Leave her alone!"

"You!" I said savagely. "You! You, shut up! Just shut up!"

I turned back to Linnet.

"Do you understand this? Your father is nothing to them. *Nothing!* They hate black men. Everybody does. It's the national pastime. To hate black men. I am a black man. I am not an animal!"

"Daddy!" Linnet screamed. "Daddy, get out of here! Get out! Get out!"

Ida ran into the room. "Have you gone crazy, Gerald? Have you gone crazy? What are you doing to this child?"

I looked around, completely bewildered, at their astonished faces. They had never seen me act this way before. I had never said "shut up" to my children before. I felt cornered and frightened, and the people who stared at me at that moment were as much strangers to me as I was to them. I felt as if I were losing my mind completely; I could hardly believe how I was acting. Suddenly, my blood felt coldly dammed in my veins; I was struck dumb by the horror of what I had been doing. What had I wanted, coming into this room and badgering my daughter like this? What had I proved except that I wanted a certain kind of power over my children—not approval, but power? My outburst, partly a result of the enormous stress and public scrutiny I was experiencing, was not, finally, about racism, or my daughter's racial consciousness or lack thereof. It was perhaps about my own insecurities about race and maybe even about my insecurities as a parent, as a father. I might just as well have been trying to ravish that poor child, I thought later. At that moment, I felt as though I had. When we abuse our children it is often not from hate or dislike or even some rooted evil in us as adults, but rather some unintelligible outburst of ferocity, of longing. One is horrified by one's own loneliness, by one's child's loneliness, too.

"I—I—I," I started stammering, "I mean, I was just trying to explain . . . You don't understand . . . They think I'm an animal . . . I—oh, what the hell is the use?" I pushed past them and ran from the house.

✳

It was a few days before Christmas, and the Frontenac incident, for better or for worse, was over. Ida and I made a conscious effort not to talk about it again after we received the "apology" from the mayor.

It was a cold day, but clear and bright. The sun was shining with a glassy brilliance. There were small mounds of dirty ice, trace memories of a small snowstorm. Linnet, wearing her "cool" jacket, and I, with my tweed cap, loafers, and blue wool jacket, walked along a street in Webster Groves. I told her a story.

"When I was in junior high school, well, it was a pretty bad school, largely black, with a lot of street gangs and that sort of thing. Well, one day, after school, which was when street gang wars most commonly erupted, this boy was killed, stabbed to death, right in front of the school. He was a white boy, a retarded boy. You see, they used to hold special-education classes for retarded kids in my junior high school. We hardly noticed these retarded kids because they were on a different schedule from the rest of the school, so they would usually be gone by the time we were dismissed.

"I don't know what happened that day or why the bus was late or how that kid got tangled up in our dismissal. But he was and a fight erupted and he was stabbed to death. Probably he was just in the way and no one had really intended to stab him at all.

"Well, the next day at school, the place is crawling with cops. They bust open all the lockers and search them for weapons. They walk up and down the hallway in a show of force.

"We had a special assembly that day and the vice principal, Mr. G., was reading us the riot act. I'm not paying that much attention, you know. I mean, I felt bad that that kid was killed, but I didn't do it and I couldn't have prevented it no matter how much I didn't want it to happen. Maybe the cops and all the white folks and everybody else was all upset because they couldn't have prevented it either and maybe they felt guilty and mad about that.

"Anyway, somewhere in this vice principal's harangue he said—and I'll never forget this—'You act like animals, and we're going to treat you like animals.' I was just stunned. I couldn't believe what I heard. Well, the rest of the kids, you know, it was kind of like water rolling off a duck's back. They didn't care what the vice principal was talking about. But I never forgot that. And for the rest of the day I went around saying to myself, 'I'm not an animal.' "

"Did they catch the boys who killed the retarded boy?" Linnet asked.

"Yes, they caught them and put them away."

We were silent for a long time.

"It was bad," Linnet said finally, "to tell somebody that."

"Yes," I agreed, "it was too bad."

Linnet was quiet for a time. Then, suddenly, she blurted out, pleadingly:

"I'm sorry, Daddy. I'm sorry I wasn't with you that night at the mall. If I was, then this wouldn't have happened. The guy wouldn't have called the police if I was walking with you."

It was a common practice for me to take my children with me whenever I went shopping, out for a walk in a white neighborhood, or just felt like going about in the white world. The reason was simple enough: if a black man is alone or with other black men, he is a threat to whites. But if he is with children, then he is harmless, adorable, the dutiful father. ("Only black men have to go around finding ways of defusing their presence in public all the time," one bitter black man said to me once, and I sadly agreed.) After all, as Robert Frost suggested, no one takes his family with him on a robbery. Although I did this, I never thought that my children were ever aware of why I took them with me so much or that they would ever see the "political" significance of their presence. And especially I would never have thought Linnet would realize this, as she seems so willfully oblivious to race and racial matters in this world. I was touched and humbled, moved not only by what she said, but by the depth of the realization it revealed.

"Thank you," I said, putting my arm on her shoulder, "thank you. It's nice to know I've got a daughter who can protect me."

Sports

Obama Victory Raises Social Significance of Basketball

Scoop Jackson

It's been a long time coming. Too long. Yeah for that too, but this is about something different. Finally, for America's "other" game, the time has come. *You ready? Stand still. Pose. Look happy. Live the moment. Smile. FLASH!* Finally . . . the game of basketball is ready for its official close-up.

Hope won? It's more than that.

Twenty-one presidents and 117 years after Naismith invented the game, basketball has finally found a place inside the place that best symbolizes America—inside *the inside* of America. Other presidents have only concerned themselves with basketball when necessary, such as playing host to NBA and NCAA champions at the White House. Barack is about to change all of that.

Obama's predecessors all treated the game as a spectator, embraced it from a distance, considered it an afterthought. All the while, over the decades the sport has become more and more intertwined into the socio-fabric of America, slowly symbolizing what this country really is, what it's really about.

This makes Obama's election that much more revealing. His connection to basketball and inclusion of the game in his campaign is a testament to his message of change and the love he has for the least elitist sport to be held in high regard by anyone to occupy the White House.

"In any basketball game you can go from the leader, to a follower, to a team, all in the span of a few trips up and down the court," ESPN's Stuart Scott said after watching and playing with Obama. "That's the beauty of it. And that's what I noticed about Barack Obama. I think that's what basketball has taught him. He's got to be the leader of this country. But sometimes he's going to have to step back and let other people give him advice, let other people lead in moments, and he's always going to have to be a part of a team—Senate, Congress, his cabinet, his most trusted advisers—*team*.

"He has to be involved in all of that, but mostly he has to be the leader. And that's one of the things that having played basketball is going to benefit him greatly. I think that's how basketball has shaped him."

Yes, it's well documented that Barack balls, that his game is nice, that his brother-in-law is the men's basketball coach at Oregon State, that his wife used the game to "find out what type of person he was" before they started seriously dating. He went so far as to make it a "rule" to play the days of primaries, a ritual he continued on election day.

But it would have been so easy for Obama to distance himself from the game, to rise above it because he'd risen so high. No one who's ever run for president has had a close relationship with basketball. Why should Barack be the first? He was *different* enough.

But there's a deeper investment in the game of basketball that represents how he possibly views the country. Very open, flawed but of promise, accessible to all. Think about it. Of all of the sports which have played a role in the lives of our commanders in chief, how many of those sports are as diverse as basketball in terms of economics, race, culture and gender?

George Washington rode horses. George H.W. Bush played college baseball. Gerald Ford, Ronald Reagan and Richard Nixon played college football. Nixon was so immersed in football, he was reputed to call Redskins coach George Allen and Dolphins coach Don Shula with play ideas. Many presidents had a passion for golf.

For whatever reason, basketball was the one sport that none of them brought with them to 1600 Pennsylvania Avenue.

The game finds itself in the one place in America it has yet to impact, a place where it's never been wanted. The running joke for almost two years among Obama's crew who play ball with him regularly was if he won the election, he'd have to destroy the bowling alley and put up a hoop in the White House instead.

"His character is totally revealed when he's on the ball court," said Chicago Public Schools CEO Arne Duncan, a friend of Obama who plays basketball with him regularly. "Basketball reveals who you really are. You can't fake it."

What becomes evident about the future president through the game of basketball can possibly give great insight into how he's going to run the country.

"What the outside world doesn't see in (Barack) when he's playing are three things," said Duncan. "One is how much of a competitor he is. I think the country underestimated him on that. Two, how he has real courage, that he will step up with the game on the line and take the big shot when others won't. And three, how really, really smart he is. His intellectual capacity is amazing. And that translates to how he does things off the court as well."

The game lends itself to the definition of not only Obama's character, but the inclusive direction he'd like the country to take.

"All sports bring people together, but none so like basketball," said Illinois State Treasurer Alexi Giannoulias, days after his team went undefeated against Barack's on election day. "Playing hoops is a great way to interact, and as a team sport it really says a lot about who he is and how he wants to bring people together. If he goes to another country or if he just goes to North Carolina like he did earlier and plays basketball with the people, it shows that he is a real guy."

So, finally, the game that has come to most represent urban America while being responsible for handing out some of the largest contracts in professional sports is about to become America's "First" sport. Because of Obama's passion for basketball, the game will gain the attention bestowed upon other sports that have shared the White House experience over the next four (maybe eight) years.

In *The Games Presidents Play*, author John Sayle Watterson wrote, "Increasingly, sports have defined the presidency." If that's true, the change that occurred with Obama's victory might transcend politics and policy. Basketball could finally be looked upon as something more than just a game of escapism from the ghetto and be seen for what it honestly is—the most democratically open sport in the country.

It could be seen as a game that "people of every creed and color, from every walk of life . . . young and old, rich and poor, Democrat and Republican, black, white, Hispanic, Asian, Native American, gay, straight, disabled and not disabled" can help prove, as Barack said, "that in America, our destiny is inextricably linked, that together our dreams can be one."

This we hope. Because just as the country proved it was ready for Obama, it will prove it's ready for a different sport to define this presidency.

Can basketball finally find that embrace? Can it finally and truly become America's game because one person won an election?

Yes it can.

"Joe Louis Moment"

William C. Rhoden

For the better part of fifty years, my father has tried to get me to feel the power of what he called a Joe Louis moment. Louis, the former heavyweight champion of the world, was the first universally embraced black American hero.

In a time of war, Louis united a divided country, not by words but with deeds. My father frequently described happy street scenes in Chicago and New York after Louis won a big fight. Now ninety-one, my father holds on to vivid memories of exactly where he was seventy years ago when Louis defeated the German heavyweight Max Schmeling in a grand rematch at Yankee Stadium.

I've seen photographs of those happy faces, watched documentaries, read books about it. But on Tuesday night, I finally understood. After Barack Obama's victory in the presidential election, I felt what my father described as that Brown Bomber moment.

On the way back to Manhattan after reporting on the Nets game against the Phoenix Suns, I drove home to Harlem and found the giddy excitement of horns honking and streets overflowing with celebration. At Londel's, the popular gathering spot at 139th and Frederick Douglass Boulevard, crowds fanned out with joy, tears and relief, singing and dancing—the way they must have danced and shouted for Louis in 1938. The passing cars added to the celebration with shouts and honking horns, a scene duplicated in neighborhoods across America.

Tuesday's crowd was more diverse than the old photographs I've seen, with more white faces dancing shoulder to shoulder with neighbors from surrounding housing projects and the restaurant regulars.

The restaurateur Londel Davis cautioned that the struggle was only beginning. On Wednesday, we would face the same poverty, the same widening divide between haves and have-nots.

"Obama began his career as a community organizer," Londel said. "We're going to all have to be community organizers if there's any hope of saving our kids."

Perhaps this is the postelection call to action for athletes, so many of whom come from underserved and economically devastated communities where hope is often in short supply.

Earlier, Grant Hill, the veteran Suns forward, said that aside from the obvious history of the Obama victory, he was encouraged by the involvement of so many colleagues.

"What's interesting," Hill said, "is that I've seen a lot of athletes lending their support—either way, for both candidates. Just seeing athletes playing more of a role in the political process is something we haven't really seen for a while. I've seen athletes really coming out, lending their support, giving money, going to events, hosting fund-raisers. You really haven't seen a lot of that in the last twenty, thirty years."

In 1990, when Michael Jordan was asked why he failed to publicly support Charlotte's former mayor Harvey Gantt, an African American, in a Senate race in North Carolina against the conservative Republican Jesse Helms, he responded, "Republicans buy sneakers, too."

Jordan's response became the anthem of profit-based neutrality for professional athletes and cemented the perception that athletes simply wanted to avoid controversy as they played to a largely white fan base by not saying or doing anything that could be construed as offensive.

All that may be changing now. This presidential race created a free space for activism without risk. Many athletes played an active role in encouraging young fans to register and vote. In Boston, the Celtics star Ray Allen worked on voter-registration drives. Los Angeles Clippers guard Baron Davis spoke at a fund-raiser for Obama in California and acclaimed him on his blog. Curt Schilling, the Red Sox pitcher, made the case for John McCain at 38pitches.com, where he wrote Tuesday night that he was, misspelling aside, "proud to know more Americans voted yesterday than at any time in this countries history."

But what will all of this mean moving forward? Will professional athletes take a more active role in advancing and driving real causes—and not just their own?

They can practice by being more active in the politics of their sports. Will NFL players finally become involved in league affairs, especially in identifying and electing a new executive director? Will NBA players, seventy percent of whom are African American, express their preference for whom the next league commissioner should be?

Hill was cautiously optimistic that they would.

"If you look at the election process, you see a lot of young athletes who felt vested in the process and feel that they played a part," he said. "This younger generation feels they can do whatever; they don't need to wait, they don't need to wait their turn. 'I want it all now. I can do my part.' It's a different mind-set. I've seen it as I get older. It's different, and it's kind of refreshing."

Around midnight on election day, I called my father in Las Vegas and let him hear the crowds shouting, horns blaring and sobs of joy in the Harlem night. I'd finally experienced my own, long-awaited Joe Louis moment.

Still Crazy After All These Years

L. Jon Wertheim

"Now is the moment you've all been waiting for," the baritone emcee bellows over a scratchy P.A. "They've spent eight decades entertaining billions and now they're here tonight. I need you on your feet and ready to greet the world famous . . . *HAAAAARLEMMM GLOOOOOOBE-TROTTERS!*"

With that, the roar of the crowd thickens, the lights dim, the fog machine belches, and eight men dribbling striped red-white-and-blue balls storm onto the court at Brookdale Community College in Lincroft, N.J. Ant, Special K, Bam Bam, Bear, El Gato, Scooter, Rocket and a seven-footer with the obligatory nickname Tiny go through an elaborate five-man weave, a braid of beauty, before forming their ritual Magic Circle. As they show off their ball handling sorcery at midcourt, the air is pierced by the familiar strains of . . . Madonna's "4 Minutes"?

This is how it goes for the Globetrotters in 2009 A.D. So long, "Sweet Georgia Brown"; hello, hip-hop.

You remember the Globetrotters, right? Two or three decades ago they were among the hottest touring acts going, a troupe that not only filled the biggest arenas but also island-hopped with Gilligan, joked with

Johnny Carson, showboated on *Sesame Street* and endorsed McDonald's. They had their own Saturday morning cartoon and, if you missed that, they often appeared later in the day on ABC's *Wide World of Sports.* "Man," recalls Curly Neal, the sixty-seven-year-old former Globies star who's now an advance publicity man for the team, "we were everywhere."

The Globetrotters never picked up their dribble, so to speak. But for a variety of reasons—the rise of the NBA; the decline in popularity of *Wide World of Sports;* the birth of And1 tours; and the availability on YouTube of countless monster dunks and crazy crossovers—the Globetrotters' brand started to collect some dust. The team flirted with bankruptcy in 1993 and a few years later made the tone-deaf decision to face college teams in competitive games, disappointing fans who had come for the slapstick and got matchup zones instead.

Now they're back, serially drubbing the Washington Generals on three tours simultaneously. As they barnstorm from Dubai to Dubuque, they're negotiating the challenge of contemporizing a classic brand, blending elements familiar and new. At a Trotters show you still get the ball-on-the-string gag, the buckets of confetti, the half-court hook shots and eventually "Sweet Georgia Brown." You'll also get references to Terrell Owens and the Wii, a cellphone routine and a chance to text your vote on whether the opposing coach should wear a tutu or a hot-dog costume if his team loses. It's all part of an act that a comedy writer has "punched up." The goal: Make sure the kids watching the Globetrotters today will want to take their kids to a game in the future.

It seems to be working. The myth that sports are recession-proof has eroded in the past few months, but the Globetrotters are thriving. *Sports Illustrated* boarded their bus last week, accompanied them for five games on the current Spinning the Globe tour and watched them play before sold-out crowds ranging from 2,000 to 12,000 fans. The Trotters, owned since 2005 by Shamrock Holdings, a private Burbank, Calif., investment fund, report that revenues are up eighteen percent from last year and record profits are expected in 2009. It helps that the average ticket price is twenty-five dollars, which barely covers parking at an NBA game. There's no violence or profanity. And the good guys always win. It's the sports equivalent of comfort food. "I say we work in the smile factory," says Kevin Daley, a.k.a. Special K. "And people need all the smiles they can get these days."

When the Harlem Globetrotters were founded in 1926, the players were neither Harlemites nor world travelers. The founder, Abe Saperstein, thought that *Harlem* connoted entertainment; the team actually was made up of the best African American players in Chicago. They played "real games," mostly in Illinois and the midwest, before eventually traveling around the country. During a 1939 game the Globetrotters were clinging to a 112–5 lead and began goofing around. The crowd ate it up. Before long the antics became their calling card and the Trotters gave new zest to the term *court jesters*.

There was also a subtle challenge to the status quo in the act. Here was a team of African Americans putting one over on the Man, the predominantly white opponents whose very name, the Washington Generals, implied establishment power. As Barack Obama put it during a documentary interview, "Whenever the Globetrotters came into town it was just a wonderful, fun-filled afternoon, but it had, I think, some deeper meaning to it."

Today, with an African American in the White House—and town houses in parts of Harlem going for $3 million—the cultural dynamic has changed. The Globetrotters' twenty-nine-man roster is entirely black or Hispanic, the Generals' an even mix of black and white. As such, a Globetrotters game feels less like sports-as-social-commentary than simply well-choreographed entertainment. Yes, the Trotters are exceptionally talented players, but to a man they are also performers, improv specialists with irrepressible personalities, smiles all but carved onto their faces.

Take Daley, a six-foot-five-inch slasher who played with Baron Davis at UCLA in the late nineties. He is a longtime member of the Panamanian national team and—talk about globetrotting—pinballed among pro teams in Costa Rica, Taiwan, Iceland, Australia and Turkey. He joined the Globetrotters in 2005 and has graduated to the role of Showman, tasked with controlling the performance. He's the closest approximation to Meadowlark Lemon that the Globies have today.

While Daley, thirty-two, grew up idolizing Michael Jordan—and played a twenty-three-year-old Jordan going one-on-one against the thirty-nine-year-old real thing in a memorable 2002 Gatorade commercial—he now includes Martin Lawrence and Chris Tucker among his inspirations. "To do this job, you have to love basketball, but you really have to love entertaining," he says. "If you're not outgoing or don't like interacting with people, you may as well not know how to dribble."

The other occupational requirement is a high threshold for travel. The current North American tour—on which two teams are wending their way through 210 cities while another unit tours Europe—began the day after Christmas and ends the last week in April. After that, half of the players, who can earn up to the mid-six figures depending on their experience, will get a few days off before going to Europe for a month.

On Friday night, March 13, the Globetrotters played in Hershey, PA. By the time they had wrapped up the standard thirty-minute postgame autograph session, showered and hopped aboard the bus, it was nearly 11:00 p.m. Slowed by an accident on the highway, the bus didn't roll into Washington, D.C., until 2:00 a.m. The players were up at eight for a shootaround and a game before a crowd of 12,350 at the Verizon Center that afternoon. (The team tends to play small venues during the week and large arenas on weekends.)

After the show there were no groupies outside, no Saturday night out at a D.C. club awaiting. The team reboarded the bus—a vessel painted bright blue with giant images of the players arrayed on the sides—and headed for Fairfax, VA, and a night game on George Mason's campus.

Each Globetrotter treats his row of seats like a private hotel room, icing his knees, catching some shut-eye or curling into a fetal position to use his iPhone. While the players started with basketball aspirations recalled by the ACC tournament games and March Madness discussion shows that played on an overhead TV, more TVs were tuned to Martin Lawrence videos.

"As a kid you might dream of playing [in the NBA], but . . . now I can't imagine playing anywhere else," says Anthony (Ant) Atkinson, a former Division II star at Barton College in Wilson, N.C. "You're making people happy, entertaining every night, maybe changing their outlook a little bit. You see the world, you see the kids and you get their e-mails, and you think, This is what I was meant to do."

✳

The Globetrotters travel in style compared with the Generals, a separate business entity, subcontracted to play the collective role of straight man. The Generals are still owned by eighty-eight-year-old Red Klotz, who retired as a player at age sixty-three and as coach twelve years later. They travel independently in a plain bus and stayed two to a room at the Comfort Inn in Towson, MD, while their opponents were in singles at the Sheraton. This mirrors a larger disparity between the two teams. Consisting mostly of former Division II and Division III players—capable ballers, but ultimately not threatening—the Generals insist the outcomes aren't fixed and that they play to win. Yet Washington hasn't done so since 1971. "We know our role," says Ammer Johnson, a longtime Generals player, once a starter at Idaho State. "Let's put it that way."

That means getting mocked, dunked on and, on occasion, divorced from their shorts. The Generals' coach, Reggie Harrison, is particularly game, an irascible sort who talks a lot of (sanitized) trash during games, flecks of spit flying from the corners of his mouth. He goes to great lengths to cheat and, of course, gets what's coming to him in the end.

If this resembles the pageantry of professional wrestling, it's no coincidence: The Globetrotters' CEO, Kurt Schneider, is a former WWE executive. When Schneider took over the Trotters in 2007, he replaced nearly half the roster with players possessing superior showbiz chops. And since good-guyness is so central to the Globetrotters' image, Schneider went so far as to hire a consultant to provide background checks on players before signing them to one-year deals.

One key to growth, he says, is minting stars, a new generation of Curlys and Meadowlarks with distinct personalities. "It used to be, A Globetrotter is a Globetrotter is a Globetrotter," he says. "But we want these guys to have identities." Schneider also claims that the Globies need to remain on the consumers' radar between appearances. To that end the team has a staff devoted to getting the Globetrotters back on TV shows and on lunch boxes, as well as on mobile applications and social networking sites.

On this Wednesday night in central Jersey, though, the game, the so-called "in-arena experience," was plenty captivating. The Globetrotters alternately entertained with their gags and their legerdemain. Shane (Scooter) Christensen, who was working as a video coordinator for the Phoenix Suns when he was discovered in a pickup game by a Globetrotters scout, put on a dribbling exhibition that included spinning a ball on his nose. Ant Atkinson hit an underhand shot from half-court. There were a few entertainment equivalents of air balls—playing the tired eighties' anthem "I Love Rock 'N' Roll" is probably not the best way to attract the younger set—but no one in the packed house of 2,450 asked for a refund.

In the end the Globetrotters prevailed 79–75, extending the winning streak against the Generals to 12,857 and bringing the Globetrotters lifetime record to 23,136–345. As the Washington coach donned a tutu, the Globetrotters remained on the court signing autographs. They could have stayed all night, but after half an hour, their shift at the smile factory was over. The team bus backed up to the loading dock, motor humming, ready to head off to the next night's show in Pittsfield.

Ethical Treatment for a Quarterback

Phil Taylor

Leo, a caramel-colored pit bull with soft brown eyes, greets every visitor to his new home in Los Gatos, CA, the same way—warmly and playfully, with a tail that won't stop wagging. If Michael Vick walked in, he would get the same welcome, even though Leo was one of the fifty-one dogs seized by authorities from Vick's infamous Bad Newz Kennels. "His reaction to Michael Vick today would be, Want to have fun? Will you pet me? Can I sniff you?" says Marthina McClay, Leo's new owner. "Canines don't look for revenge. They don't go on *Oprah* to talk about their rough childhood. They don't hold grudges."

Not so easy for some of us, is it? It's hard to think of Vick without being repulsed anew by the unspeakable cruelty of his dogfighting operation. The stories of drownings, of electrocutions, of savagery masquerading as sport are so sickening that it would be understandable to feel that his punishment should last forever—and in a sense, it will. Vick will live with that awful stain for the rest of his days. But his other sentence, the twenty-three months in prison at Leavenworth, KS, on dogfighting-related charges, is nearing its end. Vick has been cleared to move to home confinement in May, and if all goes as expected, he will be a free man and eligible for reinstatement to the NFL by July 20, right around the opening of training camps. It is anyone's guess as to whether commissioner Roger Goodell will allow his return to playing quarterback.

People for the Ethical Treatment of Animals (PETA) are looking for more than just the words of apology and remorse Vick has offered so far; he must prove that he is a changed man. The organization has urged Goodell to require that Vick submit to psychological testing before being reinstated, including a brain scan that purportedly will reveal whether he has psychopathic tendencies. "We don't think the NFL should just take him at his word," says PETA spokesman Dan Shannon. "We certainly don't. He has offered to do public service statements promoting the humane treatment of animals, and that would be great, but we would need to see some harder evidence from him that this is genuine." If Vick declines such testing or the results indicate that he could still be a danger to animals, would PETA picket any team that acquires him? "We haven't taken anything off the table at this point," says Shannon.

The accuracy of brain-scan techniques in spotting a psychopath is a debate unto itself, as is the question of whether it would be fair to deny Vick the chance to play based on the mere possibility of future misdeeds. Could it be that animal-rights activists and others horrified by Bad Newz simply begrudge him the luxuries of being a pro athlete, that they feel he doesn't deserve to be cheered for anything, ever again? "It's not like this guy's going back to laying brick," says Shannon. "For better or worse, young people look up to well-known athletes as models of behavior. So, yes, it's a little different from a guy who's returning to a nine-to-five job."

For an NFL organization just to bring Vick in for a workout, it will have to withstand not only the possible PETA protests but also the media maelstrom and the disgust of potential ticket buyers. The Falcons plan to trade Vick's rights; already the QB-needy Bucs, Lions and Jets have declared that they have no interest. Last week, a day after coach Mike Singletary said that the 49ers wouldn't completely rule out the possibility of acquiring Vick, the team closed that window with a statement that didn't include the term "ten-foot pole," but might as well have.

Such is the unforgiving climate Vick faces. He has been brought to his knees, stripped of his freedom and fortune, and as satisfying as it might feel for some to see him like that, he has been down for as long as the law requires. It's time to let him try to get back up. Vick's return to the NFL shouldn't require that we judge him to be fully redeemed; many of us never will. But we need to acknowledge that as with most other offenders who have fulfilled the terms of their punishment, he ought to be allowed to pursue his old career, if he's still qualified for it.

That's no small if: Vick will be twenty-nine years old by the start of next season, with two years away from football. He may have been erratic on the field, but given his physical skills when he left—in 2006 he threw for 2,474 yards and ran for 1,039—there surely must be one team willing to give him a set of pads and find out how much of his old talent remains.

Perhaps the real change in Vick will come when he finds that the creatures he once treated so cruelly, like Leo, are now far more accepting of him than are most humans. That's the sort of realization that can help a man who so clearly has anger issues. But then, he's not the only one who has them, is he?

Rita Dove

The Fire This Time*

Rita Dove

Disaster enthralls us. Aghast, we lean toward the diorama of the TV set to peer at the victims in their cursed worlds: rivers of silt and exploded debris, gathered into the camera's voracious caress. We shudder at the images—a silver Mercedes wrapped around a stone embankment in Paris, a smattering of sequins alongside a ripped airplane wing, the killing fields of Cambodia, Rwanda, Kosovo, the Twin Towers collapsing in clouds of deadly dust and smoke. We are both moved to compassion and repelled by the contemplation of such human misery, but we look nonetheless. In hushed tones we compare the prurient details of kidnappings or senseless accidents, war crimes, terrorist attacks or incidents of domestic terror, thinking: There but for the grace of God (or fate or chance or privilege) go I.

Accompanying each witnessing is speculation: How would I react if a tornado snatched my house into the sky? If a tsunami suddenly rose up and licked my village clean? If I were the housewife clutching my robe against the night chill as sirens descended on the wasps' nest of flames that

---

was once my home, what would I try to save? Would I try to run back in for the dog? Would I cry?

Ten years ago, these thoughts were as far from my mind as the mythical gardens of Babylon. A recent medical scare had preoccupied me for the better part of a year, but the latest test results were cause for cautious celebration. Having already survived one disaster, I let down my guard; surely lightning doesn't strike twice.

Or does it? Labor Day, 1998: My husband and I had just returned from Staunton, Virginia, one hour away, where we'd attended the opening reception of a friend's art exhibit at Mary Baldwin College, an occasion doubling as an excuse to see our daughter Aviva, who was starting her sophomore year there. By the time we had returned home it was getting dark; we shed our sticky clothes (in the South, the dog days of summer take on apocalyptic proportions), and had settled into air-conditioned bliss as a soft stuttering at the windows announced the first rain in weeks, hopefully the harbinger of the new season.

Where were you / when the lights went out / in New York City? So went the refrain of a popular song from the Seventies. Where were you when Kennedy was assassinated and Martin Luther King—then Malcolm, then Bobby, and what about Kent State? Where were you when the world changed forever?

I was in two places: in our bedroom, where *Star Trek: The Next Generation* was blasting away in full color; and across the hall in my study, pecking sporadically at a questionnaire my publisher hoped would provide stimulus for the upcoming publicity planned around my new poetry book. Whenever there was a commercial, I would scurry back to the computer to answer another marketing question: addresses of bookstores I frequented, names of newspapers and reviewers sympathetic to my work. Although it was hours before I planned to go to bed, I had changed straight from street clothes into my recent birthday present, a peach silk nightgown and robe, extravagantly printed with Gauguinesque fruit.

And then, the lights went out—with a bang so loud I couldn't think, the explosion so intense it seemed to happen inside me: All thoughts were blasted clear of my body, so that I felt only a mild wonder when I discovered, seconds later, that if I blinked my eyes I still saw nothing; although through the scattered sounds of beeping back-up systems, hard rain on the skylight, and the delayed tinkling of glass—glass?—I could hear, faintly, my husband's panicked shout.

The next sequence of events happened as if in a dream: Fred and I found each other in the hallway—he had been hurled across his room by the blast, hence the outcry—and went downstairs together in search of candles and flashlights; then, flashlights in hand, we hurried into the basement to shut off the main fuse box, thinking that lightning had struck nearby and caused an electrical surge that had blown his computer. (Who imagines actually being struck by lightning?) But when we returned to his study, the computer was running again on its backup battery. We stared at the glowing green "on" switch, then slowly fanned our flashlights across the room until the beams touched the V-shaped hole in the wall behind his desk—an opening extending up through the ceiling and into the attic. Through a scrim of smoke we could just make out scattered clouds along the southwestern horizon, while the nighttime sky in the northwest was an impenetrable black over the Blue Ridge Mountains, where the thunder was now in retreat. Baffled by the sight of sky where it shouldn't be—a deep gray drizzled with stars, framed by a zigzag gash— we stood silent, contemplating the pieces of a puzzle that refused to coalesce, though lightning's cartoon signature was scribbled all over it.

We were about to start back downstairs to grab a fire extinguisher— just in case—when the sound of something crackling took us into the hallway and guided our eyes up to a flickering rectangle of orange light rimming the trap door to the attic. Fire—with flames obviously beyond the range of a simple handheld extinguisher. Shocked into action, we raced to the garage; I called 911 from my cell phone while Fred, after a short panic trying to remember how to open the garage doors mechanically, drove the cars to the bottom of our driveway. The fire department responded within minutes, but since there were no hydrants in our countrified neighborhood—why hadn't we ever noticed?—and the firefighters' portable pumps weren't powerful enough to overcome the long steep distance from our pond, for the next several hours water had to be brought in by an endless chain of tankers from the high school, a mile up the road.

This was the moment I called Ground Zero, because everything from then on was a slow upwards climb: huddling at the foot of our driveway past midnight as rain continued to fall gently; our neighbors standing around too, trying to console us while the flames leapt, settled back to hopeful smoke, then flared up again in another spot, higher, leapfrogging from one air pocket to the next. The closets with all our clothes went off like Molotovs. Bulky in his asbestos suit and oxygen tank, a firefighter stood backlit against the flames consuming Fred's study, high up inside a large hole where the window had been, and tossed the burning antique mahogany desk out that hole so it shattered on the concrete walkway two stories below. A paramedic administered oxygen to another firefighter prostrate on the front lawn while neighbors shielded me from a reporter wandering among the clustered umbrellas. I watched for over an hour, imagining the progress of the fire inside the house while mentally bidding good-bye to our accumulated lives: the books on the hallway shelves, including Fred's first editions and my poetry collection; Aviva's baby clothes and stuffed animals and beloved Breyer horses; bedsheets and comforters, night table knickknacks, CDs, tourist T-shirts, prescription pills, my favorite purple bra. As each room was consumed by flames, I said to myself: *Okay, that's gone. I guess I can live without that.*

And when I realized that I was willing to let it all go—because the real Ground Zero, after all, would have been to stand alone at the bottom of that driveway with either Fred or our daughter still inside the burning house—another emotion began to push its way to the surface. It took me a while to find the right word for it. It was not *relief* but stranger, more unsettling, inappropriate. Gradually, it occurred to me: *Exhilaration.*

✳

Eventually I was led to a neighbor's house for the night. It seemed like everyone expected me to become hysterical and had girded themselves for support, moral and material; I was offered wine, cookies, bourbon. But all I wanted was a few books to get lost in and a computer—the computer because Fred had been working on a brief essay when the lightning knocked him across the room; I had looked through a draft of the piece only hours before and remembered fragmented passages, which I was anxious to put on disk. After reconstructing much of the essay on my neighbor's Mac (although I belonged to the PC universe, desperation made me a quick study), I placed the requisite calls to family voice mailboxes, took a bath, drank a glass of wine, and began reading a junk novel until I fell asleep. Fred came in around 8:00 a.m., a Tweedledee *cum* chimney sweep with his sooty face and borrowed clothes, bearing the astonishing news that the house had not entirely burned to the ground. I got out of bed and began to dress. Perhaps I could face this day after all.

✳

The facts: Over fifty firefighters—most of them from Albemarle County's volunteer companies—battled the blaze for six hours. By shooting tens of thousands of gallons of water into the flames, they were able to save some of the exterior structure, keeping damage to the first floor at bay until the original art works, photo albums, video archives and most of the furniture on that level had either been secured or carried outside. The attic had vanished; most of the second floor was decimated, and Fred's study had burned out totally. Along with his mahogany desk, all of his papers (unpublished manuscripts in handwriting and typescript, including 350 pages of an abandoned novel; piles of handwritten notations, ideas, revisions, etc., for another novel), the first editions of his own works as well as those books and magazines in which he had appeared over the years, were gone. Backup tapes, zip drives, keyboard and monitor had undergone meltdowns and vanished without a trace, and the blackened and twisted CPU that had been thrown out with the desk onto the walkway looked as if it had been fire-bombed. My computer and both our laptops were drenched in water. (Incredibly enough, after weeks of anxiety, a data retrieval service was able to recover nearly all important files from the hard drive that had been pried from Fred's computer wreck.)

Parts of my early literary and personal archive—drafts, correspondence—had been incinerated in the attic. Although many of the thousands of books in our upstairs hallway library, liberally doused by the firemen's hoses, seemed at first glance to have survived, most of them subsequently mildewed, warped, then fell apart. We also lost several valuable paintings and sculptures, innumerable mementos, our entire wardrobe, and all furniture and electronics on the second floor. The bedrooms were simply no more; our daughter's stuffed animals, dolls, CDs and video movies had disappeared or were badly damaged as well as favorite childhood books, photographs taken with celebrities (Aviva with Derek Walcott and Toni Morrison, Morgan Freeman and Robin Williams), the framed handwritten notes she had received from Bill Clinton and Al Gore that used to grace the wall above her desk.

✳

Every morning that first week, I woke up clutched by a vague terror, registering the unfamiliar surroundings—the plush bedclothes, sunlight filtered through somebody else's curtains, the shadows somehow different, wrong . . . and would remember. This was real; we were sleeping in a neighbor's bed because we had nowhere else to go, our house was no more. Then the survival mechanism would kick in: roll over, put your feet down on the floor, brush your teeth, shower.

We live in a neighborhood that, despite its four-acre lots, managed to maintain friendly and sometimes close relationships even after the children had grown up and a few of the properties changed hands. Before the first morning-after dawned, the neighbors had collected a bag of clothes to tide us over: shorts, T-shirts and tennis shoes, even a bra. For the rest of the week they came straight from work, forming a human chain through the muck and ashes to transport boxes of partly burned treasures outside, until night and the lack of electric power stopped them. Polly showed me how to find gemstones in the ashes on the ground directly beneath the spot in the second floor where the jewelry cabinet had stood; Ester and Richard called from their vacation home in Florida to offer the use of their house. Every evening a different neighbor delivered a full-course dinner to our borrowed doorstep, microwaveable so that we could eat whenever we decided to call it quits.

On the third morning a wrecking crane arrived and proceeded to rip off the last blackened rafters. Jagged beams toppled into the wreckage, puncturing books and manuscripts still buried there, before the director of the University of Virginia Library showed up in her crisp gray suit, stepping through the rubble yelling "Stop!" An argument with the insurance adjuster—he saw no value in retrieving "papers"—ensued; it was infinitely easier for him to order the mess bulldozed into a dump truck and get on with the rebuilding. The librarian, however, taught us how to read the topography of disaster: Where the piles of drywall and ash were greatest, there promised to lurk the sweetest treasures—collapsed walls and ceilings shielded anything they chanced to fall down on, as long as those things weren't prone to shatter. A rectangular chunk of charcoal could be a manuscript; all one had to do was carefully pry the charred layers apart to reveal the pristine center of a page, a glistening oval as astonishing and legible as a carefully framed daguerreotype.

We demanded to be allowed to keep on sorting through the debris; the salvage workers, who had found out we were writers, declared themselves willing to continue the demolition by hand. A team of people from the university library arrived to help sort and pack some sixty boxes of partially burned and waterlogged material (books, letters, manuscripts), which, to arrest further deterioration, were taken to and frozen in a commercial meat locker and then shipped via freezer truck to a freeze-drying facility in upstate New York.

How often have we seen photographs of survivors picking through the ruins of their lives? *How sad,* we say, *how devastating.* I learned that there can be jubilation in the scavenging, because when you are the one struck down—when it's *your* charred and sodden possessions buried under rubble—what you are looking at is not disaster, but recovery. Fred and I spent nine days combing through the debris, searching for anything that might have survived the conflagration. Each discovery—a brass Christmas tree ornament, a clutch of old Polaroids unscathed beneath a massive chunk of drywall—was like stumbling upon a miracle, a nugget of memory as precious as any diamond. Curiously, I never thought long about the writing I had lost—what inspirations had burned up in old notebooks, which fountain-penned entries had washed away. Besides, time was of the essence: mildew was brewing, the dump truck was waiting. So we kept on poking, sifting, hunting, recovering.

✳

The smallest things: a bar of perfumed turquoise soap, gift from my German mother-in-law, still glistening in its shrink-wrapping. A plastic model of the Goodyear blimp, buried under a foot of wet ashes around my desk. The shelves of Breyer horses in our daughter's room, which miraculously had survived, protected behind the door we kept open to pretend she was still there instead of in a dorm room an hour away, studying genetics while indulging her retro love for the Eurythmics.

On the other side of the equation, however, there were little losses that conspired to break me: one charred paw and half a furred chest of Rocky Raccoon, the stuffed animal we had bought to celebrate the news of my pregnancy, sixteen years before, who went with us to the hospital to oversee thirty-six hours of labor, tears and laughter. One pearl earring. The jungle green brilliance of my favorite summer dress, reduced to a scrap of chewed cloth protruding from a tangled lump of wire, melted hangers and carbonized fabric.

And then there were the things no longer in this world, objects that had vaporized inside the magician's black hat appeared in dreams or popped up unbidden in those moments when the conscious mind slips into the cracks of distressed memory: a writing notebook, black with red corners, left on the bed when the lightning struck, the lines of that nascent poem forever erased. The huge Plexiglas case that housed one of our most ephemeral pieces of art, blue brushstrokes on muslin, the Polish artist Ewa Kuryluk's tribute to Hurricane Hugo. How could so much Plexiglas simply disappear? For that matter, how could an entire Xerox machine vanish without a trace? Or the large computer monitor we had seen lit by backup power in those last few moments before we realized that nothing would be the same again?

But there were also stunning survivals: a copy of Strindberg's *Dream Play,* found on the floor where the bedside table used to be, next to where the bed once stood. Two notebooks plucked intact from the attic's inferno, comprising a faithful record of my dreams during my Fulbright scholarship in Germany a quarter century earlier, complete with color illustrations. These were moments of translucent peace: sitting down together on a pile of shredded drywall where Fred's study had been (the outer walls entirely gone, a huge plastic sheet replacing the ceiling) to decipher a scrap of a letter written to Fred during my last semester of graduate school, chuckling as the sun beat down on the plastic overhead, heating us up like orchids. The delicious sensation of stepping into the shower at the end of the day and watching the gray water swirl down the drain. Applying makeup for the first time in a week.

Both Fred and I are proverbial packrats. Theater ticket stubs, banquet menus, restaurant matchbooks—such items are *de rigueur* when packing the return bags after a summer vacation or business trip. Add to this sentimental list literary memorabilia such as publicity brochures, reading announcements, posters, and bookmarks, and the clutter rapidly becomes unmanageable. A grand portion of that noteworthy detritus had suddenly disappeared, and we did not miss it. Even the thought of first drafts and early jottings, old letters and mimeographs I had gathered and sorted in anticipation of a major university's interest in acquiring my papers (some of which I had neatly boxed up and stored in the attic just that summer) failed to bring me to tears; after all, like an explorer, a writer is most intrigued by the unknown territory up ahead, that next line or phrase or entire book.

✳

Reactions of acquaintances tended to fall into rather diverse categories: Spontaneous Sympathy, Horrified Babbling, Denial/Revulsion, and what

I would call Creative Rapacity. Sympathy was easiest to deal with, and
Babbling was simply a more psychosomatic manifestation of commisera-
tion; a few reassuring remarks would becalm the recipient of such bad tid-
ings, for the burden of consolation often falls upon the shoulders of the
victim: Yes *of course* it was horrible, but *at least* we're alive; well, and the
photo albums were saved; hey, now we have an excuse to go shopping!
The third reaction, Denial/Revulsion, was one of the oddest, not infre-
quently erupting from the ranks of literati—lovers of literature who simply could not stomach the image of so many mildewed and incinerated
books. Upon hearing of our predicament, colleagues at the National
Book Awards ceremony in New York in November of that year (my first
"professional" appearance after the fire—I'd served as a juror) would either quickly change the subject, or make an awkward joke and *then*
change the subject. One sensitive soul actually backed away, shaking his
head as he muttered, "I'm sorry. I just can't bear the thought." He kept his
distance the rest of the evening.

But the most confounding reaction belonged to the fourth category,
cropping up with a regularity I found as mind-boggling as the bad taste it
revealed. First came a dollop of sympathy, followed by wistful musing: "I
can't wait to see what poems will come out of this." My god, didn't they
realize that poetry was the last thing on my mind? Even Fred, who had
lost so much more of his work than I, didn't mention writing for a long
time. At first we thought we were simply numbed by the enormity of the
ordeal, but for as long as a year afterwards our emphasis lay with the practical aspects of rebuilding a normal existence so that we could get back to
work rather than pillaging our emotional salvage for creative material.
Of course, eventually we expected the fire to do *something* to our writing,
just as it had altered our perspectives, but living was and remained more
important. Besides, we'd been lucky—neither of us lost a nearly
completed book, like Ralph Ellison's *Juneteenth*, or like Maxine Hong
Kingston during the 1994 Oakland fires. Our most acute privation was of
Time. I was scheduled to be on leave from the university for the fall semester, free from teaching, advising and committees for the last four
months of the year—a precious chunk of freedom I had guarded jeal-
ously, refusing all lecture invitations that would have fallen during that
period so that I might only write, write, write.

All in all, we managed to achieve a version of normalcy fairly quickly.
After the first week in Richard and Ester's house, we moved into a residence hotel; another couple of weeks later we "settled" into a lovely older

furnished home near the UVA campus, property of a retired engineer and his wife who lived in Yorktown and occasionally rented their second home in Charlottesville to visiting faculty. Chris and Faith proved to be the nicest and most accommodating landlords anyone could hope for, rearranging furniture to convert two of the bedrooms into offices, introducing us to our new neighbors and arranging for lawn service.

Fred's new study rapidly turned into the crisis center for the rebuilding effort: a mess of blueprints, tile samples, and brochures transformed the formerly Victorian bedroom into a mole's lair. Fighting the frustrations and reversals of construction became Fred's mission—the madness of contractor deadlines missed again and again and again, supplier promises broken over and over as a matter of course. I developed a method of non-listening whenever Fred launched into explanations of electrical routings, the comparable merits of different security systems, or the geometric configurations of roof trusses. For the next nine months, he went by our house at least once a day, whereas I avoided site visits, unable to bear looking at what to me appeared to be a flimsy matchstick framework—how was that supposed to support a dwelling?

In an attempt to forge ahead, I duly adorned my own study with new lamps, sofa, file cabinets and photos, but it was difficult to work there—not because the environment was strange (after all, I'd written a novel, a play and my first two books of poetry in rental properties), but because I not only knew it was temporary, I knew what awaited me on the other end of this interim. I was in physical and emotional limbo, and no matter how I tried to apply the seat of my pants to the seat of the chair, my creative engine idled, waiting obediently for the green light that would set it loose again. The few poems I wrote were either fables based on Adam and Eve (transparent, yes: Paradise lost and the burden of starting over) or verses relentlessly grounded in the present—an ode to my old desk, waterlogged and buried in rubble, a description of the fox-trot I was just learning in dance classes. Instead of writing myself, I taught my creative writing seminars and read the books given to me by colleagues or that arrived, unrequested, in the mail, for I couldn't imagine building up a new library until I was able to arrange my selections on my own bookshelves.

Yet to the outside world I might have seemed quite prolific. All autumn I proofed galleys and discussed jacket copy for my new book, *On the Bus with Rosa Parks*, but it was a ghostly activity, as if those poems had been written in another time and country. By April, during the customary author's book tour, I felt more and more like an amnesia victim with each appearance, reading the story of a life I could not remember.

I poured my nervous energy more and more into dance. Not the Saturday-night-lights-are-low-and-the-music's-blasting type of dancing, but *ballroom*—tango, waltz, fox-trot, quickstep, cha-cha, rumba, bolero, mambo, swing, salsa. As long as I was out on the dance floor, I didn't have time to think. As long as I could count beats and practice Cuban hip motion until the perspiration dripped, I felt alive and happy in the here and now. (My husband, bless him, went along with this mania. Ninety minutes of group instruction, five nights a week, plus private lessons. Sometimes we went back to the dance studio at 1:00 or 2:00 a.m. to review steps, since the proprietors had entrusted us with a key.) When our daughter came home for Christmas vacation, she started ballroom dancing, too. Even now, whenever we're in an elevator or at the supermarket, any one of us might blurt out at the opening strains of some Muzak: "Mambo." "Slow Rumba." "Another Fox-trot!"

✳

Late August 1999; another Labor Day was approaching. We had just returned from six weeks in Europe, ready to move back into the rebuilt house. (All year long I'd stumbled over differentiating between the house we'd rented while rebuilding and our actual home. "The old house" sounded as if we had given up on it as a residence; "the burned house" was too flamboyant, or desperate, or both; "our house" was too precious. Finally, as the time for reentry loomed, I settled on The House.)

The House was empty save for the boxes stacked in closets and piled in the center of two rooms upstairs. Late afternoon sunlight cut through, serene: a pale yellow balm. I had forgotten, but now it was coming back. This is why I always loved this house—the banks of windows, the views of the Blue Ridge and the row of Leyland cypresses and the pond below choked with algae—but most of all the light, this lemony benediction. Standing in the upstairs hallway, I could barely remember the ashes and rubble, chunks of drywall shoveled into corners, charred rafters jutting out at all angles, the baleful blue of the sky unfurled like a fluorescent tarp above the muck. Now that I was back, even the six weeks in Europe seemed a bit like a dream—a sojourn fraught with mosquitoes, traffic jams and the occasional wistful lane in a remote village.

Tomorrow the movers would back up the driveway, and the furniture salvaged from the first floor would be returned to our lives. The past would brush us with its iridescent feathers; inevitably, fresh clutter would slowly accumulate. But this day, The House was ours alone. The light was sweet, and birds had repopulated the trees. We sat down on the bedroom floor and listened, charmed, to the familiar sounds around us.

On Rita Dove*

Erika Meitner

In the beginning, her fingernails were enough to convince me that she was cool. With Rita, as with every time we started a semester with a new teacher, our graduate writing workshop examined her with exceptional scrutiny, although we weren't exactly sure what we were looking for. We all knew the quirky things about Rita that we had scavenged from interviews on her Web page—that she wrote from three to six in the morning, that her father had been a chemist, that she wrote standing up at a long-legged desk. But we had real questions: How would she handle X's impenetrable language poetry, Y's ecstatic religious verse, and Z's misogynist statue poems? Would she call us on our bullshit? Would she actually *read* our poems before workshop? Would she notice who was sleeping with whom and who had gone off his antidepressants? Rita's nails spoke volumes about her workshop street cred; they looked like Keith Haring and Paul Klee had gone on a bender, and then given her a manicure. Each nail was carefully filed into a long oval, and painted dif-

*Erika Meitner, "On Rita Dove," *Women Poets on Mentorship*, ed. Arielle Greenberg and Rachel Zucker (Iowa City: University of Iowa Press, 2008) 111–117. Reprinted by permission of the University of Iowa Press.

ferently than the one next to it, in a riot of color and abstract detail—
swirls and triangles, stripes and dots in metallic hot rod blue, gobstopper
pink, rubber duck yellow, and tulip red. These were not grown-up nails.
I kept expecting to hear carousel music with a Brazilian backbeat every
time Rita waved her hands during that first class meeting.

In 1999, I was living in Brooklyn and teaching English at a public middle school, where most of my students were illiterate and borderline violent. It was then that it first dawned on me that I wanted to go back to
school for an MFA in poetry. I was burned out from yelling for five hours
a day and growing increasingly sure that getting Julio to stop kicking
Maritza during third-period Language Arts was probably not the best use
of my talent. I had done my undergraduate work in creative writing and
English literature at Dartmouth College, and when I consulted my undergraduate mentor, Cleopatra Mathis, about my MFA plans, she advised
me wisely in her thick Louisiana drawl to avoid going into debt for a
graduate degree in poetry writing. She recommended three schools that
had generous funding for their writing students, including the University
of Virginia, which ended up accepting me in late spring of that year because the girl ahead of me on the wait list was hiking through Honduras
and couldn't be reached by phone.

I didn't know much about Virginia except that, according to the
bumper stickers, it was apparently for lovers. I knew even less about the
writing program at the university other than the names of the poets who
taught there: Charles Wright, Greg Orr, Rita Dove. In retrospect, it was
probably shameful that I didn't try to find out as much as possible about
who would be guiding me through the next step of my writing future, but
I was so distraught about leaving my hip New York neighborhood for a
place I imagined to be filled with strip malls and humidity that I didn't
have much energy left to ponder the academic part of the scenario.

Rita Dove was the most familiar member of the faculty to me only because I distinctly remembered her from my dog-eared copy of *Contemporary American Poetry*, an updated, fifth edition of the 1971 anthology
edited by A. Poulin, Jr., that included photos of its poets. Rita was sand-
wiched between a terrifying picture of James Dickey, who looks as if he
is growling, and a forlorn shot of Alan Dugan. Of the fifty-five poets in
the book, Rita was one of thirteen women and the only writer to use the
word "vagina" in a poem, which was why her work caught my eye in the
first place. I spent a vast portion of my undergraduate writing career getting flak from my classmates for writing poems that included heavy help-

ings of both sex and genitalia. My work in college, and for a long time afterward, was (and often still is) obsessed with the pleasures and dangers of women's bodies. Rita's poem "After Reading *Mickey in the Night Kitchen* for the Third Time Before Bed" had the bravest and most glorious opening I had ever read: "My daughter spreads her legs / to find her vagina."

After being surrounded by a close-knit community of friends in Brooklyn, the transition to graduate school and the move to a very small town was rough. In New York I went out almost every night and interacted with people constantly during the day in my various career incarnations as corporate computer consultant, teacher, documentary film production assistant, and office temp. When I started at UVA, I lived in an anonymous condo development where I spent so much time alone in my apartment that, some weeks, the only person I spoke to outside of writing workshop was the cashier at the grocery store. I was so homesick for New York that I started to watch television—I hadn't even owned a TV for the six years before grad school—and became addicted to any show that included glimpses of the city: Hot dog carts on *NYPD Blue*! Firefighters with Queens accents on *Third Watch*! A Lower East Side Dumpster on *Law & Order SVU*! I developed raging insomnia and an inexplicable fear of getting lost around Charlottesville while driving. Just the trip to the CVS for toothpaste became a major accomplishment. By spring semester of my first year, I had almost gotten used to the crushing isolation of my new life and the pressure of the fact that my entire sense of self-esteem depended on what everyone thought of my latest workshop poem. I didn't begin to feel a real sense of community at UVA until workshop with Rita kicked into high gear.

Before we started working with her I had asked my friend Kevin, a second-year, what workshop with Rita was like. He told me, with a tinge of awe in his voice, that if you went to see her during office hours about your poem, days before it was going to be workshopped, she could refer to parts of it off the top of her head. She not only read our work but read it repeatedly, and she gave each student at least a half-page of typed comments for each poem handed in. The idea was wonderful but also intimidating—what if she spent more time reading and commenting on one of my poems than I had actually spent writing it? Guilt inspired me to work harder than I ever had. I wanted my poems to be Rita-worthy.

Rita had all the MFA students over to her house for workshop each week, where she'd seat us at her dining room table and ply us with hot taquitos and colas called Dr. Thunder and Southern Lightning, which she got, she told us, because the names sounded poetic. Her generosity was infectious, and soon we all began trying to out-snack each other every week with ethnic dishes, fresh-plucked fruit, home pickling projects, and elaborate baked goods. Rita's home, for me, became a haven, a sanctuary where we were cared for and fed and where we pushed each other artistically.

At the start of the spring that Rita was my workshop instructor, a very famous male poet came to UVA to be our visiting writer, a weeklong position wherein he was meant to read our poems, mentor us, and offer different insight into our work than our regular instructor might. Our particular poet was quite old and seemed alternately to be either very drunk or trembling uncontrollably from lack of alcohol. When it came time for my one-on-one meeting with him, we sat in an empty office, and he picked up the stapled packet of ten poems I had submitted to him months before. He flipped through the pages. I wondered if he had even read them. He cleared his throat. "None of these are really worth discussing," he said. "So, how would you like to use our time together today?" I was stunned. I stutteringly asked him if there were any he thought might be salvageable; he relented and offered pointers on one of the ten. Later, I relayed the experience to Rita during her office hours, trying hard not to cry. "I am so sorry that happened," she said quietly. She didn't bad-mouth the poet, she didn't act outraged. She asked me a simple question: "Is his project your project?" I thought about the trite, absurdist, novelty verse he had read the evening before. His project was definitely not my project. My poems tended to be rambling narratives that tackled subjects people shy away from: the detritus of the urban industrial landscape, birth control accidents, awkward one-night stands. After spending the year writing and simultaneously worrying obsessively about what my workshop would think about my poems, I felt loosed, as if someone had cut my strings. Whatever my project was, I suddenly realized, not everyone had to like it.

Halfway through spring semester, Rita handed me a sealed manila envelope—one of her famous "wild card" assignments. This was a personalized instruction pack that she presented to each of her students sometime around midterm, which involved writing a poem as a result of strange and very specific directives. The assignment was mandatory and meant to actively push us out of our comfort zones. It had to be turned in to Rita at a particular time, in a sealed envelope. My friend Jen had al-

ready warned me that hers involved crafting a poem as if it were a series
of notes dropped on the way to her grave. Kevin's mission was to bring a
purple object and an orange object outside to write about them. I felt like
a CIA operative when I opened my packet, which instructed me to wait
until the darkest and creepiest hour of the night, free-write a paragraph
on my computer without stopping, print it out, cut it up the middle verti-
cally with scissors, and put it in a drawer for one full day. When I took it
out of the drawer, I had to pick a half and form it into a poem without
adding any words to the chosen half. She said it was meant to break me
out of the narrative style I had been working in both before and since I
had come to UVA. She laughed when she finally looked at the poem that
I had made from my half-page. I had somehow still managed to form the
disparate fragments into a narrative.

During the silent moments of our workshops, Rita's new house would
creak in its joints, moan, and settle into its foundation. Her old house had
burned to the ground the year before when it was struck by lightning. She
wrote in a poem "House Fire" that "the unspeakable moved through me
like a pageant / . . . despair holding me up like a torch." But rather than
falling into inconsolable paralysis over the loss of her house and manuscripts, Rita and her husband Fred took up ballroom dancing. The spirit
and details of their hobby infuse her most recent book, *American Smooth*.

Every time I've seen Rita over the past six years she's just undertaken
something new: target practice at the local shooting range, singing lessons, touring Australia in an RV. As I was finishing up my MFA in the
spring of 2001, I found out I had received a fellowship from the University of Wisconsin Institute for Creative Writing to teach and write in
Madison for the year. Once again, I had to pack up and move to an unfamiliar place. This time, inspired by Rita, I vowed to take up some sort of
new pastime. Madison was the epicenter of all things craft-related; I decided I would learn to throw pots and fantasized about gifting friends
with the symmetrical sake sets and smoothly styled bowls I would both
design and execute. While working with clay on a wheel was a fantastic
idea, my kinesthetic abilities and coordination generally top out somewhere between "flailing" and "spastic," especially when an activity involves using my hands and feet at the same time. Mark, my bearded,
gnomelike pottery instructor, turned out lovely vases and platters. I
struggled for five weeks just to center my slimy hump of clay on the
wheel. I hadn't truly sucked at an activity since archery at camp in 1987. I
had forgotten the feeling of frustration and disappointment that left me

near tears each time I went home from the pottery studio caked in stiff gray clay.

I was also a poetry instructor that year. I had taught beginning poetry writing at UVA, but at the University of Wisconsin I was assigned the intermediate poetry students. My Virginia students had needed instruction in the basics: imagery, metaphor, line breaks, punctuation. For the most part they weren't yet at the phase of breaking out of writing ruts; the strongest of them were just beginning to develop a distinctive personal style in their work. At Wisconsin, for the first time, I struggled to help my students find and hone their individual voices while simultaneously trying to challenge them to move in new directions. It was tempting to avoid pushing them to change their writing: as in my beginning pottery classes, there was more of a chance that their work would be awful during the transitions.

I was grappling with this issue in my own poems, too. Narrative had come easily to me when I was out in the world sleeping with near-strangers, working weird jobs, and generally collecting experiences that might later be processed into poems. After three years of being ensconced in academia and solitude, my work became more internal. My stories of inner-city school kids and bodega dwellers dried up. One of my closest friends committed suicide, and suddenly the chaos of my world was less easily arranged into stories with redemptive endings, or with any endings at all. I tried to write lyric poems—tried to crack myself out of narrative, as Rita had attempted to get me to do the year before—and for that entire long year failed miserably. My Wisconsin work was nonsensical and disjointed, and it lacked music. I didn't know how to go about making poems that hung together without a plotline; I never knew when these new pieces were finished; I couldn't figure out how to work the turns. Rita always told me you had to write the bad poems to get to the good ones. Her philosophy was that the pieces that didn't work were absolutely necessary in ultimately producing the poems that did. So I wrote more bad poems. And every time I pondered giving up on a student, considered taking the path of least resistance and simply praising her work to avoid the hard job of opening her to the new, I channeled Rita. I pretended that I was infinitely patient, wise, and generous with my time. I sent my most difficult poems on field trips to the organic farm or the bowling alley, asked the reductive students to listen to Allen Ginsberg and the expansive one to read Robert Creeley, tricked the absurdist kid into writing something sincere, and assigned the freestyle rappers sonnets.

When people write about their poetic mentors, they often focus on how their work influenced them. As a Pulitzer Prize winner and former U.S. poet laureate, Rita has a formidable body of work. Her poems have wide-ranging styles, often give voice to the voiceless, and manage to imbue personal experiences with a larger sense of history and culture. I've absorbed many lessons from her work, but Rita was a mentor to me in a different way. She taught me that writing and living are the same thing. In order to write, she said, you have to learn how to truly inhabit and push against the world rather than move through it as an afterthought. Poetry isn't something that happens in a vacuum. If you are shuttered to all the work has to offer, your work will be narrow, uninteresting, and lacking a crucial spark. You have to pick yourself up and dance when your house burns, respect your self, and seek out new experiences. Rita reminds me of the quotation I scrawled in a journal once in college, from the Buddhist teacher Chogyam Trungpa: "We must continue to open in the face of tremendous opposition. No one is encouraging us to open and still we must peel away the layers of the heart."

Often when I'm sitting in a conference hotel room in a humorless business suit for an academic job interview, in the hopes of landing a gig teaching poetry, I think of Rita's nails. She never lets society dictate who she is, what she should look like, what her schedule should be, how she writes, or what she writes about. She gives me the courage to wear red stilettos with my suit slacks, to be uncompromising in my interview answers about my projects, to read poems with the word "fuck" in them at job talks, and to feel unapologetic when groggily answering the phone at noon after a night of writing. Most important, she taught me to be relentless in my pursuit of something I've since termed "the delta factor." We each have in us the infinite possibility and capacity for change. We must change to stay alive as artists and as writers.

African American Literature

———————— ✳ ————————

Chester Himes:
Exile & 125th Street

Michael A. Gonzales

Eleven years ago, dreadlocked and recently divorced writer Darius James quietly stacked boxes in a rusty garden shed in the backyard of his father's house in New Haven, Connecticut.

A few days before he was due to leave the country for Berlin, the Black bizarro author of 1993's *Negrophobia* (a cult classic that author Dennis Cooper once called "one of the most extraordinary and undervalued novels to come out of the East Village scene") was sifting through thirty years of stuff. Indeed, the then forty-two-year-old was ready to jet away for his own ex parte experience.

Certainly, the perceived romance of dwelling in Europe had always held a certain allure for folks of color. Be them stories of Negro war vets, diva Josephine Baker, jazz musician Sidney Bechet, painter Beauford Delany, artist Lois Mailou Jones, nightclub owner Bricktop or lit-genius Richard Wright, the mythology of being "on the other side of the ocean" was one that I too had once embraced.

In author Tyler Stovall's splendid *Paris Noir: African-Americans in the City of Light* (1996), he points out: "Both French officials and ordinary citizens often reacted with surprise and dismay to the bigoted attitudes of white Americans. Many simply could not understand why Americans would treat their fellow countrymen so poorly."

However, on that spring afternoon in 1997 as I helped Darius move countless cartons, I was pleasantly startled when I stumbled across a box that contained a collection of Chester Himes' pulp fiction reprints from the seventies.

"It's a shame how they treated my man Himes," I said, gazing at the gaudy covers of *The Crazy Kill*, *The Big Gold Dream* and *Cotton Comes to Harlem*, the latter of which had been adapted into an MGM blaxploitation flick (1970) directed by famed actor Ossie Davis.

Ever since I first started collecting Himes' brilliant Harlem detective series (there were eight in total, including the incomplete *Plan B*, published posthumously in 1984) in the mid-eighties, the late Ohio native had become a lit-hero in my personal canon.

"What do you mean?" Darius asked.

"Hell, you would never have seen covers like this on *Invisible Man*. No dis to Ralph Ellison, James Baldwin or Richard Wright, but if you ask me, Chester Himes was always the better writer."

"And don't think he didn't know it either," Darius laughed.

※

Twenty years after becoming my personal patron saint of dark alleyways and damaged souls, the textual webs that Himes weaved into his fictional landscapes has inspired a generation of bleak storytellers that includes television writers Tom Fontana and George Pelecanos, comic book creators Frank Miller and Howard Chaykin and novelists Gary Phillips and Charlotte Carter.

Hell, even cultural critic and director Nelson George once suggested in his *Village Voice* essay "Hyper as a Heart Attack" that the cryptic rhythms and brutal beats heard in the music of Eric B. & Rakim would be the ideal soundtrack for Chester Himes' crime series.

With narratives filled to the brim with crazed street gangs, pistol whippings, runaway cars, shifty soul sisters, crooked ministers and sightless shooters, Himes' Harlem (which he had completely re-imagined in Paris) was a wild ride through the surrealism of his psyche and the racism of his reality.

Perhaps my favorite fictional accounts of life above 110th Street,

Chester's fiction gave the term "black comedy" a completely different meaning. Like his friend Pablo Picasso, brother Himes simply had a different way of observing the world.

"The humor in my stories is the dark humor of the ghetto," Himes said in a 1970 radio interview.

Treated as a visionary writer in Europe, who had no problem mixing brutal street poetics with urbane existentialism, Himes stated to journalist Helmut M. Braem, "I got an opportunity to make a living in Paris, using Harlem as a locale for some detective novels. I just did it to make a living, but ultimately realized that my work had become a kind of classic in the field."

Indeed, the work of this moody yet handsome lady-killer (in the symbolic sense) has always stood tall next to criminal-minded contemporaries David Goodis and Jim Thompson as one of the most hard-boiled storytellers of his generation. By embracing the *Black Mask* magazine template that had been perfected by his crime-lit muse Dashiell Hammett ("*he placed his stories against a stark background; peopled them with men and women who seemed truly to sweat, bleed and ache; and made the pursuit of justice a noble as well a necessary goal*"), Himes figuratively spiked his prose with a hit of cocaine and a Count Basie soundtrack.

"I would say that Chester was more significant to France than Miles Davis," says French-born novelist and translator Thierry Marignac. "We took pride in the fact that Himes lived in France, that it was a French editor (Marcel Duhamel) who had given him his first real chance to be a writer of significance. Chester Himes and Iggy and the Stooges were, to our drugged minds, the real definitions of Frog taste."

Despite the lean boldness of Himes' Harlem novels (as opposed to the sometimes overwrought James Baldwin texts written about the same locale), the writer is still treated less seriously in literary discussions than either big-daddy Richard Wright or relative newcomer Colson Whitehead.

As biographer James Sallis (who himself is also a first-rate crime novelist) pointed out in *Chester Himes: A Life* (2000), the author still remains, "one of America's most neglected and misunderstood major writers."

✳

In our age of ghetto-lit novelists writing about their misadventures in the butt-naked city of "da hood" and prison, Chester Himes' early life has the concrete jungle boogie of a narrative in a Terri Woods or Relentless

Aaron book. Nevertheless, unlike the current crop of "hip-hop" novelists, Himes wrote passionately about the inner city, but he wasn't raised ghetto.

Born into a bourgeois, yet highly dysfunctional family of educators, Chester had been through so much Gothic shit one would have sworn that some witch had put a mojo on him from birth. His ordeals with his parents' hatred for each other as well as blaming himself for an accident that blinded his brother, always stayed with him.

Though he enrolled in Ohio State University in 1926 to study medicine, Chester spent more time prowling the streets than studying. Hanging out with "Cleveland's gamblers, hustlers and high rollers," he later ended-up in prison for an eight-year stretch for a jewel robbery charge.

Explaining his jail stint in his 1972 autobiography *The Quality of Hurt*, Himes wrote, "I found the convicts like idiot children, like the idiot giant in Steinbeck's *Of Mice and Men*, intensely grateful for small favors and incomprehensibly dangerous from small slights . . ."

Going behind bars at nineteen and coming out when he was twenty-six, it was while serving time that Himes decided to become a writer. Moreover, as the best writing teachers have always suggested, Himes wrote about the people that he knew best.

Influenced, as critic Robert Skinner later put it, by "men with violence deeply imbedded in them," he began submitting stories to *Abbott's Monthly* (founded by Robert Sengstacke Abbott, owner of the *Chicago Defender*) and the *Atlanta Daily Word* in 1933.

"There was nothing to do," Himes told *The New York Times* in 1969. "All you had to do was tell it like it is." Yet, it wasn't until *Esquire* editor Arnold Gingrich bought two of Himes' prison stories in 1934 ("Crazy in the Stir" and "To What Red Hell") that the incarcerated scribe finally felt like a real writer. "After that, until I was released in May 1936, I was published only in *Esquire*," Himes declared.

Contemporary mystery writer, teacher and editor Christopher Chambers (*The Darker Mask*) separates Himes' penitentiary writings from modern day prison scribes. "Unlike some jailhouse writers I could name, Chester never wrote characters that were caricatures," Chambers explained. "Most of these new-school ghetto writers are into depicting stereotypes, but Himes put so much complexity, angst and fear into his work, which is why his works are classic literature."

Having written two novels about FBI Agent Angela Bivens, including 2003's *A Prayer for Deliverance*, the D.C.-based writer continued: "When

I started writing, Chester was who I was trying to emulate. He had his finger on the pulse of damaged people just trying to survive in the world with nothing but hardness and humor."

Publishing two naturalist "protest" novels after his release, *If He Hollers Let Him Go* (1945) and *Lonely Crusade* (1947), it wasn't until a backlash over the politics of the latter tome ("Hate runs through this book like a streak of yellow bile," the *Atlantic Monthly* wrote) that Himes stopped writing for five years.

Following the death of his father in 1953, Himes decided to leave America by ship that April. A week later, Himes had finally arrived in France. In the interim, Chester wrote countless short stories and two more novels in a four-year span.

Still, it wasn't until 1957 when he met editor Marcel Duhamel, the director of Gallimard Press' detective line La Série Noire, that Himes was encouraged to write his first so-called police procedural.

Though at age forty-seven Himes was hardly a spring chick, he wrote with the fierce fearlessness of a man in his twenties. Fueled by Faulkner, rum, blues music, Dostoyevsky, beautiful women, café conversations with Wright and moonlit memories of various American ghettos, Himes embarked on a literary journey that equated pleasure and anger, laughter and sin into 220 typewritten pages originally called *The Five-Cornered Square*. The book title changed to *For Love of Imabelle* when it was released in America and later flipped again, this time to *A Rage in Harlem*.

Three months later, he turned in the manuscript and was already working on a follow-up called *The Real Cool Killers*.

In 1958, the Parisian government awarded Himes their highest literary award, the Grand Prix de Littérature Policière for his debut crime novel. It was the first time a non-French-speaking author had won the award.

Until his death from a stroke in the Orwellian year of 1984 while living in Spain, Chester Himes continued to change the game of literature while always playing by his own rules.

Racial Identity, Enslavement, and the Law

---- ✳ ----

Multiracialism and the Social Construction of Race: The Story of *Hudgins v. Wrights*

Angela Onwuachi-Willig

Introduction

In the case of *Hudgins v. Wrights*,[1] the Supreme Court of Appeals of Virginia[2] delivered an important lesson on the non-genetic nature of race—the manner in which race is socially determined by both physical and

---

[1] 11 Va. (1 Hen. & M.) 134 (Va. 1806).

[2] The Supreme Court of Appeals of Virginia, which served as a model for the United States Supreme Court, was created in 1779 as one of four superior courts in Virginia. Though initially judges never rendered written opinions, the Virginia Constitution was amended in 1851 to require judges to state, in writing, the reasons for their rulings. The name of the court was changed to its current title, the Supreme Court of Virginia, by the Virginia Constitution of 1970. *See* The Supreme Court of Virginia, History, http://www.courts.state.va/scov/cover.htm (last visited February 4, 2007).

non-physical proxies. *Hudgins* involved the legal battle of three women—a grandmother, a mother, and a granddaughter—who struggled to prove that they were free citizens, not slaves, by offering evidence to refute a white slaveowner's claim that they descended from an enslaved black woman instead of a free American Indian woman.[3]

The social context in which the *Hudgins* decision was issued is critical to understanding its impact and enduring lessons. Beginning in the late seventeenth century, disputes about the racial background of individual persons in Virginia became significant. Due to a rapidly growing system of bondage that presumptively marked all blacks as slaves, persons who could "earn" the racial label of white or American Indian in Virginia worked hard to capture one of those labels because such racial identities essentially placed them outside of a life of slavery and on the side of either freedom or indentured servitude. Thus, for Jacky, Maria, and Epsabar Wright, who, like others after them, were seeking to prove their freedom by disclaiming blackness, the determination of their racial identity was transformative in that it would signify either their independence or their enslavement.

Hudgins v. Wrights demonstrates the impact of a growing multiracial population on Virginia's racial classification laws in a society that required segregation to preserve slavery. Specifically, this story analyzes how *Hudgins* helped to establish a system of racial definitions that entrenched a black class of enslaved labor within the tobacco economy. The chapter begins with the emergence of the slave system in Virginia and details how definitions of race shifted with the growth of a mixed-race population that threatened the stability of segregation and slave labor. This account also illustrates how the small numbers of American Indians and their propensity to escape intensified the need to isolate blacks, who generally could be identified by the most commonly used proxy for race—skin color—in a system of long, hard enslavement. Thereafter, the chapter tells the story of *Hudgins v. Wrights* from trial through appeal, culminating in a finding that the Wrights were free women because they descended from an American Indian on their maternal side. As the litigation makes clear, the three women's fate was determined not just by their appearance, which complicated the task of categorizing them because of their mixed racial heritage, but also by their families' reputation and conduct within their communities. Finally, the chapter ends with a discussion

---

[3]*Hudgins*, 11 Va. (1 Hen. & M.) at 136–38.

of the contemporary significance of the *Hudgins* decision, highlighting an enduring societal belief in pure biological classifications of race even in the face of a growing multiracial population and a continued practice of identifying race based on both physical appearance and community perceptions.

Slavery and Freedom in Virginia

Hudgins was decided in 1806, a time when the determination of a person's race as black in Virginia was life-altering in a way that could establish bondage or freedom, and, in some cases, life or death. The burden of blackness in Virginia was not always so heavy. Although the first group of blacks arrived in Virginia in 1619,[4] the enslavement of blacks was not officially sanctioned by law until 1661.[5] Before then, although some blacks were unofficially enslaved by whites, it was not unusual to find blacks who toiled in Virginia's tobacco fields alongside whites as indentured servants.[6]

Changing mores and economic imperatives laid the foundation for the 1661 slave law. As a moral matter, many white Virginians viewed enslavement as an acceptable practice to inflict on blacks, whom they believed to be inferior heathens.[7] When the law was passed, the black population in the colony had grown to approximately 950 residents, making blacks three to four percent of the state's population—a fairly large increase from the small population of only twenty-three blacks in 1625.[8]

---

[4] Robert S. Cope, *Carry Me Back: Slavery and Servitude in Seventeenth Century Virginia* 5–6, 11 (1973).

[5] *Id.* at 11; *see also* Betty Wood, *Slavery in Colonial America 1619–1776*, at 8 (2005) (noting that blacks had not immediately been enslaved by the English and that "their legal status remained somewhat ambiguous until the late seventeenth century"); Adele Hast, *The Legal Status of the Negro in Virginia 1705–1765*, 54 J. Negro Hist. 217, 218 (1969) ("The first Negroes brought into Virginia in 1619 were probably considered similar to indentured white servants."). *But see Hudgins*, 11 Va. (1 Hen. & M.) at 137 ("From the first settlement of the colony of *Virginia* to the year 1778, . . . all *negroes*, *Moors*, and *mulattoes*, except *Turks* and *Moors* in amity with *Great Britain*, brought into this country by sea, or by land, were SLAVES."). Two other states had legally sanctioned slavery before Virginia—Massachusetts in 1641 and Connecticut in 1650. *See* Cope, *supra* note 4, at 11.

[6] *See* Cope, *supra* note 4, at 11.

[7] *See id.* at 9 ("Since the English commonly associated the color black with sin, it was all too easy to arrive at the conclusion that God had decreed perpetual bondage as part of Africans' punishment."); Hast, *supra* note 5, at 219 ("In its early years in Virginia, slavery was justified as permissible with heathen people.").

[8] *See* Wood, *supra* note 5, at 8.

In the eyes of many white Virginians, blacks had become a readily available and plentiful pool of labor. More importantly, as a social and financial matter, white Virginians viewed slavery as economically rational and necessary. To their minds, white indentured servants were too costly in an agricultural economy because of social customs that required payment for their work with wages and future land grants. American Indians were too impractical due to their susceptibility to disease and their familiarity with the land, which made it easy for them to escape from their masters.[9] Indeed, in 1661—the same year in which the enslavement of blacks officially became legal—the Virginia Assembly passed a statute that prohibited the sale of American Indians as slaves and permitted American Indians to be used only as indentured servants for no "longer time than English of the like ages should serve by act of assembly."[10]

Under this system of legalized slavery, blackness became a life-changing status in the state of Virginia. Although a few blacks in Virginia were born free or were able to purchase freedom for themselves or their family members,[11] the vast majority were relegated to a life of harsh, forced slave labor within the state's tobacco economy. In most instances, slaveowners provided their slaves with only minimal amounts of food, clothing, and shelter.[12] For example, slaves generally lived in sparsely furnished log cabins of about twelve by fourteen feet with mud filling the spaces between the logs.[13] Additionally, slaveowners often failed to give their slaves any shoes to wear and provided no more than two sets of clothing per year: one set to wear in the summer and the other to wear in the winter.[14] The food provided to slaves was sparse, too, often consisting of a standard weekly provision of corn and, at times, a piece of pork.[15]

---

[9] *Id.* at 9–10.

[10] Laws of Virginia, Mar. 1661, 14th Charles II, at 143. ("*And be it further enacted* that what Englishman trader, or other shall bring in any Indians as servants and shall assigne them over to any other, shall not sell them for slaves nor for any longer time than English of the like ages serve by act of assembly.")

[11] Anthony S. Parent, Jr., *Foul Means: The Formation of a Slave Society in Virginia, 1660–1740*, at 107 (2003) (noting that some blacks "even became freeholders and slaveholders").

[12] *See* Wood, *supra* note 5, at 46–47; *see also* Damian Alan Pargas, *Work and Slave Family Life in Antebellum Northern Virginia*, 31 J. Fam. Hist. 335, 344–46 (2006) (describing conditions of slavery during eighteenth century Virginia).

[13] *See* Kenneth Morgan, *Slavery and Servitude in North America, 1607–1800*, at 81 (2000); Wood, *supra* note 5, at 46–47.

[14] *See* Wood, *supra* note 5, at 46.

[15] *See id.*

Socially, slaves faced the routine loss of loved ones because slave families easily could be separated by the sale of one or more relatives.[16]

The atrocities of slavery in Virginia were visited not only on monoracial blacks but also on people of mixed racial heritage—black and white or black and American Indian. Being of "partial white blood" did not change one's status from black slave or servant to free person. Confronted with an increasing population of mixed-race children—primarily born as a result of the brutal sexual assault and rape of black women by white slaveowners[17]—the Virginia Assembly in 1662 passed an act declaring that mixed-race children inherited the status of their mothers.[18] Under this act, the mixed-race child of a black slave mother became the property of the mother's owner.[19] For the first time, Virginia categorized individuals of multiracial ancestry by placing the vast majority of them on the side of blackness and thus slavery. In 1691, the Assembly declared that even the small population of mixed-race children of white mothers would

---

[16]*See id.* at 43 ("[S]lave families had absolutely no guarantee that their [marriages] would be a lifetime relationship. . . . [I]t was a relationship that could be destroyed at any time and for any reason. In their legal capacity as property, enslaved people could be sold, given away in wills or as gifts, and even gambled away."); Angela Onwuachi-Willig, *The Return of the Ring: Welfare Reform's Marriage Cure as the Revival of Post-Bellum Control*, 93 Cal. L. Rev. 1647, 1656 (2005) ("In fact, because slave families were so frequently ripped apart by the slave market, slave couples often recited vows such as 'until death or distance do us part.' " (quoting Leon F. Litwack, *Been in the Storm so Long: The Aftermath of Slavery* 240 (1979))); Andrew T. Fede, *Gender in the Law of Slavery in the Antebellum United States*, 18 Cardozo L. Rev. 411, 416 (1996) (" 'The separation of slave families was possibly the most inhumane aspect of chattel slavery.' " (quoting Andrew Fede, *People Without Rights* 221 (1992))).

[17]*See* Rachel F. Moran, *Interracial Intimacy: The Regulation of Race and Romance* 24, 27–28 (2001); *see also* Mitchell F. Crusto, *Blackness as Property: Sex, Race, Status, and Wealth*, 1 Stan. J. C.R. & C.L. 51, 67, 81–82 (2005) (enslaved blacks "were legally classified and treated as 'property' under their master's control" and "were expected to 'breed' enslaved children, adding to their master's wealth"); Eugene D. Genovese, *Roll, Jordan, Roll: The World the Slaves Made* 415 (1976) (noting the way in which black women were raped and sexually assaulted during slavery); Randall Kennedy, *Interracial Intimacies: Sex, Marriage, Identity, and Adoption* 42–46 (2003) (describing the sexual assault of black women by their slavemasters); Kate Manning, *Crossing the Color Line*, L.A. Times, Mar. 30, 2003, at R3; Robert P. McNamara, Maria Tempenis, & Beth Walton, *Crossing the Line: Interracial Couples in the South* 24 (1999) (describing black women's vulnerability to rape during the antebellum period); *accord* Nancy F. Cott, *Public Vows: A History of Marriage and the Nation* 58–59 (2000) (describing the role that sexual violations against slave women played in the abolitionist movement and abolitionist literature).

[18]Cope, *supra* note 4, at 11; Hast, *supra* note 5, at 220.

[19]*See* Wood, *supra* note 5, at 44 (noting that because of this law, "every slave child represented a potentially lucrative capital asset as well as a potentially valuable worker").

become indentured servants until age thirty, thereby cementing the non-whiteness of multiracial people.[20]

Being born free or buying one's freedom did not necessarily save individuals with black ancestry, whether multiracial or not, from the horrors of slavery. A free black could be made a slave if, at any given moment, he or she could not produce documents that established a claim to freedom.[21] Some free blacks were relegated to bondage despite their proof of freedom. Additionally, they suffered some of the same hardships that their enslaved counterparts endured. Free blacks were frequently separated from loved ones who were sold to owners in other regions, and even worse, free blacks sometimes had to purchase their family members and keep them as slaves.[22] Finally, free blacks held few of the privileges enjoyed by free white citizens, having no right to testify against whites in court, own firearms, attend school, or roam freely in their surroundings.[23]

Given the cruelty of slavery and the ease with which free blacks' free-

---

[20] See Trina Jones, *Shades of Brown: The Law of Skin Color*, 49 Duke L.J. 1487, 1503–04 (2000); *cf.* Moran, *supra* note 17, at 21 ("As slavery hardened the lines between whites and blacks, the racial tax on mulattoes increased. Their curtailed privileges clearly identified them as nonwhite. . . ."). White women who gave birth to mixed-race children were either heavily fined or sentenced to indentured servitude for five years. *Id.;* Marie-Amélie George, *The Modern Mulatto: A Comparative Analysis of the Social and Legal Positions of Mulattoes in the Antebellum South and the Intersex in Contemporary America*, 15 Colum. J. Gender & L. 665, 674 (2006); Carter G. Woodson, *The Beginnings of Miscegenation of the Whites and Blacks, in Interracialism: Black-White Intermarriage in American History, Literature, and Law* 42, 47 (Werner Sollors ed., 2000); *see also* Hast, *supra* note 5, at 222 ("The most severe punishment was given any white woman having a child by a Negro or mulatto father. . . ."). The drafters of the Act, however, knew that a white woman would rarely submit herself to the social ostracization and punishment that would come with bearing the children of a black man. *See* George, *supra*, at 674 (discussing various other reasons for regulating white women's sexuality).

[21] Cope, *supra* note 4, at 34.

[22] *See id.* at 32. Free blacks' practice of keeping family members and friends enslaved began as a way for free blacks to procure the freedom of their loved ones. Before 1806, purchases of enslaved family members were generally followed by immediate manumissions. After passage of an 1806 Virginia law requiring manumitted blacks to leave the state within twelve months, free blacks "continued to purchase their relatives but held them as slaves, refusing to decree their banishment by executing a deed or will of manumission." Samll Goldsmyth et al., *Colored Freemen as Slave Owners in Virginia*, 1 J. Negro Hist. 233, 239–41 (1916). In 1712, after one Virginian planter freed sixteen of his slaves, the Virginia General Assembly was asked to enact legislation to prohibit manumission. Such a law was passed in 1723, officially forbidding "the freeing of any slave, on any pretense, 'except for some meritorious service,' as judged by the governor and Council." Hast, *supra* note 5, at 220–21; *see also* Ellen D. Katz, *African-American Freedom in Antebellum Cumberland County, Virginia*, 70 Chi.-Kent L. Rev. 927, 942 (1995) (citing "revealing a conspiracy" as one example of meritorious service).

[23] Paul Finkelman, *The Centrality of the Peculiar Institution in American Legal Development*, 68 Chi.-Kent L. Rev. 1009, 1014–15 (1993).

dom and limited rights could be stripped away,[24] no white person in Virginia—including indentured servants—desired the usual fate of any blacks—free or enslaved.[25] Similarly, although American Indians were not enslaved as systematically as blacks were,[26] no white person was envious of the position of tribal members.[27] Like blacks, American Indians were forced into hard labor as captives of war beginning in the second half of the seventeenth century—though their labor was primarily as indentured servants.[28] Prior to Bacon's Rebellion in 1676, it was illegal for whites to enslave American Indians, but American Indians could still be held in indentured servitude.[29] In this sense, until 1676, the laws of Virginia worked to maintain a racial hierarchy of enslavement and labor—with whites as free persons, American Indians as hard laborers, and blacks as slaves. In fact, from 1670 to 1676, legislation racialized the two classes of forced labor by categorizing them as either black slaves or American Indian servants. Specifically, a 1670 colonial enactment provided that non-Christians who were imported into Virginia by shipping (usually Africans) would be slaves for life, while those non-Christian children who came by land (usually American Indians) would be servants until age thirty, and those non-Christian adults who came by land (again, usually American Indians) would be servants for twelve years.[30]

---

[24]Cope, *supra* note 4, at 34.

[25]*Id.* at 40 ("The most congenial companion of the free Negro aside from his own class was the Negro slave. The free Negro seldom regarded slavery as a social class status inferior to his own position during the seventeenth century in Virginia."); George, *supra* note 20, at 676–77 ("Over the course of the seventeenth and eighteenth centuries, free mulattoes and blacks were forged into the same legal category, one that was prohibited from exercising many of the fundamental rights of citizenship, including the right to vote, hold office, possess firearms, convene meetings, and be protected from unlawful searches and seizure." (footnote omitted)); *accord* Finkelman, *supra* note 23, at 1014 ("Free blacks in the South were better off than enslaved blacks, but they remained second class members of society."); Hast, *supra* note 5, at 235 ("In many important areas of civil rights and citizenship, free Negroes were classified with slaves.").

[26]Cope, *supra* note 4, at 42 ("At no time in Virginia's history, however, was there any great number of Indians held either in temporary or permanent bondage.").

[27]*See id.* at 41 ("In the overall view of colonial society, nevertheless, the Indian was regarded as inferior to the White, but somewhat higher than the Negro.").

[28]Much of the resistance to the enslavement of American Indians before the mid-century was due to fears that, in retaliation, American Indians would enslave whites who were captured during wars. *See id.* at 45.

[29]*Id.* at 45–46 ("In March, 1662, the Assembly passed a law stating that no Indian accepted in the colony as a servant should be sold as a slave or held for a longer period than English servants of like age or condition of servitude."). *But see id.* at 45 (noting that slavery of American Indians was practiced by colonists during this time despite its illegality).

[30]Cope, *supra* note 4, at 12; Laws of Virginia, Oct. 1670, 22d Charles II, at 283.

This racially coded system of hard labor disappeared briefly between 1679 and 1691 when the colony of Virginia allowed white slaveowners to hold American Indians in bondage along with blacks. In 1676 and 1679, the Virginia Assembly formally legalized the enslavement of American Indians who were captured during war.[31] In 1682, all restrictions on the enslavement of American Indians and blacks in Virginia were removed, legitimating the sale and trade of both blacks and American Indians.[32]

With fewer restrictions on slavery, the slave trade grew in prominence in Virginia, and the black population there increased from 23 in 1625, to 300 in 1655, and to 20,000 in 1702.[33] At the same time that black slavery was expanding exponentially, the Virginia Assembly was working to increase trade between whites and native American Indians by fostering mutual goodwill. Consequently, in 1691, the same year that the Assembly determined that mixed-race children of white mothers were no longer born free, Virginia prohibited the enslavement of American Indians who were brought to or arrived in the colony after 1691.

In essence, by 1691, and certainly by 1705,[34] the Virginia legislature had cemented the lines of difference among white, black, and American Indian by enacting a statute to allow free trade with American Indians, thereby making it illegal for an American Indian to be born or brought into slavery after that critical year.[35] Under the statute, a declaration that one's maternal ancestor was an American Indian who was either born or arrived in Virginia after 1691 became critical to the freedom of those who had white or native-looking appearances and were alleged to be slaves descended from black women. As the stakes associated with racial identity took on profound significance, disputes over the classification of individuals with an ambiguous appearance or ancestry made their way into the courts. These battles over the color line and who was slave or free bring us directly to the story of *Hudgins v. Wrights.*

---

[31]Parent, *supra* note 11, at 114; Cope, *supra* note 4, at 14, 46; *see also Hudgins v. Wrights,* 11 Va. (1 Hen. & M.) 134, 138 (Va. 1806); *see, e.g.,* Laws of Virginia, June 1676, Bacon's Laws, at 346; Laws of Virginia, Feb. 1676–77, 29th Charles II, at 404.

[32]Parent, *supra* note 11, at 114; Cope, *supra* note 4, at 14, 46; *see* Laws of Virginia, Nov. 1682, 34th Charles II, at 491; *see also Hudgins,* 11 Va. (1 Hen. & M.) at 139.

[33]Cope, *supra* note 4, at 23–26.

[34]*See infra* notes 46, 51, and 69–70 and accompanying text.

[35]*See* Laws of Virginia, Apr. 1691, 3d William & Mary, Act IX, at 69; Laws of Virginia, Oct. 1705, 4th Anne, Ch. L2, at 468.

A Struggle for Freedom by Disclaiming Blackness

At issue in *Hudgins* were the rights of a mother, a daughter, and a grand-daughter who had sued for their freedom from Holder Hudgins, a white slaveowner in Virginia. While Jacky, Maria, and Epsabar Wright[36] maintained that they were descended from a free American Indian woman and were therefore free themselves, Hudgins claimed that they were descended from a black female slave and were therefore his slaves. Specifically, Hudgins proclaimed "that they [were] descended from a negro woman by an *Indian*."[37] The power of race in Virginia's slave economy was so great that it influenced every aspect of the legal proceedings, even the evidentiary rules that governed the case. The courts struggled to determine who should bear the burden of proof when individuals had a phenotypically ambiguous appearance that left them in the perilous space between bondage and freedom.

The Trial: A Surprising Victory and a Referendum on Slavery

At trial, the parties presented evidence of ancestry, appearance, and reputation before Chancellor George Wythe of the Richmond District Court of Chancery. The Wrights offered proof that their genealogy could be traced back to Butterwood Nan, an American Indian woman. Additionally, they drew on the testimony of various witnesses, one of whom swore that he had seen Butterwood Nan and that she was "an old Indian," and another of whom described Butterwood Nan's daughter, Hannah, as a woman with long, black hair and "the right *Indian* copper colour."[38] A third witness, Robert Temple—in fact, a witness of Hudgins'—testified that Butterwood Nan's father was known to be an Indian; Temple was silent, however, about her mother.[39] The witnesses also ex-

---

[36]Peter Wallenstein, Indian Foremothers: Race, Sex, Slavery, and Freedom in Early Virginia, *reprinted in The Devil's Lane: Sex and Race in the Early South* 65 (Catherine Clinton & Michele Gillespie, eds. 1997); Jason A. Gillmer, *Suing for Freedom: Interracial Sex, Slave Law, and Racial Identity in the Post-Revolutionary and Antebellum South*, 82 N.C. L. Rev. 535, 601 (2004).

[37]*Hudgins,* 11 Va. (1 Hen. & M.) at 134.

[38]*Id.*

[39]*Id.* at 134, 142 (noting with suspicion that the appellant witness's "memory seem[ed] only to serve him so far as the interest of the appellant required").

plained the basis for their inferences, all declaring that they often had seen American Indians.[40]

At the trial's end, Chancellor Wythe denied Hudgins' claim and declared each of the three women to be free on two grounds: (1) The women did not look black, but instead had the appearance of a person of white and American Indian ancestry; and (2) Slavery violated Virginia's Declaration of Rights and thus was illegal in the state.[41] Because of his opposition to slavery, Chancellor Wythe found "that whenever one person claims to hold another in slavery, the *onus probandi* lies on the claimant."[42] This presumption against bondage placed the burden of proof squarely on Hudgins, regardless of the Wrights' appearance, and the ambiguities surrounding their identity made it impossible for him to prevail.

The Arguments on Appeal: Debating the Basis for Determining Racial Identity

On appeal, the parties once more staked out their positions on the three women's racial identity. Hudgins, through his attorney Edmund Randolph,[43] made two different arguments. First, Randolph contended that the women had not sufficiently proven their genealogy to warrant a presumption that they were free. Randolph insisted that Chancellor Wythe had been improperly influenced by the plaintiffs' white appearance because "the whole of the testimony proved [the three women] to have been descended from a slave." Their physical appearance was not an appropriate basis for decision, for "[w]hether they are *white* or not, cannot appear to this Court *from the record*."[44] Alternatively, Randolph argued that even if the women were found to have descended from an American Indian woman, the women still should be identified as slaves since such "female ancestor was brought into this country between the years 1679 and 1705,

---

[40]*Id.* at 133–34 ("[A]ll those witnesses deposed [stated] that they had often seen *Indians*.")

[41]*See* Finkelman, *supra* note 23, at 1020 (citing *Hudgins*, 11 Va. (1 Hen. & M.) at 141). Interestingly, Chancellor Wythe had previously freed his own slaves. *See* Paul Finkelman, *The Dragon St. George Could Not Slay: Tucker's Plan to End Slavery*, 47 Wm. & Mary L. Rev. 1213, 1218 (2006).

[42]*Hudgins*, 11 Va. (1 Hen. & M.) at 134.

[43]John J. Reardon, *Edmund Randolph: A Biography* 353 (1975).

[44]*Hudgins*, 11 Va. (1 Hen. & M.) at 134–35.

and under the laws then in force, might have been a slave."[45] Rejecting 1691 as the year when Virginia first prohibited the enslavement of American Indians, Randolph maintained that no such rule was in effect until 1705. He argued that "[i]n all the cases decided by this Court on the present question, the act of 1705 has been considered as restricting the right of making slaves of *Indians:* and those cases are authority with me."[46]

In response, the three women again declared their freedom as originating from a native American Indian in the maternal line. Suing *in forma pauperis,*[47] the women, through attorney George K. Taylor, stressed the most commonly used proxies for race—skin color and outward appearance—to establish their claim to freedom.[48] Importantly, Taylor asked, "What more than strong characteristic features would be required, to prove a person *white?*"[49] Then, turning to the evidence, Taylor highlighted those parts that, he said, "clearly proved the appellees to have descended from *Indian stock.*"[50] He focused particularly on the testimony regarding the appearance of Butterwood Nan's daughter, Hannah. After noting that American Indians were legally free persons in Virginia, except between 1679 and 1691—or at the latest 1705—Taylor offered proof that the women descended from Indians brought into Virginia after 1705, making it "incumbent on the appellant to prove that they [were] slaves; the appellees [were] not bound to prove the contrary."[51]

In his final reply, Randolph shot back at Taylor for again invoking what he saw as an inappropriate reliance on outward appearance, proclaiming that "[t]he circumstance of the appellees' being *white,* has been mentioned, more to excite the feelings of the Court as *men,* than to address them as *Judges.*"[52] Randolph then went on to argue that the burden of proof in the case lay with the women because the "original *Indian* stock from which [they] descended, was derived from the *paternal* line."[53] Consequently, he maintained, the three women, and not Hudgins, had the

---

[45] *Id.* at 135.

[46] *Id.*

[47] *Id.* at 134.

[48] *Id.* at 135 (declaring to the court, "This is not a common case of mere *blacks* suing for their freedom; but of persons perfectly *white.*").

[49] *Id.*

[50] *Id.*

[51] *Id.*

[52] *Id.* at 136.

[53] *Id.*

burden of proving that they descended from a free American Indian woman. According to Randolph, Chancellor Wythe incorrectly placed the burden on Hudgins because "the maternal line must be established before the *onus probandi* is thrown on the other side."[54]

The Author of the *Hudgins* Opinion: A Study in Contradictions

The author of the Virginia high court's decision in *Hudgins* was none other than Judge St. George Tucker, who, in 1796, had publicly proposed an end to slavery in the state of Virginia.[55] Tucker, a former law professor at William and Mary, had argued in his dissertation for the eventual abolition of slavery in Virginia, noting that human bondage is "perfectly irreconcilable. . . . to the principles of a democracy, which form the foundation of our government."[56] Specifically, Tucker advocated a gradual process of abolition over 105 years.[57] Rather than an immediate end to slavery, Tucker pushed for this slower approach because of his concerns about unavoidable economic losses to slavemasters, the potential for damage to Virginia's economy,[58] and the risk of allowing freed blacks to become "a numerous, starving, and enraged banditti, upon the innocent descendants of their former oppressors."[59]

Having learned about the progressive abolition of slavery from revered and educated men in the North—such as Zephaniah Swift, a Federalist congressman and opponent of slavery[60]—Tucker proposed the emancipation of slaves in stages. The first stage would occur through the freedom of all female children of current female slaves; these children, as

---

[54]*Id.*

[55]*See* Finkelman, *supra* note 23, at 1020 (citing St. George Tucker, *A Dissertation on Slavery: With a Proposal for the Gradual Abolition of It, in the State of Virginia* (1796)).

[56]*See* Katz, *supra* note 22, at 928 & n.4 (quoting St. George Tucker, *A Dissertation on Slavery: With a Proposal for the Gradual Abolition of It, in the State of Virginia* 48 (reprinted 1861) (1796)).

[57]Finkelman, *supra* note 41, at 1229, 1235 (citing St. George Tucker, *A Dissertation on Slavery: With a Proposal for the Gradual Abolition of It, in the State of Virginia* 101 n.22 (Negro Univ. Press 1970) (1796)) (but noting that, contrary to Tucker's estimates, the process would actually take more than 120 years).

[58]Finkelman, *supra* note 41, at 1229 ("Without labor, the land of the Virginia elite would be worthless and useless.").

[59]*Id.* at 1229, 1235 (quoting Tucker, *supra* note 57, at 88).

[60]*Id.* at 1223–24.

a means of compensating slaveowners, would then be required to serve as indentured servants until age twenty-eight.[61] After this period of servitude, the women would receive "twenty dollars in money, two suits of clothes, suited to the season, a hat, a pair of shoes, and two blankets."[62] The male children of current female slaves, on the other hand, would become slaves for life.[63] Eventually, however, both the male and the female children of the female descendant would be born free, subject thereafter to twenty years of indentured servitude.[64]

Although Tucker wanted slavery to end gradually in Virginia, he also wanted all free blacks to leave his beloved state immediately. Were freed blacks to remain in Virginia, Tucker believed, they would become " 'idle, profligate, and miserable,' " and would potentially " 'become hordes of vagabonds, robbers, and murderers.' "[65] He recommended severe restrictions on emancipated blacks to push them out of Virginia (and ultimately America).[66] Tucker proposed curtailing their rights, including many political rights—such as voting, holding office, serving in the army, owning weapons, serving on a jury, and being a witness in court.[67] More important, Tucker proposed that free blacks be excluded from an important means of livelihood in Virginia—the purchase and transfer of land:

> *Let no Negroe [sic] or mulattoe [sic] be capable of taking, holding, or exercising, any . . . freehold, franchise or privilege, or any estate in lands or tenements, other than a lease not exceeding twenty-one years. . . . Nor be an executor or administrator; nor capable of making any will or testament; nor maintain any real action; nor be a trustee of lands or tenements himself, nor any other person to be a trustee to him or to his use.[68]*

---

[61] *Id.* at 1229, 1235 (citing Tucker, *supra* note 57, at 89).

[62] *See* Katz, *supra* note 22, at 928 n.6 (quoting Tucker, *supra* note 56, at 48).

[63] Finkelman, *supra* note 41, at 1229, 1235 (citing Tucker, *supra* note 57, at 89).

[64] Katz, *supra* note 22, at 928 n.6 (quoting Tucker, *supra* note 56, at 48).

[65] Finkelman, *supra* note 41, at 1233 (quoting Tucker, *supra* note 57, at 77, 84).

[66] *See* Katz, *supra* note 22, at 928–29 nn.5, 7–8; *see also* Phillip Hamilton, *Revolutionary Principles and Family Loyalties: Slavery's Transformation in the St. George Tucker Household of Early National Virginia,* 55 Wm. & Mary Q. 531, 536 (1998).

[67] Finkelman, *supra* note 41, at 1238 (quoting Tucker, *supra* note 57, at 88, 101 n.22); Hamilton, *supra* note 66, at 536 ("Tucker confessed that he chose to 'accommodate' racism in order to 'avoid as many obstacles as possible to the completion of so desirable a work, as the abolition of slavery.' ").

[68] *See* Katz, *supra* note 22, at 928 n.8 (quoting Tucker, *supra* note 56, at 91–92) (alterations in original).

These conflicting principles about slavery and the rights of blacks would shape Judge Tucker's approach to *Hudgins*. He had, after all, authored his dissertation on the gradual abolition of slavery only ten years earlier.

The Decision: Multiracialism and the Contingencies of Identity

Writing for the Supreme Court of Appeals of Virginia in *Hudgins,* Judge Tucker affirmed the trial court's decision to identify the Wrights as free women on the basis of their ancestral heritage—as women descended from native American Indians on their maternal side. Before declaring the court's ultimate conclusion, Judge Tucker established that 1691, not 1705, was the date after which American Indians could no longer be brought into slavery in the state of Virginia:

> *By the adjudication of the General Court, in the case of* Hannah *and others against* Davis, *April term, 1705, all American Indians brought into this country since the year 1705, and their descendants in the maternal line, are* free. *Similar judgments have been rendered in this court. But I carry the period further back,* . . . *to the 16th day of* April, *1691, the commencement of a session of the General Assembly at which an act passed, entitled* "An Act for a free trade with Indians," . . . *the enacting clause of which, I have reason to believe, is in the very words of the act of 1705, upon which this Court have pronounced judgment in the cases referred to.*[69]

From this interpretation of Virginia's statutes, Judge Tucker declared that American Indians were prima facie presumed to be free. So long as there was evidence to show maternal American Indian ancestry, the claiming slaveholder had to show that this ancestor was brought to Virginia after 1679 (the point at which the enslavement of American Indians had become legal in the state) and before 1691 (the point at which an act made all American Indians arriving thereafter free).[70]

---

[69]Hudgins v. Wrights, 11 Va. (1 Hen. & M.) 134, 137–38 (Va. 1806) (footnote omitted).
[70]*Id.* at 138–39.

Unlike Chancellor Wythe, Judge Tucker allocated the burden of proof depending on the physical appearance of the parties. Where white persons or American Indians, or their descendants in the maternal line—meaning those who physically appeared to belong to one of those groups—were alleged to be slaves, the burden as to their status rested with the party who claimed ownership.[71] On the other hand, if the plaintiffs were black (or physically appeared to be black), the burden of proof rested with the individuals who sought their freedom. As stated by Judge Spencer Roane in a separate concurrence:

> In the case of a person visibly appearing to be a negro, *the presumption is, in this country, that he is a slave, and it is incumbent on him to make out his right to freedom: but in the case of a person visibly appearing to be a white man, or an* Indian, *the presumption is that he is free, and it is necessary for his adversary to shew [sic] that he is a slave.*[72]

In *Hudgins,* because of the white-looking appearance of the granddaughter, and the gradual shades of difference in color of the mother and the grandmother,[73] the court declared that the women, as American Indians, were presumptively free.[74] The burden then fell on Hudgins, the purported owner, to prove that the three women were in fact descended from either a black female slave or from an American Indian female slave who had been brought into Virginia between the years of 1679 and 1691.

In reviewing the trial court's decision, Judge Tucker held that there was sufficient evidence to substantiate the trial court's determination that the family of women descended from an American Indian through the maternal line. That evidence included testimony from Mary Wilkinson

---

[71]*Id.* at 139 ("If one *evidently white,* be notwithstanding claimed as a slave, the proof lies on the party claiming to make the other his slave." (emphasis added)); *see also* Mark V. Tushnet, *The American Law of Slavery 1810–1860,* at 157 (1981) (discussing the differing burdens of proof based on physical appearance); George, *supra* note 20, at 677–78 (same).

[72]*Hudgins,* 11 Va. (1 Hen. & M.) at 141 (Roane, J., concurring) (first emphasis added).

[73]*Id.* at 134.

[74]*Id.* at 139 (majority opinion) ("[A]ll *American Indians* are prima facie FREE: and . . . where the fact of their nativity and descent, in a *maternal* line, is satisfactorily established, the burthen of proof thereafter lies upon the party claiming to hold them as slaves. To effect which, according to my opinion, he must prove the progenitrix of the party claiming to be free, to have been brought into *Virginia,* and made a slave between the passage of the act of 1679, and its repeal in 1691.").

and Robert Temple that revealed that "the plaintiffs [were] in the maternal line descended from *Butterwood Nan*, an old *Indian* woman" who was approximately sixty years old in 1755; testimony from Robert Temple that Butterwood Nan's father was an American Indian; and testimony from several witnesses that Hannah, the daughter of Butterwood Nan, "had long black hair . . . and [was] generally called an *Indian* among the neighbours. . . ."[75]

Judge Tucker also relied, however, on his observations of the laws as connected "with the natural history of the human species."[76] One view of this history included the reputation of the women among their neighbors, all of whom testified that the women's maternal ancestors were American Indians.[77] Thus, in many ways, the question in *Hudgins* was, did the white community regard and accept these women as American Indian rather than black?[78] The witnesses repeatedly gave a positive response to this question. Judge Tucker further elaborated on his understanding of natural history, which allowed a judge the ability and the right to decide if a challenged individual was white, American Indian, or black "from his own view."[79] After all, the physical features of blacks and American Indians were so distinct that they could not be confused with one another any more easily than "the glossy, jetty cloathing [sic] of an *American* bear

---

[75]*Id*. at 137.

[76]*Id*. at 139.

[77]*Id*. at 142 (Roane, J., concurring) ("This general reputation and opinion of the neighbourhood is certainly entitled to *some* credit: it goes to repel the idea that the given female ancestor of *Hannah* was a *lawful* slave; it goes to confirm the other strong testimony as to *Hannah's* appearance as an *Indian*. It is not to be believed but that *some* of the neighbours would have sworn to that concerning which they *all* agreed in opinion. . . .").

[78]*See* Ariela J. Gross, *Litigating Whiteness: Trials of Racial Determination in the Nineteenth Century South*, 108 Yale L.J. 109, 118–21 (1998) (detailing how determinations of race by juries during the nineteenth century often turned on witness testimony regarding hair color, hair texture, facial features, and social performances); *see also* Daniel J. Sharfstein, Essay, *The Secret History of Race in the United States*, 112 Yale L.J. 1473, 1479–80 (2003) (discussing how "scholars have shown how scientific notions of race such as genealogy or physical appearance have never been the courts' sole or even preferred type of evidence for determining race").

[79]Hudgins, 11 Va. (1 Hen. & M.) at 140 (majority opinion). Although disagreeing with the Judge on other points, Judge Spencer Roane agreed with Judge Tucker that "[t]he distinguishing characteristics of the different species of the human race are so visibly marked, *that those species may be readily discriminated from each other by mere inspection only*." *Id*. at 141 (Roane, J., concurring) (emphasis added). Professor Adrienne Davis has termed "this physical component scopic in that it relies on the inspecting and scrutinizing gaze of a (white) individual in order to discern and assign racial identity." Adrienne D. Davis, Essay, *Identity Notes Part One: Playing in the Light*, 45 Am. U. L. Rev. 695, 705 (1996).

[could be confused with] the wool of black sheep. . . ."[80] Specifically, Judge Tucker noted that persons of African descent had been stamped with three distinct characteristics that would not and could not readily disappear: dark skin, a flat nose, and woolly hair—the strongest "ingredient in the African constitution"—which

> *predominates uniformly where the party is in equal degree descended from parents of different complexions, whether white or* Indians; *giving to the jet black lank hair of the Indian a degree of flexure, which never fails to betray that the party distinguished by it, cannot trace his lineage purely from the race of native* Americans.[81]

All of these observations of law commingled with natural history eventually led Judge Tucker and his colleagues to reach the conclusion that Hannah could not possibly have had long, black hair, been of copper complexion, or been reputed to be an American Indian in her community unless "her mother had . . . an equal, or perhaps a larger portion of *Indian* blood in her veins."[82] Thus, Hannah was presumptively free.

In a separate concurrence, Judge Roane made clear that he did not agree that descent from the maternal or paternal line could be determined from a judge's view. However, he did agree that Hudgins had failed to meet his burden of proof by failing to show that the three women descended from either a black female slave or a rightfully held American Indian female slave.[83] Like Judge Tucker, Judge Roane was especially persuaded by the evidence regarding the appearance of Hannah. He found that "[n]o testimony can be more complete and conclusive than that which exists in this cause to shew [sic] that *Hannah* had every appearance of an *Indian*."[84] Judge Roane argued that if "*Hannah's* grandmother . . . were a *negro*, it [would have been] impossible that *Hannah* should have had that entire appearance of an Indian which is proved by the witnesses."[85] In essence, as Professor Ian Haney López has indicated, "[a]fter

---

[80]*Hudgins*, 11 Va. (1 Hen. & M.) at 140.

[81]*Id.* at 139.

[82]*Id.* at 137; *see also id.* at 143 (Roane, J., concurring) (stating that "[t]he mother and grandmother of *Hannah* must therefore be taken to have been *Indians*").

[83]*Id.* at 141–42.

[84]*Id.* at 142. Judge Roane also seemed to be influenced by the appearance of the three women themselves, noting in his opinion: "In the present case it is not and cannot be denied that the appellees have entirely the *appearance* of white people. . . ." *Id.* at 141.

[85]*Id.* at 142.

unknown lives lost in slavery, Judge Tucker freed three generations of women because Hannah's hair was long and straight."[86]

Notably, however, Judge Tucker—who, despite owning slaves,[87] taught his law students that slavery was a moral wrong—failed to give any weight to his own intellectual and political views on slavery[88] in the *Hudgins* opinion. He rejected his former teacher Chancellor Wythe's decision at the trial level to grant the Wrights freedom on the grounds that slavery was illegal in Virginia. Judge Tucker asserted that Virginia's Declaration of Rights did not outlaw slavery because it did not apply to those who were not free. He declared:

> *I do not concur with the Chancellor in his reasoning on the operation of the first clause of the Bill of Rights, which was notoriously framed with a cautious eye to this subject, and was meant to embrace the case of free citizens, or aliens only; and not by a side wind to overturn the rights of property, and give freedom to those very people whom we have been compelled from imperious circumstances to retain, generally, in the same state of bondage that they were in at the revolution, in which they had no concern, agency or interest.[89]*

After the *Hudgins* decision, a panel of judges delivered a decree of the Supreme Court of Appeals of Virginia, ordering the permanent status of blacks as slaves.[90] Thus, although the three women would be free, the enslavement of blacks would endure for more than half a century longer—

---

[86]Ian F. Haney López, *The Social Construction of Race: Some Observations on Illusion, Fabrication, and Choice,* 29 Harv. C.R.-C.L. L. Rev. 1, 2 (1994).

[87]Finkelman, *supra* note 41, at 1216–18 (describing Tucker as a man conflicted about slavery and noting that Tucker owned more than 100 slaves and negotiated the purchase and sale of human beings as part of his work as an attorney); Hamilton, *supra* note 66, at 531 ("St. George Tucker . . . faced conflicting loyalties: he wished to eliminate slavery to fulfill the Revolution's ideological promise, but he also wanted to safeguard his family's property to preserve its wealth, power, and prestige.").

[88]Finkelman, *supra* note 41, at 1222–23. Tucker declared in his dissertation: "Slavery not only violates the Laws of Nature, and of civil Society, it also wounds the best Forms of Government: in a Democracy, where all Men are equal, Slavery is contrary to the Spirit of the Constitution." *Id.* at 1222 (quoting Tucker, *supra* note 57, at 1).

[89]*Hudgins*, 11 Va. (1 Hen. & M.) at 141.

[90]*Id.* at 144 (Lyons, P.J., concurring) ("This Court, not approving of the Chancellor's principles and reasoning in his decree made in this cause, except so far as the same relates to white persons and native *American Indians,* but entirely disapproving thereof, so far as the same relates to native *Africans* and their descendants, who have been and are now held as slaves by the citizens of this state, and discovering no other error in the said decree, affirms the same.").

until the issuance of the Emancipation Proclamation in 1863.[91] In the end, at the same time that *"Hudgins* may have secured freedom for Virginia's tiny and dwindling population of Indians, . . . it simultaneously tightened the chains of bondage on the Commonwealth's huge black population."[92] Indeed, in 1812, Judge Tucker further tightened the chains by preventing his stepson, Charles Carter, from taking action to emancipate his own slaves.[93]

Larger Lessons about the Challenges of Multiracialism

The primary lesson of *Hudgins v. Wrights* is one often repeated by scholars: Race is not biologically defined but is instead socially constructed.[94] As Professor Ian Haney López has highlighted, "[t]here are no genetic characteristics possessed by all Blacks but not by non-Blacks; similarly, there is no gene or cluster of genes common to all Whites but not to non-Whites."[95] Likewise, Professor Adrienne Davis has described ways in which space and place may alter a person's identity in the view of the surrounding community members, detailing how she is perceived as black in some places, but non-black in others.[96]

Years earlier, William D. Zabel unknowingly demonstrated the social construction theory of race in his paper *Interracial Marriage and the Law,* in which he discussed states' varying standards for determining which multiracial individuals were black for purposes of enforcing antimiscegenation statutes. Zabel clarified that, in the face of a growing mixed-race population, determinations of individuals' blackness varied from state to

---

[91]The Proclamation did not translate into true freedom for many slaves until long after the Civil War's end when the federal government forced plantation owners to acknowledge the freedom of blacks. *See* Litwack, *supra* note 16, at 173, 181–83.

[92]Finkelman, *supra* note 41, at 1214. By 1756, fifty years before the *Hudgins* decision, 120,156 of 173,316 Virginia residents were black. *See* Hast, *supra* note 5, at 218.

[93]Finkelman, *supra* note 41, at 1242.

[94]*See* Davis, *supra* note 79, at 696–719 (specifically exploring the construction of whiteness); Angela P. Harris, *Foreword: The Jurisprudence of Reconstruction*, 82 Cal. L. Rev. 741, 774 (1994) (" '[R]ace' is neither a natural fact simply there in 'reality,' nor a wrong idea, eradicable by an act of will."); Michael Omi & Howard Winant, *Racial Formation in the United States: From the 1960s to the 1990s*, at 55–60 (2d ed. 1994) (analyzing race as an evolving set of social meanings that are formed and transformed under a constantly shifting society); Angela Onwuachi-Willig, *Undercover Other*, 94 Cal. L. Rev. 874, 883–84 (2006) (noting that "[s]ociety imposes identities on people").

[95]Haney López, *supra* note 86, at 11.

[96]*See* Davis, *supra* note 79, at 697–701.

state, not based purely on scientific distinctions, but rather on local customs of acceptable racial mixtures. He asked:

> *Who is a Negro under [these] laws? There is no uniform definition, so it is difficult to know. The different definitions create racial chameleons. One can be Negro in Georgia because he had a one-half Negro great-grandmother, and by crossing the border into Florida, become a white because Florida makes him a Negro only if he had a full Negro great-grandmother. The most common definition uses an unscientific percentage-of-blood test usually classifying a Negro as "any person of one-eighth or more Negro blood." If a blood test is to be used and one-eighth Negro blood, whatever that means, makes you Negro, why does not one-eighth of white blood make you white?*[97]

As Zabel's account of multiracialism suggests, the Wrights, as women of mixed ancestry, challenged the very assumption that races are entirely separate as a biological matter. Through their court case, they delivered an important lesson about racial fluidity. After all, their race was not determined by any unique gene, known to exist only in American Indian women. Rather, it was influenced by commonly held social beliefs among the judges about how American Indian women looked and behaved. For the Wrights, their fate as either free American Indian women or legally defined black slaves depended not just upon the fairness of their skin or the straightness of their hair but the exercise of their non-black identity and their recognition as non-black by neighboring whites.

Indeed, the performance of a non-black identity was critical to determinations of race during a period in which people resided in relatively small

---

[97]William D. Zabel, *Interracial Marriage and the Law, in Interracialism: Black White Intermarriage in American History, Literature, and Law,* at 54, 57 (Werner Sollors ed., 2000). Even white citizens during the eighteenth and nineteenth centuries, including slaveholders, understood the non-biological nature of race, as demonstrated by newspaper advertisements searching for runaway slaves. *See* Sharfstein, *supra* note 78, at 1476 (noting that whites in the post-Reconstruction South "had a basic awareness that racial identity was something that could be disputed and creatively argued, at least in the courtroom"). For example, on January 6, 1836, slaveowner Anderson Bowles published an advertisement in the *Richmond Whig* searching for a slave who had run away, describing the young man as a "negro" with "straight hair," who was "nearly white" such that "a stranger" would suppose there was "no African blood in him." William Goodell, *Slavery and Anti-Slavery: A History of the Great Struggle in Both Hemispheres* 265 (1852). Similarly, on April 22, 1837, in his advertisement in the *Newbern Spectator,* Edwin Peck offered 100 dollars for the return of a slave named Sam, described as having "light sandy hair, blue eyes, [a] ruddy complexion," and being "so white as very easily to pass for a white man." *Id.*

communities, from which courts could enlist testimony about the different parties' reputations and ancestries. Although urbanization, industrialization, and immigration complicated this means of classifying persons according to race, conduct remained important to these racial trials for centuries. For example, Professor Ariela Gross has extensively detailed how the performance of whiteness—the way in which a person exercised the privileges of white citizenship and was accepted by other whites in the community—"positively" affected a court's determination of his or her status as white or black during nineteenth-century trials.[98] In her account, Gross demonstrated that a person's behavior and reputation figured almost as much as appearance in decisions about racial status in these trials.

Concerns about racial ambiguity and the dilemmas of classification in a segregated society persisted into the twentieth century. During this period, racial passing was becoming more prevalent, and racial classifications were becoming increasingly contingent upon and subject to individual manipulation. This fact concerned many white citizens, who feared racial fraud by intruding blacks.[99] Nevertheless, white citizens, on some level, were willing to acknowledge the lack of precision in biological determinations of race and maintained flexibility on standards of challenged whiteness because of one major driving force: the fear that they, or any other persons with the physical appearance of whiteness, could also fall prey to a determination of non-whiteness.[100] A quote from a railway conductor in the 1920s clearly reveals the ways in which many white Americans understood the fluidity of the color line. When the railway conductor was asked whether he had "any difficulty about classifying people who are very near the [color] line," he responded, "I give the passenger the benefit of the doubt."[101]

At the same time, however, underlying the legal determination of the

---

[98]Gross, *supra* note 78, at 156–57; *see also* Sharfstein, *supra* note 78, at 1479–80 ("In part, the color line was established, in the words of the South Carolina Supreme Court, by 'evidence of reputation as to parentage; and such evidence as was offered in the present case, of the person's having been received in society, and exercised the privileges of a white man.' " (quoting *State v. Davis*, 18 S.C. L. (2 Bail.) 558, 560 (1832))).

[99]Moran, *supra* note 17, at 44–45 (detailing how some "light-skinned mulattoes" "[c]apitaliz[ed] on the influx of immigrants from southern Europe" to "pass themselves off as dark-skinned ethnics from the Mediterranean"); *see also* Kennedy, *supra* note 17, at 298 ("The most thoroughgoing effort in American history to prevent and punish passing began in Virginia in the 1920s. . . .").

[100]*See* Davis, *supra* note 79, at 706–07 (noting that one judge's main focus in *Hudgins* seemed "to be the safeguarding of whites from accidentally falling into the perils of slavery").

[101]Sharfstein, *supra* note 78, at 1500 (quoting Charles W. Chesnutt, *Remarks of Charles Waddell Chesnutt, of Cleveland, in Accepting the Spingarn Medal at Los Angeles* (July 3, 1928), in *Charles W. Chesnutt: Essays and Speeches* 510, 514 (Joseph R. McElrath, Jr. et al. eds., 1999)).

Wrights as American Indian, instead of black, was an enduring belief in biological race. For many white Virginians, including Judge Tucker, there were "ingredients in the African constitution"[102] that could not readily disappear. These genetic ingredients made Judge Tucker confident that whites could ascertain race by physical appearance.

The fact is that, although whites understood the way in which multi-racialism made phenotype ambiguous and subverted the reliability of community reputation, they deeply desired the determinism of biological race.[103] The 1896 decision of the U.S. Supreme Court in *Plessy v. Ferguson*[104] is a good example of the undying faith by whites in genetic-based racial distinctions. There, the Court upheld a Louisiana statute requiring separate railway cars for whites and blacks in the face of Homer Plessy's challenge to his categorization as black. Plessy was seven-eighths white and one-eighth black, and in his case, "the mixture of colored blood was not discernible."[105] As a result, he alleged that his segregation on an all-black car was arbitrary and improper. The Supreme Court noted that determinations of racial status as black or white varied from state to state and that it could "become a question of importance whether, under the laws of Louisiana, [Plessy] belongs to the white or colored race." At the same time, the Court reinforced the notion of race as biological and fixed by declaring that "[l]egislation is powerless to eradicate racial instincts, or to abolish distinctions based upon physical differences. . . ."[106]

During the early 1900s, this idea of race as biologically fixed would become further entrenched by numerous states' adoption of the one-drop rule,[107] which provided that any person with one drop of black blood is

---

[102] *See supra* notes 79–81 and accompanying text.

[103] Haney López, *supra* note 86, at 6 (defining biological race as the view "that there exist natural, physical divisions among humans that are hereditary, reflected in morphology, and roughly but correctly captured by terns like Black, White, and Asian (or Negroid, Caucasoid, and Mongoloid)").

[104] 163 U.S. 537 (1896).

[105] *Id.* at 541.

[106] *Id.* at 551–52.

[107] For example, the Census Bureau adopted the rule in 1920, stating:

> The term "white" as used in the census report refers to persons understood to be pure-blooded whites. A person of mixed blood is classified according to the nonwhite racial strain. . . . [t]hus a person of mixed white . . . and Negro . . . is classified as . . . a Negro . . . regardless of the amount of white blood.

Christine B. Hickman, *The Devil and the One Drop Rule: Racial Categories, African Americans, and the U.S. Census*, 95 Mich. L. Rev. 1161, 1187 (1997) (quoting 3 Bureau of the Census, U.S. Dep't of Commerce, Fourteenth Census of the United States: 1920, at 10 (1923)).

black.[108] Again, as Judge Tucker hinted in his opinion in *Hudgins,* the belief was, and still is, that whiteness is so pure and blackness is so degrading that "ingredients in the African constitution" would "never fail to betray . . . the party distinguished by it."[109] Under the one-drop rule, no amount of whiteness, no matter how great, could save an individual of black ancestry from what was viewed as the pollution of blackness, no matter how small.[110] Noted African American author Langston Hughes once proclaimed, "[H]ere in the United States, the word 'Negro' is used to mean anyone who has any Negro blood at all in his veins."[111]

In the end, whites still held fast to the idea of race as highly visible and easily recognizable, especially for blacks. This belief persisted despite a seemingly contradictory acceptance of race as defined by factors other than skin color, including conduct. No case demonstrates this point more strongly than *Rhinelander v. Rhinelander,*[112] a 1920s New York lawsuit in which Leonard Kip Rhinelander, a wealthy white socialite, filed for the annulment of his marriage to Alice Beatrice Jones, a woman of racially ambiguous heritage, on the ground that Alice had misrepresented her race. According to Leonard, Alice committed fraud by failing to inform him that she possessed colored blood.[113] To everyone's surprise, Alice chose not to litigate her whiteness, but instead admitted that she was of colored descent and argued that Leonard was aware of her race before the

---

[108]Neil Gotanda, *A Critique of "Our Constitution Is Color-Blind,"* 44 Stan. L. Rev. 1, 26 (1991) ("The metaphor is one of purity and contamination: White is unblemished and pure, so one drop of ancestral Black blood renders one Black. Black ancestry is a contaminant that overwhelms white ancestry.").

[109]*See supra* note 79–81 and accompanying text.

[110]*See* Nadine Ehlers, *Hidden in Plain Sight: Defying Juridical Racialization in* Rhinelander v. Rhinelander, 4 Comm. & Critical/Cultural Stud. 313, 316 (2004) (explaining that " 'mixing' was imagined as that which polluted 'pure whiteness' because it introduced foreign non-white 'blood,' a fluid of 'racial essence' that was represented as a pathogen that both contaminated and degenerated the 'integrity of whiteness' "); Robert Westley, *First Time Encounters: "Passing" Revisited and Demystification as a Critical Practice,* 18 Yale L. & Pol'y Rev. 297, 311 (2000) ("Being white was a matter of blood, just as being Black was the pollution of blood.").

[111]Langston Hughes, *The Big Sea: An Autobiography* 11 (1940).

[112]The Association of the Bar of the City of New York, New York Supreme Court: Appellate Division—Second Department, Leonard Kip Rhinelander *against* Alice Jones Rhinelander, Case on Appeal, at 889 (Nov. 26, 1924–Dec. 5, 1925); *Rhinelander v. Rhinelander,* 157 N.E. 838 (N.Y. Ct. App. 1927); *Rhinelander v. Rhinelander,* 219 N.Y.S. 548 (S. Ct. App. Div. 1927); *see also* Angela Onwuachi-Willig, *A Beautiful Lie: Exploring* Rhinelander v. Rhinelander *as a Formative Lesson on Race, Marriage, Identity, and Family,* 95 Cal. L. Rev. 2393 (2007).

[113]*See* Jamie L. Wacks, *Reading Race, Rhetoric, and the Female Body in the* Rhinelander *Case, in Interracialism: Black White Intermarriage in American History, Literature, and Law* 162, 163 (Werner Sollors ed. 2000).

marriage. In support of her claim, she said that Leonard knew of her colored background because he had seen her naked body during premarital sexual relations. Playing upon the notion of race as easily recognizable, Alice's attorney offered as evidence Alice's bare skin.[114] Presumably, he agreed with Judge Roane in *Hudgins* that "[t]he distinguishing characteristics of the different species of the human race are so visibly marked, *that those species may be readily discriminated from each other by mere inspection only.*"[115]

Ultimately, the jury returned a verdict for Alice, denying Leonard's request for an annulment. No doubt each juror wanted to believe, as Judge Tucker did in *Hudgins,* that he could tell the race of a person "from his own view."[116] This belief was comforting because it reinforced a racial hierarchy and hence whites' ability to preserve their favored position. Otherwise, as author Jamie Wacks notes, "The notion that a lower-class woman like Alice Jones . . . could trespass into the world of a wealthy white man like Leonard Rhinelander questioned the boundaries between white and black . . . [and] suggested the vulnerability of alleged white dominance."[117] Although many whites realized that race was not genetically decipherable, they also gravitated to a notion of fixed biological difference—they desired to believe that they would know race "when they saw it."

Today, the widespread societal belief in pure biological classifications of race persists, even as the multiracial population in this country continues to grow. Despite changes in the 2000 Census that allow individuals to mark more than one racial category in identifying themselves, many multiracial individuals are still not entirely "free to forge a unique identity, regardless of what strangers expect or how other family members define themselves."[118] As Professor Rachel Moran has indicated, "Even when individuals with mixed black and white ancestry try to disregard racial

---

[114] *See* Earl Lewis & Heidi Ardizzone, *Love on Trial: An American Scandal in Black and White* 159–60 (2001) ("Alice's lawyers resorted to the comforting belief that race was easy to determine and differentiate. Alice, they repeated, was clearly black, for anyone with reasonable intelligence to see."); Wacks, *supra* note 113, at 164 ("Later that same day, over the objection of Leonard's attorney, Alice's attorney requested that Alice take her clothes off to allow the all-white, all-male, all-married jury and Leonard to inspect her skin color.").

[115] Hudgins v. Wrights, 11 Va. (1 Hen. & M.) 134, 141 (Va. 1806) (Roane, J., concurring) (emphasis added).

[116] *See supra* note 79 and accompanying text.

[117] *See* Wacks, *supra* note 113, at 166.

[118] Moran, *supra* note 17, at 160.

boundaries, the overwhelming reality of segregation reinstates them."[119] This reality remains especially true for blacks, who continue to be segregated by neighborhood and marriage in ways that other racial and ethnic groups are not.[120]

In sum, despite a plethora of literature on the social construction of race, a longing for biological race lingers. In fact, business is booming for companies, like DNA Print Genomics, that claim to be able to determine a person's ancestral heritage. Throughout the country, increasing numbers of college applicants are trying to uncover their ethnic ancestries through genetic testing in order to assert a minority identity and gain an "advantage" in the college admissions game.[121] Indeed, many teenagers who grew up with a socially and phenotypically white identity are being tested so that they can claim a "biological race" on application forms that does not match their personal experience.[122] After exercising all the privileges of white citizens,[123] these students are staking a claim not to their genetic race, but to the preferential treatment that they view as coming with that genetics (without the social disadvantages).

For example, Matt and Andrew Moldawer, twins who knew that both of their birth parents were "white" and grew up in an adoptive white family, engaged in genetic testing, through which they learned that they were nine percent Native American and eleven percent North African. They then used that information to garner a better financial aid package for college.[124] Likewise, the sister of Ashley Klett, whom DNA tests showed to be two percent East Asian and ninety-eight percent European, checked the "Asian" box on her college application, an act she believes helped her earn a scholarship.[125]

---

[119]Moran, *supra* note 17, at 175.

[120]*See* Rachel F. Moran, *The Mixed Promise of Multiculturalism*, 17 Harv. BlackLetter L.J. 47, 47–55 (2001).

[121]*See* Amy Harmon, *Seeking Ancestry, and Privilege, in DNA Ties Uncovered by Tests*, The New York Times, April 12, 2006, at A1 (noting that "[p]rospective employees with white skin are using the tests to apply as minority candidates"); *see also* Angela Onwuachi-Willig, *The Admission of Legacy Blacks*, 60 Vand. L. Rev. 102, 182–85 (2007) (discussing the racial fraud of college applicants based on genetic testing).

[122]As Lester Monts, senior vice provost for student affairs at the University of Michigan, asserted, "If someone appears to be white and then finds out they are not, they haven't experienced the kinds of things that affirmative action is supposed to remedy." *Id.*

[123]In 1831, the South Carolina Supreme Court even described social experience as important evidence for determining racial identity. *See* Sharfstein, *supra* note 78, at 1479–80 (quoting State v. Davis, 18 S.C.L. (2 Bail.) 558, 560 (1832)).

[124]*Id.*

[125]*Id.*

This newly popular view of genetic race has done far more than simply satisfy personal curiosity or conveniently alter college applications and scholarships. As Professor Lisa Ikemoto has highlighted, "race is back on the biomedical research agenda . . . [,] emerging as a legitimized explanation for medical and social issues."[126] For scholars like Ikemoto and Dorothy Roberts, a law professor who specializes in reproductive rights, this fascination with genetic race raises fears of a return to eugenics, which was used in the past to support laws—such as compulsory sterilization—that deeply discriminated against racial minorities.[127] In fact, both Ikemoto and Roberts decry the harm that could result from the ethnic- or race-based packaging of prescription drugs.[128] For example, BiDil has been advertised as treating heart failure specifically in African Americans.[129]

Similarly, critics have attacked the return to the notion of biological race in criminal law enforcement. Increasingly, DNA tests are being used, both in the United States and in the United Kingdom, to assist police in determining what a crime suspect looks like.[130] Despite repeated expressions of concern about how poorly DNA predicts physical appearance and about how such testing could lead to "genetic racial profiling, or promote the idea that certain races are more inclined than others to commit crimes," several law enforcement agencies are praising these new efforts, claiming that such testing has enabled them to solve violent crimes.[131] In fact, recently, the London police requested DNA samples from officers of Afro-Caribbean descent to compare them with evidence from nine unsolved rapes, declaring that such information put them " 'on the right track' in their investigation."[132]

---

[126]Lisa C. Ikemoto, *Race to Health: Racialized Discourses in a Transhuman World*, 9 DePaul J. Health Care L. 1101, 1101 (2005).

[127]*See id.* at 1102; Dorothy E. Roberts, *Legal Constraints on the Use of Race in Biomedical Research: Toward a Social Justice Framework*, 34 J.L. Med. & Ethics 526, 526–28 (2006).

[128]*See* Ikemoto, *supra* note 126, at 1124 ("Attempts to market products to particular racial groups—e.g. BiDil—may legitimize biological race."); Roberts, *supra* note 127, at 528–29 (proposing "that the legal regulation of race in biomedical research should aim to promote social justice. . . . [which] holds that race is a socially constructed category without scientific basis that continues to produce health inequities, that these inequities require race-conscious legal remedies, and that biomedical research should be subject to legal regulation that promotes racial justice").

[129]*See* BiDil-Prescription Drug for African Americans with Heart Disease, http://www.bidil.com/.

[130]*See* Richard Willing, *DNA Tests Offer Clues to Suspect's Race*, USA Today, August 16, 2005, *available at* http://www.usatoday.com/news/nation/2005-08-16-dna_x.htm.

[131]*Id.*

[132]*Id.*

Reliance on the idea of genetically based race has polluted various areas of the law, resulting in a kind of schizophrenic analysis of issues of discrimination. On the one hand, at least a minority of courts recognize (with undesirable consequences) the social construction of identity in their determinations of when to apply the Indian Child Welfare Act to a child removed from his home for adoption. The Act does not apply to a child whose American Indian parent has failed to develop any significant social, cultural, or political relationship with the Indian community.[133] This relationship can be established by showing that the parent has privately described herself as an Indian, observed tribal customs, voted in tribal elections, or maintained social contacts with other tribal members.[134] In applying the Act, courts at least acknowledge, despite their questionable practice of determining native authenticity, the ways in which performance—the exercising of community privileges and culture—can determine race in our racially polarized society. On the other hand, as Professor Mario Barnes and I have noted, some courts simultaneously have rejected the social construction of race in Title VII employment discrimination cases. Judges have refused to recognize proxies for race (such as names and accent) and have ignored the role of race and racism in the prohibition of certain hair styles and clothing in workplace grooming codes.[135] In these decisions, courts treat race as a biological fact and overlook the ways in which it is defined through social practice.[136]

Conclusion

In the context of our post-slavery and post–civil rights world, the case of *Hudgins v. Wrights* may seem like a distant memory of the past. In truth,

---

[133] *See* Solangel Maldonado, *The Story of the* Holyfield *Twins:* Mississippi Band of Choctaw Indians v. Holyfield, *in Family Law Stories* (Carol Sanger ed., 2007).

[134] *In re* Santos Y., 112 Cal. Rptr. 2d 692 (Cal. Ct. App. 2001); *In re* Bridget R., 49 Cal. Rptr. 2d 507, 527 (Cal. Ct. App. 1996), *cert. denied,* Cindy R. v. James R., 519 U.S. 1060 (1997); *In re* Adoption of Crews, 825 P.2d 305 (Wash. 1992); *see also* Hampton v. J.A.L., 658 So.2d 331, 336 (La. Ct. App. 1995) (applying the existing Indian family test where a child's mother was 11/16th Indian, was an enrolled tribal member, and had lived on a reservation until she was nine years old, but had not maintained significant tribal ties since then).

[135] *See* Angela Onwuachi-Willig & Mario L. Barnes, *By Any Other Name?: On Being "Regarded as" Black, and Why Title VII Should Apply Even If Lakisha and Jamal Are White,* 2005 Wisc. L. Rev. 1283.

[136] *See* Jones, *supra* note 20, at 1497 ("With racism, it is the social meaning afforded one's race that determines one's status.").

however, its lessons are growing each day. *Hudgins* provides an excellent example of the way in which those in power have worked to define and control race in order to maintain systems of racial oppression and hierarchy. As we saw in *Hudgins,* the very burdens of proof for different parties depended upon their racial appearance and thus stations in life, with those who looked black bearing the burden of proving their freedom and those who looked white or American Indian possessing a presumption of freedom.

Today, biological race is making a comeback. But, as *Hudgins* demonstrates all too well, race is defined not by biology, but by proxies, both physical and social—performance and authenticity. The law must adapt to these understandings if we as a society are ever to achieve complete equality. For example, although the census has formally recognized mixed-race identity, multiracial persons with a black appearance have almost no practical claim to the non-black parts of their racial identity. As Ward Connerly proclaimed about his own multiracial identity, people laugh "if he tries to identify himself as Irish based on the fact that he is 37.5 percent Irish, 25 percent French, 25 percent black, and 12.5 percent Choctaw."[137] The fact is that the one-drop rule remains a powerful force in identifying those who look black in the United States.

At the same time, *Hudgins* exposes the problems and challenges that multiracialism poses for racial classifications and order. The Wrights were able to capitalize on a situation in which phenotype was an unreliable guide to racial identity. In their lawsuit, the Wrights relied not just on their racially ambiguous appearance but also on their and their ancestors' performances within their communities to prove their non-blackness and thus gain their freedom. At the same time that *Hudgins* revealed an intense need to enforce the color line in a segregated system of slavery, the case also revealed the permeability of racial lines. Although the imperatives of policing racial boundaries through the one-drop rule continue to confine the racial options for those who are phenotypically black, multiracialism holds out more promise for multiracial individuals of non-black descent—or at least of indiscernible black descent—such as Japanese Americans, American Indians, and white Latinos. These groups cannot

---

[137]Moran, *supra* note 17, at 175; *see also* Amos N. Jones, *Black Like Obama: What the Junior Illinois Senator's Appearance on the National Scene Reveals about Race in America, and Where We Should Go From Here,* 31 T. Marshall L. Rev. 79, 85 (2005) (asserting the same about Barack Obama's ability to claim a white identity).

only claim their mixed origins on the census but also may enjoy recognition as white or multiracial in their everyday lives. As Professor Rachel Moran has explained, to some extent, for these groups, the challenge has become one of maintaining a distinct racial or ethnic identity in the face of pressures to assimilate to a white identity.[138] *Hudgins* presages some of the difficulties of forging an identity that is neither black nor white in a society that still remains committed to these racial distinctions. Yet, the case also demonstrates that multiracialism can subvert the color line. As the multiracial population in the United States continues to grow, it is certain to challenge, through its very existence, the notion of race as biological and rigid, steadily destabilizing the assumptions that construct and preserve racial hierarchy.

---

[138]Moran, *supra* note 17, at 167–69.

In Memoriam:
John Hope Franklin

---- ✳ ----

The Dilemma of the American Negro Scholar

John Hope Franklin

The problems of the scholar who belongs to a particular group, ethnic or otherwise, must be considered in the context of the general problem of the scholar in the United States. In America the scholar's role in the community and the nation has always been limited. Indeed, his role has been rather carefully defined by the history of the country. Questions have often been raised about the effective use of the scholar in a society whose fundamental preoccupation has been with problems that have had little or nothing to do with the life of the mind. Intellectual prowess and mental acumen, it was argued almost from the beginning, could make no substantial contribution to the tasks of clearing the forests, cutting pathways to the frontier, and making a living in the wilderness. The intellectual life was reserved for those whose task it was to preserve and promote the moral and religious life of the community. In the early days of the nation there was a widespread feeling, moreover, that these aspects of life could

Originally published in Herbert Hill (ed.), *Soon One Morning: New Writing by American Negroes, 1940–1962* (New York, 1963).

be kept separate from the other aspects. Meanwhile, the rest of the community could live in blissful ignorance, with little or no concern for the great world of scholarship and learning that might be flourishing as far away as London and Paris or as close as the nearest county seat.

This was a mere fiction, but Americans liked to believe in it. In the final analysis, however, those who devoted themselves to intellectual pursuits became forces in the community in spite of the community itself. The lack of respect for learning or the lack of concern for it melted before the exigencies of conflict, when ideological justifications and rationalizations were needed for actions that had already been taken. Thus, when the patriots were fighting for independence, the scholars came to the rescue of the polemicists and agitators, and Locke and Hume and Dickinson and Jefferson became household words among groups considerably larger than those who could be described as learned. It was at this juncture that the peculiar ambivalence that was to characterize American attitudes became evident. On the one hand, there was little regard, if not downright contempt, for the scholar and the serious thinker. On the other hand, there was the acknowledged need for the talents and resources of the man who was devoted to the intellectual life; and there was a willingness to call upon him to strengthen the hand of those who had decided upon a particular course of action.

There has always been some acknowledgment, from that day to this, of the importance of the role of the scholar and intellectual in American life. Too often it has been begrudgingly conceded and too often the pervasive influence of scholarship in policy making and decision making is wholly unrecognized. We have been inclined to discount this influence and to insist that theorizing is the pastime of less practical-minded people. As for ourselves, we move, we act, we get things done, we have no time for indulging in the fantasies that emanate from the ivory tower. We do not seem to care that for this attitude we may be branded unintellectual or even anti-intellectual. We prefer to be known and recognized as practical-minded, down-to-earth. After all, our constitution is a practical, workable document. Our economy reflects our hard-headed approach to exploiting our resources and developing effective and efficient means of production. Even our social order and our institutions are evidence of our pragmatic orientation. I would suspect, however, that the more generous and broad-minded among us would recognize the fact that an untold amount of scholarship went into the writing of our constitution; that theoretical scientists as well as technicians and businessmen helped to make our economy what it has become; and that many scholarly hands contributed to the formulation of our social order and the institutions of which we boast.

The point is that, whether he wanted to or not, the American scholar has been drawn irresistibly into the mainstream of American life, and has contributed his knowledge and his ingenuity to the solution of the major problems that the country has faced. Jonathan Edwards *Freedom of the Will*, with all its scholarship, good and bad, was primarily an effort to preserve the unity of the older religious institutions in the face of powerful currents of change. Thomas Jefferson was a close student of eighteenth-century political theory, but the most significant manifestation of his scholarship in this area is to be found in the Declaration of Independence, whose practical-mindedness can hardly be surpassed. Even Ralph Waldo Emerson's *American Scholar*, while embodying some remarkable generalizations about the intellectual resources and powers of mankind, was in truth a declaration of American intellectual independence, calling the American scholar to arms in the war against ignorance and in behalf of the integrity of American intellectual life.

In recent years the story has been essentially the same. It was Woodrow Wilson, the former professor at Princeton, testing his theories of congressional government while president of the United States. It was James MacGregor Burns, of Williams College, adding scholarship and a new dimension to the traditional campaign biography with his life of John F. Kennedy. It was John Kenneth Galbraith descending from the insulation of a Harvard economics chair to make searching and stimulating observations on the industrial and business community of the nation. If these and scores of other scholars were faced with dilemmas—of whether to satisfy themselves in attacking the theoretical problems of their fields or to grapple with the fundamental problems of mankind—they resolved them fearlessly and unequivocally by applying their disciplines to the tasks from which they felt that they could not escape. In that way they gave meaning, substance, and significance to American scholarship.

It is in such a setting and context that we must examine the position of the American Negro scholar. The dilemmas and problems of the Negro scholar are numerous and complex. He has been forced, first of all, to establish his claim to being a scholar, and he has had somehow to seek recognition in the general world of scholarship. This has not been an easy or simple task, for, at the very time when American scholarship in general was making its claim to recognition, it was denying that Negroes were capable of being scholars. Few Americans, even those who advocated a measure of political equality, subscribed to the view that Negroes—any Negroes—had the ability to think either abstractly or concretely or to assimilate ideas that had been formulated by others. As late as the closing years of the nineteenth century it was difficult to find any white persons in the labor or business community, in the pulpit or on the platform, in the field of letters or in the field of scholarship, who thought it possible that a Negro could join the select company of scholars in America.

The Negro, then, first of all had to struggle against the forces and personalities in American life that insisted he could never rise in the intellectual sphere. Thomas Nelson Page, the champion of the plantation tradition and the defender of the superiority of the white race insisted that "the Negro has not progressed, not because he was a slave but because he does not possess the faculties to raise himself above slavery. He has not yet exhibited the qualities of any race which has advanced civilization or shown capacity to be greatly advanced." In 1895, a future president of the United States, Theodore Roosevelt argued that "a perfectly stupid race can never rise to a very high plane, the Negro, for instance, has been kept down as much by lack of intellectual development as anything else." If one were to thumb through the pages of the most respectable journals of the early years of this century—*Atlantic, Harper's, Scribner's, Century, North American Review*—he would find the same spirit pervading the articles published there. Industrial and vocational education, they contended, was peculiarly suitable for the Negro. Negroes, they argued, were childish, simple, irresponsible, and mentally inferior. It was the same wherever one looked.

The Negro who aspired to be a scholar in the closing years of the nineteenth century and the opening years of this century must have experienced the most shattering and disturbing sensations as he looked about him in an attempt to discover one indication of confidence, one expression of faith in him and his abilities. If he doubted himself, it would be understandable, for he had been brainwashed, completely and almost irrevocably, by assertions of Caucasian superiority, endorsements of social Darwinism, with its justifications for the degradation of the Negro, and political and legal maneuverings that lowered the Negro still further on the social and intellectual scale. But the aspiring Negro scholar did not doubt himself, and he turned on his detractors with all the resources he could summon in the effort to refute those who claimed he was inferior.

In 1888, a Negro, William T. Alexander, published a whole volume to support the claim that the Negro was the intellectual equal of others. "By the closest analysis of the blood of each race," he argued with eloquence, and futility, considering the times, "the slightest difference cannot be detected; and so, in the aspirations of the mind, or the impulses of the heart, we are all one common family, with nothing but the development of the mind through the channel of education to raise one man, or one people above another. . . . So far as noble characteristics are concerned, the colored face possess those traits to fully as great a degree as do the white."

Alexander and numerous contemporaries of his had faced their dilemma, and they had made their choice. They *had* to combat the contentions of Negro inferiority. They *had* to demonstrate that Negroes were capable of assimilating ideas and of contributing to mankind's store of knowledge. They made their argument simply and directly. It was as though whites had said they could not count, and Negroes then counted from one to ten to prove that they could. There were subtle, more sophisticated ways of proving their mental acumen, but if Negroes thought of them, they must have been convinced that such methods would have no effect on those whose arguments were not based on fact or reason in the first place.

It must have been a most unrewarding experience for the Negro scholar to answer those who said that he was inferior by declaring: "I am indeed *not inferior*." For such a dialogue left little or no time for the pursuit of knowledge as one really desired to pursue it. Imagine, if you can, what it meant to a competent Negro student of Greek literature, W. H. Crogman, to desert his chosen field and write a book entitled *The Progress of a Race*. Think of the frustration of the distinguished Negro physician C. V. Roman, who abandoned his medical research and practice, temporarily at least, to write *The Negro in American Civilization*. What must have been the feeling of the Negro student of English literature Benjamin Brawley, who forsook his field to write *The Negro Genius* and other works that underscored the intellectual powers of the Negro? How much poorer is the field of the biological sciences because an extremely able and well-trained Negro scientist, Julian Lewis, felt compelled to spend years of his productive life writing a book entitled *The Biology of the Negro?*

Many Negro scholars, moreover, never entered any of the standard branches of learning. Perhaps they would have been chemists, geologists, essayists, critics, musicologists, sociologists, historians. But they never were. From the moment of their intellectual awakening they were drawn inexorably, irresistibly into the field that became known as Negro studies. Here they were insulated from the assaults of the white scholars, who could be as vicious and as intolerant in their attacks and in their attitudes as the out-and-out racists were. Here, too, they would work relatively unmolested in a field where they could meet, head on, the assaults of those who would malign them and their race. In a sense, they could establish not only a professional standing by dealing objectively and in a scholarly fashion with the problems related to them and their race, but also the value and integrity of the field of Negro studies itself, which they had brought into being.

The careers of three Negro scholars—W. E. B. Du Bois, Carter G. Woodson, and Alain L. Locke—epitomize the history of Negro scholarship in the first half of the twentieth century. All three were carefully trained and held degrees of doctor of philosophy from Harvard University. After writing a doctoral dissertation that became Volume I in the Harvard Historical Studies, Du Bois moved on from his path-breaking work on the suppression of the African slave trade to a series of studies that not only treated many aspects of the Negro problem but also covered a number of areas in the social sciences and the humanities. He produced *The Philadelphia Negro,* a modern sociological study; he was the editor of the Atlanta University *Studies of the Negro Problem,* called a pioneering work in the field of the social sciences; he wrote *The Souls of Black Folk,* a critique of approaches to the solution of the race problem, *Black Folk Then and Now,* a history of the Negro in Africa and the New World, *Black Reconstruction,* a study of the Negro's part in the years following the Civil War, and literally dozens of other works. In his ninety-fourth year, he completed an epic three-volume novel about the Negro experience, *The Ordeal of Mansard.*

Woodson's first scholarly work, *The Disruption of Virginia,* was a rather general study. He soon settled down to a systematic study of the Negro, however. Successively, he produced his *Education of the Negro Prior to 1860,* his studies of the free Negro, his *Century of Negro Migration, The History of the Negro Church, The Negro in Our History, African Background Outlined,* and many others. In 1915 he organized the Association for the Study of Negro Life and History, and shortly thereafter became editor of the *Journal of Negro History,* which became one of the major historical publications in the United States.

Alain Locke's career was, in several important respects, different from that of Du Bois and Woodson. He was an honor graduate of Harvard

College, where he was elected to Phi Beta Kappa. He was a Rhodes Scholar at Oxford and later studied at the University of Berlin. Trained in philosophy, he soon became involved in the literary activity that was later called the "Negro Renaissance." Although he maintained his interest in the theory of value and cultural pluralism, he became a powerful force in articulating the position and aspirations of the new Negro. Thus, his *The New Negro: An Interpretation, The Negro in Art,* and *Plays of Negro Life* eclipsed his "Values and Imperatives," "Ethics and Culture," and "Three Corollaries of Cultural Relativism." After 1925 he never gave very much attention to purely philosophical problems.

Under the shadow and influence of these three figures and others, there emerged a large number of Negro scholars who devoted themselves almost exclusively to the study of some aspect of the Negro. Soon recognized fields emerged: the history of the Negro, the anthropology of the Negro, the sociology of the Negro, the poetry of the Negro, the Negro novel, the Negro short story, and so on.

In moving forthrightly in this direction, what had the Negro scholar done? He had, alas, made an institution of the field of Negro studies. He had become the victim of segregation in the field of scholarship in the same way that Negroes in other fields had become victims of segregation. There were the Negro press, the Negro church, Negro business, Negro education, and now Negro scholarship. Unhappily, Negro scholars had to face a situation, not entirely their own creation, in the perpetuation of which their stake was very real indeed. In the field of American scholarship, it was all they had. It grew in respectability not only because the impeccable scholarship of many of the Negroes commanded it, but also because many of the whites conceded that Negroes had peculiar talents that fitted them to study themselves and their problems. To the extent that this concession was made, it defeated a basic principle of scholarship— namely, that given the materials and techniques of scholarship and given the mental capacity, any person could engage in the study of any particular field.

This was a tragedy. Negro scholarship had foundered on the rocks of racism. It had been devoured by principles of separatism, of segregation. It had become the victim of the view that there was some "mystique" about Negro studies, similar to the view that there was some "mystique" about Negro spirituals which required that a person possess a black skin in order to sing them. This was not scholarship; it was folklore, it was voodoo.

The Negro scholar can hardly be held responsible for this sad turn of events. He had acted in good faith, and had proceeded in the best traditions of American scholarship. American scholarship had always been pragmatic, always firmly based on need. Du Bois and Woodson and Locke were in the same tradition as Jonathan Edwards and Thomas Jefferson. Here was a vast field that was unexplored. Here was an urgent need to explore it in order to complete the picture of American life and institutions. Here was an opportunity to bring to bear on a problem the best and most competent resources that could be commandeered. That the field was the Negro and that the resources were also Negroes are typical irrelevancies of which objective scholarship can take no cognizance. One wonders what would have happened had there been no Du Bois, no Woodson, no Locke, just as one wonders what would have happened had there been no Jonathan Edwards, no Thomas Jefferson. Du Bois could have moved toward imperial or colonial history or toward literary criticism; and Woodson could have moved toward political history or economic geography. Locke could have become a leading authority on values and aesthetics. Perhaps they would have been accepted in the mainstream of American scholarship; perhaps not. Their dilemma lay before them, and their choice is evident. It is not for us to say that American scholarship suffered as a result of the choice they made. We *can* say, however, that it is tragic indeed, and a commentary on the condition of American society, that these Negro scholars felt *compelled* to make the choice they did make. Had conditions been different, had they been free Americans functioning in a free intellectual and social climate, they might well have made other choices. Nothing, however, can degrade or successfully detract from the contributions they made, once they had chosen.

There were other Negro scholars, however, who did not take the road to Negro studies, who preferred to make their mark, if they were to make one at all, in what may be termed the mainstream of American scholarship. When W. S. Scarborough graduated from Oberlin in 1875 with a degree in Greek and Latin, it was widely thought that the only suitable pursuit for Negroes was in the area of vocational studies. Scarborough neither followed such a course nor yielded to the temptation to become a student of Negro life. In 1881 he published his *First Lessons in Greek,* and several years later he brought out his *Birds of Aristophanes: A Theory of Interpretation.* Then he translated the twenty-first and twenty-second books of Livy, published other works in Latin and Greek, and became a competent student of Sanskrit, Gothic, Lithuanian, and Old Slavonic.

But there was no place for him in American scholarly circles, not even at the predominantly Negro Howard University, where the white members of the Board of Trustees took the position that the chair in classical languages could be filled only by a Caucasian. Three generations later, the fate of William A. Hinton, one of America's most distinguished syphilologists, whose discoveries revolutionized the techniques for the detection and cure of dread social diseases, was almost the same. Despite his signal accomplishments, Harvard University Medical School kept him on for many years as a nonteaching clinical instructor. Not until he neared retirement and not until the position of the Negro in American society had significantly changed after World War II was Hinton elevated to a professorial rank. Scarborough and Hinton wore down their knuckles rapping at the door of American scholarship. Whenever the door was opened, it was done grudgingly and the opening was so slight that it was still almost impossible to enter.

The wide gap that separates the white world from the Negro world in this country has not been bridged by the work of scholarship, black or white. Indeed, the world of scholarship has, for the most part, remained almost as partitioned as other worlds. The Negro scholars that have become a part of the general world of American scholarship can still be counted on the fingers of a few hands. The number of Negro scholars on the faculties of non-Negro American colleges and universities is still pitifully small. The lines of communication between the two worlds are few and are sparingly used. Thus, the world of scholarship in America is a mirror of the state of race relations generally. Perhaps the world of scholarship is a step or two ahead of the general community; but the vigor and the pragmatism that characterize the American approach to other problems are missing in this all-important area. The Negro scholar is in a position not unlike that of Ralph Ellison's Invisible Man; he is a "fantasy," as James Baldwin puts it, "in the mind of the republic." When he is remembered at all he is all too often an afterthought. When his work is recognized it is usually pointed to as the work of a Negro. He is a competent *Negro* sociologist, an able *Negro* economist, an outstanding *Negro* historian. Such recognition is as much the product of the racist mentality as the Negro restrooms in the Montgomery airport were. It was this knowledge of racism in American scholarship, this feeling of isolation, that drew from Du Bois this comment: "I sit with Shakespeare and he winces not. Across the color line I move arm in arm with Balzac and Dumas, where smiling men and welcoming women glide in gilded halls. From out the caves of evening that swing between the strong-limbed earth and the tracery of stars, I summon Aristotle and Aurelius and what soul I will, and they come all graciously with no scorn nor condescension. So, wed with Truth, I dwell above the Veil. Is this the life you grudge us, O knightly America? Is this the life you long to change into the dull red hideousness of Georgia? Are you so afraid lest peering from this high Pisgah, between Philistine and Amalekite, we sight the Promised Land?"

The path of the scholar is at best a lonely one. In his search for truth he must be the judge of his findings and he must live with his conclusions. The world of the Negro scholar is indescribably lonely; and he must, somehow, pursue truth down that lonely path while, at the same time, making certain that his conclusions are sanctioned by universal standards developed and maintained by those who frequently do not even recognize him. Imagine the plight of a Negro historian trying to do research in archives in the South operated by people who cannot conceive that a Negro has the capacity to use the materials there. I well recall my first visit to the State Department of Archives and History in North Carolina, which was presided over by a man with a Ph.D. in history from Yale. My arrival created a panic and an emergency among the administrators that was, itself, an incident of historic proportions. The archivist frankly informed me that I was the first Negro who had sought to use the facilities there; and as the architect who designed the building had not anticipated such a situation, my use of the manuscripts and other materials would have to be postponed for several days, during which time one of the exhibition rooms would be converted to a reading room for me. This was shocking enough, but not as crudely amusing as the time when the woman head of the archives in Alabama told me that *she* was shocked to discover that despite the fact that I was a "Harvard nigger" (those are her words) I had somehow retained the capacity to be courteous to a southern lady. She ascribed it all to my Tennessee "seasoning" before going into the land of the Yankee!

Many years later, in 1951, while working at the Library of Congress, one of my closest friends, a white historian, came by my study room one Friday afternoon and asked me to lunch with him the following day. I reminded him that since the following day would be a Saturday, the Supreme Court restaurant would be closed, and there was no other place in the vicinity where we could eat together. (This was before the decision in the Thompson restaurant case in April, 1953, which opened Washington restaurants to all well-behaved persons.) My friend pointed out that he knew I spent Saturdays at the Library, and he wondered what I did for food on those days. I told him that I seldom missed a Saturday of research and writing at the Library of Congress, but that my program for that day was a bit different from other days. On Saturdays, I told him, I ate a huge late breakfast at home and then brought a piece of fruit or candy to the Library, which I would eat at the lunch hour. Then, when I could bear the hunger no longer during the afternoon, I would leave and go home to an early dinner. His only remark was that he doubted very much whether, if he were a Negro, he would be a scholar, if it required sacrifices such as this and if life was as inconvenient as it appeared. I assured him that for a Negro scholar searching for truth, the search for food in the city of Washington was one of the *minor* inconveniences.

These incidents point out not only the distress caused by physical inconveniences but also the dilemma of the scholar who, first of all, would persevere in remaining some kind of a scholar and, secondly, would remain true to the rigid requirements of equanimity, dispassion, and objectivity. To the first dilemma, the true scholar who is a Negro has no more choice than the Negro who is a true painter, musician, novelist. If he is committed to the world of scholarship, as a critic, sociologist, economist, historian, he *must* pursue truth in his field; he *must*, as it were, ply his trade. For scholarship involves a dedication and a commitment as truly as does any other pursuit in the life of the mind. If one tried to escape, as my white historian friend declares that he would, he would be haunted by the urge to fulfill his aspirations in the field of his choice; and he would be satisfied in no other pursuit. If he could indeed become satisfied by running away from his field, it is certain that there was no commitment and dedication in the first place. Thus, the true scholar who is a Negro has no real choice but to remain in his field, to "stick to his knitting," to persevere.

But in the face of forces that deny him membership in the mainstream of American scholarship and that suggest that he is unable to perform creditably, the task of remaining calm and objective is indeed a formidable one. There is always the temptation to pollute his scholarship with polemics, diatribes, arguments. This is especially true if the area of his interests touches on the great questions in which he is personally involved as a Negro. If he yields to this attractive temptation, he can by one act destroy his effectiveness and disqualify himself as a true and worthy scholar. He should know that by maintaining the highest standards of scholarship he not only becomes worthy but also sets an example that many of his contemporaries who claim to be the arbiters in the field do not themselves follow.

It is, of course, asking too much of the Negro scholar to demand that he remain impervious and insensitive to the forces that seek to destroy his dignity and self-respect. He must, therefore, be permitted to function as vigorously as his energies and resources allow, in order to elevate himself and those of his group to a position where they will be accepted and respected in the American social order. This involves a recognition of the difference between scholarship and advocacy. On the one hand, the Negro scholar must use his scholarship to correct the findings of pseudo-psychologists and sociologists regarding Negro intelligence, Negro traits, and the alleged Negro propensity for crime. He must rewrite the history of this country and correct the misrepresentations and falsifications in connection with the Negro's role in our history. He must provide the social engineers with the facts of the Negro ghetto, the overt and the subtle discriminations inflicted on the Negro in almost every aspect of his existence, the uses and misuses of political and economic power to keep the Negro in a subordinate position in American life. There is also a place for advocacy, so long as the Negro scholar understands the difference. Recognizing the importance of the use of objective data in the passionate advocacy of the rectification of injustice, the Negro can assume this additional role for his own sake and for the sake of the community. When I wrote the first working paper to be used in the briefs of the National Association for the Advancement of Colored People in their school desegregation arguments, I was flattered when the chief counsel, Thurgood Marshall, told me that the paper sounded very much like a lawyer's brief. I had deliberately transformed the objective data provided by historical research into an urgent plea for justice; and I hoped that my scholarship did not suffer.

When such an opportunity does not present itself, there is still another way to keep one's scholarly work from being polluted by passion— namely, by blowing off steam in literary efforts. A few examples will suffice: Several years ago, while waiting in the segregated Atlanta railway station, I was so mortified and touched by the barbaric treatment of Negro passengers by railway officials and city policemen that I immediately sat down and wrote a piece called "DP's in Atlanta," in which I drew some comparisons between the treatment of these Negroes and the treatment of displaced refugees in Nazi-occupied countries during World War

II. After that, I was able to go out to Atlanta University and give the series of lectures that I had been invited to deliver.

On another occasion I had a further opportunity to engage in some writing that was not particularly a scholarly effort; at the same time, it did not seem necessary to deny its authorship. In 1959, I was invited to give the Lincoln sesquicentennial lecture for the Chicago Historical Society. En route I went into the diner for my evening meal just before the crowd arrived. I thus had a choice seat, at a table for four. Soon the diner was filled and a long line of people was waiting at the entrance—singly and in groups of twos and fours. They all declined to join me, and I sat in splendid isolation for the better part of an hour. As places became vacant near me they took their seats, and I was able to hear their orders to the waiters as well as their conversations with their new companions. When I returned to my compartment, I wrote a short piece called "They All Ordered Fish." You see, it was Ash Wednesday, and these Christian ladies and gentlemen were beginning their forty days of commemoration of the agony of their Lord, Jesus Christ. Neither "DP's in Atlanta" nor "They All Ordered Fish" has ever been published. They remain in the uncollected papers of a Negro scholar who has faced his share of dilemmas.

I suspect that such a repression of one's true feelings would not be satisfying to some, and it may even be lacking in courage. I do not commend it; I merely confess it. It is doubtless a temporary escape from the painful experience of facing the dilemma and making the choice that every Negro scholar must sooner or later make. For the major choice for the Negro scholar is whether he should turn his back on the world, concede that he is the Invisible Man, and lick the wounds that come from cruel isolation, or whether he should use his training, talents, and resources to beat down the barriers that keep him out of the mainstream of American life and scholarship. The posing of the question, it seems, provides the setting for the answer. I have said that the American scholar has been drawn irresistibly into the mainstream of American life, and has contributed his knowledge and ingenuity to the solution of the major problems his country has faced. I now assert that the proper choice for the American Negro scholar is to use his knowledge and ingenuity, his resources and talents, to combat the forces that isolate him and his people and, like the true patriot that he is, to contribute to the solution of the problems that all Americans face in common.

This is not a new and awesome prospect for the Negro. He has had to fight for the right to assist in the defense of his country when his country was locked in mortal struggle with its enemies. He has had to fight for the right to discharge his obligations as a voting citizen. He has had to fight for the right to live in a community in order to help improve that community. It is the same wherever one looks—in education, employment, recreation, scholarship. It is, therefore, a goodly company the American Negro scholar joins as he chooses to make of the course he pursues a battleground for truth *and* justice. On the one hand, he joins those of his own color who seek to make democracy work. On the other hand, he joins his intellectual kinsmen of whatever race in the worthy task of utilizing the intellectual resources of the country for its own improvement. A happier choice could hardly be made. A happier prospect for success, even in the face of untold difficulties, could hardly be contemplated.

Acknowledgments

I wish to thank my research assistant, Keya Kraft, for all her hard work in helping me find material for *Best African American Essays/Best African American Fiction* by culling through countless magazines, newspapers, and books. I also wish to extend my gratitude to the staff of the Center for the Humanities at Washington University for their assistance: Robbie Jones, our bookkeeper, and especially Barb Liebmann and Jian Leng, without whose help and organizational skills the book you hold in your hands would never have come into being. They are great people and I owe them a lot.

Notable essays for which there was no room:

The controversial, the personal, the informative, the polemical,
the decorous, the radical

1. "Fellow Traveler" by Neil deGrasse Tyson, from *Natural History,*
   October 2007
2. "White Boy Music" by Michael Gonzales, from *Blackadelic Pop,*
   February 27, 2008
3. "The Devil and Ike Turner" by Donald Fagen, from *Slate,* December 17, 2007
4. "The Literary Ivory Tower" by Esther Armah, from *New York Amsterdam News,* November 13, 2008
5. "The End of Race As We Know It" by Gerald Early, from *The Chronicle of Higher Education,* October 10, 2008
6. "The Color of Politics" by Peter J. Boyer, from *The New Yorker,* February 4, 2008
7. "My Old Man: A Voyage Around Our Fathers" by Chimamanda Ngozi Adichie, from *The Observer,* June 15, 2008
8. "Most Likely to Succeed" by Malcolm Gladwell, from *The New Yorker,* December 15, 2008
9. "The Obama Bargain" by Shelby Steele, from *The Wall Street Journal,* March 18, 2008
10. "Post-Race Scholar Yells Race" by Ishmael Reed, from *Counterpunch,* July 27, 2009
11. "The King and Us" by Margo Jefferson, from *The Washington Post,* June 21, 2009
12. "Obama, the African Colonial" by L. E. Ikenga, from *American Thinker,* June 25, 2009

Permissions and Credits

The Presidential Election of 2008

"A More Perfect Union" by President Barack Obama. This is the full text of President Barack Obama's speech, as prepared for delivery.

"A Deeper Black" by Ta-Nehisi Coates. Copyright © 2008 by *The Nation*. Reprinted by permission from the May 1, 2008, issue of *The Nation* magazine.

"Obama No" by Adolph Reed, Jr. Copyright © 2008 by *The Progressive*. Originally published in *The Progressive* in the May 2008 issue. Reprinted by permission from *The Progressive*, 409 E. Main St., Madison WI 53703. www.progressive.org.

"Who Died and Made Tavis King?" Copyright © 2008 by Melissa Harris-Lacewell. Originally published in *The Root*, May 15, 2008. Reprinted by permission of the author and the author's agent, Anderson Literary Management, LLC.

"What Obama Means to the World" by Gary Younge. Copyright © 2009 by *The Nation*. Reprinted by permission from the January 15, 2009, issue of *The Nation* magazine.

"Finally, a Thin President" by Colson Whitehead from *The New York Times*, November 6, 2008. Copyright © 2008 *The New York Times*. All

Our Michelle

Reverend Wright Revisited

The United States, Past and Present

Personalities

Profiles

Race Talk

Sports

Rita Dove

African American Literature

Racial Identity, Enslavement, and the Law

In Memoriam: John Hope Franklin

About the Editors

GERALD EARLY is a noted essayist and American culture critic. A professor of English, African and African American Studies, and American Culture Studies at Washington University in St. Louis, Early is the author of several books, including *The Culture of Bruising: Essays on Prizefighting, Literature, and Modern American Culture,* which won the 1994 National Book Critics Circle Award for criticism, and *This Is Where I Came In: Black America in the 1960s.* He is also editor of numerous volumes, including *The Muhammad Ali Reader* and *The Sammy Davis, Jr. Reader.* He served as a consultant on four of Ken Burns's documentary films, *Baseball; Jazz; Unforgivable Blackness: The Rise and Fall of Jack Johnson;* and *The War,* and appeared in the first three as an on-air analyst.

RANDALL KENNEDY, the Michael R. Klein Professor of Law at Harvard University, focuses his research on the intersection of racial conflict and legal institutions in American life. His books include *Sellout: The Politics of Racial Betrayal* and *Nigger: The Strange Career of a Troublesome Word.* Additionally, Kennedy has published numerous collections of shorter works. Many of his articles can be found in periodicals such as *The American Prospect, The Nation, The Atlantic,* and *The Law Journal.*

About the Type

This book is set in Fournier, a typeface named for Pierre Simon Fournier, the youngest son of a French printing family. He started out engraving woodblocks and large capitals, then moved on to fonts of type. In 1736 he began his own foundry and made several important contributions in the field of type design; he is said to have cut 147 alphabets of his own creation. Fournier is probably best remembered as the designer of St. Augustine Ordinaire, a face that served as the model for Monotype's Fournier, which was released in 1925.